SEASON OF TERROR

TIMBERLINE BOOKS

STEPHEN J. LEONARD AND THOMAS J. NOEL, EDITORS

The Beast, Benjamin Barr Lindsey with Harvey J. O'Higgins

Colorado's Japanese Americans, Bill Hosokawa

Colorado Women: A History, Gail M. Beaton

Denver: An Archaeological History, Sarah M. Nelson, K. Lynn Berry, Richard F. Carrillo, Bonnie L. Clark, Lori E. Rhodes, and Dean Saitta

Dr. Charles David Spivak: A Jewish Immigrant and the American Tuberculosis Movement, Jeanne E. Abrams

Enduring Legacies: Ethnic Histories and Cultures of Colorado, edited by Arturo J. Aldama, Elisa Facio, Daryl Maeda, and Reiland Rabaka

The Gospel of Progressivism: Moral Reform and Labor War in Colorado, 1900–1930, R. Todd Laugen

Helen Ring Robinson: Colorado Senator and Suffragist, Pat Pascoe

Ores to Metals: The Rocky Mountain Smelting Industry, James E. Fell, Jr.

Season of Terror: The Espinosas in Central Colorado, March–October 1863, Charles F. Price

A Tenderfoot in Colorado, R. B. Townshend

The Trail of Gold and Silver: Mining in Colorado, 1859–2009, Duane A. Smith

Season of Terror

The Espinosas in Central Colorado

March–October 1863

Charles F. Price

University Press of Colorado
Boulder

Published by University Press of Colorado
5589 Arapahoe Avenue, Suite 206C
Boulder, Colorado 80303

First paperback edition 2018
Printed in the United States of America

The University Press of Colorado is a proud member of the Association of American University Presses.

The University Press of Colorado is a cooperative publishing enterprise supported, in part, by Adams State University, Colorado State University, Fort Lewis College, Metropolitan State University of Denver, Regis University, University of Colorado, University of Northern Colorado, Utah State University, and Western State Colorado University.

∞ This paper meets the requirements of the ANSI/NISO Z39.48-1992 (Permanence of Paper).

Library of Congress Cataloging-in-Publication Data

Price, Charles F., 1938–
Season of terror : the Espinosas in central Colorado, March/October 1863 / Charles F. Price.
pages cm. — (Timberline books)
Includes bibliographical references and index.
ISBN 978-1-60732-236-8 (hardcover : alk. paper) — ISBN 978-1-60732-804-9 (pbk : alk. paper) — ISBN 978-1-60732-237-5 (ebook)
1. Espinosa, Felipe Nerio, –1863. 2. Espinosa, José Vivián, –1863. 3. Vincente, José, –1863. 4. Serial murders—Colorado—History—19th century. 5. Murder—Colorado—History—19th century. 6. Serial murderers—Colorado—History—19th century. 7. Murderers—Colorado—History—19th century. 8. Frontier and pioneer life—Colorado. 9. Colorado—History, Local—19th century. 10. Colorado—Race relations. I. Title.
HV6533.C6P75 2013
364.152'320922788—dc23

2013012711

Design by Daniel Pratt

For my dear wife Ruth, who knows why.

And for Mike Perschbacher, who drove me all over Central Colorado helping me locate murder sites.

And for Christie Wright, fellow enthusiast of Colorado outlawry who knows more about the bad actors in old-time South Park than anybody but the robbers and shootists themselves.

Contents

Figures

Foreword

Season of Terror springs from the intersection of two obsessions. The first emerged early in 1863 when two Espinosa brothers, Felipe Nerio and José Vivián of San Rafael, a village near Conejos in Colorado's San Luís Valley, launched a vendetta that in eight months led to the murder of perhaps as many as thirty-two Anglo-Americans as well as the deaths and decapitations of the brothers themselves and their nephew, José Vincente. The second passion flared more than a century and a quarter later when author Charles F. Price resolved to plumb the Espinosas' bloody doings that terrorized pioneer Coloradans and put the perpetrators among the worst serial murderers in the nineteenth-century American West.

Season of Terror is more than a detailed and gripping account of a raft of killings. It also places the Espinosas in the broader context of centuries of Hispano-Anglo conflict, sharpened by the Mexican-American War (1846–1848), which saw the United States seize more than half a million square miles of Mexican territory, including lands that thirteen years after the war's end would form much of Colorado Territory. By revealing the bigger picture, weighing conflicting stories, and analyzing complex evidence, Price presents a clear account of the Espinosas and their adversaries. Moreover, he tells much about Colorado in 1863, a place with fewer than 50,000 inhabitants and so different from today's state of more than five million that we can imagine it only with the help of an insightful guide.

Despite Price's meticulous research, lost or overlooked evidence may surface to shed new light on the story. For example, consider a couple of sentences from page 89 of a booklet titled *Souvenir: Dedication of the Masonic Temple, Denver Colorado . . .* (Denver: W. F. Robinson, 1890). In his recollections of the Knights Templar, a Masonic organization that counted some of Colorado's leading Anglo-American Protestants among its members, Webster D. Anthony, who served as Governor John Evans's secretary in the 1860s, tells of one of the dead Espinosas' contributions to the Knights' mysterious doings.

> Espanosa [*sic*] was his name, and many Sir Knights have the happy reflection that their 5th libation was taken by the aid of what was left of this murderous chief. Other Knights who have followed, not being subjected to the same test, have been given the opportunity to "reflect" over it, and in all probabilities [*sic*] these occasions are the only ones when any portion of "Espanosa" or his memory have ever served anything like a good purpose.

Yet, even if more details crop up, Price's account will likely long remain definitive because it is unlikely that anyone else will develop such an obsession with the Espinosas. Fortunately, obsession in the pursuit of history is not necessarily a vice.

Charles F. Price, a resident of Burnsville, North Carolina, is a man of many careers, including journalist, lobbyist, novelist, and urban planner. His Colorado connection comes, in part, through his wife, Ruth, a native of Salida, to whom he has dedicated the book. His passion for accuracy and love of mountains led him to tramp parts of the state as he traced the Espinosas' haunts. Thanks to his wanderings and obsessions we have another worthy work to add to the University Press of Colorado's Timberline Series, which aims to publish or republish significant books on Colorado and the West.

Stephen J. Leonard, Professor of History and Chairperson of the History Department at Metropolitan State University of Denver

Coeditor with Prof. Thomas J. Noel of the Timberline Series, University Press of Colorado

Acknowledgments

I am deeply indebted to many people who helped me prepare this book. Foremost among them is my wife, Ruth, who not only tolerated my years-long obsession with the Espinosas but even came to share it, ending by materially assisting in the research; it was she who discovered the whereabouts of the Ethan W. Eaton papers, leading us into a fascinating, labyrinthine, and previously unsuspected byway of the Espinosa story. And as always, Ruth served as my most implacably honest critic and editor.

Ruth also selflessly devoted many hours—with my own well-intentioned but often inept assistance—to reviewing the copyedited text and making the many needed corrections and additions, despite her already challenging professional work schedule as a consultant to caregivers whose loved ones suffer from dementia. I'm indebted also to Karl Yambert, the meticulous copyeditor who steered me through the dangerous minefields of endnoting and source referencing.

Nor could I have understood the context of my topic—or, more accurately, my obsession—as fully as I have if not for the generosity and counsel of Dr. Jerry D. Thompson, Regents Professor of History at Texas A&M International University in Laredo, Texas, an expert on the Civil War period in the Southwest and author of many books on that subject, who made available to me countless copies of relevant military correspondence bearing on the hunt for the Espinosas and its consequences in the officer corps of the Volunteer Service of the US Army. He was also kind enough to read and comment on selected portions of the manuscript bearing on the cultural and military aspects of the New Mexico–Colorado region during the Civil War period.

I also owe an immense obligation to Christie Wright of Highlands Ranch, Colorado, president of the Board of Directors, Park County Local History Archives, who secured for me copies of old newspaper and magazine articles that I was unable to locate in person or online and who served as a fount of information for all things historical pertaining to South Park, that magnificent space in the heart of Colorado, redolent of so much that is stirring in the past of the Centennial State.

Nelson Walker of Cañon City, Colorado, a retired forester who served twenty-six years with the US Forest Service and five years with the Bureau of Land Management, courteously but firmly debated with me by email the movements of John McCannon's California Gulch posse and the location of Vivián Espinosa's death site in the canyon lands of Fremont County, and brought his intimate and invaluable knowledge of that rugged terrain to bear on both questions in a way that considerably enlightened me. Though neither of us changed the other's mind, I always found his arguments cogently and clearly stated, and have been happy to include his views in Appendix A to this book.

Mr. Walker has read and commented on the manuscript, and the book would have been poorer without his valuable assistance.

I am further indebted to Mr. Walker, and to some of his friends, for yet another valuable service. One July day he, along with Bradley K. Nelson, Steve and Bryan McAllister, and my nephew, John Perschbacher, nursed my aging, out-of-condition self through a hike in and out of the rough terrain of Espinosa Gulch to explore Nash Spring, Mr. Walker's choice for the place where Vivián Espinosa died. That I survived is wholly due to the patience and encouragement of these good men, though I am sure what seemed to me an ordeal was for them but a wholesome stroll.

As I drew near the end of this work, I was also privileged to make the acquaintance by email and telephone of James E. Perkins, author of the fine book *Tom Tobin: Frontiersman*, the work that had originally inspired me to investigate the lives and times of the Espinosas. Mr. Perkins shared with me his ideas about the death site of Vivián Espinosa (also summarized in the appendix), the location of Sangre de Cristo Canyon, and several other aspects of this compelling period in frontier history. He, too, has been kind enough to read and comment on my manuscript, and the work has benefited from his matchless command of all things related to the past of Colorado and New Mexico.

I also owe thanks to Mike and Colleen Perschbacher for making it possible for me to tour many of the old haunts of the Espinosas and their victims, and Mike deserves special recognition for helping me find the Harkens grave and the probable location of the Bruce farm, not to mention tolerating my gimpy leg after I pulled a calf muscle crawling out of a ravine in search of the former. I must also thank my father-in-law Ray Perschbacher, whose devotion to Colorado history set an example for me; to the late Ed Quillen and his wife, Martha, former publishers of *Colorado Central Magazine*, and the current publisher, Mike Rosso, who invited me to write articles about the Espinosas and the aftermath of their outbreak.

The acquisitions editor of the University Press of Colorado, Jessica D'Arbonne, patiently and with unfailing good humor guided me through the unfamiliar territory of academic publishing, and on many a day bolstered my flagging confidence. Our working relationship also benefited from the fact that we shared an unlikely affinity for "cowboy guns." I owe her a debt of thanks I can never repay. In fact every staffer at the University Press of Colorado whom I encountered proved to be an eminently reasonable and respectful collaborator with a novelist trying to become a historian. I must especially single out for sincere thanks Editor-in-Chief Laura Furney, Production Manager Daniel Pratt, and Sales and Marketing Manager Beth Svinarich. All these good people treated me as a friend and colleague as well as a fledgling writer of nonfiction.

Many other friends, archivists, historians, and documentarians deserve my heartfelt gratitude for their assistance, including Ed and Nancy Bathke for allowing me to use their rare photograph of Wilbur Fisk Stone ("Dornick") as a young man; the late Claude W. Sánchez, descendant of Felipe Espinosa; Rick Manzanares, director, Fort Garland Museum, Colorado, and his assistant, Joey Gallegos; Dorothy Brandt of the San Luís Valley Museum of Alamosa, Colorado, and her husband, Captain John Brandt; Jay Warner of Antonito, Colorado, director of the San Luís Valley Historical Society; Dr. David Sandoval of Colorado State University in Pueblo, Colorado; Wanda Edwards, collections manager, Palace of the Governors/The New Mexico History Museum; Tomas Jaehn, librarian, Daniel Kosharek, photo archivist, and Mark Scharen, digital imaging specialist, Fray Angélico Chávez History

Library, Palace of the Governors, Santa Fe, New Mexico; Sarah Gilmor, photo research librarian, History Colorado (formerly the Colorado Historical Society); Elena Cline, Colorado State Archives; Marcia Kehl, archives specialist, Special Collections and Archives, Penrose Library, University of Denver; Lisa M. Studts, archivist/curator, Royal Gorge Museum and History Center, Cañon City, Colorado; Brooke Traylor, archivist assistant, Starsmore Center for Local History, Colorado Springs Pioneer Museum; Coi Drummon-Gehrig, photo research librarian, Western History Section, Denver Public Library; T. Juliette Arai, Textual Archives Services Division, National Archives and Records Administration, Washington, DC; Mary McCarthy, support and collections specialist, Colorado Virtual Library; Jane Gilsinger, archivist, Park County, Colorado, Local History Archives; Eric Bittner, archivist, National Archives and Records Administration, Rocky Mountain Division; Barbara Dey, reference librarian, Stephen H. Hart Library, History Colorado, Denver, Colorado; Scott Cossel and Libby Funk of the Rights and Reproductions Section, University of Arizona Library, Tucson, Arizona; Susan K. Forbes, Research Section, Kansas State Historical Society, Topeka, Kansas; Julie R. Monroe and Jennifer Gedert, University of Idaho Library Special Collections and Archives; Stephanie Hodges, research assistant, Archives, University of Colorado at Boulder; Cindy Tyson, administrative assistant, *New Mexico Historical Review*; Christine Trujillo, library director, El Rito Public Library, El Rito, New Mexico; Kelly Murphy, Research Coordinator, Starsmore Center for Local History, Colorado Springs Pioneer Museum; Robert W. Philbrook, genealogist of the Philbrick–Philbrook family, and Dr. Jeffrey J. Safford, professor emeritus of history at Montana State University and author of *The Mechanics of Optimism: Mining Companies, Technology, and the Hot Springs Gold Rush, Montana Territory, 1864–1868* (University Press of Colorado, 2004), both of whom helped me narrow down identification of one of the Espinosa victims who survived; Karen Mitchell of Colorado City, who maintains the excellent Huerfano County, Colorado Resources page online; and Sherry Roane Ellis of the Buncombe County, North Carolina, Public Libraries, who facilitated my numerous interlibrary loan requests. I'm also honored to have been the recipient of generous advice from the person Ed Quillen has called Colorado's unofficial historian laureate, the distinguished Virginia McConnell Simmons, author of countless books and articles about the history of the Centennial State, who was kind enough to advise me about Penitente *moradas* in the San Luís Valley of southern Colorado.

Thanks also go to Susan Martin, who helped me with the Spanish language I had allowed to deteriorate since my college years. I must also thank two men I deeply admire but have never been fortunate to meet: Hampton Sides, author of *Blood and Thunder: The Epic Story of Kit Carson and the Conquest of the American West*, and David L. Dorrance, who wrote the unpublished thesis *Archibald H. Gillespie in the Department of New Mexico.* Both works sparked and sustained my interest in various aspects of the Espinosa story and are cited in the bibliography.

I absolve all these fine people of any responsibility for mistakes I have made in using the information they supplied.

I also acknowledge a great debt to the excellent website *Colorado Historic Newspapers Collection*, operated jointly by the Colorado State Library and History Colorado. This online archive of many old-time papers, including *The Rocky Mountain News* and the *Weekly Commonwealth,* provided me with an invaluable running account of the Espinosas' story as it unfolded week after week in the accounts of various correspondents for Denver's rival organs.

Finally, I must thank my good friend Ed Sheary, director, Asheville–Buncombe County Public Library System, North Carolina, who greatly expedited my research and has given steadfast support to my writing from the first; his life partner, Peggy Weaver, who in an earlier incarnation as a branch library director helped launch my literary career and has cheered me on ever since; polymath and literary critic Seabrook Wilkinson, who read every chapter and demichapter of my lengthy manuscript as my computer spat them out and whose remorseless copyediting and never flagging faith in the merit of the work buoyed me up on many an occasion when I was ready to sink beneath the waves of self-doubt; and Marlin Barton of Montgomery, Alabama, one of America's finest writers of literary fiction, for his unflagging belief that my writing deserved to be read.

ESCALANTE MOUNTS
NORTH PARK
ELKHEAD MT
OLD PARK
RABBIT EARS MTS
Bear River
PACIFIC RAIL ROAD
White River
MIDDLE PARK
SUMMIT CO.
EGERIA PARK
BOOK MTS
SOUTH
PARK
Developed Gold
LAKE CO.
UNCOMPAGRE PARK
SAWATCH
HOMAN PARK
UNCOMPAGRE MOUNTS
ANIMAS PARK
COSTILLA CO
RIO GRANDE DEL NORTE
SIERRA LA PLATA
SIERRA SAN JUAN
SAN LUIS PARK
CONEJOS CO.
MESA VERDA
Rio Dolores
Rio La Plata

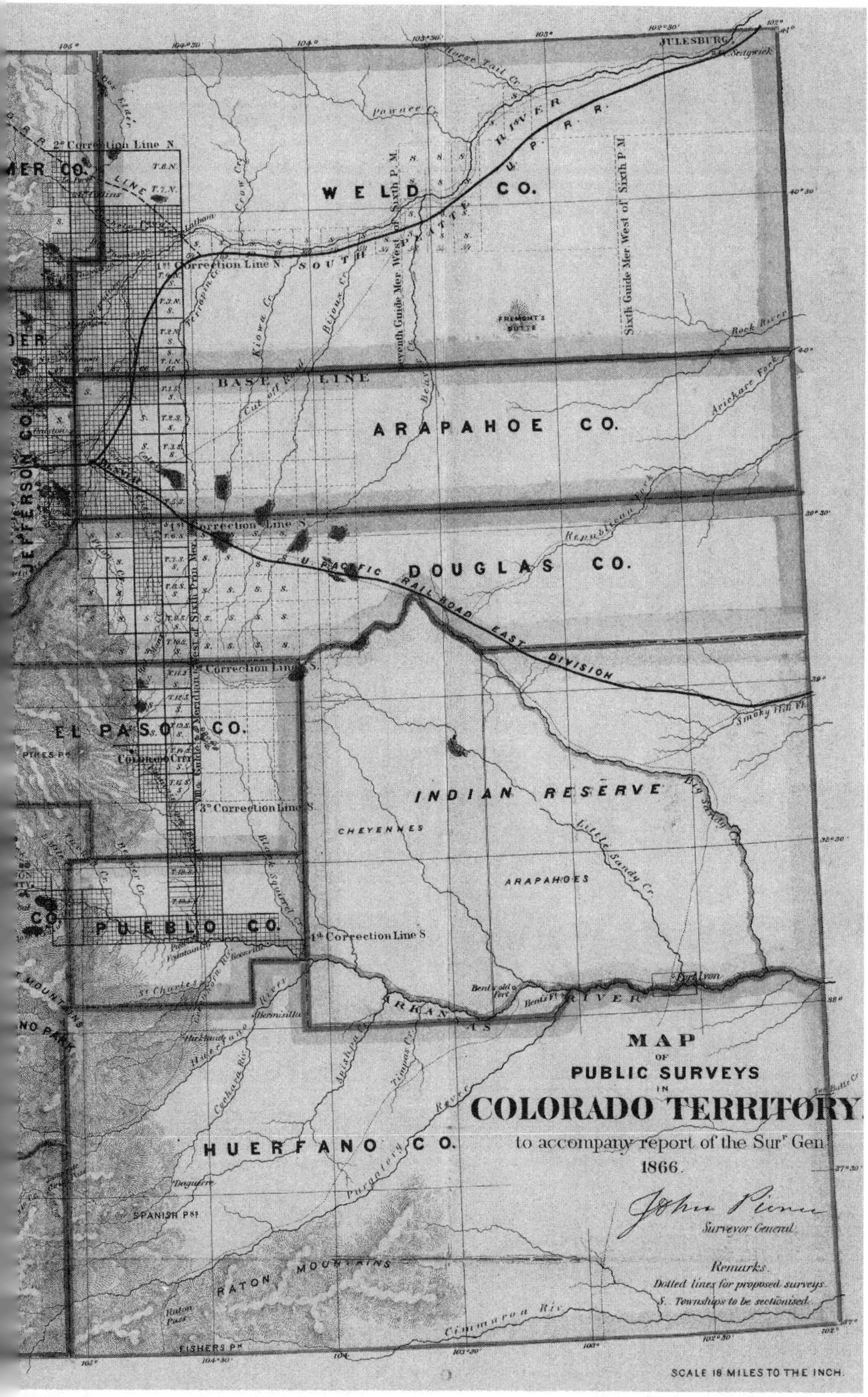
MAP
OF
PUBLIC SURVEYS
IN
COLORADO TERRITORY.
to accompany report of the Surr Genl
1866.
John Pierce
Surveyor General.
Remarks.
Dotted lines for proposed surveys.
S. Townships to be sectionised.
SCALE 18 MILES TO THE INCH.
WELD CO.
ARAPAHOE CO.
DOUGLAS CO.
EL PASO CO.
PUEBLO CO.
HUERFANO CO.
JEFFERSON CO.
INDIAN RESERVE
CHEYENNES
ARAPAHOES
JULESBURG
BASE LINE
1st Correction Line N.
2d Correction Line N.
1st Correction Line S.
2d Correction Line S.
3d Correction Line S.
4th Correction Line S.
SOUTH PLATTE RIVER
U. P. R. R.
U. PACIFIC RAIL ROAD EAST DIVISION
ARKANSAS RIVER
Seventh Guide Mer. West of Sixth P. M.
Sixth Guide Mer. West of Sixth P. M.
FREMONT'S BUTTE
Republican Fork
Arickaree Fork
Rock River
Pawnee Cr.
Horse Tail Cr.
Crow Cr.
Kiowa Cr.
Bijou Cr.
Big Sandy Cr.
Little Sandy Cr.
Smoky Hill Fk.
Fort Lyon
Bent's old Fort
Bent's Ft.
Purgatory
Timpas Cr.
Apishpa Cr.
Huerfano River
Cucharas Riv.
Cimmaron Riv.
RATON MOUNTAINS
Raton Pass
SPANISH P'KS
FISHERS P'K
PIKES P'K
Colorado City
Denver
Daguerre
St Charles
NO PARK
MOUNTAINS
Black Squirrel Cr.
Cut off road

Introduction

> "In the spring of the year mentioned, the entire region of country between Pueblo and Park counties, indeed all sections of the Territory, became in a measure panic stricken by accounts of terrible and mysterious massacres of travelers on the lonely roads leading from the southwest to the South Park. Every little while, residents of certain localities disappeared, and upon search being instituted by friends, their dead bodies were found. Who committed these horrible deeds no one could comprehend, since all traces were lost."[1]

The "year mentioned" was 1863. The place was the newly organized Territory of Colorado. The inexplicable carnage lasted eight months. No one knows how many were murdered; the generally accepted count is ten or eleven but the killers themselves boasted of having slain thirty-two, and such a number is far from implausible. They also tried to take the lives of two other men and they raped a woman. "Ask in New Mexico," one of them wrote, "if any other . . . men have ever been known to have killed as many . . . as the Espinosas."[2]

There were three of them: a pair of New Mexican–born brothers, Felipe Nerio and José Vivián, and their nephew, José Vincente. In their short but vicious eruption into frontier history no other malefactors inspired more fear and dread over a greater expanse of country than this trio, yet today they and their grisly rampage are largely forgotten, save in the local and regional lore of Colorado.

And even in the Centennial State the Espinosas are not widely remembered. When they are, sensationalism has been the order of the day. As recently as the 1970s, the then-director of the museum at old Fort Garland[3] regularly staged reenactments of the dramatic moment when famed plainsman Tom Tobin dumped the severed heads of Felipe and José Vincente out of a gunnysack in front of the commandant's office—in the case of the reenactment, heads especially fashioned of *papier-maché*—much to the disgust of many Hispanic Coloradans. The museum's current director, Rick Manzanares, says people still stop by asking to see the real heads, which they imagine have been preserved. (They haven't.)[4]

Why have the Espinosas escaped widespread notoriety when their atrocities far exceeded the crimes of figures better known in the annals of Western outlawry? One reason might be that their actions did not fit neatly into any of the frontier stereotypes. They were not gunmen like John Wesley Hardin, "Texas Billy" Thompson, or "Wild Bill" Longley; they killed no one in straight-up confrontations but always by stealth, from hiding. They were not feudists like the Earps and the Clantons, or the Tewksburys and the Grahams, nor were they caught up in range wars like Billy the Kid. Though they stole, they were not rustlers in the mold of John Kinney's band, or robbers of banks and trains such as the James–Younger gang. Nor were they cowboys gone wrong like Butch Cassidy or Tom Horn. They were, as best we can determine, only *labradores*, poor Hispanic farmers who became what we would call serial killers, a category of crime more readily associated with our own time than with the nineteenth-century Western frontier.

Their obscurity may also be attributable in part to an accident of historical timing. Their murders occurred during a pivotal phase of the Civil War back East. While they were killing Coloradans, the attentions of most Americans were riveted on the great campaigns and battles of Chancellorsville, Gettysburg, Vicksburg, Chickamauga, and Chattanooga, which yielded up butcher's bills on a scale previously unimaginable. With such torrents of blood being shed on the battlegrounds of the East, who except those directly concerned was going to notice a string of violent deaths in a remote Western territory?

Another reason they are not better known is that credentialed historians have not told their story in any detail. There exists no single comprehensive, book-length account of their activities that adheres strictly to the principles of historiography. Local and regional histories and some historical journals tell portions of the story; one well-documented biography of Tom Tobin offers a good deal more, though that account is confined to but a single chapter of a book crowded with the other exploits of its remarkable subject.

It may be that some scholarly historians have preferred to dwell on what are perceived as the more wholesome aspects of Colorado's past—mining, railroading, and the like—and to turn away from any topic smacking of the lurid or unseemly, most especially the depredations of the "Bloody Espinosas." Yet to examine frontier outlawry in serious fashion is not to promote cheap melodrama; it is to make a considered effort to understand lawless behavior and to honor those who were its innocent victims or who, like Tom Tobin, chose to stand against it. Conflict of this sort is, after all, at the heart of history; it is through conflict that progress is made. Colorado did not escape this struggle. Yet it was a very nearly complete lacuna in the scholarly historical record of the Espinosas that prompted the author to undertake this study.

Readers may reasonably ask why the writer believes the Espinosas, more than other old-time murderers, deserve to be dragged from relative obscurity into the light. In an age glutted with gory tales of Ted Bundys and Jeffrey Dahmers and John Wayne Gaceys and a hundred other monsters of like kind, is it really necessary to probe the doings of these neglected nineteenth-century killers? After all, Gacey took more victims; Dahmer was more fiendish; Bundy more diabolical. With these horrific examples before us, what can we possibly learn from two men and a boy of Hispanic heritage who, almost 150 years ago, set out to "exterminate the Americans"?[5]

Part of the answer must lie in that last phrase. The Espinosas set out to kill all Anglos. Their stated motive implicitly suggests a twisted version of Hispanic patriotism. One far-fetched surmise says they were once lordly New Mexican *hacendados* until, after the American takeover in 1846, a supposed patriarch, Don Juan Espinosa, was dispossessed of his vast herds and lands and outlawed by the new Anglo rulers.[6] Another blames their vendetta on the Americans who crushed the 1847 Pueblo–New Mexican revolt and hanged its suspected leaders, enraging the young Felipe, who may have witnessed the events.[7] A different theory is that José Vivián, most widely known as Vivián, hated Anglos because two Americans whom the Espinosas had granted food and shelter repaid them by raping a sister.[8]

A member of a civilian posse who helped chase the Espinosas offered a more mercenary motive: he wrote that one of the brothers, in 1860, had traveled to the Anglo mining camp of California Gulch (now Leadville) where a gambler paid him fifty cents to murder a miner with whom the gambler had quarreled. "He then went to Mexico [*sic*] and got his brother and came back to Colorado three years later and resumed his work."[9]

Even more fantastic is a rumor that Pedro Ignasio Espinosa, father of Felipe and Vivián, had been convicted of murder in Mexico and Felipe felt impelled by his patron saint to expiate the sin by killing fifty Americans.[10] Perhaps the most preposterous yarn of all claims that the verifiably New Mexican Espinosas[11] were actually natives of Veracruz in Old Mexico and that during the American bombardment of that city in March 1847, Felipe's parents, grandparents, brother, and sister were all killed. (The 1860 Territorial Census locates the entire family, alive and presumably well, in the *plaza* of San Rafael in the San Luís Valley[12] of what is now southern Colorado.) As a result, Felipe is said to have conceived a deep hatred for all *gringos*, later exacerbated by a vision in which the Virgin Mary commanded him to kill "one hundred Americans for each of his . . . slain relatives."[13]

Equally far-fetched is the fantasy that Felipe, described as "a man of recognized ability and learning," had been a member of the New Mexico legislature until "some reference was made to his nationality that stirred up his resentment and when adjournment came the wound still rankled." Felipe then resolved on "wholesale vengeance against the whites."[14]

Whatever the real source of their animosity, the Espinosas could be viewed, as some Chicano activists regard them even today,[15] as patriotic figures resisting Anglo oppression. A case could be made that they were, for Hispanics, what Eric Hobsbawm has termed "social bandits."[16]

But were they bandits? And if so, what kind? Banditry is defined as the taking of property by force or the threat of force.[17] While the Espinosas began by stealing, they ended as mankillers who also stole. Did they kill and steal because they were crazy? According to Tobin's biographer,[18] Felipe, the oldest, was by nature a violent and mentally unstable individual, so, as is the case with all serial killers, the possibility exists that he might have been criminally insane.[19] But if he was, the condition seems to have come over him later in life than one would expect; he was about forty-two when the murder spree began.[20] Generally acknowledged as the leader, he was a remarkably late bloomer in the business of killing.

When news of their initial outbreak began to spread, the brothers were described in the Denver press as "desperate and lawless bravos, known over the entire country."[21] That claim is difficult to take seriously, since at that time writers for the Denver newspapers paid small heed to goings-on in Conejos and Costilla counties, on the Espinosas' home ground, the San Luís Valley. On the rare occasions when editorialists and correspondents did take note, they tended to dismiss the area as an alien land inhabited almost exclusively by what were often disparagingly called "Greasers."[22] Cultural misunderstandings fed suspicions and disrespect on both sides of the ethnic line. To the Anglos clustered in the gold-bearing areas in and near the Front Range, "southern Colorado" was Pueblo and Colorado City; everything below the Arkansas River Valley was regarded—or, more accurately, dismissed—as "Mexican."[23]

So if the Espinosas had earned a certain reputation for banditry, their depredations must have been confined to the southern region of Colorado and the northern part of New Mexico. But prior to January 1863 their only recorded offenses seem to have been an unknown number of horse thefts, one robbery and assault,[24] and evidently some involvement in a tax revolt by Hispanic farmers that Anglo authorities considered a treasonous conspiracy.[25] If the Espinosas were bandits, social or otherwise, up until the time they commenced killing, no record of their prior exploits has survived beyond those few mentioned. Finally, it is worth noting that as far as we know they never killed anyone until the January day when they were assaulted in their homes by troops of the US Army. Before then, they appear to have been no more dangerous than run-of-the-mill, small-time *bandidos*.

Because they were thought to have been members of a lay religious order not well understood by Anglos, they have often been portrayed as militant agents of a radical faith-based ideology. It was believed they had set out to destroy an alien culture they regarded as greedy, racist, imperialist, and godless. Perhaps, it was often suggested in their own time, they believed themselves to be acting as warriors of faith against the *gringo* infidel.

Tobin's biographer believed, on the basis of information given him by an Espinosa descendant, that Felipe was indeed a member of the Sacred Brotherhood of Our Father Jesus, or the Penitentes,[26] a secret but benevolent offshoot of New Mexican Catholicism whose culture of self-flagellation has at times been suspected of giving rise to violence against outsiders.

Thus, instructive lessons for our times can perhaps be drawn from a close examination of the bloody swathe the Espinosas cut through old-time Colorado.

Their crimes can be seen as foreshadowing the resistance ideology of the Chicano *Movimiento*, the symbolism of the social bandit as hero of the oppressed, the serial killings we wrongly think of as peculiar to our own age of neurosis and alienation, or finally even a fanatical terrorism akin to that of twenty-first-century jihadists.

But are these sufficient reasons to pluck the dread Espinosas from the dustbin of history and parade their massacres before the reader who, already jaded by every day's budget of evil news, has at least been spared, until now, any knowledge of these long-ago renegades? The writer thinks they are, and not simply because the Espinosas were verifiably the worst serial killers in frontier history. Consider how Felipe Espinosa himself explained the killing spree: "They ruined our families. . . . Seeing this we said, 'We would rather be dead than see such infamies committed on our families.' These were the reasons we had to go out and kill Americans—revenge for the infamies committed on our families."[27]

Felipe's assertion weakens all the loftier excuses. Here is no religious rant. No pan-Hispanic screed against generalized Anglo oppression. No self-serving exculpations such as the social bandit Jesse James loved to dole out. Only revenge. Revenge for a single specific trespass on the sanctity of home.

Whatever other motives may have driven them, the Espinosas were wreaking private vengeance. And the vengeance tale is one of the oldest and most compelling of human stories, always worth the telling and hearing, most especially when it teaches, as this one does, a tragic cautionary lesson that resonates in the world we inhabit.

But it is also worth noting that any historical event is nothing but real life set in the past, and that real life is never entirely consistent. Human actions are not resolvable to single causes but instead swarm with mixed and ambiguous impulses. That is why, after sifting through all their possible motives, we are left to ponder the fact that the first and the last victims of the Espinosas were not despised *gringos* at all. They were Hispanos.[28]

And perhaps here is the best reason for this study. Is it not always important to remind ourselves that theories and ideologies can never explain everything, that in the final analysis the human heart is always an insoluble mystery?

NOTES

1. Frank Hall, *History of the State of Colorado* (Chicago: Blakely Printing Company, 1889), 1: 378.

2. *Weekly Commonwealth*, October 28, 1863.

3. Fort Garland in the San Luís Valley of Colorado was the army post from which Tom Tobin was dispatched to hunt down the last two Espinosas. The fort has been restored and includes a well-stocked museum and library.

4. Personal Interview, June 2, 2008.

5. *Weekly Commonwealth*, May 21, 1863.

6. *Albuquerque Tribune*, November 27, 1953.

7. James E. Perkins, *Tom Tobin: Frontiersman* (Pueblo West, CO: Herodotus Press, 1999), 127.

8. Kenneth Jessen, John Lamb, and David Sandoval. "Colorado's Worst Serial Murders: The Espinosa Story," *The San Luís Valley Historian*, Vol. XXVII, No. 4 (1995): 26.

9. Letter of Joseph M. Lamb to J. A. Israel, March 9, 1897, Tom Tobin File, Stephen H. Hart Library, Colorado Historical Society, MSS 224, FF3, Denver, CO.

10. Jessen et al., "Colorado's Worst Serial Murders," 26.

11. The 1845 Mexican census shows the Espinosa family living in El Rito, New Mexico Territory; Virginia Langham Olmstead, *New Mexico Spanish and Mexican Colonial Censuses, 1790, 1823, 1845* (Albuquerque: New Mexico Genealogical Society, 1975). The 1850 US Territorial Census shows them in Santa Ana County and lists their places of birth as New Mexico; 1850 Federal Census of Santa Ana County, New Mexico Territory, http://webcache.googleusercontent.com/search?q=cache:http://files.usgwarchives.net/nm/santaana/census/1850/index/indx02ca.txt.

12. Will Trujillo, "The Espinoza [*sic*] Brothers," *Raices y Ramas*, Vol. I, No. 5 (Winter 1999): 172–175.

13. Christopher O'Brien, *Secrets of the Mysterious Valley* (Kempton, IL: Adventures Unlimited Press, 2007), 304–309.

14. *Rocky Mountain News*, February 27, 1897.

15. George Hartley, Assistant Professor of English, Ohio University, *"I Am Joaquín": Rodolfo "Corky" Gonzales and the Retroactive Construction of Chicanismo*, online at http://epc.buffalo.edu/authors/hartley/pubs/corky.html, accessed January 17, 2013. Hartley argues that Gonzales's 1967 epic poem was "the inaugural work . . . of the Chicano Literary Resistance," fusing into a single unifying force all past Spanish, Mexican, Mestizo, and Native American influences on contemporary Chicano culture. The poem approvingly cites famed Hispanic outlaws who resisted oppression, including the California bandit Joaquín Murieta and the Espinosas.

16. Hobsbawm, in his 1965 work *Primitive Rebels* (New York: Norton, 1965), coined the term to denote those operating outside the law who are seen by the oppressed as heroes of popular resistance. His model has since been challenged by other scholars who point to a lack of solid evidence that peasants have celebrated bandits contemporaneously, though they may have done so retrospectively. Hobsbawm has also recently moderated

this concept. See Richard W. Slatta, ed., *Bandidos: The Varieties of Latin American Banditry* (Westport, CT: Greenwood Press, 1987). However, David J. Weber, in *Foreigners in Their Native Land: Historical Roots of the Mexican Americans*, rev. ed. (Albuquerque: University of New Mexico Press, 2004), 204–205, points out that violence "was the most extreme and probably the least common response of outraged Mexican Americans to Anglo domination." This did not mean that certain *bandidos,* like Tiburcio Vásquez, did not intentionally pose as "social bandits" (see Vásquez's statement on page 227 of Weber's work attributing his crimes to deprivation of his "social rights" by the Anglos). John Boessenecker has convincingly shown in his biography *Bandido: The Life and Times of Tiburcio Vásquez* (Norman: University of Oklahoma Press, 2010), 371–376, that Vásquez, as a native Californio, had little more use for Mexicans than he did for Anglos and preyed on both as a thief and killer, even admitting as much before he was hanged.

17. Slatta, "Eric J. Hobsbawm's Social Bandit: A Critique and Revision," *A Contracorriente: A Journal on Social History and Literature in Latin America*, 2004, at www.ncsu.edu/project/acontracorriente/spring_04/Slatta.pdf, accessed January 17, 2013.

18. Perkins, *Tom Tobin*, 127–128.

19. *The Rocky Mountain News Daily* of February 11, 1872, in a retrospective piece on the Espinosa murders, called Felipe a "monomaniac," but cited no evidence to support the assertion.

20. In the 1860 Federal Census of Conejos County, Taos County, NMT, Felipe Nerio Espinosa, Laborer, Household 1625, reported he was 39 years old. See Trujillo, "The Espinoza Brothers," 172.

21. *Rocky Mountain News Weekly*, February 12, 1863.

22. *Rocky Mountain News Weekly*, March 19, 1863; *Denver Weekly Commonwealth*, October 28, 1863.

23. *Weekly Commonwealth*, April 16, 1863, referred to a development in Pueblo County as "News from the South" and in another article mentioned that the colonel of the First Colorado Volunteers had gone "into the Southern part of the Territory," e.g., Pueblo County, to look after "military affairs in that section."

24. Perkins, *Tom Tobin*, 129.

25. *Rocky Mountain News Weekly*, February 12, 1863.

26. Marta Weigle, *Brothers of Light, Brothers of Blood: The Penitentes of the Southwest* (Santa Fe: Ancient City Press, 1978), 64, 93. There is scant evidence of violent activity by this devout and philanthropic lay fraternity, though Anglos encountering the brotherhood in the nineteenth century often confused its secrecy and bloody penitential exercises with sinister intent. However, there can be little doubt the exercises of the brotherhood were exceedingly brutal, and in the case of volatile personalities like Felipe Espinosa, may have facilitated violent behavior toward others. Michael P. Carroll, in *The Penitente Brotherhood: Patriarchy and Hispano-Catholicism* (Baltimore, MD: Johns Hopkins

University Press, 2002), 189–223, makes an intriguing but ultimately unconvincing case that the flagellations of the brotherhood were manifestations of misdirected Oedipal guilt and rage felt by younger members against their elders, but does not establish a link between these supposed feelings and any violent action against outsiders.

27. *Weekly Commonwealth*, October 28, 1863, quoting the contents of an undated letter written by Felipe Espinosa to Colorado governor John Evans, found on Espinosa's body at his death.

28. A Hispanic corporal of the First New Mexico Volunteer Cavalry, killed, and a Hispanic woman, raped.

1 "Alarming Intelligence and Intense Excitement"

First Murders in the Pike's Peak Country

That year, spring came early to the Front Range of the Rockies and to the great cleft in the mountains to the south where the Arkansas River broke out onto the plains. While frosts were still common at night, by the middle of March the weather had warmed and the grass had started and some of it was standing an inch or two high. "Already its emerald tinge is mellowing down the dark brown of the prairies," one newspaperman exulted. By every account the winter then passing had been the mildest since the settlement of Colorado Territory, "remarkable for the evenness of temperature and slight fall of snow."

To be sure, storms and winds had been unusually severe in the mountains themselves, but even given the turbulence on the high peaks, some observers thought accumulations of snow up there had been only two-thirds the quantity of the previous year. At the foot of the range, snow had not been uncommon but had usually melted away under bright sunlight within a day of falling. An exception was a "severe storm" of snow over a two-day period in mid-December, which "seriously delayed" the mail coaches.[1] Still, not once all winter had the temperature in Denver City dropped below zero.[2]

In fact, wrote Thomas Gibson, editor of Denver's *Weekly Commonwealth*, on the first day of March, a Sunday, "Spring came upon us . . . as the swelling buds

DOI: 10.5876/9781607322375.c01

of the cotton-woods show, and they know their business better than anyone can tell them, and have stood too long in this latitude not to be well aware when the time has come to start their young leaves out into the open air."[3]

The unseasonable weather seemed miraculous, so much so that one Thursday in mid-March the editors of both the Mile-High City's weekly newspapers, normally at daggers drawn on any issue of substance, found in it a rare comity. "Saturday was one of the most lovely and beautiful days which mortals anywhere were blessed with," Gibson rhapsodized. "The air was mild as June, and all nature seemed in the highest enjoyment of the Spring Life which was warming into being everywhere. Overcoats were a burden, and men actually spoke of the necessity of ice."[4]

Nor was Gibson's rival and gadfly, William Byers, editor of *The Rocky Mountain News Weekly,* inclined to stint on the ecstatic hyperbole. "A lovelier day than yesterday never smiled upon the inhabitants of this mundane sphere. The sun shone all day undimmed by a single cloud, and just enough air was moving to pleasantly fan the cheek through open casements. No June weather in the Eastern States ever excelled it in balmy brightness and sunny magnificence. The afternoon was unusually hot, more like July than March. Spring is upon us. Improve the time."[5]

Farmers on the Fontaine qui Bouille[6] in the valley of the Arkansas were already obeying that injunction. They were sowing their wheat. Earlier an agrarian enthusiast there, who signed himself R. Stubbs, had written to the *News Weekly* from near Colorado City:

> Spring is opening under favorable auspices for the people of this section. Many new farming claims are being taken, and old ones further improved. . . . A greatly increased breadth of land will be cultivated in the coming season. Reapers, threshing machines, corn shellers, &c., will be introduced before another harvest, and now that we have got such a good flouring mill in our midst, may not the people of this valley congratulate themselves that they are entering upon a career of usefulness and prosperity, second to none in the whole country.[7]

Little more than a fortnight after Stubbs penned this letter,[8] and only fourteen miles south of Colorado City on a tributary of the Fontaine qui Bouille, a family named Priest was improving their time by settling on their own claim in a narrow, roadless canyon "filled with majestic pines," a place becoming known as Saw Mill Gulch because a group of enterprising men were building a new mill there. One of these, fifty-five-year-old "Uncle" Henry Harkens, was an acquaintance of the Priests. So was the owner of the property, Murdoch McPherson. Helping with the construction of the mill were Alden Bassett, a man named Judd, and four other laborers McPherson had employed in Cañon City.

Almost three years before, Harkens, with McPherson and his extended clan and a family headed by Franklin William Bruce, had set out together from Wisconsin to prospect for gold in Colorado Territory. Harkens and McPherson prospected at the boom camp of Buckskin Joe in South Park,[9] where the Priests came to know them, and the Bruces settled in at California Gulch on the west side of the Snowy Range, today's Mosquito Mountains. Now, on a clear, frosty evening,[10] after a pleasant reunion with old friends, Harkens guided the Priests to the location of their new home, a mile from the site of McPherson's unfinished mill.[11]

A surround of softly pleated hills sheltered the canyon, their summits mostly bare, composed of ruddy earth and outcrops of cinnamon and pale pink rimrock. *Piñon*, dwarf oak, juniper, and scrub pine speckled their girths, and the growth thickened lower down so the bases of the hills were darkly cloaked with the big pines that were going to feed the saws of the new mill. A fast-running creek wended its way through the canyon; its force would be enough to turn the wheel of the mill. The canyon floor was still choked with sage, greasewood, and pale gray clumps of aspen yet to leaf out. A wildly beautiful but brooding and lonely place was this Saw Mill Gulch. The Priests agreed to pitch in and help hack a road through the canyon "to haul lumber away from the mill when it got to running."[12]

It happened that the Bruces, too, were farming now only twenty-odd miles south of Saw Mill Gulch on the other side of the Arkansas, at a place on the prairie known as Hardscrabble.[13] The fifty-eight-year-old Bruce, his wife, Ruth, and their four children were holding a claim on Hardscrabble Creek. They had settled there in 1861 after leaving California Gulch and laying over for a winter in Cañon City. Bruce had built a house six miles south of the Arkansas and taken an irrigation canal out of the creek, one of the earliest such diversions recorded in the Arkansas Valley.[14] He had successfully grown crops for two seasons and beginning this spring he planned on bringing in another.

The Bruce farm stood on a broad unbroken plain sloping almost imperceptibly down to the Arkansas, seamed and wrinkled with deep arroyos. The soil was a light tan, spotted in places with white patches of alkali left behind where ponds of winter snowmelt had dried up in the sun. Dwarf junipers and *cholla* cactus grew here and there. But the arid appearance was deceptive. Around his farm, Bruce's irrigation canal had made this bleak-looking prairie yield a green bounty. And the setting was a breathtaking one. In the distance among the hills north of the Arkansas, snowcapped Pike's Peak seemed to float suspended, more like the dream of a mountain than the thing itself. On the south frowned the low, olive-colored summits of the Wet Mountains. Arching over it all was a vast blue vault of sky.

But Franklin Bruce, as he was known, had seen an opportunity beyond farming to better his prospects; he would supply finished lumber to the new settlers roundabout the Hardscrabble. So as the fine weather continued, he and his sons, Russell and Thadeus, were knowingly or unknowingly following Murdoch McPherson's lead by building their own sawmill amid thick stands of spruce and fir on the upper reaches of the stream six miles south of their farm. All about them stood a forest of ponderosa, a wood less suitable for building material than their chosen spruce and fir. Above them rose the red sandstone ramparts of the Wet Mountains.[15] Like McPherson, Harkens, and the Priests, they, too, were improving their time.

We do not know whether these men, all linked by former connections but separated by the different choices they had made upon arriving in Colorado, had come together in the Arkansas Valley by prearrangement or by happenstance. The distance between them suggests their decisions may not have been collaborative. The only firsthand account we have is that of Priest's son, Henry, told to a woman named Elsie Keeton some two-thirds of a century after the fact. Henry, who must have been very young at the time of the events he describes, confirms that Harkens was a friend from their days at Buckskin Joe but makes no such mention of McPherson, though one historian has shown they were indeed well acquainted.[16]

Whether Bruce and the Priests had previously met, we do not know. What we do know is that the population of central Colorado just then was in flux and many others were making similar new choices. Though the Territory was immense, its white population, always small, had actually dwindled over the past three years. The 1860 Federal Census had enumerated approximately 43,500 people,[17] but by the time of the special Territorial Census the following year, only 25,331 were counted.[18] By 1863 that total must have dropped even further.

Why? The gold strikes of 1858–59 had ignited a stampede from the East into the Golden, Clear Creek, California Gulch, and South Park fields, but placer mining had reached its pinnacle in 1862 and now was declining as more and more of the placers played out and hard-rock mining, requiring costly equipment to break through cap rock and extract the ore, became necessary. Disillusioned gold-seekers gave up and left the Territory to pursue more promising options elsewhere; hardier souls disdained them as "go-backers."[19] Union and Southern sympathizers returning East to join the respective Civil War armies, and increasing depredations by hostile Indians, also accounted for a portion of the exodus. And as mining activity fell off, so did business in the mercantile centers such as Denver, Cañon City, and Colorado City that had furnished the boom. The latter two towns "virtually disappeared" during the war.[20]

With so few people concentrated in only a handful of settlements, it was not remarkable that nearly everybody in Colorado seemed to know everybody else, or know *of* everybody else, in the same way the Bruces knew Murdoch McPherson and Henry Harkens as fellow travelers westward[21] and the Priests knew Harkens and McPherson from the Buckskin Joe goldfields. Nor was it strange that some of those who had lingered in the Territory were now forsaking the long chances of quick wealth and were choosing instead to settle on the land and work it for a living, as had the Bruces, the Priests, McPherson, and his partner, Harkens.[22]

Whether it was by chance or according to plan, these once peripatetic friends were now settling down within forty miles of each other, probably with as much of an eye to permanence as such restless spirits could muster. But before this supernal month of March was done, they would be linked not only by companionship and memories of shared adventures in the gold camps, but also by a catastrophe that would shatter their lives and consume all central Colorado with a contagion of fear.

On Wednesday, March 18, nearly a week after their arrival in the gulch, the Priests were working on the new road while Harkens, McPherson, and Bassett kept busy at the mill-site, Harkens daubing the logs of the cabin and hanging a blanket for a door while his partners applied themselves to construction of the mill. At quitting time McPherson and Bassett decided to visit the Priests to check on their progress with the road. Harkens set about cooking supper.

Returning near sunset from looking over the roadwork, McPherson and Bassett approached their cabin expecting to find supper waiting. Instead, the building stood dark. "I wonder what's the matter that the old man doesn't have a light?" McPherson remarked.

Bassett replied, "You must remember he daubed the cabin today and hung a blanket for a door, so we couldn't see a light if he had one."[23]

Increasingly suspicious, they approached the cabin and, according to Henry Priest, "the first thing that met their gaze was Harkens, lying dead within six feet of the cabin door, his head split open with the ax, and two ugly gashes in his left breast. McPherson thought the murderer must still be in the cabin, so he cocked his gun, and with the barrel cautiously pushed aside the blanket which served as a door. There was no one in the cabin, but everything was topsy-turvy."

The cabin had been plundered, a suitcase of McPherson's had been cut open and the contents scattered about, and a one-hundred-pound sack of flour had been emptied just inside the door. Bassett and McPherson "thought the woods were full of Indians and . . . expected to be scalped any minute." They fled in a panic back to the Priests' where they gasped out the story that Harkens had been killed by Indians. According to Henry Priest:

> Father wanted to go right over and put the body in the cabin where it could be safe from wild beasts, but mother and McPherson and Bassett were so frightened and so sure he had been killed by Indians they would not let him go, so we stood guard all night and at daybreak father started down to the nearest ranch, five miles distant, for help. When he reported the killing a man rode on to Fountain, which was five miles further, and reported the murder there, and by noon there were twenty-five men at our house, and we all went to Harkens' cabin to see what had happened to him and whether there were any Indians about. We found Harkens had been shot in the middle of the forehead with a Colts [*sic*] Navy revolver, then the murderers had taken the ax and split his head open from the top to the mouth, and then, judging from the appearance of his head and the ax, they had hit him on each side of the head with the head of the ax, and two pieces of skull and his brains lay on the ground at the top of his head. He was also stabbed twice in the left breast; two four-inch gashes about three inches apart. He must have been killed shortly after McPherson and Bassett started down the canon, for he had not yet cut the wood with which to cook supper.[24]

It may be reasonably asked how, in the absence of modern-day ballistics, the murder weapon could be identified at once by manufacturer and model, especially since the bullet hole in the forehead, possibly but not necessarily useful in establishing its caliber, would have been eradicated by the ax wounds Priest describes. Equally questionable, after the passage of sixty-six years, is Priest's ability to describe Harkens's other wounds so particularly. But these are trivial questions when measured against the savagery of the crime, which shocked and horrified the surrounding community.

The Priests and their neighbors searched the area of the cabin and the mill for clues:

> The murderers must have still been ransacking the cabin when they heard McPherson and Bassett returning, for judging from their pony tracks they had mounted them and hastily ridden away toward the red cliffs west of the cabin. They had ridden right through the pine tree tops, which were scattered about where the logs for the cabin had been cut, and in one pile of the tree tops we found a chunk of beef they had lost in their flight. They rode back to the red cliffs where there was a sheltered place in a gulch by a ledge of rock and here we found they had evidently cooked their supper; then they mounted their horses and had taken the old trail to Colorado City. This old trail passed within a few rods of father's house, and while we were standing guard the night of the murder the bandits must have passed right by us.[25]

Having satisfied themselves that the murderers had left the area, the saddened party began digging a grave for Harkens. While they were so engaged, two horsemen came down the canyon "at a brisk pace." They proved to be peace officers, identified by Priest as "a sheriff and his deputy from Hardscrabble." They were trailing two men who, they reported, had murdered McPherson's old Wisconsin friend, Franklin Bruce, at his mill-site in the Wet Mountain foothills the day before the killing of Harkens, and at about the same hour. The group gathered around Harkens's half-dug grave was thunderstruck. Bruce, the sheriff related, had been shot several times after walking to the door of his blacksmith shop.[26]

A modern historian relates a slightly different version of Bruce's death. In this account Bruce had left his mill and was climbing out of a gulch toward a meadow where his saddle horse was grazing when two men rode up close to him and shot him through the heart. Then one of his assailants mutilated the body by carving a large cross on his chest with a knife. As at the Harkens place, the murderers then vandalized the mill and its outbuildings. Bruce's horse was left grazing in the meadow.[27]

A Cañon City correspondent signing himself "N.F.C." sent another version of the Bruce slaying to the *Weekly Commonwealth* dated March 19, the day after Harkens's death:

> Last Monday morning, Mr. Bruce left home for the purpose of visiting his saw mill, some six miles away, stating to his family his intention to return immediately. His protracted absence alarming his family, they sent his son, a little boy, to ascertain his whereabouts. He found his father lying upon his face dead, and a portion of his clothing removed. Subsequent examination, by his neighbors and friends, revealed the fact that [the] deceased had been most brutally murdered—most probably for the purpose of robbing him of a valuable horse that he had ridden from home. At the place where the deceased was lying were evidences of a recent struggle, as though he had attempted to prevent his property being taken from him. He was shot through the heart, the direction of the wound being such as to warrant the presumption that the shot had been given by some person on horseback.
>
> As soon as information of the above transaction reached this place, several of our citizens started in pursuit, and it is hoped will succeed in capturing or killing the perpetrators of this damnable deed.[28]

In a postscript, "N.F.C." added, "Since writing the above, the report of another murder has just come in. Mr. Harkins [*sic*], a former highly respected citizen of this town, was found yesterday at his place of residence at the head of the Fontaine-qui-Bouille, shot dead. No particulars."[29]

The peace officers mentioned by Henry Priest as trailing the murderers were in all likelihood Fremont County sheriff Egbert Bradley and an unknown deputy. Fremont County had been organized and its boundaries defined in 1862, and the location of the Bruce killing would have been within Bradley's jurisdiction,[30] though that of Harkens may have lain in El Paso County. Undoubtedly Bradley and his deputy were also the "citizens" who, "N.F.C." wrote, had "started in pursuit" of the murderers.

Henry Priest told Elsie Keeton, "the sheriff and his deputy did not stop long and were soon off again on the trail of the bandits." He claimed they followed the killers "to Colorado City, up through Manitou and on up through Ute Pass, and were the first to find two men the bandits had murdered at the stage stand up Ute Pass the morning after they had murdered Harkens . . . and

The Arkansas River Valley, looking north from near the Franklin Bruce farm. The snowcapped summit of Pike's Peak is faintly visible in the far distance. (Author photo)

they returned to Colorado City and reported that murder there."[31] Of course the town of Manitou did not yet exist,[32] and if the news of killings at Ute Pass was current in March 1863 and not the fruit of the garbled memories of an old pioneer in the 1930s, this may have been the first of a host of false rumors that were to spread panic among the miners and settlers of the young territory in the wake of the deaths of Bruce, Harkens, and, soon, many more.

In fact no one had been killed at Ute Pass. Sheriff Bradley and his deputy lost the trail of the murderers along the Colorado and Tarryall Road[33] somewhere near Ute Pass and seem to have turned back just as Priest reported, since there is no further word of them in the record. By chasing the outlaws as far as Ute Pass, Bradley had already exceeded his authority. Apparently believing he had done all he could, he properly turned the matter over to the authorities of El Paso County and returned home to Cañon City.

Back in Saw Mill Gulch, after the departure of Bradley and his deputy, the Priests, Bassett, McPherson, and their friends "resumed our sad work," Henry Priest recalled. "My father took small logs, and in the grave they had dug he laid the logs as though building a cabin, only he fitted them together as closely as he could. Then we lined the box with fragrant boughs and in this rude casket

Henry Harkens's grave marker in Dead Man's Canyon. (Photo by Ruth Ellen Price)

we placed the body, covered the top tightly with little poles and boughs, then covered all with the soil, and on a rough headstone we carved the words

> Henry Harkens, Murdered Wednesday Eve.,
> March 19th, 1863."[34]

Soon afterward, people ceased calling the little canyon where Henry Harkens died Saw Mill Gulch. They began referring to it as Dead Man's Canyon. They still do.[35]

Over the following days, reports of the double murders in the Arkansas Valley began to spread, and a note of morbid fear entered the accounts, such as this one, written to the *News Weekly* on April 3 from Colorado City:

> **ALARMING INTELLIGENCE**
>
> Intense excitement is now prevailing in this community, in consequence of the several murders and robberies that have been committed quite recently. Franklin Bruce, a well and favorably known citizen and one of the worthy pioneers of our territory, was brutally murdered near Canon City . . . , his horse and a part of his clothing taken. A few days after an old gentleman

> named Hawkens [*sic*], well known at Canon City and in the South Park, as an estimable and inoffensive man, was murdered in his cabin. . . . A few days since Mr. Templeton was shot at in open day by a stranger who approached him on horseback, but this time the cowardly ruffian failed in his diabolical attempt, for Mr. Templeton returned the fire so vigorously as to cause him to wheel his horse and run for dear life.[36]

The writer of this bulletin evidently felt no need to further identify "Mr. Templeton." Thus the modern reader is left to wonder who he was and how reliable a witness he might have been. What we can believe, however, is that his experience—perhaps imaginary, perhaps not, but nowhere else substantiated—bolstered an impression that mysterious villains such as those who had felled Harkens and Bruce were abroad in the land. Tidings of his brush with death, if such it was, went forth to join the unsupported tales that may have already been circulating about the supposed Ute Pass slaughters. It did not help that the *News Weekly* stringer, in writing up Templeton's story, used sensational language he thought appropriate to his subject—"cowardly ruffian," "diabolical attempt." He could hardly be blamed for doing this; lurid characterizations were the stuff of mid-nineteenth-century journalism. But his words, and all the other dread-inducing words soon to come, only poured oil on already spreading fires of suspicion and fear.

But then, as if to mock this first spurt of panic, there would now be a strange lull in the bloodletting, at least matters would so appear. There was no news of fresh killings for another thirteen days, and then not in the immediate vicinity of Ute Pass at all but about twenty miles southwestward, near a remote crossing of the South Platte River in the rugged country verging on the great basin of South Park. Here, within seven miles of what is now called Wilkerson Pass, in the only house between Colorado City and the South Park gold camp of Tarryall,[37] lived a young man named John Addleman, a hay farmer who also kept a way station for mail riders serving between those two points.

Like Mr. Templeton in Colorado City, John Addleman has left us no description, no likeness, no life story.[38] But in his case the absence of personal information is especially poignant. Templeton had little significance for our story; Addleman is central. For he was the next man to die at the hands of the unknown destroyers.

He seems to have lived alone, a bachelor or perhaps a widower. Beyond this single fact we cannot go. We cannot tell his place of birth, his exact age, the

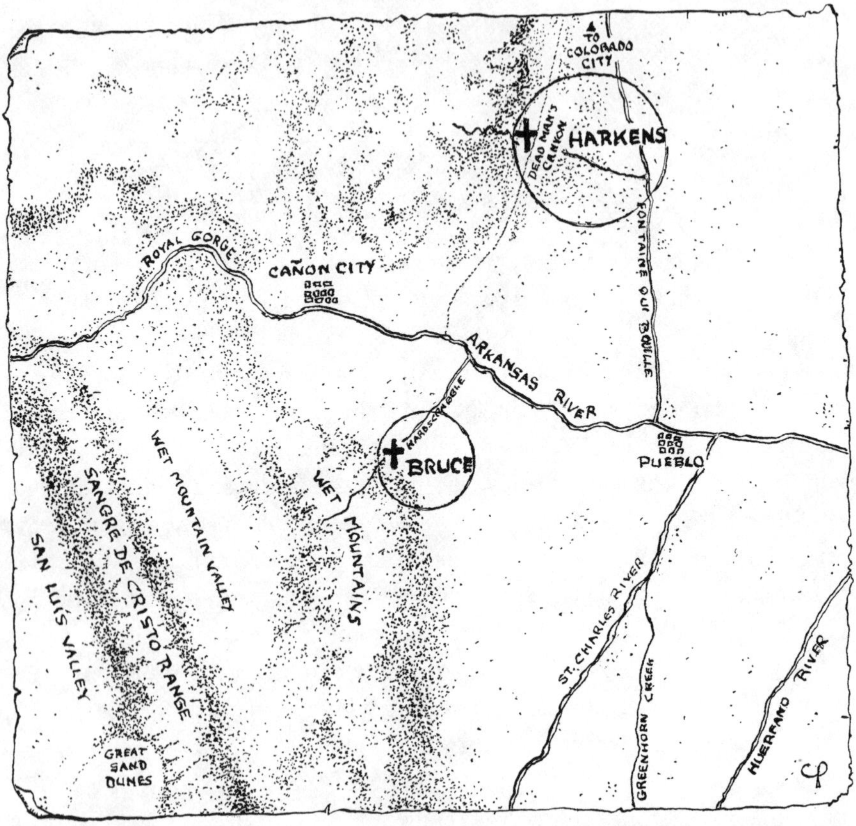

Death sites of Franklin William Bruce and Henry Harkens in the Hardscrabble and Fontaine qui Bouille country.

color of his hair and eyes, what he liked to eat, his political preferences, or why he had chosen to live in "the only house between Colorado City and Tarryall," a distance of something over one hundred very lonesome miles. Why did he choose to be a hay farmer in this remote and dangerous place? How and why did he come to operate a mail station? Intriguing questions. Unanswerable questions.

On March 31 the mail carrier between Tarryall and Colorado City, a man named Rowe, rode into the latter place and reported having made his routine stop at Addleman's only to find the place empty and "disordered." Rowe saw no sign of Addleman, presumed he had been murdered, and "decided to leave immediately."[39]

As reported later by a *Rocky Mountain News Weekly* correspondent signing himself "H.," Rowe "got but a short distance when a suspicious looking character tried to head him off, but Mr. Rowe eluded him and by riding all night arrived here in safety. Such intelligence aroused the fears of our citizens. Sheriff Shapter, with a posse of half a dozen men, repaired to the scene and found their worst fears realized."[40] Here again, as in the case of Templeton, a "suspicious character" is seen and the worst is assumed, though whoever "tried to head him off" may have been entirely innocent of ill intent.

"H." then gave further particulars of Addleman's fate, using inflammatory language calculated to whip up strong emotions, as had the writer of the April 3 article:

> Mr. Addleman had been shot but a short distance from his house, with two balls through the heart, and what seems more horrible, those fiends incarnate, seem to have worried their victim as the cat does the mouse before killing him. Mr. Addleman was a young man of great respectability, well known here, and as would be natural, his horrid murder following so soon after the others, has caused great excitement among the people here.[41]

Noting that "a company is being made up to follow and capture the murderers if possible," the *News Weekly* went on to editorialize that "an organized band of murderers and thieves are undoubtedly prowling in our neighborhood, and it behooves every citizen to be prepared for every emergency; as no one knows when his house may be entered by the midnight assassin or himself waylaid in broad daylight."

Having thoroughly alarmed the reading public, the editor then proclaimed, "We are no alarmist, yet think it proper to give the public the true condition of things here." The *Weekly Commonwealth,* in an unsigned dispatch from Colorado City dated April 3, after recounting the murders of Bruce and Harkens, had more to say about Addleman's fate. The correspondent wrote that a pony was stolen from "Tappin's [*sic*] ranche,[42] near Colorado City," the day after the death of Harkens and that "the murderers and robbers then struck for the mountains," where they followed a Mr. Gill, of the Fontaine qui Bouille, who was "going up with a team." The killers "followed him to where he camped, and while after his cattle that had strayed, they came to his wagon and took his rifle, and some things of little value." This is said to have occurred on March 29. The attack on Addleman supposedly occurred the following day.

Approximate location of the murder of John Addleman southeast of Wilkerson Pass. (Author photo)

Mr. Gill, like Mr. Templeton in Colorado City, is another otherwise unidentified source, and it is unclear how either he, or the writer of the April 3 dispatch, could have known that the persons who stole a pony from Tappan's ranch were the same ones who "struck for the mountains," followed Gill, stole his rifle, and then went on to Addleman's mail station. The *Weekly Commonwealth* reporter went on to give a few additional details of what had occurred at the murder site:

> They shot Mr. Adalman [*sic*] about one hundred yards from the house, robbed him of his boots and about $75, tore everything upside down in the house, and left before the mail rider got there. . . . He had been shot with a rifle supposed to be the one taken from Gill, as it was a double one and two ball holes were found close together, under his arm. There is no doubt but that there is a band of bushwhackers in this part of the country at the present time; so look out for them.[43]

A modern historian writes that Addleman may have been in bed asleep when the murderers called him out of his house because his bare footprints

John Addleman's grave, recently anonymously restored. (Photo courtesy of Christie Wright)

Addleman's grave inscription. (Photo courtesy of Christie Wright)

were found in his dooryard. The same author cites unnamed sources claiming Addleman was "butchered."[44] His body was buried near his cabin by "Mr. Gill and his party"[45] in a grassy meadow opposite a rocky headland. A nearby stream came, in time, to bear a variation of his name, Adalman's Creek. Later the site became known as Rocky Graveyard and Addleman's resting place was lined with stones.[46] More recently it has been enclosed with a fence and a wooden marker erected. The pine-clad, rock-studded peaks of the Puma Hills watch over him now, eternally, and the many facts and secrets of his life are buried with his bones. All that is left of him is the story of his tragic passing.

So began the most horrific spate of serial killings in the annals of the American West. As one of the authors of the *History of the Arkansas Valley* wrote retrospectively in 1881:

> In that time every man within a radius of fifty miles was a neighbor, and the effect of these events was simply appalling. The visitation of death, in the garb of murder, first here, then there, and then in two places at once, was as if the hand of the destroyer was abroad and wreaking a promiscuous vengeance on all mankind. The sense of dread insecurity which pervaded the community . . . can be realized only through an experience which none could wish repeated.[47]

NOTES

1. *Weekly Commonwealth*, December 18, 1862.

2. These references to weather conditions in the spring of 1863 come from Denver's *Rocky Mountain News Weekly* of February 19, March 19 and 26.

3. *Weekly Commonwealth*, March 5, 1863.

4. *Weekly Commonwealth*, March 19, 1863.

5. *Rocky Mountain News Weekly*, March 19, 1863.

6. This name, given by French trappers earlier in the century, means "Boiling Fountain." It was inspired by the soda and mineral springs near the headwaters of the creek at what is now Manitou Springs. In 1863 the French usage was still common, though more and more often its present name, Fountain Creek, was being heard. See Taylor, *Colorado South of the Border*, 538, and William Bright, *Colorado Place Names* (Boulder, CO: Johnson Books, 2004), 68.

7. *Rocky Mountain News Weekly*, March 19, 1863.

8. March 12, 1863.

9. George G. Everett and Wendell F. Hutchinson, *Under the Angel of Shavano* (Denver, CO: Golden Bell Press, 1863), 57–59. Among the McPhersons on the wagon train was a young girl, Annabel, later the wife of Civil War veteran and prominent south Arkansas cattleman Joseph Sykes Hutchinson, whose son, John Arthur Hutchinson, and great-grandson, Joseph D. Hutchinson, have told how, during the trip west, one of the McPherson children, Annabel's brother John, fell out of the wagon. Harkens, the driver, "looked back just as little John fell . . . and got the oxen stopped just before the great iron-tired wheel started over John, [only] bruising his side." John's mother, Helen McPherson, "a staunch Presbyterian from Scotland, always thought it was an act of God that made Harkins [*sic*] look back." Typescript, letters of John Arthur Hutchinson to Joseph D. Hutchinson dated May 21, 1935, and August 25, 1939, in which Harkens is said to have leaped from the wagon, jumped in front of the oxen, and called "whoa" just in the nick of time; also the reminiscences of Joseph D. Hutchinson, August 13, 1983, both at Hutchinson Homestead Ranch and Learning Center, National Register of Historic Places, Poncha Springs, Colorado; courtesy of Mike and Colleen Perschbacher, Older Than Dirt Construction Co., restorers of the Hutchinson home and ranch outbuildings.

10. Meteorological Chart, *Rocky Mountain News Weekly*, March 19, 1863.

11. Henry Priest, "The Story of Dead Man's Canyon and of the Espinosas," *The Colorado Magazine*, Vol. VIII (January 1931): 34.

12. Ibid., 35.

13. Janet LeCompte, *Pueblo, Hardscrabble and Greenhorn: The Upper Arkansas, 1832–1856* (Norman: University of Oklahoma Press, 1978), 109, quotes a letter of George S. Simpson, one of the 1844 settlers of the area, saying Hardscrabble took its name from the "hard scrabbling" required to get in a crop with a single plow and "half a dozen hoes among

the nine of us." Though the name suggests the soil was inhospitable to farming, in fact Hardscrabble boasted year-round springs and wells, but the stream itself tended to dry up in summer. When aided by irrigation from the creek, good crops could be grown. Famed cattleman Charles Goodnight, in 1869, found the plain around Hardscrabble "well-watered, sheltered and covered with uncropped grama." See J. Evetts Haley, *Charles Goodnight: Cowman and Plainsman* (Norman: University of Oklahoma Press, 1936), 260. Similar conditions in the 1840s had encouraged early ranchers to overgraze the grasslands, so what Goodnight saw must have reflected a recovery from that damage. Some sources assert the name Hardscrabble actually originated when the earliest settlers were chased out of the valley in 1854 by hostile Ute Indians. One of the fugitives claimed he and his neighbors had "a hard scrabble" to get out of the valley and into the Wet Mountain hills. See Bright, *Colorado Place Names*, 82, and Taylor, *Colorado South of the Border*, 520. Also see O. L. Baskin, *History of the Arkansas Valley, Colorado* (Chicago: O. L. Baskin & Co., 1881), 547.

14. Wilbur Fiske Stone, *History of Colorado* (Chicago: S. J. Clarke Publishing Co., 1918), I: 493. The earliest-priority ditch taken out of Hardscrabble was officially recorded May 1, 1860. It should be noted, however, that much of the area had been irrigated two decades before by the traders who were among the first settlers in the Arkansas Valley. See LeCompte, *Pueblo, Hardscrabble and Greenhorn*, 107.

15. Perkins, *Tom Tobin*, 132–133.

16. Ibid., 132–134.

17. Eugene H. Berwanger, *The Rise of the Centennial State: Colorado Territory, 1861–1876* (Urbana: University of Illinois Press, 2007), 8–10.

18. Frank Hall, *History of the State of Colorado*, II: 267.

19. Duane A. Smith, *The Birth of Colorado: A Civil War Perspective* (Norman: University of Oklahoma Press, 1989), 6.

20. Berwanger, *The Rise of the Centennial State*, 8–10. Berwanger estimates 15,000 to 16,000 people left Colorado Territory between 1860 and 1866.

21. Bruce, McPherson, and Harkens met by chance at a wagon-train rendezvous of gold-seekers at Sparta, Wisconsin, in June 1860. See Perkins, *Tom Tobin*, 133.

22. Evidently Harkens had also lived for a time in Cañon City. A correspondent for the *Weekly Commonwealth* of March 26, 1863, referred to him as "formerly a highly respected resident of this town." In the April 2 edition of the same paper another correspondent from Buckskin Joe in South Park called him "an old and much respected citizen, and formerly of the firm of Harkins [*sic*] & Cooper."

23. Priest, "Dead Man's Canyon and the Espinosas," 36.

24. Ibid.

25. Ibid., 36–37.

26. Ibid., 37.

27. Perkins, *Tom Tobin*, 134.

28. *Weekly Commonwealth*, March 26, 1863.

29. Ibid.

30. While Henry Priest said the sheriff and deputy were "from Hardscrabble," he evidently meant they had come from the Bruce murder scene at Hardscrabble, not that they were officials of that particular area. Perkins, *Tom Tobin*, 137, says the lawmen were from Cañon City, the seat of Fremont County. Bradley became Fremont County's third sheriff in November 1862 and seems to have served until October 1863. See *History of Sheriff's Department, Fremont County*, http://www.fremontco.com/sheriff/history.shtml, accessed January 17, 2013. See also B. F. Rockafellow, "History of Fremont County," in Baskin, *History of the Arkansas River Valley*, 567.

31. Priest, "Dead Man's Canyon and the Espinosas," 37–38.

32. Bright, *Colorado Place Names*, 111.

33. Virginia McConnell Simmons, *Bayou Salado: The Story of South Park*, rev. ed. (Boulder: University Press of Colorado, 2002), 78. In 1862, Simmons writes, the Ute Pass Wagon Road Company constructed this road from Colorado City into South Park. It is doubtful an active stage stand existed on the road at this time due to the decline in activity at the South Park goldfields.

34. Priest, "Dead Man's Canyon and the Espinosas," 37.

35. The actual death date is March 18. The website Single Graves and Abandoned Cemeteries, El Paso County, Colorado (http://files.usgwarchives.net/co/elpaso/cemeteries/single.txt) states, "the Harkens grave is located on the east side of Highway 115, about 5.8 miles south of the main entrance to Fort Carson, Southwest of Colorado Springs. Visible from the road, it is ringed by a white fence set on a small rise and crowned by scrub oak. According to GPS-derived geolocation (accurate to within 10 meters), the memorial's coordinates are latitude [38° 40' 16.3" North] and longitude [104° 51' 30.2" West]. The original marker has been embedded in a larger tombstone-shaped concrete marker. Faint lines from the original inscription are visible but not genuinely legible on the lichen-covered stone." Site accessed January 17, 2013. The author has visited and photographed the gravesite on several occasions and a photograph taken by his wife, Ruth, appears in this book. Interestingly, as the photograph shows, someone is regularly decorating the grave—at last visit it was found with a silken cross of Hispanic design wired to the fence, artificial flowers on the grave itself, and coins of American money lying on the top of the headstone.

In the May 8, 1911, issue of the *Alaska Citizen* of Fairbanks, Alaska, an article on the Espinosas began with these evocative paragraphs:

> In Dead Man's Canon where the red sandstone, rising in massive shafts against the mountain skies and the red dust flying in the roadway, calls to the imaginative mind the blood stains of the crimes committed in that primeval spot, there is a lonely grave marked with a slab of that red stained stone. Not thirty feet from the new

road, made smooth and even by the hands of convicts—on the right of way going to Canon City—rises this small shaft. The grave rests beneath the spreading fingers of an old spruce tree and on the headstone is carved in rude letters:

"H.Harkins [*sic*], murdered Wednesday Evening, March 19, 1863"

Today the automobiles, chugging between Colorado Springs and Canon City, throw the red dust over the grave of Henry Harkins . . . lying mouldering in the ground these forty-eight years across from [where] his old sawmill stood. [He] was one of the first victims of those murdering Mexicans whose mysterious and sinister influence fell upon the mountain dwellers with almost supernatural terror back in the days when the country was new. When the new Canon City road was being planned there was talk of moving the grave of Henry Harkins, but the spirit of the old pioneer, a victim of the cruel Espinosas, must have murmured through the sheltering spruce—for the red stone still remains a reminder of hideous crimes.

The piece is attributed to celebrated *Rocky Mountain News* reporter Alice Rohe. Perkins, *Tom Tobin*, 172, note 23, says the grave was moved "a short distance east" in 1947 to accommodate the widening of Highway 115. Joseph D. Hutchinson (note 9 above) says John Arthur ("Uncle Art") Hutchinson was instrumental in convincing the state highway engineers to preserve the gravesite. It is presently accessible through a break in the highway guardrail and is protected on the east by barbed wire bounding the Fort Carson Military Reservation.

36. *Rocky Mountain News Weekly*, April 16, 1863.

37. Ibid.

38. Addleman evidently came into the Pike's Peak area in 1861; *The Colorado Springs Gazette Telegraph*, March 8, 1959, section BB, pp. 8 and 10.

39. Ibid.

40. Ibid. The "Sheriff Shapter" mentioned in this article appears nowhere else in the old-time records this author has consulted. A David Spielman was sheriff in early 1865, according to his interview that appeared in the Pioneer edition's magazine section of the *El Paso County Democrat*, Colorado Springs, December 1908, 12. http://historyofthespielmanfamily.blogspot.com/2006/10/history-of-spielman-family-1730-1944.html, accessed February 20, 2013. The online history of the El Paso County Sheriff's Office identifies Rankin Scott Kelly as the first sheriff, appointed at the organization of the county in 1861, "A Brief History of the El Paso County Sheriff's Office," http://shr.elpasoco.com/Office+History.htm, accessed January 17, 2013. It is possible, though admittedly improbable, that "H." could have confused the name Spielman with that of Shapter.

41. Ibid.

42. This must have been the ranch of Lewis N. Tappan, one of the original founders of El Paso County, or perhaps of his cousin, Samuel F. Tappan, at this time lieutenant colo-

nel of the First Regiment of Colorado Volunteers; A. Z. Sheldon, "History of El Paso County," in Baskin, *History of the Arkansas River Valley*, 419, 420.

43. *Weekly Commonwealth*, April 16, 1863.

44. Perkins, *Tom Tobin*, 141. Perkins also writes that the death of Addleman occurred about April 8, after the killings of Binkley and Shoup in South Park (see Chapter 2). This date is at least a week later—and possibly even later still—than the date the newspaper sources suggest. It is not absolutely certain from the news accounts whether Addleman was murdered on March 31 or that his body was discovered on that date. The author believes he could have been killed a day or two before March 31.

45. *Weekly Commonwealth*, April 16, 1863. The gravesite is about three and a half miles west of the present Lake George just off County Road 92. The body of Franklin Bruce was taken to Cañon City and buried there, but the site has been lost. Perkins, *Tom Tobin*, 172–173.

46. Article by Park County Historian Harold Warren, "Cold-Blooded Killers Terrorized Local Folks in 1863," *Fairplay Flume*, April 18, 1990.

47. A. Z. Sheldon, "History of El Paso County," 425.

"Most Horrible and Fiendish Murders"
The Bleeding of South Park Begins 2

Remembering his entrance into South Park at the height of its first frenzied gold rush in 1859, a prospector from Kentucky named Daniel Ellis Conner later gave a somewhat prosaic description, calling it "a fine, grassy, grazing country in the summer and perhaps forty miles across it. In the winter the snow falls two or three feet deep and remains until May. It is rolling country, interspersed with clumps of trees and small open parks, and at that time a great range for wild game and the Ute Indians in the summer."[1]

But some quality beyond what Conner's matter-of-fact minimalism can convey lingers in this vast place. It seems a thing somehow implacable and indifferent. Even Conner felt it in time: "This whole land and the imposing mountains of the main divide," he wrote of a later visit, "were all covered with snow and offered a terribly bleak-looking aspect."[2] In the transitional seasons of spring and fall, what one apprehends is simply the winter that lurks amid the heights early and late, ready to sweep down without warning and turn any soft bright day into a blinding blizzard.

In March or September, from Kenosha Pass at the northeastern entrance to the Park, the eyes can sweep the mountain-bound horizon and see starkly different weather patterns at every quarter of the compass; here a storm of rain occasionally veined by lightning, trailing its gray hem over the peaks, its thunders too

DOI: 10.5876/9781607322375.c02

distant to be heard; yonder a brilliant welcoming sun in a clear sky; there, immense occluded clouds rolling darkly down from towering summits, spewing squalls of snow; and from yet another direction a constant bone-numbing wind that blows bursts of sleet that sting like birdshot.

At any time of the year, the Park can look especially sinister. Latter-day water diversion arrangements, preventing development, have left huge tracts oddly, even eerily vacant. But something else confers a bleak air of the ominous. Even in the glare of high summer, amid the tourist bustle of South Park City and the hum of traffic on Highway 285, a strange gloom can settle over its solitudes and it is not difficult to imagine that what one apprehends is the whiff of a terrible past.

From time immemorial the Park was the preferred hunting ground of the Ute Indians because immense herds of bison, antelope, and other game grazed there, but that very abundance excited the envy of other tribes, especially Arapahos and Cheyennes from down on the plains, and many battles were fought for possession of the Park's buffalo, grasslands, streams, and salt marshes. White explorers witnessed some of these fights, which continued until the early 1860s and took many lives and scalps even as the buffalo herds dwindled and eager Argonauts began pouring into the Park. With the gold rush, inevitably, came rough-and-tumble mining camps like Fairplay, Hamilton, Jefferson, Tarryall City, Mosquito, and Buckskin Joe, bringing in their wake an inevitable contagion of lawlessness: claim-jumpings, robberies, and shootings. South Park's air of menace is well earned; its ground is dark and bloody indeed.

But in the spring of 1863, with the dwindling-away of placer mining, the increasing difficulties associated with penetrating barren rock or refractory ore bodies so as to pursue successful hard-rock mining,[3] and the Civil War siphoning young men off eastward to join the ranks of the contending armies, South Park, like most of the gold-rush camps of the Territory, was losing population and, despite some lingering pockets of activity,[4] its economy was beginning to stagnate.[5] Its original air of forbidding, silent emptiness had begun to replace the feverish gush of hydraulic hoses, the thumping of stamp mills, the grinding of *arrastras,*[6] and the clang of single-jack drilling against cap rock,[7] sounds that had characterized its heyday only a year or so before.

Measuring sixty miles from east to west, forty-five miles wide, Park County proper contains something like 2,166 square miles. The Park itself is actually a geological basin covering 1,400 square miles of space, counting 900 square

Tarryall Creek Valley, likely the murderers' route into South Park. (Author photo)

miles of plain and foothills and its ring of mountains as far as their tips above timberline, slate-dark in summer, snow-mottled in winter.[8] Its elevation ranges from about 7,200 feet to more than 14,000 feet on its westernmost peaks.[9] It is bounded on the west by the Mosquito Range, known in the 1860s as the Snowy Range, and by the eastern bulge of the Continental Divide along a line of mountains now called the Park Range. On the west it is hemmed in by the Tarryall Mountains and the Puma Hills. It is drained by the headwaters of the South and Middle forks of the South Platte River and by Tarryall Creek, which flows between the Puma Hills and the Tarryall Mountains, eventually joining the Platte River in the hills of the Front Range.[10] Denver lies about fifty miles northeast, Cañon City about the same distance southeast. Coming from Denver, travelers enter the Park through Kenosha Pass; from Cañon City they use the eastern gateway, Wilkerson Pass, which pierces the Puma Hills.

In 1863, Saw Mill Gulch, where Henry Harkens died, would have lain some sixty or seventy miles distant from Wilkerson Pass, measured by the roads and trails of the day. The farm and sawmill of Franklin Bruce at Hardscrabble would have lain only a few miles farther south, across the flats of the Arkansas, at the edge of the Wet Mountains. From the lonely spot in the Puma Hills where the body of John Addleman rested, Wilkerson was only seven miles distant.

But one need not enter the Park by way of either pass through its encircling curtain of mountains. Instead, at a point about halfway between Ute Pass and Wilkerson, one can turn north and west along the broad valley of a winding watercourse called Tarryall Creek and travel upstream through some quietly stunning scenery, thirty-five to forty miles of it, and emerge at the base of Kenosha Pass at the northern end of the Park, having quartered across its easternmost edge.

This is almost certainly the route followed by the mysterious assassins who murdered Bruce, Harkens, and Addleman down in the Pike's Peak country. While the pass road was heavily traveled,[11] the remote Tarryall wilderness gave ready shelter for those who had reason to move in secrecy.[12] And these men had need of secrecy, for South Park would now be their killing ground. They would shed blood here in this imposing and baleful space, off and on, for thirty long days.

In 1863 spring came early to South Park, as it had to Hardscrabble and the Fontaine qui Bouille. "The long sunny days of spring are gliding in upon us, balmy and calorific, causing the water in the creeks to make 'a run upon the banks,'" reported the *Weekly Commonwealth*'s correspondent "Dornick," who fancied himself a wit, if punning can be considered a form of wit. He wrote from Montgomery, a mining camp in the Park at the head of the North Fork of the Platte, on March 20.[13] In his next dispatch, dated April 4, he announced "'Ye merrie sprynge tymme' which was to arrive is now arriving . . . and all nature is jubilant"; but he also complained, "the emigration to the new mines continues, slowly. Every day or two a man is taken off with Bannock [*sic*] on the brain."[14]

His reference was to recent gold strikes at Bannack and Virginia City, in what had once been the Territory of Dakota but in March had become Idaho Territory.[15] The strikes were being touted as the richest diggings yet discovered in the West. Many gold-seekers who had joined the flood into Colorado in 1859 only to see their hopes of quick riches wither away were now pulling stakes for what were universally being called "the new mines," adding

South Park, looking southwest from Kenosha Pass. (Author photo)

yet another stream to the general bleeding-off of population from Colorado. Among these were two men, Abram Nelson Shoup and Jacob M. Binkley, who set out for Bannack from the lower end of South Park on Tuesday, April 7, 1863.

As was the case with John Addleman, relatively little is known of Jacob Binkley, other than he was about twenty-three years of age, was born in Indiana, and had lived in Illinois and Iowa before coming to Denver in 1860 with an older brother.[16] He seems to have been a partner of Shoup. About Shoup we know a good deal more, mostly because he was the brother of a prominent Coloradan, First Lieutenant George Laird Shoup of the First Regiment of Colorado Cavalry.[17] Abram Shoup, a native of Slate Lick, Pennsylvania, was less than a month shy of his twenty-ninth birthday[18] when he and Binkley started out with an ox team that Tuesday morning from Philo Weston's wayside house at the eastern base of Weston Pass, one of the easier if longer routes into the Park through the Snowy Range.[19]

By Wednesday evening they had ascended Kenosha Hill at the Park's upper end and "between four and five o'clock"[20] drove past the Kenosha House, a noted hostelry on the west side of the hill[21] that offered accommodations

The Kenosha House. Binkley and Shoup were killed a short distance north and west of this location. (Photo courtesy of History Colorado; scan no. 10027856)

for travelers between Denver and the Park. Evidently choosing to spend the delightful spring night outdoors rather than take rooms at a hotel, they camped in a gulch a mile and a half below the Kenosha House and were seen that evening "by different parties, while cooking and eating their suppers, and they appeared very much elated with the prospect before them."[22]

Next morning George W. Harriman,[23] owner of the Kenosha House, noticed three oxen eating hay in front of his barn and recognized the animals as belonging to Binkley and Shoup. He assumed they had strayed, and since he already had business farther up the Denver road, he and an associate decided to drive the oxen to the travelers' camp to save them the trouble of going in search of them.

Arriving at the campsite, Harriman and his companion at first saw no sign of either man, then, to their shock, discovered the corpse of Binkley sixty-five yards from the partners' wagon, lying facedown, his pockets turned out and his money gone. He had been shot once in the back, the ball passing through his body and coming to rest just beneath the skin of his chest. Shoup was nowhere in evidence. About this time, travelers passing by on the Denver road joined Harriman in a search for the missing man. Some distance from Binkley's body they found footprints presumed to be Shoup's, and then, farther along, his coat, which had been flung to the ground.

The searchers then surmised that Binkley and Shoup might have fallen into a dispute and Shoup had killed his partner and fled. But this suspicion was erased as the search continued and Harriman eventually found Shoup's body lying nearly four hundred yards from the wagon; he had been stabbed three times in the chest and hideously mutilated about the head. He, too, had been robbed.

A South Park resident named R. Berry then arrived, having learned of the murders in Fairplay. Two days later, from the Kenosha House, he wrote a letter to the *Rocky Mountain News Weekly* describing the crime, beginning with the forbidding statement, "We are under the necessity of communicating to you intelligence of the perpetration of the most horrible and fiendish murders that has [*sic*] ever disgraced the records of our young Territory."

After giving an account of the affair and noting that Binkley and Shoup were "both well known in this community and were peaceable, quiet and respectable citizens," he expressed an opinion that the partners must have been "murdered for their money, of which they had some hundred and forty or fifty dollars. But who the murderers are is a mystery. Every effort will be made to hunt up the perpetrators, but as yet we have very little evidence to guide us in the search."

Berry's letter concluded with a now familiar exhortation. "By giving this a place in your columns you may possibly arouse the citizens of the Territory to an effort to hunt out and bring justice to those midnight murderers who are lurking throughout the country."[24]

A second account of the atrocity came to Denver from Hugh Murdock, landlord of the South Park Hotel in Fairplay,[25] whose last name the typesetter misspelled as "Muspeck." In a letter dated April 11 he related events substantially as

Berry had given them, but reflecting the hysteria that was beginning to spread in the wake of the killings, he also gave the names of Addleman and three other men said to have been lately slain (Addleman being the only proven victim). "And even this is not all," trumpeted Murdock. "We have news of seven more bodies having been found dead in this vicinity within the last eight or ten days."[26] Like the three erroneously named with Addleman, these seven victims must also have been imaginary, as no other contemporary source confirms them.

Murdock appealed to the Territorial authorities for protection: "Now, I would ask if this is not enough to stir the Pet Lambs and their officers to come to the rescue of our citizens."

The First Regiment of Colorado Volunteers (Infantry), originally formed and supplied by William Gilpin, the first Territorial governor, at the outbreak of the Civil War, were nicknamed—at first derisively by Southern sympathizers—"Gilpin's Pet Lambs." Though an unruly and disorderly lot, they had distinguished themselves during the 1862 Confederate invasion of New Mexico and by 1863 had grown fond of what had begun as a term of opprobrium. In November 1862 the unit was reorganized as the First Colorado Cavalry because the War Department believed horse troops would be more effective in Indian fighting. They also became popularly known as the "Onesters" or the "Firsters." The commanding officer was Colonel John M. Chivington, generally thought of as the hero of the battle of Glorieta Pass. Since much of Colorado still lacked organized civilian law enforcement in 1863, the First Colorado was often called upon to perform police duties.[27]

"One good day's ride will fetch them to the place of these depredations," Murdock wrote of the "Firsters." "Ask them if they will not come. If they do not, the people will leave the gulches." The miners, he averred, had no guns or ammunition or they would have gone after the murderers on their own account, "and they now call on the Colorado First to show themselves, as they did in [New] Mexico."

"There are but a few of these murderers," Murdock continued, "but they will go from road to road, and kill every man that passes. . . . If the Governor[28] won't do something for this part of Colorado, the people will all leave it." He added that the bodies of Binkley and Shoup "are at present awaiting interment in my store, and will be buried in this place tomorrow."[29]

A third account of the deaths of Binkley and Shoup also appeared in the same April 16 edition of the *News Weekly*. The editors gave it the arresting headline "Horrible Murder." It repeated much of the content and language of Berry's letter. It concluded, however, with a sentiment echoing Murdock's sense of urgency: "Two more murders added to the already startling list for the last month, and there seems no clue to the perpetrators.—Something must be done, and a terrible example made of the miscreants who infest the country."[30]

The *Weekly Commonwealth* for April 16 contained no news about the deaths of Binkley and Shoup. "Dornick," who ordinarily would have covered the story, seems to have been in Colorado City at the time of the killings, gathering information for his account of the murders of Bruce, Harkens, and Addleman, which did appear in the paper that day.[31] It was not until the April 23 edition that "Dornick" addressed himself to the South Park killings. By then he was in Central City, along with several other "honest citizens of Montgomery, Buckskin Joe and thereabouts," attending a session of the United States District Court.[32]

His reporting basically rehearsed what the *News Weekly* had offered on April 16 but added one detail not previously cited and, typically, he inserted his own editorial note: "The mail carrier on the road from Hamilton to Colorado [City] was chased by guerrillas a few days ago and barely escaped by running his horse. It is time a few of these jayhawkers were strung up to a cottonwood limb." Then, in a postscript based on "a private letter just received from Buckskin," "Dornick" wrote of the murders of Binkley and Shoup, adding nothing of substance to what had already been covered by the rival paper. As always, however, he was ready with an opinion: "[T]his seems to settle it that both the men were murdered by guerrillas for their money, as none was found on them, and they had a considerable amount when they left home two days before the murder."[33]

Finally, "Dornick," like Murdock before him, could not keep from purveying unverified rumors of other persons supposed to have been assassinated: "The letter conveying the news of the finding of Shoup also states that on Friday night last two men were murdered near Fairplay and robbed by unknown parties. The writer had not yet learned the names of the persons found dead."[34]

Nor would he, for there seem to have been no such new victims. But if "Dornick's" reputed murders were imaginary, the fears kindled by the very real slayings of Bruce, Harkens, Addleman, Binkley, and Shoup were not. They began to grip the whole of Colorado.

Much of this alarm could be attributed to what we might call a perfect storm of publicity. The April 16 edition of the *News Weekly* had carried no less than three accounts of the killings of Binkley and Shoup, all on the same page, as well as references to the earlier murders. The *Weekly Commonwealth*, scooped on April 16, soon made up for its lapse with gripping accounts in its later editions. The effect was to give a misleading impression that blood-curdling events that had happened over the course of almost a month's time had instead occurred in a much shorter period.

This was a problem inherent in frontier news reporting. Owing to the absence of telegraphic communications,[35] the Denver newspapers relied for much of their content on dispatches written by part-time correspondents like "Dornick" or public-spirited citizens like Murdock and Berry. These writers lived at various points around the Territory and sent their material to the editorial offices either by mail or by express rider. Naturally this method entailed substantial time lags between the occurrence of newsworthy events and their appearance in print. While both the *Weekly Commonwealth* and the *Rocky Mountain News* published daily editions, these sheets were slim on reporting and heavy on advertising; the meatiest news items were usually reserved for the weekly editions, which came out on Thursdays.

The editors of the weeklies collected news copy and set it in type as it arrived serially from Friday through Wednesday; then, after the Wednesday deadline, they began their press runs. Under these conditions it was impractical for compositors to break up the already typeset pages to accommodate late-breaking news. In fact, it was not uncommon in the same edition of a weekly to find on one page a story directly contradicted or corrected on another, or even on the same page; it was easier to simply slug in the new material and leave the erroneous or outdated story in place.

Consequently, though Bruce was killed on March 17, Harkens on March 18, and Addleman on or about March 30, the accounts of their deaths were not carried in the Denver press until several days after the fact. The news of Bruce's murder, sent by a Cañon City correspondent signing himself "N.F.C." two days subsequent to the event, appeared in the *Weekly Commonwealth* of March 26. His account also mentioned, in a hasty postscript, that news of the killing of Harkens had "just come in."[36] The following week's edition of the *Weekly Commonwealth* carried a short note of condolence for Harkens, dated March 28, from "Dornick," evidently an acquaintance of the victim, writing from Montgomery.[37]

The *News Weekly* did not cover the killings explicitly during that two-week period, though it did mention in its edition of April 9 that "a man was killed

The headstone of Abram N. Shoup in the old Fairplay graveyard. (Photo by Ruth Ellen Price)

on the Little Fontaine qui Bouille, then another on the Arkansas," evidently referring to Harkens and Bruce. A third man, "Mr. Ottoman," was said to have been killed "not far from Colorado City." This was obviously John Addleman, though he was mistakenly said to have lived on the Fontaine qui Bouille. The writer cited these "atrocious murders" as evidence that "a regular guerrilla organization exists" in the area he referred to as "Southern Colorado."[38] In the whole period between March 16 and April 9, neither paper referred in any detail to Addleman's death.

While two murders (or three) over a span of nine or ten days were not necessarily noteworthy in a raw frontier society, the grisly nature of the killings of Bruce and Harkens must have aroused some concern among readers in late March.[39] However, nothing like the panic seizing the Pike's Peak country seems to have broken out in Denver—not, that is, until the fateful Thursday, April 16, when subscribers of the *News Weekly* began to learn that there had now been five, not two or possibly three, heinous and unexplained killings, the last a particularly vicious double murder on the northern edge of South Park.

In a retrospective article by "An Old Timer" in a 1909 edition of the *Fairplay Flume*, the writer recalled arriving in Denver from his home in Illinois "within a day or two" of the news of the South Park killings. He "found Denver and the whole country greatly alarmed, as no clue could be had of the murderers."[40]

"I shall not forget that week or ten days of intense excitement," recalled the Reverend John L. Dyer, a minister of the Methodist Episcopal Church who served as missionary to the mining districts on both sides of the Snowy Range, often crossing the mountains on a pair of homemade skis, which he called snowshoes. Thinking of the period immediately after the Kenosha Hill killings, he wrote, "Everybody was alarmed. The . . . murdered men were buried at Fairplay. The sickening sight of the dead, and the thought, Who would be the next? set the few inhabitants almost into a panic."[41]

Nine years after the bloody events, the *Rocky Mountain News* looked back ruefully on those frightful days: "The people . . . were appalled, stricken with fear, scarcely daring to venture beyond the reach of immediate aid. It seemed like a mysterious visitation from Providence—if Providence ever sends bullets through men's hearts—and no one could tell from what concealment the messenger of death, which had never missed his mark, might reach him. The dread despair, the feeling of uncertainty, the reign of terror, the fear of an

Wilbur Fiske Stone ("Dornick"), South Park correspondent for the *Weekly Commonwealth* and other Colorado newspapers. (Photo courtesy of Ed and Nancy Bathke Collection)

unseen and unknown foe, pervaded the hearts of those sturdy pioneers who dared face any danger open and known."[42]

And worse was yet to come.

NOTES

1. Daniel Ellis Conner, *A Confederate in the Colorado Gold Fields*, edited and with an introduction by Donald J. Berthrong and Odessa Davenport (Norman: University of Oklahoma Press, 1970), 70.

2. Ibid., 93.

3. Smith, *The Birth of Colorado*, 32.

4. *Weekly Commonwealth*, April 9, 1863. The paper's correspondent, "Dornick," writing from Montgomery in South Park, asserted, "shafting goes bravely on here, night and day. The gulches, also, are beginning to look up, and soon the hydraulics will be squirting their cool demands into the banks, making said banks fork over the specie on deposit. Some prospecting is being done hereabouts." Hydraulic mining involved the use of high-pressure water hoses, flumes, reservoirs, and sluices to wash away hillsides and

stream banks in hopes of exposing ore; Smith, *The Birth of Colorado*, 31. The word *dornick*, probably Irish in origin, denotes a small round stone. Appropriately, the correspondent was in fact Wilbur Fiske Stone, who later became an attorney and illustrious jurist, serving first on the Colorado Supreme Court and then the US Court of Private Land Claims. Finally, in 1918, he published a four-volume history of Colorado, cited elsewhere in this book. He died in 1920. An article on Stone appeared in the journal *The Colorado Lawyer* for July 2002, written by Denver County judge Larry Bohning. I am indebted to Park County Local History Archives Board president Christie Wright for this information.

5. Berwanger, *Rise of the Centennial State*, 8–9.

6. A Spanish method of crushing ore with horse or mule power and rocks; Smith, *The Birth of Colorado*, 33.

7. Single-jacking was a method of drilling whereby an individual miner repeatedly struck a steel drill with a sledge, turning it slightly between strokes; double-jacking involved one miner wielding the sledge and the second turning the drill; Otis E. Young, Jr., *Western Mining: An Informal Account of Precious-Metals Prospecting, Placering, Lode Mining, and Milling on the American Frontier from Spanish Times to 1893* (Norman: University of Oklahoma Press, 1970), 182–183.

8. Park County Statistics, South Park Chamber of Commerce, March 21, 2009, courtesy of Christie Wright; Virginia McConnell Simmons, *Bayou Salado: The Story of South Park*, rev. ed. (Boulder: University Press of Colorado, 2002), 14.

9. R. Laurie Simmons and Thomas H. Simmons, *The History of Ranching in South Park, Colorado, 1859–1950* (Washington, DC: United States Department of the Interior, National Park Service, 1999), 28.

10. Ibid., 16.

11. Ed Helmuth and Gloria Helmuth, *The Passes of Colorado: An Encyclopedia of Watershed Divides* (Boulder, CO: Pruett Publishing Company, 1994), 246. The Ute Indians had used Wilkerson Pass from early times as a route from their buffalo grounds in South Park to the hot springs near what is now Manitou, Colorado, a place that they considered sacred.

12. Midge Harbour, *The Tarryall Mountains and the Puma Hills: A History* (Colorado Springs: Century One Press, 1982), 7–19.

13. *Weekly Commonwealth*, April 2, 1863. "Dornick" did not write exclusively for the *Weekly Commonwealth*; he also served as a stringer for several different papers of the time and in 1866 for the *Daily Mining Register*. Again I am indebted to Christie Wright for this information.

14. *Weekly Commonwealth*, April 9, 1863.

15. Now Montana.

16. The older brother, Jonathan, remained in Denver where he worked as a stock raiser and buyer. He died in 1924 at the age of 78. Christie Wright provided this information, for which I am grateful.

17. George L. Shoup (1836–1904) had earned a name for initiative and intrepidity in the 1862 campaign against the Confederate invasion of New Mexico and had become the regiment's commissary of subsistence on November 1 of that year. At the time of his brother's murder he was on field duty in the vicinity of Pueblo seeking out and crushing a band of outlaws—some said Confederate guerrillas—including, surprisingly, Hank Way, the sheriff of Pueblo County; *Weekly Commonwealth*, April 16, 1863. See also entry, April 10, 1863, Diary of First Lieutenant George L. Shoup, First Colorado Cavalry, Diary 1862–1863, typescript, MG 8, Box 3FF, Diary, University of Idaho Library Special Collections and Archives, Moscow, ID.

18. May 5, 1834, according to the headstone on his grave in the old Fairplay Cemetery.

19. Helmuth, *The Passes of Colorado*, 243–244. Philo's brother Algernon, a Lake County attorney, operated a ranch at the western outlet of the same pass. The pass is named for one or both of the brothers. According to a letter written by Abram Shoup's niece who had traveled to South Park in search of her uncle's grave in 1939, a local resident showed her a cabin "about three miles from Fairplay" where the two men had lived. It is possible their mining claim lay in the vicinity of Weston's ranch; perhaps that was their starting point when they left for the new mines. Letter, Laura Shoup to Walter C. Shoup, August 20, 1939, typescript, MG 8, Box 3FF, Letter, University of Idaho Library Special Collections and Archives, Moscow, ID.

20. *Rocky Mountain News Weekly*, April 16, 1863.

21. Simmons, *Bayou Salado*, 236, has a photograph of the Kenosha House as it appeared about 1870; it is reproduced in this book.

22. *Rocky Mountain News Weekly*, April 16, 1863.

23. Harriman, a native of Canada, had come to Colorado in 1860, spent time in Boulder and Central City, and in the spring of 1861 moved to South Park and opened the Kenosha House. In October 1865, disillusioned by the continuing lawlessness in the Park, he removed first to Wisconsin and then back to Colorado, eventually settling at Golden in Jefferson County, where he became a member of its board of commissioners; http://www.memoriallibrary.com/CO/1898DenverPB/pages/pbrd0432.htm (a short biography of Harriman is on p. 436), accessed January 4, 2010.

24. *Rocky Mountain News Weekly*, April 16, 1863.

25. Simmons, *Bayou Salado*, 118. Obituary, *Fairplay Flume*, June 9, 1881. The misspelling is odd because Murdock was well-known in the Territory. One of the earliest settlers in Fairplay, he was a native of Ireland, having come to Colorado in 1859. Information provided by Christie Wright.

26. *Rocky Mountain News Weekly*, April 16, 1863.

27. Ovando J. Hollister, *Boldly They Rode: A History of the First Colorado Regiment of Volunteers* (Lakewood, CO: The Golden Press, 1949), 7; Smith, *The Birth of Colorado*, 19–20, 22–23, 26–27, 112–114; M. S. Elswick, "Colorado Volunteers 1861–1865," Colorado State

Archives; http://www.colorado.gov/dpa/doit/archives/civwar/civilwar.html, accessed January 18, 2013.

28. John Evans was appointed the second governor of Colorado Territory on March 31, 1862, after the dismissal of Gilpin.

29. *Rocky Mountain News Weekly*, April 16, 1863. Binkley and Shoup are buried in the old Fairplay Cemetery on a hill overlooking the town from the west. Binkley's grave is unmarked but Shoup's is in the northeast corner of the fenced enclosure and has a headstone giving his full name, place and date of birth, and an erroneous death date of May 11, 1863. Three other victims of the South Park murders would eventually be interred there as well.

30. Ibid.

31. See Chapter 1.

32. *Weekly Commonwealth*, April 23, 1863.

33. Ibid.

34. Ibid.

35. Thomas C. Jepsen, "The Telegraph Comes to Colorado: A New Technology and Its Consequences," *Essays and Monographs in Colorado History*, No. 7 (Denver: Historical Society of Colorado, 1987), 9. The east–west Overland Telegraph Line had advanced as far as Julesburg, Colorado, in September 1861, and messages then had to be carried to Denver by riders or stagecoach. At that time no lateral telegraphic communication from Denver to other Colorado communities was possible. The line connection from Julesburg to Denver was not completed until October 1863, but Indian attacks throughout 1863–64 constantly interrupted service.

36. *Weekly Commonwealth*, March 26, 1863.

37. *Weekly Commonwealth*, April 16, 1863.

38. *Rocky Mountain News Weekly*, April 9, 1863.

39. A year earlier, the infamous Reynolds brothers had robbed the Buckskin stage in South Park, causing a brief stir in Denver when two messengers hastened into town warning that the outlaws were depredating near at hand. I am obliged to Christie Wright for pointing this out.

40. An Old Timer, "Early Days in Park County," *Fairplay Flume*, February 9, 1909.

41. J. L. Dyer, *The Snow-Shoe Itinerant* (Cincinnati, OH: Cranston & Stowe, 1890), 154.

42. *Rocky Mountain News Weekly*, February 11, 1872.

3 "There Has Been Considerable Excitement"
The First Colorado Cavalry Steps In

As reports of the five unexplained murders in the Pike's Peak country and South Park spread throughout Colorado, speculation on the identity of the killers tended to center on two theories: either they were guerrillas or they were jayhawkers. The early suspicion by the men at Saw Mill Gulch that Indians might have been responsible seems to have quickly dissipated, owing to the fact that no hostiles were known to be on the prowl.

The terms *guerrillas* and *jayhawkers* sound synonymous to modern ears, but in Civil War–era Colorado they were not. *Guerrillas* was a term applied almost exclusively to suspected bands of Confederate partisans. *Jayhawkers*, a pejorative initially coined by Southerners during the Kansas–Nebraska troubles of 1854–56 to denote antislavery gangs, had, by 1861, somehow taken on a different connotation, that of criminal activity undignified by any association with the respective sides in the fraternal conflict. By this definition the crimes of rustling, robbery, and murder for profit were referred to as "jayhawking."[1]

The Territory had some reason to fret about Rebel guerrillas. The first gold strikes in Colorado had been made by Georgians and in the initial mad rush of 1859 into the diggings, Southerners were heavily represented.[2] At the outbreak of war a Confederate flag had been raised in Denver but it was torn down almost at

DOI: 10.5876/9781607322375.c03

once by Unionists.[3] While large-scale violence between the factions did not break out, there were individual instances of fights and disturbances involving adherents to either side of the national dispute.[4]

But overall, Colorado escaped anything resembling the bitter partisan warfare that afflicted border regions like Missouri and the Southern Appalachians, where Unionists and Confederates, former neighbors, turned on each other with a terrible ferocity. Of course an unknown number of the Territory's males traveled east to join the regular armies of North or South; others stood fast and made an effort to fit in, whatever their sympathies, usually nursing persistent hopes of striking it rich in the diggings. But very early in the war Colorado Territory, politically and editorially, became firmly attached to the cause of Union, though reactions to President Lincoln's Emancipation Proclamation and to the draft law were mixed[5] and there was always an undercurrent of pro-Southern feeling in an apparent minority of the population.

This is not to say the Territory was entirely free of actual Confederate activity. In the late summer of 1862 a band of thirty-five men under a Captain George Madison, "supposedly a detachment sent out by the rebels to capture government trains" and to interrupt the mails, was active at Raton Pass, near the headwaters of the Huerfano River and near the Spanish Peaks. The "avowed object of this band" was "to harass and rob the government in every possible way." Madison was said to be a part of the Texas army that had invaded New Mexico earlier in the year, and was thought by some to be the precursor of yet another such foray.[6] Army troops were sent out from Fort Garland in Costilla County in a vain effort to capture these guerrillas[7] but Madison soon disappeared[8] and the rumored Texan invasion did not materialize.

In early 1863 another Rebel gang headed by one Charley Harrison, formerly a Denver gambler and saloon owner,[9] made a serious effort to ride west from Kansas with several like-minded souls, intending to raise a body of Confederate troops along the way and seize Colorado's gold for the Southern cause. But this group ran afoul of Osage Indians on whose land they unwisely trespassed. Fortunately for the Union cause in Colorado, the Osages killed and beheaded all but two of Harrison's party.[10]

A third Confederate effort—almost comedic compared with the activities of Madison and Harrison—centered on a place called Mace's Hole in the Greenhorn section south of the Arkansas River, where an eccentric named Alexander ("Zan") Hicklin operated a ranch serving as a secret rallying point for Rebel recruits. Hicklin played a sly double game with Union command-

United States Marshal Alexander Cameron Hunt. (Photo courtesy of Colorado State Archives)

ers at Forts Lyon and Garland, feigning loyalty to the United States while secretly fostering the activities of a Confederate officer, Colonel John Heffner, whom Rebel authorities in Texas had sent to Mace's Hole to organize and train a corps of Southern troops.

Heffner's soldiers were to cooperate with the 1862 invasion of New Mexico and help hold Colorado for the South. However, the scheme fell apart after the destruction of the Texans at Glorieta Pass. One of the minor participants in the failed Mace's Hole plot was Daniel Ellis Conner, the Kentucky-born prospector who had once worked the goldfields in South Park.[11]

In view of these and other fifth-column activities, it is not unusual that some Coloradans, confronted by the atrocities at Hardscrabble, Saw Mill Gulch, and South Park, were quick to ascribe the crimes to roving Confederate guerrilla bands. Others, accustomed to the prevalence of frontier lawlessness, thought the culprits might be a gang of particularly savage jayhawkers simply intent on mayhem for its own perverse sake. Whatever they believed, they seem to have expected little or no remedial action from civilian law enforcement. Murdock appealed to the First Colorados, "Dornick" to lynch law, and other writers, more vaguely, to a need for action by "the citizens."[12]

As we have seen, the sheriffs of Fremont and El Paso counties made brief but abortive efforts to track the killers of Bruce, Harkens, and Addleman, but no contemporary report mentions any investigative activity in nearby Park County. Why? The sheriff of that jurisdiction, a man named Cullen Farnham, had recently resigned over a dispute with the presiding judge of that district, Charles Lee Armour.[13] Therefore, Park County itself was at that moment without a senior law enforcement officer and though the Park County commissioners had appointed a replacement, one Theodore H. Robertson of Buckskin Joe, neither he nor any other officer appears in the record as active in the manhunt. One officer certainly was there—territorial US marshal Alexander Cameron Hunt. District court duty was mandatory for such an officer. Hunt seems to have been conscientious—the press of the day is full of reports of his activities and those of his deputies, and he was continually busy with responsibilities in and out of court. But with Sheriff Farnham gone, his successor only days on the job, and Marshal Hunt preoccupied with court duties,[14] the people of Park County were forced to look either to the First Regiment of Colorado Volunteers or, more ominously, to themselves to apply the law.

Historian Ken Jessen, in a study of Colorado lawlessness, has noted, "what is disturbing about early Colorado justice is the lack of due process. Citizens were constantly taking matters into their own hands, often because of frustration with an ineffective judicial system. Sentences of capital punishment were not in style in the late 1800s, and the populace wanted a more certain end to a given criminal than life in prison."[15]

In fact, the time was not distant when Judge Lynch would actually be called into play in South Park. But that time was not quite yet. First, the "Pet Lambs" would take a hand, and presumably they would have special reason to be zealous in their search for the killers of Abram Shoup, whose brother, First Lieutenant George L. Shoup, was one of their most respected officers.

Already, as noted earlier, Lieutenant Shoup had been busy in the Pueblo area rounding up an outlaw party suspected of being Rebel irregulars.[16] Colonel Chivington had traveled from Denver down to Colorado City to supervise those operations.[17] Lieutenant Shoup's diary, in the Special Collections of the University of Idaho Library, shows he received news of his brother's death on April 14 while at Colorado City trying to prevent the citizens from lynching his prisoners.[18] It must have been a traumatic time for him. He wrote, "Received intelligence that my Brother Nelson has been murdered by the Lawless Desperado in S. Park. My brother was a very quiet inoffensive Man, the Murder a cold-blooded Butchery."[19] Evidently he requested immediate leave to attend to the tragedy, as he writes on April 20, "Was sworn in to act as Deputy US Marshal—am Sent to South Park." On April 27 he returned from the Park and proceeded "to Huerfano to Search for the Murderer Espinosa."[20]

Since the identity of the killers was not known until after May 8, this entry must be a retrospective one, but it shows the lieutenant was eager to avenge his brother's death. His search in the Huerfano country proved fruitless and after four days he gave it up, returning on April 30, apparently to Colorado City.[21] He later caused a headstone to be placed on his brother's grave in the Fairplay Cemetery.[22]

It is fair to assume the men of the First Colorado shared the lieutenant's feelings about the death of Abram Shoup. They were certainly capable of dealing out rough justice; the unit was notorious for indiscipline. One of their own admitted in his regimental history that the Firsters had fairly earned their reputation as "chicken thieves, jayhawkers, turbulent and seditious, a disgrace to themselves and the country,"[23] though he blamed this misbehavior on their disappointment at not being sent east to fight the Confederacy and on the monotony they had endured during the long interval between recruitment and their deployment to New Mexico to confront the Texan invasion. The regiment had indeed covered itself with glory in New Mexico, and the same writer who mentioned their "jayhawking proclivities" also concluded, "there is not a manlier, better disposed thousand men in the United States service than the First Colorados."[24]

On April 15 a detail of volunteers—twenty men each of Companies E and F under the command of First Lieutenants Luther Wilson of Company F and John Oster, Jr., of Company K—left Denver to move into the Park to provide security to the population and hunt down the supposed guerrillas.[25] Territorial Governor John Evans and/or Colonel Chivington must have ordered the movement, though it is not known for certain which officer was responsible or whether the act was a joint one. At this time or possibly later, the governor is said to have offered a substantial reward for the capture or death of the supposed guerrillas.[26]

Luckily for posterity, one of the soldiers accompanying the South Park detachment was a diarist, Private Romine H. Ostrander of Company F. Then about twenty-six years old, Ostrander was a native of Roseville in Warren County, Illinois. We do not know the date of his enlistment, but it is clear from his writings that he had served during the New Mexico campaign.[27] He began his diary on February 26, 1863, and his is the only contemporary personal account of the activities of the Firsters in South Park.

At the outset Ostrander portrays the South Park duty as a routine one. But then, many of his earlier and later entries convey an impression of the diarist as self-absorbed, bored, and oddly detached from or even unaware of large events.[28] Whether this was the result of complacency, depression, or some

Colorado Governor John Evans. (Photo courtesy of Colorado State Archives)

other preoccupation, he would soon be jolted out of his ennui and would provide graphic firsthand accounts of developments over the coming weeks.

After a three-day march from Denver, the forty-man detachment arrived at the Kenosha House, and the following morning, April 18, from Kenosha Hill, even the matter-of-fact Ostrander—like everyone else before or since who has gazed upon the sweeping vista of the Park—felt compelled to try to describe it:

> It does not look as I expected it would. It is a kind of bason [*sic*] of prairie surrounded by high mountains on three sides and covered with hills in the Southern part of it. It is about 80 miles long . . . and twenty to thirty miles wide. The hills are capped with pine and look black in the distance and they are all over it except the northern end. We left Tarryall about three miles to our right and came into Fairplay twenty-five miles. It is a very small town of log houses and dirt roofs. It has been pretty windy to day and quite cold.[29]

Lieutenant Wilson later told the *Weekly Commonwealth* how the detachment was deployed. Details of soldiers were quartered at "a dozen different ranches and stations in the Park and regularly escort[ed] the mail, and parties of citizens requesting it, to the extent of their capacity. While tracing the demoniac miscreants who have spread terror through that section, details have frequently rode [*sic*] fifty miles per day."[30]

Ostrander's diary confirms Wilson's account of diligent scouting but also shows that the men managed to find time to amuse themselves. While Ostrander and ten troopers of Company E did track a pair of supposed guerrillas to Buffalo Springs, a mining settlement south of Fairplay on April 19, they lost the trail there. Next day he and his messmates "had some fine sport shooting trout." On April 21 Ostrander slept late but eventually roused himself,

George Laird Shoup, in 1863 a first lieutenant in the First Colorado Cavalry. In this 1864 likeness he appears in the uniform of a colonel of the Third Colorado Volunteers. (Photo courtesy of History Colorado; scan no. 10031856)

joined his patrol, and went looking in vain for "payhamkers" (jayhawkers?), camping that night on Trout Creek. "We killed some rabbits this afternoon which we eat [*sic*] for supper. I saw deer sign." The detail had, however, traveled seventy miles in two days' time.[31]

If Ostrander's first week of guerrilla hunting had yielded little more than saddlesores, the following two days, Wednesday and Thursday, April 22 and 23, would bring him face-to-face with the stark panic then afflicting the Park. On Wednesday he and another soldier rode into the mountains to search for evidence of guerrillas and, finding none, were returning to camp, having traveled an astonishing fifty-eight miles, when "we saw four mounted men coming toward us which we took for guerrillas but they proved to be soldiers from Fairplay. They took us for guerrillas and came to take us."

That unsettling mistake cleared up, the six troopers then rode to Weston's ranch, where the full command was camped. There they learned that "two men who . . . are suspected [of being guerrillas]" had been captured that day by Third Duty Sergeant Jesse F. Keel. Ostrander's entry for April 23, typically understated, nevertheless captures the drama that unfolded next: "There has been considerable excitement here about the two prisoners the boys took yesterday. Carle Man and Dutch Mike. They would like to get hold of them and hang them. Carle Man was released this evening as it was ascertained that nothing could be proven against him."[32]

The fate of "Dutch Mike" went unrecorded. Ostrander's account fails to make clear which "boys" wanted to lynch both prisoners. Were they "the boys" of the First Colorado eager to avenge the murder of Abram Shoup? Or a mob of South Park miners gone berserk with dread of the mysterious murderers? It is hard to say. We may have a somewhat less dramatic account of this same incident from the pen of the *Weekly Commonwealth*'s stringer "Dornick," who wrote on April 30:

> The soldiers sent up here from Denver gobbled a couple of men in the Park a day or two ago, suspected of connection with jay hawkers. A couple of men, and one individual who aint [*sic*] a man to any great extent. One has since been released, nothing appearing against him, so we understand. The other, Mike Conrad, is a little butcher who was out on bail for larceny in this county, and is more than strongly suspected of complicity in some of the late murders hereabouts. He is in irons in Fairplay and in custody of the soldiers. The other fellow, not exactly in the image of a man, is named "Dutch Moll," was taken in company with the two men, and is suspected of "not being any better than she ought to be." Several head of stock were taken with them, supposed to be stolen. A squad were out on a scout yesterday after some more gentlemen of the jayhawking persuasion. I presume there is no more danger to be feared in future from this craft.[33]

If the affair occurred as Ostrander described, the attempted hanging of Dutch Mike and Carle Man, together with the previous day's potentially deadly misunderstanding between two parties of guerrilla-hunting soldiers, gave evidence that the tide of panic in South Park was running high.

Then, two days after the Dutch Mike / Carle Man affair, on Saturday, April 25, the killers struck again, not at some secluded spot in secret as had been their habit, but brazenly in broad daylight, four miles west of Fairplay on the main road between Montgomery and Buckskin Joe, and this time before witnesses.

NOTES

1. See for instance *Weekly Commonwealth*, May 7, 1863: "Mr. Lehman was a German from whom ten mules were jayhawked last fall at Frying Pan Gulch by the Leper [Leeper?] Gang." It is ironic that the antislavery jayhawking in Kansas and Missouri before the Civil War later came to be seen as rank outlawry in staunchly Unionist Colorado Territory. Proslavery guerrillas during the Kansas troubles were known as Border Ruffians. After the outbreak of sectional warfare back East, all guerrilla units North and

South tended to be known as *bushwhackers*, though the term also covered gangs holding no allegiance to either cause, or to both or neither depending on circumstances. During the Kansas troubles and later in the Civil War, Colonel Charles R. Jennison's Seventh Kansas Cavalry proudly boasted the name "Jennison's Jayhawkers," and lived up to its bloody connotation. See Michael Fellman, *Inside War: The Guerrilla Conflict in Missouri During the American Civil War* (New York: Oxford University Press, 1989), 32, 34–35; and Jay Monaghan, *Civil War on the Western Border, 1854–1865* (New York: Bonanza Books, 1955), 17–106.

2. Hollister, *Boldly They Rode*, 5.

3. Smith, *The Birth of Colorado*, 12.

4. Ibid., 13–14.

5. Ibid., 110.

6. *Rocky Mountain News Weekly*, August 14 and 21, 1862.

7. Report of Captain E. W. Eaton, commander, Co. D, First New Mexico Volunteers, to Commander, Fort Garland, C.T., September 5, 1862, Letters Received, Department of New Mexico, Record Group 393, Adjutant General's Office, National Archives and Records Administration, Washington, DC.

8. Parkhill, *The Law Goes West*, 124, notes, "an indictment was returned in the Third District [Court] against George I. Madison, Snaggletooth Jones, William M. Pierson, Dolly Stine, and Snap Mitchell," charged with "larceny on June 28, 1862, at Cuchara in Huerfano County of an $80 bay horse and a $15 saddle from Thomas J. Barnham, and of a dragoon revolver, a Bowie knife, and a pair of spurs from George O. Austin. The case was dropped when the suspects could not be found."

9. Robert K. DeArment, *Knights of the Green Cloth: The Saga of the Frontier Gamblers* (Norman: University of Oklahoma Press, 1982), 43–44. Harrison, DeArment writes, was the "undisputed leader" of the gambling element in Denver from his arrival in 1859. "In addition to his outstanding generosity, gambling ability, and leadership qualities . . . he was renowned for his skill with the fancy cap-and-ball pistols he always wore and which he called his 'pets.'" The handle of one of Harrison's pistols was said to have been notched eleven times to denote his male victims and the butt of its mate three times as a record of the women he had shot. Generosity and leadership qualities evidently did not rule out indiscriminate homicide.

10. DeArment, *Knights of the Green Cloth*, 64–67. After a number of shooting escapades and other adventures, Harrison made his Southern sympathies known at the outbreak of war and was eventually charged with treason and conspiracy to overthrow the government. Found guilty, he was banished from Colorado Territory. He repaired to Leavenworth, Kansas, where he joined the Confederate Army; became captain of Company A, Fourth Missouri Cavalry; fought at the battles of Cane Hill, Reed's Mountain, and Prairie Grove, Arkansas; was promoted lieutenant colonel; and eventually attained the rank of colonel,

assuming command of the Fourth Missouri. Eventually he conceived a plan to organize a guerrilla force and lead it to Denver. He put the plan into action; however, on Lightning Creek in southeastern Kansas. Harrison's party encountered Osage warriors under Chief Little Bear and Harrison died from a bullet wound and a lance thrust; his companions were also killed. Smith, *Birth of Colorado*, 146; *Weekly Commonwealth*, July 2, 1863.

11. Taylor, *Colorado South of the Border*, 66–70; Conner, *A Confederate in the Colorado Gold Fields*, 126–168. Conner, like many other "recruits" in the Mace's Hole plot, made his escape to Arizona Territory.

12. See Chapter 2.

13. The presiding judge of the Second District, Charles Lee Armour of Maryland, appointed March 28, 1861, became extremely unpopular within his first year on the bench, evidently owing to obnoxious behavior. By July 6, 1863, Farnham had had enough of trying to deal with Judge Armour and resigned because, he wrote the Park County Board of Commissioners, "I believe that we shall never have a Court in that County while he [Armour] is Judge of our District and [I] cannot do the business and wait until there is a change in the Administration for my pay." On March 5, 1864, the Colorado Legislature finally gerrymandered Armour out of the Second District and transferred him to the Third District (Costilla and Conejos counties), but he refused to acknowledge the transfer and remained at Central City until 1865, acting "as a gentleman of leisure" before returning east; "A History of the District Courts of the San Luis Valley," La Plata County Government Records, Series 18.5, Collection M-028, nd, Center for Southwest Studies, Fort Lewis College, Durango, Colorado. I am indebted to Christie Wright, president of the Park County Local History Archives Board, for locating this information.

14. Hunt would eventually serve as the fourth governor of Colorado Territory, 1867–69.

15. Ken Jessen, *Colorado Gunsmoke: True Stories of Outlaws and Lawmen on the Colorado Frontier* (Loveland, CO: J. V. Publications, 1986), 248. Seven of the twenty-three instances of outlawry in Jessen's book ended with lynchings—eight if the notorious Jack Slade is counted. Slade first operated in Colorado but was actually hanged by the Montana Vigilantes after leaving Colorado. Stephen J. Leonard, *Lynching in Colorado, 1859–1919* (Boulder: University Press of Colorado, 2002), 2–13, counts at least 175 people killed without benefit of law in Colorado during the years he studied. Leonard believes the subject of lynching in Colorado has been understudied, in part due to a reluctance by academic historians to explore the participation by some of Colorado's leading citizens, such as William Byers, editor of *The Rocky Mountain News*; A. C. Hunt, US marshal during the 1860s; and Colonel John M. Chivington, all of whom, along with other "pillars of the community," saw themselves as representatives of law and order and not as men engaged in illegal killings.

16. See Chapter 2, note 17.

17. *Weekly Commonwealth*, April 16, 1863; Romine H. Ostrander, *This Soldier Life: The Diaries of Romine H. Ostrander, 1863 and 1865, in Colorado Territory*, annotated by Paul A.

Malkoski (Denver: Colorado Historical Society, 2006), entry of April 6, 1863, 12: "The Lieutenant says that the General [*sic*] is going down the country to look after those gurillies [*sic*] and that we may have some fun before we get back. I hope we will."

18. Yet another instance of the propensity of Coloradans to resort to lynch law; see note 21 above. Lieutenant Shoup's diary entry for April 11 reads in part: "Arrived at Colorado City with prisoners. Citizens wish to have them turned over to them that the citizens may hang them. I persuaded them to wate [*sic*]"; Diary entry of April 11, 1863, First Lieutenant George L. Shoup.

19. Ibid., entry of April 10, 1863.

20. Ibid., entry of April 27, 1863.

21. Ibid., entry of April 30, 1863.

22. Letter, Laura Shoup to Walter C. Shoup, August 20, 1939.

23. Hollister, *Boldly They Rode*, 7.

24. Ibid.

25. Ostrander, *This Soldier Life*, 14.

26. Taylor, *Colorado South of the Border*, 213, says the Territorial Legislature offered a $1,000 reward; Governor Evans posted another $1,000; and relatives of the murder victims collectively offered another $500. Tom Tobin, who eventually killed two of the murderers, claimed Col. Samuel F. Tappan, commander of Fort Garland in October 1863, told him Governor Evans had offered a $2,500 reward and that the announcement had appeared in *The Rocky Mountain News*, but no such account could subsequently be found; Tom Tobin, "The Capture of the Espinosas," *The Colorado Magazine*, Vol. IX, No. 2 (March 1932), Historical Society of Colorado. See also Appendix B.

27. Ostrander, *This Soldier Life*, iv, 1–4.

28. For instance, he makes no mention of the Sand Creek Massacre, or the capture of the infamous Reynolds gang of guerrillas in 1864, or of the Lincoln assassination in 1865; ibid., v.

29. Ibid., 15.

30. *Weekly Commonwealth*, May 21, 1863.

31. Ostrander, *This Soldier Life*, 15–16.

32. Ibid., 16. At some point during this period, according to his diary, Lieutenant Shoup must have been in South Park in his capacity as deputy US marshal searching for his brother's killers. It is an intriguing but unanswerable question whether he played any role in the activities of the First Colorados during the period from April 20, when he left Colorado City for the Park, to April 27, when he set out for the Huerfano.

33. *Weekly Commonwealth*, April 30, 1863.

4 "The People Are Scared Nearly to Death Here"

The Murderers Strike at the Vitals of South Park

The gold camp of Montgomery, home to "Dornick," the garrulous correspondent of the *Weekly Commonwealth*, lay in a high valley dominated by the rugged mass of a peak in the Snowy Range that residents had named Mount Lincoln. The settlement lay at the foot of Hoosier Pass, which crosses the Continental Divide toward Breckenridge, then a thriving camp of miners working the gold deposits along the Blue River in what is now Summit County.

Despite its forbidding location high in the mountains, in an economic sense Montgomery was far from isolated; a branch of the grandly named Breckenridge, Buckskin Joe and Hamilton Wagon Road Company served it, linking it not only with the diggings on the other side of Hoosier Pass but with all the camps along the Middle Fork of the South Platte down to Fairplay. Colorado Territory had granted a charter for the toll road over to Breckenridge in November 1860.[1] Traffic up and down it on the eastern side was constant; in a very real sense it could be called the heart of the mining activity in the upper section of South Park.

The settlement boasted five sawmills[2] and on Saturday, April 25, 1863, three men were busy at one of them loading lumber into a wagon. One of these, Bill Carter, was a resident of the Mosquito Mining District, which lay several miles to the southwest but was also

DOI: 10.5876/9781607322375.c04

The gold camp of Montgomery. (Photo by William G. Chamberlain, ca. 1880s; courtesy of Park County, CO, Local History Archives)

served by a branch of the main road. The other two seem to have been from Fairplay. Evidently the trio had climbed this high in the mountains to obtain wood because most of the timber lower down had already been cut since the rush of 1859 to make flumes, sluice boxes, rockers, and the other paraphernalia of placer mining.

Late that afternoon Carter decided he'd had enough of the hard work of shoving the heavy boards into the wagon. He declared his intention to return to Fairplay on foot, perhaps to enjoy some of the night life there, but would stop at Mosquito to retrieve his overcoat to protect himself against the chill of the evening.

It may seem strange that a man might set out alone near twilight, even along a heavily traveled road, at a time when the whole of South Park was

A Montgomery sawmill with stacked logs, Hoosier Pass in the distance. Bill Carter would have worked at such a mill. (Photo by T. C. Miller, ca. 1880s; courtesy of Park County, CO, Local History Archives)

on the alert for prowling assassins. Perhaps his companions even warned him of his danger. If they did, he ignored them. Maybe he believed the presence of the Colorado Volunteers had made solitary travel safer. He may have reassured himself that most of the killings to date had happened in remote wilderness locations quite unlike the busy placer mining operations all along the Fairplay road and down the next drainage of Beaver Creek northeastward.

Even Binkley and Shoup had been murdered in a gulch some distance from the Kenosha House and off the Denver road. Whatever his reasoning, he started off alone as the sun was sinking, leaving the other two to finish the task of loading the wagon.

That same afternoon a Mr. Metcalf was getting his mail at the Montgomery post office. We know little about Metcalf; not even his first name has come down to us. We can assume he lived somewhere in the vicinity of Montgomery since he received mail there, and we know from a newspaper account that he, like Carter and his friends, had accumulated a wagonload of lumber that he intended to take down to Fairplay, perhaps to sell. Presumably he was a Republican and maybe an abolitionist, since his mail that day contained a copy of President Lincoln's Emancipation Proclamation, some explanatory reports, and a communication from Hiram Pitt Bennett, Colorado's congressional delegate. Leaving the post office, Metcalf slipped the papers into his left breast pocket, mounted to the box of his ox-drawn wagon, and began his trip down the mountain toward Fairplay.

At some point on the descent Bill Carter overtook Metcalf's slow-moving outfit, passed it, and continued on his way. Four miles west of Fairplay, just below a spot where a road forked off to the right toward Buckskin Joe and within sight of a hostelry called the Cottage Grove House, Carter was surprised to encounter two mounted men, one large and formidable-looking, the other smaller. One wore a white broad-brimmed hat. Both appeared dark-complexioned, as if they were Mexicans or blacks, or perhaps white men who had smeared their faces with burnt cork. One of these shot Carter in the chest, killing him instantly. His body was then dragged a short distance from the road and thrown into a snowbank; his head was viciously hacked as if with a tomahawk. The killers rifled his pockets and stole his overcoat.

About this time Metcalf was approaching the scene in his ox wagon. The murderers concealed themselves in some brush by the roadside and when Metcalf was within about a hundred yards of their ambush site, one of the assailants fired a shot and struck Metcalf in the left breast, providentially striking the thick packet of papers he had pocketed after getting his mail, leaving him bruised but unhurt. The report of the gun and the smell of Carter's blood spooked Metcalf's ox team and the frightened animals bolted. One of the killers fired a second shot just as a wheel of Metcalf's careening wagon struck a rock, causing the rig to rebound. Metcalf fell backward and the bullet missed—a second time fate saw fit to spare the good Republican's life.

A man named Allen, who was staying at the nearby Cottage Grove House, heard the gunfire, snatched up his rifle, and ran out into the main road just as Metcalf's wagon hurtled past. Dusk was falling but Allen got a good look at the killers and may have even fired at them, but they made a safe escape.[3]

Private Ostrander's diary tells what came next:

> A man[4] came running into town, this evening about dark, and said that he had been shot at, and chassed [*sic*] by two men, three miles from here towards Buckskin Joe's. He said that he saw a man that lives in this town [Fairplay] by the house of McCarter a little while before and he thought that he was killed. A half dozen men and some citizens went to look for him and found him shot in the breast and cut in the forehead with the but [*sic*] of a gun or some sharp instrument. He has a brother living here.[5]

A participant later recalled that the search for Carter's body went on for two hours before it was located, "mainly through the untiring efforts of his brother," who was "overcome with grief" once the mutilated corpse was found.[6] The same source described the reaction of the populace around Fairplay:

> The whole town was aroused, and a party formed to scour the country. As soon as it was fairly light on Sunday morning . . . messengers were sent to Buckskin, from where a large force turned out to aid in the search for the murderers. The country for miles around was searched. . . . The murderers were tracked from the scene of the murder to Platte River, a large track leading, and a smaller following. They took up Platte River in the water, and their trail was lost.[7]

Ostrander's diary entry for that Sunday tells how the Firsters also took up the hunt for the killers:

> Some citizen thought he heard a couple of gunshots in a northeast direction about seven o'clock last night and it was thought that the murderers had possibly gone over into veever [Beaver] gulch, and killed somebody. So Lieuten't Oster, and five of us went over to see about it. Nobody had been killed and there had no gunshots been heard in the neighborhood. Ten of us with Lieu't Wilson, and about a dozen citizens went to look for the trail to day. We found it, and followed it, till about the middle of the afternoon when we lost it. We hunted about three hours for it and then gave it up as a bad job and came home. The people are scared nearly to death here none but the bravest dare go out at all.[8]

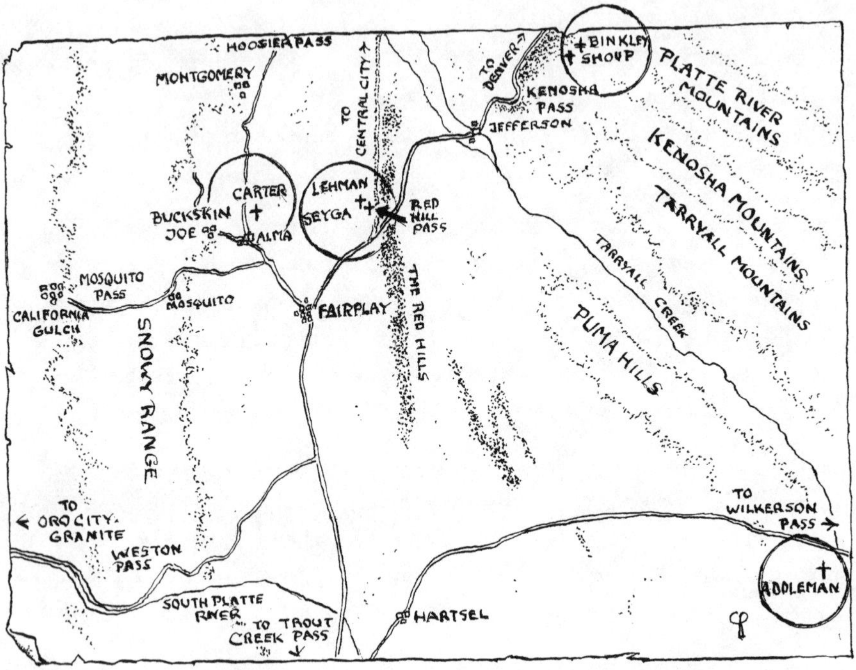

Death sites of the six victims in and around South Park.

Incredibly, that same evening, only about twenty-four hours after killing Carter, the murderers attacked again, killing and mutilating two more victims at Red Hill Pass on the main road between Denver and Fairplay, another central and very exposed location in the middle of the South Park goldfields, with witnesses nearby. Clearly the murderers intended a bold stroke, slaying three men in two days within a compass of only five or six miles, in the thick of the region's most populated area. It was an attack calculated to exacerbate the terror Carter's murder had already stirred up.

The dead at Red Hill Pass were Fred Lehman and Sol Seyga,[9] residents of California Gulch[10] on the western side of the Snowy Range. They and a group of neighbors were returning from Central City, where Lehman had testified in US District Court against one George W. Brown, thought to be a member of an outlaw gang that had rustled ten of Lehman's mules at Frying Pan Gulch the previous fall.[11]

Red Hill is a long, pine-clad Dakota Hogback formation running north–south, bisecting the South Park basin.[12] Today's Highway 285 cuts through this

Red Hill Pass, where Lehman and Seyga died, was near the point of dark timber extending from the right about a mile distant. (Author photo)

ridge at a place now called Red Hill Pass, but in 1863 the pass of that name was located one mile due north of the present one.[13] Its name apparently referred to the salmon-colored rock present in the ridge and especially noticeable in the cut of today's highway. At the time of the killings the original pass was "wooded and rocky on the top and the road crosses . . . (at a place) just wide enough to admit a wagon."[14] Even now that ridge has a forbidding air, wearing its dark shroud of pine forest fringed in early spring with stands of bone-white aspen not yet ready to bear leaves, these dismal hues contrasting with the livid tint of the exposed rock, which at times suggests the color of strawberry pulp—or of blood.

Lehman and Seyga had passed Stubb's ranch a mile or so east of Red Hill about four o'clock and an hour later were walking their horses up the hill and had nearly reached the narrow slot of the pass at the summit when they were ambushed. Seyga was shot in the breast and instantly killed. Lehman was not so fortunate. He was wounded in one arm and, equipped with a Colt's Navy revolver, evidently engaged the killers in a running fight back down the hill until he was fatally shot through the body.

The Fairplay graveyard; the town of Fairplay in the distance. (Photo by T. C. Miller, ca. 1870s; courtesy of Park County, CO, Local History Archives)

Three other men had been traveling a short distance behind Lehman and Seyga. They too had been in attendance at the Central City court session. One of them, Nathan S. Hurd, who had built the first road into the Mosquito holdings, had once employed Lehman and Seyga at a quartz mill he operated. He and his two companions came upon the blood-splashed scene while the bodies were still warm and saw to their horror that in addition to being shot, Lehman and Seyga had been savagely tomahawked. The bodies had been stripped and their horses taken. Hurd and the other two tentatively searched the immediate area. They found Lehman's paper collar pinned to a tree, "upon which something was written in Mexican . . . saying that vengeance was to be wreaked upon Americans as a sacrifice to the Virgin."[15]

This evidence, together with the eyewitness accounts of Metcalf and Allen, confirmed at least the physical appearance of the mysterious assassins and clarified their purpose. They were not Rebel guerrillas or rampaging jayhawkers at all but Hispanos apparently conducting some sort of vendetta against Anglos, seemingly for religious reasons. We can guess what effect this realization must have had on the miners in South Park, who were accustomed to seeing "Mexicans" as meek, humble, illiterate, superstitious, and above all harmless laborers, operating the *arrastras* that ground their ore, selling the firewood they burned to keep warm in their cabins, or herding the sheep that furnished the meat they ate. Overnight that dismissive attitude would change. By Monday, every Hispano in South Park—indeed, every person whose coloring was dark—would be regarded with fear and suspicion.

For reasons that are unclear, Hurd and his friends seem not to have spread word of the killings that Sunday night. Some of them could have kept watch over the bodies while others carried the word into Fairplay, but evidently this did not happen. Perhaps they were afraid to hang about in the darkness of the pass with the killers possibly lingering nearby in search of fresh victims. Maybe they simply stampeded for home. Whatever the reason, news of the atrocity at Red Hill Pass did not reach Fairplay until the next morning at about nine o'clock when, according to Ostrander:

> One of the boys came rushing in . . . and said, two more men killed Lieutenant, whereupon he jumped up from a game of poker and sung out *saddle up!* Which was done in about the time it takes me to write it. Lieu't Oster with three of us sent down to Guirand's ranche about 12 miles from Fairplay to watch from a hill, while Lieu't Wilson went to look for the corpses, and the trail. He found them at the red hills. One shot through the heart, lying in the road, and the other a little to one side, shot in the arm, and cut in the head with a hatchet. He found the trail of one man, and he had macisins [moccasins] on, as every trail we have followed has been, which he followed till dark and then came in here about 8 o'clock.[16]

The Reverend John Dyer, the Methodist missionary, found himself caught up in the whirlwind of events precipitated by the discovery of the dead men at

The Reverend John L. Dyer, the "Snow-Shoe Itinerant" who saved Foster from a lynching. (Photo courtesy of History Colorado, scan no. 10027605)

Red Hill Pass. He has left us a description of what occurred. "At this time there were a few soldiers at Fair Play," he wrote, speaking of Wilson's and Oster's detachment. "A number were sent to bring in the dead bodies, and try, if possible, to capture the murderers. Just as the soldiers passed the second dead body, they saw a man coming on the road, whom they first thought to be a traveler. But he, seeing them about the same time, and having heard of the numerous murders . . . thought they would surely kill him; and dropping his coat in the road, put out south."[17]

Was the lone traveler perhaps dark-complexioned? Whatever his pigmentation, the fact that he had fled aroused the troopers' suspicions, already sharpened by the tensions and anxiety pervading the Park. The Firsters mounted up and gave chase "at full speed." Reverend Dyer wrote that the fugitive was "a man in the prime of life and active, especially on this occasion," and "made a good race." What had begun as a comedy of errors now took a sinister turn. "The word came to Fair Play that they were after the murderer," Dyer remembered, "and another company started on horses to try to head him off."[18] With two parties of agitated riders closing in on the terrified stranger, the grim possibility of a lynching was taking shape.

Dyer wrote: "But Mr. John Foster—for that was his name—evaded them all. At one time his pursuers were very close on him, as he passed over a sharp ridge, but he got over before they got quite to the top, and that gave him a chance to turn his course and throw them off his track." Dyer made the preposterous claim that Foster covered "fifteen or twenty miles" in his marathon run, reaching Fairplay "in his socks, without coat or hat."[19]

It is impossible to know exactly what the terrain was like in 1863 between Red Hill Pass and Fairplay, but today, from the wooded heights of the old pass southwest to the edge of town, the land is flat and treeless except at one point where a low ridge covered with aspen slopes down from the north; this might have been Dyer's "sharp ridge," though it doesn't look sharp to modern eyes.

There would have been impediments, though. Perhaps there were structures that have long since disappeared, which Foster would have had to dodge. Depending on the desperate runner's route, there might have been at least two creeks to cross, Crooked Creek, a small one, and Beaver Creek, a larger one, closer to Fairplay; and in late April, with snow still on the ground in places and the soil boggy from melt, the going for men and horses would have been heavy.

Even so, and bearing in mind the fact that terror gave wings to Foster's feet, it is hard to understand how men on horseback could not manage to overtake him—unless the ruffianly Firsters had spent the morning verifying their reputation for imbibing spirituous liquors at all hours of the day and night. At any rate, the distance between today's Red Hill Pass and the edge of Fairplay on Highway 285 is almost exactly two miles; Foster had farther to go, perhaps as much as three but hardly more than four miles, and certainly not Dyer's fifteen or twenty.

Private Ostrander, still based at Guiraud's "French Ranch" south of Fairplay, spent that Monday patrolling without success, but the next night "came across some citizens from Fairplay, who said the trail we were following was that of a man who saw the boys yesterday and took them for guerrillas and ran all day and came in after dark. He was scared nearly to death and threw away his coat hat comfiter [*sic*] and handkerchief."[20] Thus if Foster did not cover fifteen or twenty miles, Ostrander's diary confirms he certainly ran a good long way.

The Reverend's account continues:

> As the people saw [Foster] in his plight, they halloed: "There comes the murderer!" But I recognized him, as he kept a "Methodist Hotel" in California Gulch, and kept in between them and him until he got to the first house. The door being open he went in, and it was some time before he could relate his feat, as he was very short of breath and badly scared, and did not know till then but it was the murderers that had been running him so close. After a while his pursuers came, feeling mortified that he had got away from them; but when the facts were known, they felt relieved, for although they had been outrun, they had been saved from killing an innocent man.[21]

One wonders whether the charitable preacher correctly divined the temper of the mob. It is more than likely, given events about to unfold, that they felt cheated of the chance to hang somebody, anybody, simply to relieve the oppressive tension that each new day in South Park seemed to deepen.[22]

The Rocky Mountain News Weekly of May 7 gave voice to the feelings of outrage, dread, and frustration now pervading the Territory: "All [the murders], from the first, have been marked with a peculiar singularity—the most fiendish and diabolical atrocity. . . . There is today, no more known about, or who are the perpetrators, than when tidings came of the first one. . . . These acts will probably go on until the people take the matter in hand and make a terrible example of some of the suspected."[23] Evidently the writer of this piece was unaware that Metcalf and Allen had at least identified the killers of Carter as either Mexicans or blacks. But apart from that small lapse, he had correctly judged the mood of the people of South Park.

On the same day an editorial note in the *Weekly Commonwealth* also summed up the prevailing mixture of paranoia and resolve:

> It seems to us some organization of the Vigilance Committee or secret police style is needed among our mountain friends to detect and punish the thieves and murderers swarming in the Park and adjacent portions of the Territory. The soldiers undoubtedly do their best. But they are easily eluded. If these robbers *have* any organization it is secret, permitting them to appear in the community as good citizens, and the only way to ferret them out is for all honest men to band together and spare neither vigilance in detecting nor rigor in punishing, whenever they can be caught. It was done in San Francisco, in Denver, and many other localities in the West. What man has done man can do.[24]

NOTES

1. Simmons, *Bayou Salado*, 78, 81; Helmuth, *The Passes of Colorado*, 108–109.

2. Ghost Towns and History of the American West, http://www.ghosttowns.com/states/co/montgomery.html, accessed January 18, 2013.

3. This account of the attacks on Carter and Metcalf is a composite of three primary sources, one a contemporary newspaper account and two later reminiscences. "Dornick" wrote a description from Montgomery on May 2, 1863, one week after the fact, which was carried in the *Weekly Commonwealth* of May 7. The first reminiscence is from an article entitled "Early Days in Park County" in the *Fairplay Flume* of February 9, 1900, written by an unidentified person known as "An Old Timer," who was personally

involved in the incident. The second is from the Reverend John L. Dyer, the Methodist minister who served several years in South Park and was well placed to know the parties involved. There are small discrepancies between these versions. "Dornick" and Dyer have Carter merely passing Metcalf on the road and later being killed, implying that they were strangers; "An Old Timer" says that Metcalf, Carter, and another man were all part of the same wood-collecting party; that Carter went on ahead; and that the other two men followed in the ox-drawn wagon, only to come upon Carter immediately after he was murdered. According to this version, both Metcalf and his friend were tumbled backward when the ox team bolted and the wagon wheel struck a stone in the road. Dyer's account agrees with "Dornick's" that Metcalf was alone. Though both he and "An Old Timer" wrote many years after the events they describe, their memories are remarkably detailed, especially as regards the events subsequent to the killings, and in the main all three accounts coincide. It is Dyer who gives the important information that one of the assailants wore a white broad-brimmed hat and that both were "either negroes or blackened," though his additional comment, "I suppose he [Metcalf] had never seen a Mexican," is nonsense, as Mexicans were working the goldfields and herding sheep throughout South Park at the time; Dyer, *The Snow-Shoe Itinerant,* 152. In the narrative above the author has attempted to reconcile the small differences among these three sources.

4. This could have been either Metcalf or Allen, the witness at the Cottage Grove House.

5. Ostrander, *This Soldier Life*, 17.

6. The brother was named Charles Carter. "An Old Timer" wrote in the *Fairplay Flume* article that "the brother was so overcome with grief and so shocked, that long after he would awake from his sleep and exclaim: "Oh, my brother, my brother!" Bill Carter's body was taken into Fairplay that night and was eventually buried in the Fairplay Cemetery along with Binkley and Shoup. His burial place is unmarked.

7. Ibid.

8. Ostrander, *This Soldier Life*, 17.

9. "Dornick's" article in the *Weekly Commonwealth*, May 7, 1863, unaccountably calls Seyga "Vinton," though the name is Seyga in the cemetery listing of the Park County Local History Archives (Park Country cemetery records, http://www.parkcoarchives.org/Cemetery_Records_Name.pdf, accessed January 18, 2013) and also appears in other contemporary sources. Interestingly, Ostrander also calls this victim Vinton, which perhaps was a first name; he refers to Lehman as Leland, obviously a phonetic spelling (Ostrander, *This Soldier Life*, 18).

10. The present location of Leadville, Colorado.

11. See Chapter 3, note 15. On April 13, Brown, Isaac Roberts, Jonathan Leeper, and two men known only as Slatten and Harrison had been indicted for larceny by a grand jury of the US Second District Court in Central City. They were charged with stealing several mules, the property of Frederick and Ernst Lehman and Leonard Kirscht, on September 12, 1862, in Lake County. Second District Court records indicate a trial jury found the

defendants guilty but do not show the sentences imposed. Brown sought a new trial, arguing that the crime, if it occurred, took place outside the proper jurisdiction of the court. The records do not show the final disposition of the case, nor do they include a list of witnesses; Record Group 21, Records of the US District Court of the US Territory of Colorado, Bankruptcy, Civil and Criminal Case Files, 1862–74, Case #54, *United States of America vs. George W. Brown, Isaac Roberts, Jonathan Leeper, Slatten and Harrison*, National Archives and Records Administration, Rocky Mountain Division, Denver, CO. See also Parkhill, *The Law Goes West*, 42–43. Parkhill, who examined US District Court records in the 1950s, found a true bill of indictment charging "Vincent Moore, a disloyal citizen, with conspiring on September 12, 1862, with Jonathan Leeper, George W. Brown, John Haffner, James Richie and others, to give aid and comfort to the rebellion by providing rebels with pistols, blankets, horses, mules, bacon, 1,000 pounds of flour, and $50 in cash." The Lehman mule-stealing case against some of the same individuals must have been related to this charge, since the date of the offense, September 12, 1862, is the same in both instances.

12. Simmons, *Bayou Salado*, 16.

13. Helmuth, *The Passes of Colorado*, 178.

14. *Weekly Commonwealth*, May 7, 1863.

15. Ibid.; *The Alaska Citizen*, May 8, 1911, citing an interview with Hurd. A correspondent for the Black Hawk *Daily Mining Journal*, in a letter published July 23, 1864, told of traveling through Red Hill Pass over a year after the murders. He wrote, "The shirt collar which Lehman wore when killed was nailed to a poplar sapling, and there remains to the present day."

16. Ostrander, *This Soldier Life*, 17–18.

17. Dyer, *The Snow-Shoe Itinerant*, 152–153.

18. Ibid.

19. *Rocky Mountain News Weekly*, May 7, 1863, credited Foster with "remarkable speed and endurance," having made "a six hours' run over the mountains and through the woods."

20. Ostrander, *This Soldier Life*, 18.

21. Dyer, *The Snow-Shoe Itinerant*, 153.

22. It should be noted that "Dornick," in his long article in the *Weekly Commonwealth* of May 7, believed Foster was shot at and chased by the real murderers. Despite this lapse, his piece correctly linked the killings of Bruce, Harkens, Addleman, Binkley, Shoup, Carter, Lehman, and Seyga to the same killers. By coincidence, the *Rocky Mountain News Weekly* drew the same conclusions, also in its issue of May 7, the first time these connections were made.

23. *Rocky Mountain News Weekly*, May 7, 1863.

24. *Weekly Commonwealth*, May 7, 1863.

"Fallen into the Hands of Hard Men in an Evil Hour"

5

The Lynching of Baxter

John McCannon of Frying Pan Gulch[1] regarded himself as a leader of men. It was an opinion that may well have been justified. When he first appears in the historical record of Colorado Territory he already seems to have carried the title *Captain*, a rank he may have earned while supporting the antislavery side in the "Bleeding Kansas" troubles before coming west; he had served as quartermaster for the Kansas Free State Militia.[2] Or it may be that the men who later wrote about his activities during 1863 conferred on him retroactively a rank he did not actually earn until the following year when, in November 1864, as a captain in the Third Colorado Regiment, he participated with unapologetic relish in what came to be known as the Sand Creek Massacre of a peaceful band of Cheyenne Indians.[3]

Whether he bore the title before April 1863 may be uncertain; what is sure is that he *became* a captain, if not a military one, shortly after the news of the murders of Fred Lehman and Sol Seyga made its way over the Snowy Range into California Gulch, where he and others were trying to eke their fortunes in gold out of the heavy red sands and stubborn granite boulders and black rock that—ironically, had anybody known it—actually concealed an unimaginable bonanza of silver that would not be discovered for another fourteen years and finally give birth to the boomtown of Leadville.

DOI: 10.5876/9781607322375.c05

Captain John McCannon, center, with other officers of the Third Colorado Volunteers, in 1864. (Photo courtesy of History Colorado, scan no. 10039646)

McCannon must have offered a commanding presence. Certainly his letters, preserved in the files of the Kansas Historical Society, are full of a brash, self-assured belligerence.[4] His 1864 photograph shows a high-cheekboned, dark-browed countenance with a lofty forehead and pale, penetrating eyes; the mouth and chin are concealed behind a thicket of mustache and chin-whiskers. Three upper buttons of his military tunic are undone, the better to slip a hand into his bosom, Napoleon-like, but on the occasion of having his likeness taken he has restrained himself from actually making the gesture, almost as if he senses it would look absurd and he has no desire to risk making such an obvious impression of vanity.[5] It is tempting to call his appearance hard and uncompromising, but that might be a reading not so much of his physical being as of what we know he did, and caused to be done.

On April 28 two men from Mosquito arrived in California Gulch to report that Lehman and Seyga had been cruelly slain in South Park and, according to a *Rocky Mountain News Weekly* correspondent in Oro City, "to request us to send out a sufficient force to cooperate with parties from Mosquito and Buckskin Joe, in pursuit of the murderers."[6]

A meeting was called in Oro City at White's Hall,[7] in McCannon's words, "for the purpose of raising men and funds to ferret out and bring to speedy justice the murderers of their comrades."[8] Resolutions were passed to raise a company of volunteers and to defray its costs. McCannon himself, in a later reminiscence, names seventeen fellows who volunteered to make up the avenging party, putting his own name at the end of the list. "The last-named," he modestly wrote, "was selected as Captain of the company."[9]

Just then California Gulch was playing out. In the fall of 1860, at the height of the rush into the then-new diggings, 10,000 men were estimated to have swarmed the place.[10] However, "after the first year of the gold excitement the population decreased so rapidly that, in 1866, there were but 150 permanent residents."[11] But if the allure of the gulch was fading, the nature of the miners who stubbornly kept picking away at its scant remnants of color had not softened one whit. As an early historian wrote:

> [T]here was so little of the ordinary work of a public character to be performed that the officers found little to do and were not particular whether that was done or not, as the inhabitants were of that class of men, who, if they wanted anything done for their own convenience, did it, and saved themselves the trouble of going through the formula of legal authority.[12]

Such appears to have been the attitude of McCannon's posse. Not only could they requite the tragic loss of their neighbors, the task offered the agreeable diversion of sport—hunting down murderers looked far more satisfying than continuing to toil in the increasingly unrewarding gulch. One of the stalwarts, Joseph M. Lamb, recalled in later life how, if there were killers abroad in the land, "the camp thought it was time to take up killing also." To this end, "the party was supplied with a complete outfit by public spirited citizens. It was decided to travel afoot, owing to the rough nature of the country, and to carry bedding and food on pack animals."[13] Lamb himself "shouldered a trusty double barrel gun."[14] The decision to travel by shank's mare rather than on horseback sounds counterintuitive, but two different sources confirm it,[15] and, surprisingly, the strange-seeming choice proved a productive one.

McCannon and his posse crossed Weston Pass into South Park on April 29.[16] Before setting out, McCannon had sent a man to Cache Creek[17] "to get Alexander Morse[18] to join me at Weston's ranch, and to bring some pack-animals with him, and to cross the range that day or night at all hazards."

Morse complied, and brought with him to Weston's ranch four more men eager to join in the hunt.[19]

At Philo Weston's wayhouse McCannon expected to meet the promised contingents from Buckskin Joe and Mosquito but

> when I got there, to my surprise, ten men only presented themselves, and they were sent by one N.J. Bond, of Buckskin Joe . . . without pack animals, provisions or money, and with the request that we furnish them provisions and animals; this I had no right to do, and should not have done so if I had. The Buckskin Joe delegation then returned home [leaving us] to our own resources.[20]

The McCannon party "laid over one day at Weston's ranch, while I [McCannon], with a team, went to Fairplay for a supply of provisions."[21] Here McCannon found some troopers of Colorado Cavalry, queried them, and determined they had little to offer save conjecture regarding the identity or whereabouts of the killers. "Nothing authentic could be ascertained," he curtly concluded.[22]

Private Ostrander's diary notes that Lehman and Seyga (Vinton?) were buried in the Fairplay cemetery on April 29.[23] McCannon had crossed the Snowy Range that morning and Fairplay lay only four or five miles distant from Weston's, so it is possible he may have been present for the interment and gained from that sad event an additional incentive to deal out rough justice to the killers. What is certain is that while in Fairplay he encountered four more men, one of whom was Charles Carter, the bereaved brother of Bill Carter,[24] who "were on the same errand—looking up the foulest of the most foul perpetrators of crime." Carter and his companions joined the California Gulch posse at Weston's ranch.[25]

Now Captain McCannon made a consequential decision. "I sent seven mounted men in a northerly direction *to clean out a gang of known thieves* [emphasis added] and to scour the country to the northeast."[26] Up to this moment his announced intention—indeed, his principal mission as given him by the Oro City committee—had been to find the murderers of Lehman and Seyga, though it is true the chairman of that body, one Captain S. D. Breece, had, in his opening remarks at the public meeting, "drawn particular attention to the numerous murders *and robberies* . . . lately committed in the South Park."[27] Clearly common thievery should have taken second place to serial murder, but in view of what was to come, it is possible McCannon and his compatriots may have thought they had reason to treat the two crimes as one.

The names of the seven vigilantes McCannon sent north are worth recording. C. T. Wilson was "Commandant." The others were Alexander Morse of Cache Creek, William R. McComb, J. A. Hamilton, John Brown, John J. Spaulding, and a Doctor Bell.[28] Private Ostrander seems to have encountered them on April 30 and his account tells us something of their temper:

> Five or six citizens went on the . . . trail this morning. They wanted some of our horses for packing. Would not have the ponies, said they wanted good horses or none. Had not sence [*sic*] enough to know that the ponies were the best. Thought things were at a pretty pass when government horses could not be had for such a purpose.[29]

In his reminiscence McCannon goes on to relate that "Commandant" Wilson's impatient party "succeeded in capturing some of the gang." In his near-contemporary report to the Oro City committee he said this group "did good service in routing a den of thieves."[30] What gang? What thieves? What about the killers of Lehman and Seyga? Without explaining further, he next writes dismissively, "One Baxter was hung by some recruits of the Second [*sic*] Colorado Regiment near Fairplay."

Who was Baxter? Why was he lynched? We will not learn that from John McCannon. For something approaching the truth we must turn from him to other sources having less to hide—though it must be borne in mind that whatever we do, we can come no nearer than what some historians have called rhetorical or subjective truth. Multiple narratives exist and no two agree in all respects. But if each account must be considered with caution, each also contains some elements of fact, some of supposition, some of rumor, and even one or two of deliberate evasion, and we must weigh all these factors before we guess—for guess is all we *can* do—what *might* have happened. Each version must also be studied with an eye toward its proximity to the event in time, allowing for the distortion of memory over the passing years.

One account, for instance, comes to us at first hand, within four days of the incident, and explicitly links "Commandant" Wilson's California Gulch detachment—not the soldiers—with the lynching. A Mr. Richards, identified as the postmaster at Parkville,[31] told the *Rocky Mountain News Weekly* that on May 2, while he was staying at the Kenosha House, Hamilton and Spaulding of Wilson's group "rode up and asked for an assisting party to return with them to Snyder's ranch . . . for the purpose of arresting a man named Baxter who was supposed to be there secreted."[32]

The two possemen said they and five others had stopped by the ranch "for the purpose of warming themselves," only to be denied entry by Mrs. Snyder under circumstances the possemen found suspicious—she claimed to be alone but some of Wilson's men heard the clumping of heavy boots within and, "as they were in quest of Baxter, they began to feel he was there concealed." Why was Baxter known by name? Who had named him? Why was he sought? By this time Metcalf's and Allen's description of the murderers as Mexicans or blacks must have been widely known. Was Baxter of dark coloring? We do not know the answers to any of these questions. All we know is that Wilson's men were intent on laying hold of him. They persisted in their appeals to Mrs. Snyder to admit them, and during this parley someone inside the house fired two shots through a window "into the crowd outside," killing a mule belonging to the posse.

At this point the seven members of Wilson's detachment withdrew to a distance, conferred, and uncertain how many armed inmates of Snyder's house they might be confronting, agreed to send Spaulding and Hamilton to the Kenosha House for reinforcements. Postmaster Richards and six other men who were staying at the hostelry responded at once, "and in an hour the party, increased to fourteen, again came forward and demanded admission at Snyder's."

Richards was an acquaintance of Snyder and eventually persuaded the terrified rancher to come out, "pushing his wife in front of him as a living shield against a fire which he feared might be opened upon him." Richards then glimpsed a man inside the house, heard the clicking of a cocked gun, got the drop on the fellow, and demanded and obtained his surrender. This proved to be the much-sought-after Baxter. Richards's story continues:

> [Baxter] and Snyder were then taken to the Kenosha House, where both were subjected to three or four successive hangings by the neck, in the hope to obtain something from them by confession. Nothing, however, was elicited, farther than a confirmation of what was generally believed, that Snyder and Baxter were both bad characters. Baxter confessed to having escaped from the sheriff of Park county five or six weeks ago.

Snyder was given twenty-four hours to leave the country, and Baxter was taken up and delivered to the miners of California Gulch, to be dealt with as they might see fit.[33]

Our next source is the Reverend John L. Dyer, the savior of poor John Foster.[34] Though Dyer wrote in the 1890s, his memory—and his conscience—

were clear, and his description of what the California Gulch posse saw fit to do was unsparing. At about the time of the burials of the victims at Fairplay, he recalled, word came "that a man was harbored at a ranch some fifteen miles east, and a company went over about night and demanded him." Dyer confirms in broad outline Postmaster Richards's description of the various attempts by "Commandant" Wilson's squad of McCannon's posse to gain admittance to the house, the shots that killed the mule, and the withdrawal of the besiegers to wait for morning.

At sunup, Dyer writes, the posse—or, more properly, the mob—gave the inmates of the house "just a few minutes to surrender the man, under the alternative of having the house burned." This threat sufficiently cowed those within to open up, and the mob rushed in, captured the stranger, forced the ranchman to pay for the dead mule, and ordered him to leave his own home.[35]

> They took the prisoner near to Fairplay, and without trial or jury, hanged him, although he denied being guilty of any crime for which he deserved death. But poor Baxter had fallen into the hands of hard men in an evil hour. This was a mob, and nothing better ever comes of such work.[36]

Next we consider the account of "Dornick," the stringer for the *Weekly Commonwealth*, replete with faux-Latinate puns and bursting with ghoulish glee. It is worth repeating in its repellent entirety:

> From Dornick,
> May 8th, 1863
>
> I have the pleasure of informing you that one of the notorious jayhawkers has been captured, and like
>
> "Zachariah he
> Clum a tree."
>
> "his lord and master (the devil) for to see," and is now non est, up a limb-i-bus, neck in rope-i-bus, et dangling in the air-i-bus. On last Saturday evening some citizens got on the track, as they had reason to think, of suspicious characters, and went to Snyder's Ranch in the Park at the junction of the Tarryall and Jefferson roads, and when they attempted to enter the house were denied permission by the woman, who told them her husband, Snyder, was away and she was alone. The citizens persisted in entering, and in the act of doing so,

were met by several shots fired from within, one of which took effect upon one of the horses at the door, killing it instantly. The party then surrounded the house and guarded it until morning, when they succeeded in entering and corralled Snyder and a man named Baxter, and took them away towards Fairplay and examined them both by a little choking process with a rope to elicit any confession of crime they felt disposed to make under the pressing circumstances. Not much was got out of Snyder who was liberated. Baxter was found to be one of the gang which jayhawked the mules with Leeper, Brown and others last fall, from the Lehman brothers at Frying-pan gulch. He also had on him a coat which was identified as that worn by Carter, who was shot at the Cottage Grove, Baxter himself acknowledged it to be Carter's coat. In his pocket were found some bullets which corresponded with those found in several of the murdered bodies, in size, weight and a peculiar mark made by the moulds in moulding. Satisfied of his criminality, the citizens delivered him over to the soldiers at Fairplay, who took him out on the road about two miles east of Fairplay, and about noon (Monday) his body might have been seen suspended by a rope to the limb of a tree—no breath of life visible to any great extent in said body. The habeus corpus was suspended; he "struck the cap" and went up the spout, to the place where jayhawkers ought to go. It is some consolation to the friends of Lehman to know that this notorious scoundrel took his last look at this earth in sight of the bloody Red Hill where poor Lehman was murdered. Every one justifies this act, and wishes that more of the same sort may be had to "hang dangling in the air" like the body of the ancient J. Brown. The scouts are on the track of the others and it is hoped the country will soon be rid of these diabolical outlaws.

There are some laughable circumstances growing out of the present excitement to one who has an eye for the ridiculous side of things. For instance, while every one when going a mile from his own door is watching on all sides for outlaws, two neighbors meet at a distance; they approach each other cautiously and fail to recognize each other; one stops to reconnoiter, and the other becomes alarmed; each is certain the other is a jayhawker, and both crouch down and run dodging in opposite directions as if the Old Harry was after them and report having narrowly escaped at the hands of a villain.

Since the life of Metcalf was saved by the public document in his pocket, in which the ball that was fired at him lodged, everybody is practicing on pamphlet targets, and no one goes from home now, without arming himself with a double-barrelled shot gun, loaded with buck shot, three or four of

Bennett's documents in each vest pocket, and a bottle of schnapps in case of a truce.

Ever, DORNICK[37]

Here at last, buried in Dornick's sardonic prose, we catch a glimpse of a reason for the otherwise inexplicable fury of the mob against Baxter and their haste to execute him. The correspondent wrote, "Baxter was found to be one of the gang which jayhawked the mules with Leeper, Brown and others last fall, from the Lehman brothers at Frying-pan gulch." How and when this discovery was made is not disclosed. But we do know that Baxter was being sought, by name, at the time "Commandant" Wilson's vigilantes first approached the Snyder ranch. Why were they looking for this particular man?

An intriguing possibility is that even before McCannon's party left California Gulch, a man named Baxter was thought to have been a member of the Leeper mule-rustling band and was suspected of lurking about South Park—hence, Breece's instructions to McCannon that "particular attention" be paid to the "numerous murders *and robberies* . . . lately committed." But why would Baxter's presumed association with robberies in general or with the "Leeper gang" in particular have implied a link to the murders of Lehman and Seyga?

We have seen in Chapter 4 how Lehman, at the time of his death, was returning from US District Court in Central City where he had testified against several of the suspected mule rustlers[38]—George W. Brown, Isaac Roberts, Jonathan Leeper, and two men named Slatten and Harrison, whose first names were unknown to the grand jurors who indicted them. Baxter's name does not appear among those indicted. Whatever the reason, there is a high probability that "Commandant" Wilson's mob believed Baxter to be an associate of the Leeper crowd if not one of the five indicted.

The extant court records are incomplete as to the trial verdicts in the cases of Roberts, Leeper, Slatten, and Harrison. It is possible one or more of these men were exonerated. But the records do show that Brown was found guilty, largely on the basis of Lehman's testimony and that of his brother, Ernst.[39] "Commandant" Wilson's party must have known this and concluded that Baxter had followed Lehman from Central City to South Park and murdered him at Red Hill Pass in revenge for his damaging testimony against Brown. This gives new emphasis to Dornick's assertion, "It is some consolation to the friends of Lehman to know that this notorious scoundrel took his last look at this earth in sight of the bloody Red Hill where poor Lehman was murdered."

While all this goes to suggest there may have been something of a pretext for the lynching of Baxter in the minds of "Commandant" Wilson's vigilantes—something beyond simple lynch fever run amok—in the end there was no solid proof of the victim's complicity in the murder of Lehman, though it may have been true that he had rustled some mules with Leeper and the others. And it cannot be overlooked that rustling, by itself, was often a hanging offense on the frontier. No official records have survived to substantiate Richards's claim that Baxter had recently escaped from the Park County sheriff or to explain why he was in custody, though as we will see, Ostrander repeats the assertion. But even were it true that Baxter was some sort of criminal, the circumstances of his fate lend the whole affair a foul aftertaste, and it is no surprise that in McCannon's recollections he gave it short and cryptic shrift.

The charitable Reverend Dyer had drawn a veil over some of the worst of the incident, such as the repeated near-strangling of poor Snyder, a detail "Dornick" so delighted in. There is no telling what effect this treatment had on the unfortunate ranchman; it is worth remembering that Reuben Samuel, the foster father of Jesse James, was subjected to this same treatment in Missouri early in the Civil War, and never fully recovered his mental or physical faculties.[40] As regards the nature of Baxter's crimes, Dyer does not proclaim his entire innocence; he simply tells us the man had done nothing to merit death.

The suspicions of Baxter's complicity in the deaths of Lehman and Seyga apart, it is hard to know what to make of the incriminating evidence "Dornick" says the mob found on the man, except to adduce the fact that, in a few days' time, the real murderers would be found, and Baxter would be shown to have been innocent of the South Park killings, whatever else he might have been guilty of. Whether he had ever been a member of "the Leeper Gang" we cannot know.

In one other respect "Dornick's" report, revolting as it is, shies away, as McCannon's also does, from the one damning fact that Reverend Dyer was willing to confront: that it was not the disreputable toughs of the First Colorados who hanged Baxter; it was in fact the mob, and very likely "Commandant" Wilson's mob, which is to say, John McCannon's mob.[41] Private Ostrander saw it all, and what he saw shattered his habitual eerie calm.

His diary entry for May 2 mentions that two prisoners were taken by "the boys, that is, the First Colorados . . . but they were released an hour afterwards." Next day, a Sunday, "we were just this side of Snider's with a prisoner by the name of Baxter, who they[42] had taken this morning at Snider's. They went there last night to take them and were fired on from the house, having a mule killed. They watched the house till daylight and then arrested them. I was ordered to go back with the t[w]o men and help guard them."[43]

On Monday, May 4, Ostrander's diary reads as follows:

> We stopped at McLaughlin's last night and left there this morning at nine o'clock, when within a mile of Fairplay *we met some of the citizens to whom we delivered the prisoner* [emphasis added]. He was known to be an outlaw having escaped mail [jail?] in Dinver [*sic*] once and from the sheriff once. They took him out in the timber and hung him to a tree. Oh it was a horrible sight to see the poor fellow hung and he was all the time protesting his innocence even to the last breath. But I don't know but it was justice, for he was undoubtedly an outlaw and all outlaws are dangerous characters now.[44]

The various versions of Baxter's fate cannot all be reconciled. But Ostrander's diary is probably our most unbiased source. He makes it clear that at some point the First Colorado Cavalry had custody of Baxter and that at a later time they handed their prisoner over to the mob. It is a loss to history that he fails to describe why and how this atrocity happened. Unlike many of his messmates, Ostrander seems to have been a reserved and conscientious fellow if remarkably unreflective, and his reticence leaves us in the dark at a critical juncture. The hanging wounded him deeply but he did not see fit to explain precisely how the transfer of the prisoner came about, fraught as that was with dire consequences.

The majority of the Firsters were a hard lot. Already they had shown themselves eager to chase down and lynch John Foster, Reverend Dyer's parishioner. Hanging, for them, might have seemed an agreeable way to break the monotony of their seemingly endless patrol duty. But even granting that the enlisted men, the rankers, of the "Pet Lambs" were largely a set of ruffians, what of their officers, Lieutenants Wilson and Oster? Did they acquiesce in what happened? Lead it? Withdraw and ignore it? The record does not tell us.

Baxter may not have been the only one to swing. The *Rocky Mountain News Weekly*, in wrapping up Postmaster Richards's story, had this to say:

> On the return of the [Wilson] party, another suspicious character was arrested, who, after a few administrations of the hangman's noose around

Wilkerson Pass, looking west into South Park. McCannon and his posse would have left the Park coming eastward in their search for the murderers. (Author photo)

> his neck, promised to reveal the hiding place of several of the gang who have been committing outrages in the Park. At the time Mr. Richards left, the party sent out in company with this last prisoner had not returned. It is altogether likely, however, that we shall in a day or two hear of a hanging in the above vicinity. Vengeance will soon overtake the band of cut-throats which has been holding a carnival of blood in the southern and south western parts of this territory.[45]

The *Weekly Commonwealth*'s May 14 edition, in a report separate from "Dornick's," seems to confirm Richards's surmise:

> We learn from a gentleman just down from the South Park, that three men were lately arrested in that vicinity for being connected with the recent depredations thereabouts, and the gentle but effective arguments of Judge Lynch prevailed over their minds to such an extent that they made confessions which it is hoped will lead to the ferreting out of the whole gang. There is nothing like a few feet of rope, a stout tree and a man's neck, to bring out the "gab."[46]

NOTES

1. A small gulch draining into Colorado Gulch, which in turn fed what was then known as the West Fork of the Arkansas River. This was a short distance west of the future location of Leadville, Colorado.

2. Territorial Kansas Online—Transcripts, http://www.territorialkansasonline.org/~imlskto/cgi-bin/index.php?SCREEN=show_document&documentid=102477&SCREEN_FROM=show_location&county_id=4 (item no. 102477, call no. James Abbott Collection, Box 2, Folder 11), accessed February 27, 2013.

3. *Rocky Mountain News*, January 26, 1881, interview with McCannon entitled "Scenes at Sand Creek."

4. Territorial Kansas Online, http://search.ku.edu/search?q=McCannon&btnG=Search&site=TKO&sort=date%3AD%3AL%3Ad1&output=xml_no_dtd&ie=UTF-8&oe=UTF-8&filter=0&client=default_frontend&proxystylesheet=TKO (item no. 6975, call no. James Abbott Collection, Box 2, Folder 11), accessed February 27, 2013.

5. National Park Service, http://www.nps.gov/sand/historyculture/people.htm, accessed January 18, 2013.

6. Report dated May 21 in the *Rocky Mountain News Weekly*, May 28, 1863.

7. Ibid.

8. John McCannon, "An Account by a Participant," in Captain B. F. Rockafellow, "History of Fremont County," in Baskin, *History of the Arkansas Valley*, 576.

9. Ibid. The others named include Joseph M. Lamb, Julius Sanger, McCannon's brother O. T., Thomas S. Wells, C. F. Wilson, William R. McComb, John Gilbert, Frank Miller, Frederick Fredericks, William Youngh, James Foley, John Landin, Charles Nathrop, John Holtz, John Endleman, and William Woodward. The *Rocky Mountain News Weekly* report of May 28 says there were eighteen men in the party.

10. R. G. Dill, "History of Lake County," ibid., 213.

11. Ibid., 208.

12. Ibid.

13. *The Denver Daily News*, February 24, 1894.

14. Ibid.

15. *Weekly Commonwealth*, May 21, 1863.

16. Ibid.

17. Located a few miles west of the town of Granite, Cache Creek was the location of one of the first gold deposits discovered along the Arkansas headwaters.

18. Morse's identity is not known.

19. These were J. A. Hamilton, J. J. Spaulding, John Brown, and a Dr. Bell.

20. *Rocky Mountain News Weekly*, May 28, 1863.

21. McCannon, "An Account by a Participant," 576–577.

22. Ibid., 577.

23. Ostrander, *This Soldier Life*, 18.

24. Ibid. The others were Benjamin Griffith, Charles Low, and "another man."

25. McCannon, "An Account by a Participant," 577.

26. Ibid.

27. *Rocky Mountain News Weekly*, May 28, 1863; emphasis added.

28. Ibid.

29. Ostrander, *This Soldier Life*, 18.

30. *Rocky Mountain News Weekly*, May 28, 1863.

31. Seat of neighboring Summit County, 1861–1862.

32. *Rocky Mountain News Weekly*, May 7, 1863.

33. Ibid.

34. See Chapter 4.

35. Dyer, *The Snow-Shoe Itinerant*, 154.

36. Ibid.

37. *Weekly Commonwealth*, May 14, 1863.

38. Chapter 4, note 11.

39. Record Group 21, Records of the US District Court of the US Territory of Colorado, Bankruptcy, Civil and Criminal Case Files, 1862–74, Case #54, *United States of America vs. George W. Brown, Isaac Roberts, Jonathan Leeper, Slatten and Harrison*; Stephen J. Leonard, *Lynching in Colorado*, 105–106; and Rockafellow, "History of Fremont County," 580–585, tell of a Jonathan Leeper held in the Denver jail against whom unspecified charges were dropped but who refused to leave his cell because he enjoyed the free meals. Only after a jailer told him a lynching party was on its way to hang him did Leeper flee, only to be shot by soldiers who assumed he had broken jail. It is not known whether this is the same Jonathan Leeper charged in the mule-stealing case.

40. T. J. Stiles, *Jesse James: Last Rebel of the Civil War* (New York: Alfred A. Knopf, 2003), 89–91. Leonard, *Lynching in Colorado*, 97–122, notes that repeated hangings to induce confessions, or simply to inflict torture, were quite common in frontier Colorado. One victim was hanged six times before confessing. Ordinarily those who were repeatedly hanged but later freed seem not to have suffered long-term ill effects but Samuels's ordeal suggests that lifelong consequences could occur.

41. The *Rocky Mountain News Weekly* of May 7 also made it plain the First Colorados turned Baxter and Snyder over to "the citizens," who then tried them "according to the most approved rules of Judge Lynch's court." Baxter was recognized and convicted "as an old offender and notorious cattle thief" and was taken "back some two miles on the road between Fairplay and Tarryall, in sight of the bloody red hills, and the next morning his body was found pendant from the limb of a quaking aspen tree." Ghoulish humor was not lacking in this account either: "Whether he terminated his own existence in that manner, or was aided in 'shuffling off this mortal coil,' has not been made know[n]."

42. "They," in this instance, refers to the citizen mob, as the next lines make clear.

43. Ostrander, *This Soldier Life*, 19.

44. Ibid.

45. *Rocky Mountain News Weekly*, May 7, 1863. A tantalizing mystery is the nature of the relationship between the Parkville postmaster Richards and the unfortunate ranchman Snyder. Richards admits they were acquainted, but in the accounts of the time Snyder's name seems to give off a faintly unsavory odor. Were Snyder and Baxter friends? associates? fellow rustlers? Why was Baxter hiding at Snyder's? Why was a supposedly reputable postmaster like Richards an acquaintance of Snyder's?

46. *Weekly Commonwealth*, May 14, 1863. The lynching of Baxter was also reported as far away as Central City in the *Tri-Weekly Miner's Register* of May 9; and B. F. Rockafellow, "History of Fremont County," in Baskin, *History of the Arkansas River Valley*, 577, mentions that Baxter was hanged as a member of a gang of horse thieves; cited in Leonard, *Lynching in Colorado*, 187, note 10.

“Glorious News! The Mysterious Murders Unraveled at Last”
One of the Slayers Slain

6

After amusing themselves by lynching Baxter and repeatedly stretching the necks of Snyder and possibly another innocent victim, “Commandant” Wilson’s squad of the California Gulch posse “then scouted through the country as far northeast as Deer Creek, within forty-five miles of Denver.”[1] John McCannon later wrote he believed this movement drove the murderers from the upper end of South Park.[2] He may have been right. If the killers had originally entered the Park by ascending Tarryall Creek, it is likely they left it by taking same route downstream.[3] This valley, sparsely settled and sheltered on both sides by the rough country of the Puma Hills and the Tarryall Mountains, offered a protected outlet to the south and east. By now the killers must have realized that several parties of aroused citizens were on their trail and it was time to beat a retreat.

McCannon seems to have surmised this would be their course, for at some point[4] after sending “Commandant” Wilson and his party to the northeast, he and the rest of his company marched on foot from Weston’s wayhouse eastward, past Hockin’s ranch and Pulver’s ranch[5] to a point near the deserted mail station of John Addleman, the first of the Park’s murder victims, and there pitched camp. The following day he divided the posse into two sections, one to head east and one north, in an effort to locate some sign of the murderers who he assumed were now on the run.

DOI: 10.5876/9781607322375.c06

These movements suggest that McCannon, whatever his disagreeable qualities, owned a sound head for tactics—he had used Wilson's men to execute a flanking movement that would drive the killers down the Park, then had split and dispersed his own force to cover their only routes of escape, eastward through the Tarryall Mountains and Platte Canyon to the plains or southward down Oil Creek (now Fourmile Creek) in the direction of Cañon City and the Arkansas Valley.

Two members of the posse have left accounts of their expedition. On May 21, a fortnight after the events he described, McCannon himself wrote a report to the Oro City committee, the body that had commissioned him captain of the scouting company. Long afterward, in 1881, he wrote an article for O. H. Baskin's *History of the Arkansas River Valley* describing the events of that memorable spring. Joseph M. Lamb[6] also gave two versions, both later in life, one in 1894 during an interview with the *Denver Daily News* and one four years later in a letter to J. A. Israel, then US marshal of Colorado. All four accounts, though differing in some respects, have a similar, reinforcing contour, beginning by offering an implicit impression that the posse discovered the trail of the murderers entirely unaided.

But this was not in fact the case. They had help, and a good deal of it at that. The proof is in an article in the *Weekly Commonwealth* of May 21, which contains an interview with First Lieutenant Luther Wilson of Company F, First Colorado Cavalry, co-commander of the military expedition sent into South Park for the express purpose of capturing or killing the marauders. According to Lieutenant Wilson:

> The soldiers were frequently on their [the murderers'] trail, but were foiled several times by falling snow. They were on the trail within a few miles of Canon City when the party from California Gulch intersected them, and being nearly worn out they gave up the chase to the citizens, who from being personal friends of the murdered men, and being afoot and with pack animals, were likely to leave no stone unturned in the pursuit.[7]

This language leaves scant doubt that Lieutenant Wilson, officially charged with the duty of bringing in the murderers and actually following a fresh trail, voluntarily surrendered that responsibility to "personal friends of the murdered men," almost certainly code words for a lynch mob. The act echoed the surrender of Baxter to the crowd near Fairplay that so distressed Private

Ostrander, and that also seems to have happened with Lieutenant Wilson's tacit or even active approval.[8]

It is unclear exactly when this unwarranted transfer of accountability occurred, but when McCannon split his force, the eastern party was composed of Lamb and William Youngh. After two days of scouting, Lamb says, the pair detected horse tracks near Platte Canyon[9] and followed them a short distance to a miner's cabin. In the dooryard of the cabin they found evidence that some persons had cut kindling as if preparing to make camp but then for some reason had abandoned that plan and moved on. Their suspicions aroused, Lamb avers, they returned to the rendezvous point and reported their findings to McCannon and the balance of the posse.[10] Lieutenant Wilson's remark to the *Weekly Commonwealth* reporter raises the possibility he may have helped Lamb and Youngh "detect" the telltale tracks, or perhaps he and his troopers accompanied Lamb and Youngh back to McCannon's camp and alerted him as well.

Whatever transpired, next morning McCannon's reunited company picked up the trail that Lamb and Youngh had found (or Lieutenant Wilson had pointed out), "below the crossing of the Platte on the Colorado [City] Road going south,"[11] and followed it past what Lamb called "the petrified stumps"[12] and on to what he took to be the head of Oil Creek. "There they found fresh signs and[,] keeping on[,] found a beaver dam torn down."[13] They followed the tracks along an old Indian trail[14] past three abandoned camping places, "two of which had live coals in them."[15]

Sensing they were close on the heels of their quarry, the possemen grew anxious. "We were expecting to be led into a band of them at anytime for none of us knew how many there were," Lamb recalled.[16] All the sensational reports of the atrocities perpetrated by the mysterious murderers now came vividly to mind. Also, the possemen were ordinary miners, not experienced trackers or fighting men. They were tired, hungry, and fearful.

The strain became too much for one of them, John Endleman. McCannon and Lamb disagree about the time and place of this incident[17] but are in general concurrence about what transpired. "One of our party unexpectedly became insane from excitement and exertion," Lamb told the *Denver Daily News*, "and he was left in camp with seven men in charge of the pack animals and himself."[18] McCannon, in 1881, was characteristically blunt: "[T]o the astonishment of all of us, John Endleman began to sing and yell, by turns, and, it being a serious affair, as we could not send him back or leave him, so I detailed two of the

Representative views of the rough country north of Cañon City through which McCannon's posse searched for the murderers. (Author photos)

strongest men I had to keep a steady watch on him, and to gag him when he became too noisy."[19]

This affair is not mentioned at all in McCannon's report to the Oro City committee, perhaps in order to spare the feelings of a respected neighbor who had broken down under hard service. Lamb, in 1897, wrote that "Egeton [*sic*] had lost his mind and become very noisy . . . [so] we held a council and decided to send part of our party to Canon City with him as he was not a fit man to have along."[20]

Whenever the difficulty with Endleman occurred, by four o'clock in the afternoon of May 8 the exhausted posse made camp on Oil Creek. The trail they were following had left the creek at this point and ascended westward into a maze of canyon lands. "The country to the south was high and barren mountains, and the trail led across them," McCannon wrote, and it made sense to rest and eat their suppers before going on. They lay in camp until dark. When night fell, it was clear and with a full moon.[21]

McCannon, sensing they were close on the heels of the fugitives, asked for volunteers to undertake a forced march by night and close the distance, "as I was determined to see what and who they [the fugitives] were as quickly as possible."[22] Seven men stepped forward and resumed the pursuit by moonlight, carrying no provisions or blankets[23] in order to move more easily. The seven were Lamb, Youngh, James Foley, the murdered Bill Carter's brother Charles, Julius Sanger, Frederick Fredericks, and John Landin.[24]

Moving up the trail, the volunteers advanced about three miles to a high shale ridge. Here they could no longer read the sign and so agreed to huddle in a nearby gulch and wait for sunup. "We crawled into the brush where we passed one of the coldest nights I have ever experienced," Lamb remembered. "We did not dare build a fire for fear of giving warning of our presence."[25] When day broke, the possemen bestirred themselves despite their hunger, sore limbs, and chilled bones; they felt certain they were now "close upon the murderers."

They moved stealthily another two and a half miles southeastward and eventually reached the head of a ravine "which was canyoned up at one end and sloping off on the other side."[26] From this vantage point they could see a little park on the southern edge of the gulch with a dense thicket of willows in it and two hobbled horses grazing on the tawny winter grass. A broken-topped butte of blood-red rock stood guard over the scene.[27]

Here McCannon again resorted to a tactical maneuver. He divided his force, sending Foley, Youngh, Fredericks, and Landin to "go around the bluff and get into the cañon below, and to carefully push their way up along the cañon, while we covered the horses with our guns." Lamb, Carter, Sanger, and McCannon lay concealed among the rocks at the head of the ravine. They waited anxiously about three-quarters of an hour while the other four possemen executed their half of McCannon's envelopment.[28]

Having clambered up out of the Oil Creek bottom and over the shale ridge, the possemen had left behind the dark, narrow, icy confines of the streambed. They had emerged into a sunlit landscape of soaring openness set about on all sides by fantastic battlements of rimrock and tumbled heaps of stone. McCannon and his three companions lay waiting on a boulder-strewn slope covered with bunchgrass, junipers, willows, and the occasional mesquite bush and spiky *cholla*. From this vantage point they could see ahead of them range upon range of rugged mountains spreading southward toward Cañon City. Suddenly, well before Foley, Youngh, and the others could creep into position below, a man appeared near the willows in the little meadow, moving toward the hobbled horses. He was a big man and, McCannon says, was recognized at once as a Mexican.[29] Lamb judged him to be seventy yards distant and whispered to McCannon, "There's one a-coming. Remain still and I'll tend to him."

Although the encircling party south of the meadow might be vulnerable to gunfire,[30] McCannon decided not to wait. "Be sure to shoot low enough not to lose your charge,"[31] he advised.

"Don't be alarmed; I'll tend to that part of it," Lamb replied, taking aim with his double-barreled rifle. The man in the meadow stooped to remove the hobbles from one of the horses and at that instant Lamb fired. The man "threw up his hands with a loud cry and fell backward on the rocks."[32]

Lamb wrote:

> Then I arose and began re-loading my gun. The Captain asked me where I hit him. I told him about the third rib in the left side. He [the Mexican] then got on his elbow and started to fire his pistol. I shouted to McCannon to look out just in time for him to dodge behind some willows. By this time Sanger fired at [the Mexican] with a shot gun, hitting the horse in the neck. The victim then fired a shot at Sanger without doing any harm. Then Carter raised his rifle and fired at the Mexican's breast, hitting him in the head.[33]

This head shot was fatal; Charles Carter had avenged his murdered brother. As the man sank back in death, no one in the northern half of the posse doubted he was one of the long-sought murderers.

But how could they have been certain enough to cut him down without warning? It is possible, as McCannon wrote, that they recognized him as a Mexican, bearing in mind Metcalf's and Reed's description of Carter's killers as either Mexicans or African Americans. But being a Mexican was not necessarily the same thing as being one of the serial killers who had been tormenting central Colorado since mid-March. Nor would it have been a rarity to encounter a guiltless Hispano in the country north of Cañon City; there were cattle and sheep ranches in the bottomlands along Oil Creek where they might have been employed. Hispano woodcutters and charcoal burners could have been roaming freely in the mountains and canyons.

It is tempting to conclude the possemen acted too hastily. Not only might they have slain an innocent man, had they demanded his surrender at gunpoint instead, they might have taken the stranger captive. Then they might have either established his innocence or, if persuaded of his guilt by questioning (hopefully without the aid of a hempen noose), they might have learned the reasons for the murder raid, the identity of his partner, and much else of value not only to themselves and their contemporaries but to those of us peering back through history trying to understand these terrible crimes and the reasons they were committed. But this they did not do. Perhaps they *could not* do it.

In a perfect world they should have been more prudent. But consider their circumstances. They were a party of private citizens, volunteers all, most of whom appear to have been genuinely motivated by a sense of public duty, who had taken on a dangerous task that no one in authority was willing to perform. Park County sheriff Farnham seems never to have shown his face during the whole period of the murders; the miners of Buckskin Joe and Mosquito who had originally sought their assistance had turned up at Weston's ranch totally unequipped for a pursuit and McCannon had rightly dismissed them as useless; and the First Colorados, specifically authorized by the Territorial government to capture or kill the murderers, had simply grown weary of the hunt and turned the chore over to the civilians of California Gulch.

Furthermore, McCannon's men must have felt the suffocating atmosphere of rage, fear, and paranoia that had been building up over the past weeks like thunderheads ready to unleash a lightning storm. Ever since the deaths of Binkley and Shoup, the press and public had been whipping up lynch fever, insisting that anyone even suspected of complicity in the killings should be summarily dispatched, a mood that had already doomed Baxter and nearly resulted in death for Foster, Snyder, and possibly a third unidentified man.

As a result, the possemen suffered profoundly from tension and anxiety, witness the example of Endleman. Also, they had to be inexpressibly weary; they had left California Gulch eleven days before and in that time had covered a distance of at least one hundred and fifty or sixty miles,[34] on foot, over hard country covered in places with new snow and in others with mud and bogs of melt, dragging along recalcitrant pack mules. Beyond that, the eight men surrounding the gulch and its little meadow that morning of May 9 had crept another two and a half miles since nightfall over a steep and rocky country and spent a sleepless night in the freezing cold. Is it any wonder they were inclined to act without deliberation?

Nothing would be easier than to tar this group with the same brush that blackens the character of "Commandant" Wilson and the mob that made so free with the hanging rope near Fairplay, or to judge them by the standard of their leader, McCannon, whose traits of ambition, decisiveness, and extreme self-confidence, usually seen as virtues, somehow, in the record we have of him, smack instead of defects of character.

Whatever its justification or lack thereof, the deed was done. The big Hispano lay dead in the meadow. But, as the possemen had feared, he was not alone. Lamb continues:

> On hearing the shooting, the other murderer ran into the ravine where they were camped. I saw him and pulled up to fire at him when the Captain shouted, "Don't shoot Billy Youngh!" who had gone below to get below the camp. I lowered my gun to be sure and when I moved he saw me and dodged out of sight. He was nearly the same size as Billy Youngh and dressed the same, so it was hard to tell the difference, and as we had elected our captain to give orders, I felt it my duty to obey them, but if I had fired I would have been sure of killing the other murderer. But I do not blame the captain, for he thought he was doing what was right.[35]

Lamb gives a nearly identical version of this incident in his 1894 newspaper interview.[36] Though he denies any ill feeling against McCannon, one senses the incident galled him because it deprived him of the honor of striking down the second suspect. Interestingly, in McCannon's 1881 account, it is he who starts to shoot the second man and Julius Sanger who prevents the shot in the mistaken belief the man is Youngh. But in his near-contemporaneous report to the Oro City committee, McCannon makes no mention at all of the mix-up that allowed the second fugitive to escape, perhaps because to do so might expose the fact he had allowed Lamb to open fire while Youngh and the others were still out of position and possibly exposed. Nor does he identify Lamb, or Carter, for that matter, by name as the men firing the shots that felled the first man. They become anonymously "my men." John McCannon, it appears, could not help craving center stage, or blaming others for his own errors of judgment.[37]

The second fugitive disappeared and the posse searched the area for him in vain, but later he gained a piece of high ground and fired two shots from a distance, both at Lamb, one of which passed through Lamb's hat brim and coat and cut a furrow through two shirts he was wearing; the second struck a rock at Lamb's feet, spattering him and other possemen with fragments of rock and lead.[38]

The shooter vanished again and the posse was now too used up to think of pursuit. They rested in the abandoned camp and nibbled on the only sustenance they could find: a piece of beavertail partly eaten by the late occupants. Lamb, inspecting the dead man, found he had been correct about shooting him in the third rib of the left side. The rib was found to have been cut in two as neatly as with a knife.[39]

Lamb removed the dead man's boots as keepsakes, equipped as they were with a set of wicked-looking hand-forged spurs of Spanish design whose twelve-spiked rowels measured three inches in diameter. The spurs had chain loops fitted under the arches of the boots.[40] Though neither Lamb nor McCannon mentions it, it appears that the dead man was also decapitated and the head bagged for evidence. "The dead Mexican was left where he fell as food for wild animals."[41]

In the outlaws' camp were found articles of clothing, papers, and other items belonging to several of the known murder victims. The possemen gathered this evidence and may have used the killers' one surviving horse to carry it, then set out to meet up with the remainder of the company. But when they reached the point where McCannon had divided his force, they learned that the section of the posse with the pack animals had gone on to Cañon City, so McCannon and the others hoofed it until eleven o'clock that night when they reached a ranch on Oil Creek, having been thirty hours without food or sleep. Next morning three possemen were so done in as to be unable to travel at all and McCannon had to hire a team to carry the entire company to Cañon City, arriving there the following day.[42]

McCannon wrote that the jaded possemen "rested two days, and then returned home to Lake County. The crazy man got all right and went to

Spurs of the suspect killed by McCannon's posse, taken off his body by John Lamb. (Photo by David Ryan, Museum Registrar, courtesy of the Colorado Springs Pioneers Museum)

Montana."[43] On May 21 McCannon presented his written report to the Oro City committee. It "was received with the thanks of the citizens . . . for the successful manner in which the expedition was brought to a close." A committee was appointed to secure the reward that was understood to have been offered "for the apprehension of one of the Mexicans supposed to have been killed."[44] It was also moved, seconded, and carried that another committee be appointed "to solicit subscriptions for the purpose of remunerating the men for their loss of time while out on the expedition."[45]

Who would be present at Cañon City to report the sensational developments if not the irrepressible "Dornick," correspondent for the *Weekly Commonwealth*? But for once "Dornick" could find scant material in the extraordinary performance of the California Gulch posse from which to construct a pun. Perhaps he actually realized humor would not be his best approach. At any rate, he

John McCannon, again in the uniform of a captain, Third Colorado Volunteers. (Photo courtesy of History Colorado, no scan number)

managed to tell the story straight. The *Weekly Commonwealth*'s edition of May 21 trumpeted:

GLORIOUS NEWS! THE MYSTERIOUS MURDERS UNRAVELED AT LAST

The Principal Murderer Shot!! Our correspondent "Dornick" sends us the following intelligence:

CANON CITY, May 10.

I write a few hurried lines this morning to communicate the intelligence that the great mystery which has heretofore enshrouded the bloody murders of this community and South Park has been cleared up by the capture of the chief actor in the plot.

A party of the California Gulch boys who have been tracking the murderers for ten or twelve days past, came into this place yesterday evening saying they had at last overtaken the outlaws and meted out a just reward to one of them. The murderers are two Mexicans, and they have committed the whole of the bloody crimes. The party came upon their camp on Friday morning, about 18 miles from here, in a canon up Four Mile Creek,[46] above the Oil Springs, and shot down the large one, just as he was in the act of unhobbling their horses, preparatory to starting.

The other Mexican, the smaller one, escaped, but is still pursued. A team and wagon was procured at the Oil Spring and brought in the traps and whole outfit last night. The plunder was laid out for examination in a large building here, and a large and excited crowd gathered round and examined it till a late hour. Articles of clothing, trinkets and personal effects stripped from the dead were identified as having belonged to every one of the murdered men—Bruce, Harkens, Addleman, Binkley, Shoup, Carter, Lehman and Seyga. . . . The clothing of two or three others are among the plunder not yet identified, so that it is certain these demons have murdered at least twelve persons since, starting in with Mr. Bruce here on the Arkansas.

A memorandum book was found evidently taken from Mr. Lehman, in which are several pages written by the Mexican in Spanish. . . . [It] states that they cannot live longer in New Mexico, and intend to kill Americans while they live; that they have killed many in South Park and are going down on the Plains to kill more. A reference to the names of "Espinosa" leaves little doubt that these Mexicans are the two brothers by the name of Espinosa that left Conejos in the winter as outlaws. . . . The one who was shot died cursing the Americans. He was a large, athletic man, about 25 years old, a dead shot, had a double-barrelled rifle and two revolvers, and was the most brutal and fiendish human in expression of countenance and shape of head that was ever seen. . . . These murderers being found to be Mexicans, accounts for many hitherto mysterious things, and among them those which were taken to be blackened faces.

The annals of crime, in history, furnish no parallel to the diabolical atrocity of these two outlaws, and too much praise cannot be awarded to the citizens of the mountains who have so persistently followed them up and taken so active a part in ridding the Territory of these demon foes to the citizens of the entire country—outlaws whose career of crime will form one of the most terrible epochs in the annals of Colorado. Ever, DORNICK[47]

The badly scooped opposition paper, the *Rocky Mountain News Weekly*, was forced to cite the much reviled *Weekly Commonwealth* as its unlikely source when it too broke the biggest Territorial news story of 1863 on that same May 21. The piece was brief, containing little but the essential facts, but it too harked back to some old news that had caused hardly a ripple earlier in the year, and it mentioned a name few had noticed in February but henceforth would resound throughout Colorado history: "It is said they are two Mexicans—the brothers Espinosa, for whose apprehension we advertised a reward offered by Marshal Hunt some months ago—who have now committed at least a dozen murders."[48]

NOTES

1. McCannon, "An Account by a Participant," 577.

2. Ibid.

3. An intriguing and so far unexplored question is the extent to which the murderers were acquainted with the geography of the parts of Colorado they moved through. As

will be seen, they seem to have lived all their lives in northern New Mexico or the San Luís Valley in southern Colorado Territory (though an unlikely rumor has one of them visiting California Gulch in 1860). Were they choosing their routes at random or did they already know the lay of the land and plan their travels accordingly? Another factor that has passed without serious inquiry has to do with the phenomenal distances they traveled, on horseback, crossing several mountain ranges and traversing some of the roughest terrain in the Territory, usually moving very rapidly considering the weather and the time of year. The logistics of their murder raid would be an interesting field of study on its own.

4. The date of his departure is not given in either of his written accounts.

5. Joseph M. Lamb, Letter to J. A. Israel, March 9, 1897, Colorado Historical Society (now History Colorado), MSS 224, ff #3. The site of Hockin's ranch is not known but Pulver's ranch still exists and is on County Road 90 near Wilkerson Pass, the east rim of the Park; Christie Wright, President of the South Park Archives Board, personal communication to the author, January 31, 2010.

6. See Chapter 4.

7. *Weekly Commonwealth*, May 21, 1863.

8. Wilson was the senior officer of the detachment of the First Colorado operating in South Park; it is fair to assume he either passively allowed the hanging of Baxter to proceed or ordered his troopers to deliver Baxter to the mob. Ostrander does not clarify this.

9. A narrow gorge where the South Platte River passes through the Rampart Range onto the eastern plains, located on the border of present Jefferson and Douglas counties.

10. Lamb, Letter to J. A. Israel.

11. McCannon's Report to the Oro City Committee, *Rocky Mountain News Weekly*, May 28, 1863.

12. The present location of Florissant and its fossil remains.

13. McCannon's report to the Oro City Committee.

14. Simmons, *Bayou Salado*, 25, refers to this Oil Creek trail as a now forgotten Indian route out of South Park to the southeast.

15. Lamb, Letter to J. A. Israel.

16. Ibid. Lamb must mean here that while they were trailing only two men, they feared a large band of outlaws might be waiting farther down the canyon.

17. McCannon, in his 1881 "An Account by a Participant," 577, says Endleman's breakdown occurred at Addleman's mail station, but Lamb, in his letter to Israel, says it began at Platte Canyon and worsened when the posse reached the south end of what he called Four-Mile Park. Nelson Walker of Cañon City, who has exhaustively studied the posse's route, wrote in personal correspondence with the author on December 6, 2008, "Today, there is no geographical feature named Four-Mile Park, however, there is a park situated about 15 miles south of Florissant that is named High Park. It is possible that this is the park that Lamb was actually referencing."

18. Lamb, *Denver Daily News*, February 24, 1894.

19. McCannon, "An Account by a Participant," 577.

20. Lamb, Letter to J. A. Israel.

21. McCannon, "An Account by a Participant," 577.

22. Ibid.

23. McCannon's Report to the Oro City Committee.

24. Ibid.

25. Lamb, *Denver Daily News*.

26. Ibid.

27. The description of the murderers' campsite is a composite of McCannon's and Lamb's accounts. The actual location is a matter of dispute. James Perkins, *Tom Tobin*, 172, believes it was Grape Spring, thirteen miles north of Cañon City and about a half-mile west of Garden Park corral. Nelson Walker (see note 17 above) strongly believes it was at a place called Nash Spring, about four miles west and north of Grape Spring. Appendix A covers this dispute in detail.

28. McCannon, "An Account by a Participant," 577; and McCannon, Report to the Oro City Committee.

29. Ibid.

30. Lamb, Letter to J. A. Israel.

31. That is, waste the shot.

32. Lamb, *Denver Daily News*.

33. Lamb, Letter to J. A. Israel.

34. This is an extremely rough crow-flight estimate working from maps; it does not account for the distances traveled during the two days the posse searched the area between Addleman's and Platte Canyon or the trip McCannon made on April 30 from Weston's ranch to Fairplay and back; nor does it account for the nature of the terrain covered. The actual distance, hard to believe as it is, must have been much farther.

35. Lamb, Letter to J. A. Israel.

36. Lamb, *Denver Daily News*.

37. McCannon, "An Account by a Participant," 577; McCannon's Report to the Oro City Committee.

38. Lamb, *Denver Daily News*; Lamb, Letter to J. A. Israel. Joseph Lamb told the *Daily News* he came to Colorado in 1850 [*sic*] and soon earned a reputation as a dead shot and a fine hunter. He first worked the Russell Gulch diggings and later spent eight years at California Gulch. "I dug out several good wads," he said in his interview, "but they went as easy as they came." Rheumatism forced him to retire from "high altitude" in 1868 and he settled in the Wet Mountain Valley. Wendell Hutchinson, in George G. Everett and Wendell Hutchinson, *Under the Angel of Shavano*, 61–62, says Lamb was in the area of south-central Colorado now known as Chaffee County in the early 1860s and tells how

Lamb and another man were camped on Currant Creek northeast of the present town of Salida on a hunting and prospecting trip when a band of fifty or sixty Cheyenne Indians came to their camp and asked for food. "The band was made up entirely of bucks with no squaws along," Hutchinson wrote, "and since it was on Ute territory it was evident to Lamb and his companion that they were on a raid. Lamb was friendly to the Utes, and after the Cheyennes had left camp and it was sufficiently dark for him to travel without being detected, he made a trip to the camp of a large band of Utes under the command of Chief Colorow, some 10 or 12 miles distant. He reached Colorow's camp about midnight . . . whereupon [he] . . . awakened [Colorow], and informed him of the Cheyennes. He stated that in two minutes the camp was in an uproar. It was too dark to set out immediately, but they were after the Cheyennes by daylight and encountering them the following day defeated them. Lamb claimed Colorow never forgot the favor. Several years later, Lamb became lost while making a winter trip through the South Park country, but finally happened on Colorow's camp. Colorow extended him a very hearty welcome and fed and cared for him until he was able to continue on with his trip."

39. Lamb, *Denver Daily News*.

40. *Colorado Springs Gazette*, July 11, 1920. The spurs, complete with their leather straps, are now in the Pioneers Museum, Colorado Springs.

41. Lamb, *Denver Daily News*. The detailed description of the head and its expression, given by the correspondent "Dornick" (see note 47), leads the author to believe the head, along with other effects from the dead man's camp, had been fetched back to Cañon City and put on display by McCannon's posse.

42. McCannon, "An Account by a Participant," 578; and McCannon, Report to the Oro City Committee.

43. McCannon, "An Account by a Participant," 578.

44. It is not known whether this reward was ever paid; *Rocky Mountain News Weekly*, May 28, 1863. At the outbreak of troubles with the Cheyenne Indians in 1864, John McCannon became captain of Company I, Third Colorado Regiment. On November 29, 1864, he and his company, along with the entire regiment, attacked a peaceful Cheyenne village at Sand Creek, Colorado, "with great celerity and success," according to the report of his commanding officer, Colonel George L. Shoup, brother of the Abram Shoup murdered in South Park. "His brave company killed 26 Indians in one pit and must have killed 50 more during the engagement," Shoup wrote; Sand Creek Massacre National Historic Site, http://ehistory.osu.edu/osu/sources/recordView.cfm?Content=083/0956, accessed February 27, 2013. In 1866 Shoup moved to Idaho Territory, entered politics, was appointed territorial governor in 1889, and when statehood came in 1890, state governor. Soon afterward he became one of the state's first two senators. He became a champion of Indian rights. His likeness stands in Statuary Hall in the US Capitol; Perkins, *Tom Tobin*, 173, note 32. John McCannon faded from the limelight after

1864, only to reappear in Denver in 1881 where he consented to a newspaper interview in which he defended the Sand Creek Massacre and still insisted, seventeen years later, that 600 or 700 hostiles were justifiably killed there; *Rocky Mountain News*, January 26, 1881. He resurfaced in 1897 to claim a reward for his service, falsely asserting that the expedition had been fitted out entirely at his own expense. See Appendix B for a further discussion of his claim.

45. Ibid.

46. At this period it seems the Oil Creek usage was beginning to give place to that of Fourmile Creek, the present name.

47. *Weekly Commonwealth*, May 21, 1863.

48. *Rocky Mountain News Weekly*, May 21, 1863.

"Desperate and Lawless Bravos"
The Brothers Espinosa

7

On a bitterly cold Thursday, January 15, 1863, a detachment of ten soldiers of Company D, First New Mexico Cavalry, under the command of Second Lieutenant Nicholas Hodt, clattered into the Hispano *plaza* of San Rafael on the Río Conejos near the border separating Colorado Territory from the Territory of New Mexico.

The troops had been dispatched from Fort Garland, the American military post located thirty-five miles northeast at the base of Blanca Peak in the Sangre de Cristo Mountains, at the request of a deputy United States marshal named George Austin, who now accompanied them. Deputy Austin had called on the army for help after encountering resistance in making some arrests the week before while trying to forestall what he and the other few Anglos living in the mostly Hispano San Luís Valley were construing as "an insurrection among the people."[1]

The arrival of the detachment and Lieutenant Hodt's hapless attempts to effect the previously failed arrests sparked an outbreak of violence. Gunfire and, improbably, even showers of arrows[2] rained down on the soldiers, most of whom were, ironically, themselves Hispano volunteers. Before the engagement ended on the following day, probably on the heights of Los Mogotes ("The Antlers"), a large, sparsely treed mesa north of San Rafael, one of these, a young corporal

DOI: 10.5876/9781607322375.c07

Present-day view of Fort Garland. (Author photo)

named Decedero Abeyta,[3] was dead; Deputy Austin had suffered a broken leg; and Lieutenant Hodt had managed to shoot himself in the head by accident. Three Hispanos who were suspected of having killed Corporal Abeyta had escaped.

At some point soon after this armed clash, Colorado's US Marshal Alexander Cameron Hunt and another federal deputy named Olmstead arrived on the scene. Hunt dashed off a note to the *Rocky Mountain News Weekly* saying, "We have just had a skirmish with a party of Mexican robbers . . . in which the few troopers who were here came off second best. . . . Our casualties are Corporal Lopez [*sic*] killed; Lieut. Hutt [*sic*], wounded by a shot in the head, not dangerous; George Austin, wounded, broken leg."[4]

Hunt went on to assert, "I have arrested, and will bring to Denver, one of the chief conspirators against the Government in the late affair in this valley."[5] The marshal does not give the name of the arrested party but his statement confirms that some sort of unrest was thought to be rife among the Hispano population of the border country.

Conspiracy and insurrection of the people? Or common banditry and robbery? Ordinarily there would seem to be a large distance between these

Typical adobe dwelling, village of San Rafael. (Author photo)

two types of crimes. What was the actual cause of the deadly trouble during those two January days in the usually peaceful hamlet of San Rafael? Even the newspaper was confused, noting that Hunt was offering a reward for "certain parties, but we know not for what offence. Probably for being concerned in the disturbance down there some time since"[6]—another allusion to disaffection in the southernmost part of the Territory.

True to his word, Hunt placed a reward notice in the next edition of the paper:

> **$50 REWARD**
>
> I will give the above reward for the apprehension and delivery to me, dead or alive, of three Mexicans, described as follows: JESUS M. SANCHES, long a resident of Upper Conejos, San Luís Valley, and BROBAN and PHILIP OSPENACIA, one of them 5 feet 6 inches in height and slender built; the other a little shorter and heavier.
>
> C. HUNT
> US Marshal[7]

Los Mogotes, or "The Antlers," the mountains north of San Rafael into which the Espinosas may have escaped. Corporal Abeyta may have been killed in the rough rimrock skirting Los Mogotes, not visible in this view. (Author photo)

Two of the Hispanos who had escaped the encounter at San Rafael were mentioned more particularly elsewhere in that edition, in the body of a much more detailed reconstruction of the incident. This time no mention was made of Sánchez but his alleged confederates were better identified, their names still misspelled but at least no longer phonetically mangled as in Marshal Hunt's notice. They were men "by the name of Espanosa." Furthermore, they were "desperate and lawless bravos, known over the entire country."[8] They were brothers; their right names were Felipe Nerio and José Vivián Espinosa.

Five months later, Vivián Espinosa would be shot down by John McCannon's posse north of Cañon City; Felipe would escape to kill again for yet another five months. But before that January skirmish at San Rafael, the brothers were poor farmers, *labradores* who sometimes dabbled in enough thievery and rustling to earn a name among their own as "desperate and lawless bravos." But it was the shoot-out at San Rafael that launched them on their murderous rampage through central Colorado. At this distance in time it may not be possible for us to arrive at a complete understanding of these two men and the

The church of San Pedro y San Rafael, built in the 1920s to replace the original *jacal* (stick-and-clay hut) destroyed by fire. Here the people of San Rafael have worshipped since about 1858, presumably including the Espinosas and Hurtados. The Sangre de Cristo Mountains are faintly visible in the distance. (Author photo)

reasons for their crimes. But if we are to approach at least the beginnings of an understanding, we also need to understand who the Espinosas were, what was really happening among the Hispanos of the San Luís Valley, how and why the fight at San Rafael came about, and the immediate and bitter fruit it bore.

The Espinosa family from which Felipe and Vivián sprang first appears in a census of the province of New Mexico conducted by the Mexican government in 1845.[9] This would be the last Mexican enumeration before the American takeover of the Southwest during the Mexican War the following year. The Espinosas were recorded as living in El Rito in the Spanish grant of the same name that had been awarded in 1751 to Juan Esteban García de Noriega.[10] El Rito was situated in the lower Chama Valley, about thirty-five miles west of Taos, in what would become, in 1852, Río Arriba County, one of the nine original counties of the United States Territory of New Mexico.[11]

The head of the family was recorded as Pedro Ignasio Espinosa, farmer, 46 years of age; the wife, as María Gertrudis Chaves, age 40; and the children as Felipe Nerio, 13; María Tomasa, 11; Bivián [*sic*], 9; Juan Antonio, 7; and María Juana, 6.[12]

Five years later, in the Territorial Census of 1850 that the Americans conducted for Santa Ana County, including the section of southern Río Arriba County that contained El Rito, the Espinosas appear again.[13] Interestingly, so does a family of Hurtados, whose two daughters, María Merijilda [Secundina], 8, and María Ejinia [Eugenia], 7, would one day become intimately and disagreeably involved with Felipe Espinosa.[14]

While ages and even names are often incorrect in early census enumerations, especially when recorded, as in 1850, by Anglos[15] amid a Hispano population who distrusted outsiders, James E. Perkins, the biographer of Tom Tobin, who had access to descendants of the Espinosas, was able to show that Felipe Nerio was born in 1827 and José Vivián, the third child and second son, in 1831. A sister, María Tomasa, was born in 1829; a younger brother, Juan Antonio, in 1833; and the youngest sister, María Juana, in 1834.[16]

Felipe and Vivián were born in Río Arriba County. During the next census, that of 1860, their parents and the Hurtados said they were natives of Doña Ana County, the southernmost of the counties established by the Americans in 1852.[17] But in view of the extreme remoteness of Doña Ana County, perhaps the census enumerator misunderstood them and confused the name Doña Ana with that of Santa Ana, where they had long lived.

A typical Penitente *morada* (meetinghouse), with *maderos grandes* (great crosses) stacked outside, to be carried by the *Hermanos* (Brothers) during their religious exercises. (Courtesy of Denver Public Library, Western History Collection, call no. Z-6684)

Perkins asserts that in several ways the Espinosa children were unique. Though the family were *pobres*, subsistence farmers barely making their way in life, Felipe and Vivián, and perhaps their siblings, too, could read and write in a time and place where literacy among the poor was almost nonexistent. Felipe was from his earliest years "impulsive, irrational and volatile" and especially nursed a bitter hatred for Americans, whom he saw as conquerors, oppressors, and enemies of the Catholic faith; yet he and Vivián were "devoutly religious" and had become members of the *Santa Hermandad de la Sangre de Nuestro Señor Jesucristo* (The Holy Brotherhood of the Blood of Our Lord Jesus Christ), commonly known as the Penitentes,[18] a lay fraternity that had grown up in remote areas of northern New Mexico where the influence of the church had long been weak.

The Penitentes had evolved a pattern of religious exercises, in place of the established sacraments, through which they attempted to repeat the sufferings and crucifixion of Christ during Holy Week each year and on other occasions with religious significance, for the purpose of expiation of sin. These exercises were often bloody, especially involving severe self-flagellation, practices that made the rulers of New Mexico—who, in the executive positions,

Disciplinas, or whips made of yucca fibers, used by Penitentes for self-flagellation. (Courtesy of Denver Public Library, Western History Collection, call no. Z-6118)

Padre Antonio José Martínez, *cura propio* of Taos, New Mexico, thought to have been a superior and protector of the Penitentes. (Photo unattributed, ca. 1848; courtesy of the Palace of the Governors Photo Archives [NMH/DCA], neg. no. 010308)

were largely Anglo—nervous and suspicious, so much so that sinister rumors about their nature began to circulate, some suggesting that the simulated crucifixions were not reenactments at all but actual executions. The Brotherhood also functioned as a benevolent and philanthropic organization serving the needs of the more unfortunate people in their communities, but the Anglo outsiders rarely understood this.[19]

Some scholars believe the Penitentes, though functioning outside the immediate orbit of the church, had a powerful advocate and protector in Padre Antonio José Martínez, *cura propio*, or irremovable pastor, of Taos and senior clergyman of the Roman Catholic Church in New Mexico until supplanted by the French bishop Jean Baptiste Lamy in July 1850.[20] Rome appointed Lamy to the post of vicar of New Mexico after the creation of a provisional diocese in the new territory by the Provincial Council of the Church in Baltimore.

Assuming his office in Santa Fe, Lamy undertook to regularize Catholic worship in the new territory, bringing him into immediate conflict with Padre Martínez, who, among other native priests, preferred that New Mexico be kept under the jurisdiction of the Mexican bishop of Durango, José Antonio Zubiría y Escalante, as it had been before the American conquest. Lamy's assumption of the vicariate, and later the bishopric, and his efforts at reform also caused a backlash among native priests over other issues such as tithing, which Martínez had abolished due to the poverty of the majority of New Mexican congregants.[21]

Thus Martínez assumed the guise of a Hispano patriot resisting the imposition of foreign powers (France and the Vatican) over the religious life

Bishop Jean Baptiste Lamy, French-born primate of the Catholic Church in New Mexico whose attempts to reform practices of worship brought him into conflict with Padre Martínez and other native priests. (Photo by William Henry Brown, ca. 1870; courtesy of the Palace of the Governors Photo Archives [NMHM/DCA], neg. no. 00990)

of the population.[22] Furthermore, Martínez had been born at Abiquiú near El Rito, had served as pastor there, sympathized with the *Santa Hermandad*, and may have served as the "Superior" of the Penitentes.[23] There is a possibility that Felipe and Vivián received their education at the Abiquiú mission sanctioned by Padre Martínez.[24]

Despite his sincere religious beliefs, however, Felipe Espinosa seems to have been a violent and dangerous man. Perkins relates how, in 1854, having attained the age of twenty-six, Felipe decided he should get married. However, contemporary Anglo sources imply that his repellent looks[25] worked against him. Having no luck finding a wife in El Rito where his reputation for turbulence was well-known, he rode south to Cochití near the pueblo of Santa Ana and abducted María Secundina Hurtado, the seventeen-year-old daughter of José Salvador Hurtado and María Andrea Gallegos. Secundina had a deformed and withered arm but was otherwise quite lovely. Not content with stealing Secundina, Felipe also kidnapped her eleven-year-old sister Eugenia, though he soon dropped her off at a neighbor's house.[26]

After being abused and beaten by Felipe at his home in El Rito for some time, Secundina managed to escape and return to Santa Ana, but her father, "terrified by Espinosa," prevailed on her "to return and marry him."[27] Secundina obeyed and she and Felipe settled down in Cochití. Their first child, María Vincenta, was born in 1855 and three years later they had a son, Domingo.[28]

In 1858 all the Espinosas and Hurtados relocated north into the San Luís Valley of what is now southern Colorado but was then within the Conejos or

Guadalupe Grant of Taos County, New Mexico. They chose to live on the Río Conejos in the small *plaza* of San Rafael.[29] Their migration appears to have been part of a general movement of Penitente families into the Conejos area[30] where earlier settlement had been discouraged by the attacks of hostile Ute Indians.[31]

At the time of the 1860 United States Census for the Territory of New Mexico, the Espinosa and Hurtado families were well established in San Rafael. The enumeration shows Felipe, 39, a laborer, owning $30 in personal property but no real estate; his wife Secundina, 23; and their children Vincenta, 5, and Domingo, 2, living next door to two Hurtado households, including that of Secundina's parents, where Eugenia, 17, still lived.

The senior Espinosa had died but his widow, María Gertrudis Chávez, 65, was evidently living with Vivián, 22 [*sic*],[32] who seems to have acquired a wife, María Teresa, 24, and three children, Andrea, 4, María Cicilia, 2, and María Margarita, 1 year old. Also living in this household was one Eugenio Espinosa, 26, a farm laborer, whose relationship to Vivián and Felipe is not known. Vivián was listed as a farmer and owner of $500 worth of real property and $300 in personal property,[33] making him the most prosperous member of the linked Espinosa and Hurtado clans. How he had come by his relative wealth remains an intriguing question. Was it by means of hard work and perseverance or by illegal means as the later newspaper reports suggested?[34]

On August 26, 1862, Felipe and Secundina had a third child, a daughter, María Manuela. Her christening took place in the little church of San Pedro y San Rafael, built by the parishioners in 1859,[35] where the funeral mass for Secundina's father had been celebrated and where her sister Eugenia had recently married José Francisco Lucero.[36]

At some time during this period, while the brothers continued to be engaged in pious activities with the local Penitentes, Vivián worked his farm, and Felipe earned a scant living making adobe bricks,[37] the two also took up a life of outlawry, possibly under the leadership of the stormy Felipe. Or it may have been Vivián who took the initiative in these new ventures, thus explaining his relative prosperity. These misdeeds took the form of horse stealing[38] and similar types of thievery. Whatever they had done, their transgressions were sufficient to earn them a reputation, at least among Anglos who seem to have heard of them through possibly garbled Hispano sources, for being "desperate and lawless bravos" by the time the Denver press reported on the clash with Lieutenant Hodt's army patrol in San Rafael.

But the only account we have of an Espinosa robbery comes from Tom Tobin, a former mountain man and associate of Kit Carson who, since 1858, had been a rancher on Trinchera Creek in Costilla County providing horses and supplies to nearby Fort Garland and whose wife, María Pascuala Bernal, was a distant relative of the Espinosas:

> [T]hey stopped a wagon in New Mexico between Santa Fe and Galisteo. . . . The wagon was loaded with some goods belonging to a Priest stationed in Galisteo who had a little store there; the teamster, a Mexican, was from Conejos County, Colorado. The Espinosas took and tied him. He knew the Espinosas although they were masked. They took what they wanted out of the wagon, then tied the teamster up to a staple on the end of the wagon tongue and started the team on. The wagon was met by a man who untied the teamster and was soon overtaken by the Priest. The teamster told the Priest what had happened and who the men were and where they lived. The Priest rode back to Santa Fe and told General Carleton what had happened, that the men [were] Espinosas from Conejos County. There was another man with the Espinosas but he did not touch the wagon.
>
> General Carleton sent orders to Fort Garland to Captain Eaton of New Mexico Volunteers . . . to go to Conejos, capture the Espinosas and send them to Santa Fe.[39]

Tobin says the robbery occurred in the spring of 1863, but on the basis of other evidence we can place it sometime in December 1862.[40] The officer to whom the priest complained was Brigadier General James Henry Carleton, commander of the Military Department of New Mexico, a jurisdiction that had, until recently, included the San Luís Valley and that Carleton stubbornly continued to believe he still controlled. The "Captain Eaton" in Tobin's account was Captain E. Wayne Eaton, commander of Fort Garland and its garrison of New Mexico Volunteers. This fort, Eaton, and his troops had all, in early November 1862, been transferred out of Carleton's bailiwick and into that of Colorado by order of the War Department in Washington City, but Carleton refused to recognize the change and continued to behave as if Fort Garland, Eaton, his troops, and the entire portion of the San Luís Valley now lying in Colorado Territory[41] remained under his command. His intransigence on this point was causing serious friction and loss of coordination in the ranks of the military in Colorado and New Mexico.[42]

Carleton's order reached Captain Eaton on January 9, 1863. Regrettably no copy of it has yet been found but Eaton later had occasion to characterize it as directing him "to arrest three men" at Conejos,[43] presumably Felipe and Vivián Espinosa, and perhaps Jesús Sánchez, for the robbery and assault of the teamster. There was room for confusion, however, the same confusion noted earlier. Was the crime of the Espinosas their attack on the teamster, or was it involvement in an armed tax rebellion?

At the time Carleton's order "to arrest three men" arrived, Eaton was already dealing with what the authorities of Colorado Territory believed was a treasonous conspiracy to resist tax payments and other aspects of Anglo government among the people in the southern San Luís. The Hispanos of Conejos, Costilla, and Culebra counties had long been accustomed to their traditional status as citizens of New Mexico whom the authorities of that Territory seldom troubled due to their remoteness from Santa Fe. So it came as a shock to them when, in 1861, the Territory of Colorado was established and an arbitrary line was drawn on the map cutting them off from their accustomed ties, making them subject to new laws that were not even printed in Spanish so they could understand them.[44]

Federal and Territorial officers promptly descended on the San Luís Valley and began inflicting unwanted and disturbing changes—organizing communities into voting districts, holding elections for heretofore unknown offices, posting laws, assessing taxes, and arresting those who resisted or questioned the new order. General Carleton in Santa Fe unwittingly helped stir the cauldron of disaffection by sending an army officer, Major Archibald H. Gillespie, into the San Luís in October 1862 to conduct a "military census" of the population, arousing fears that every Hispano adult male might be conscripted into the American military. In the course of his duty Gillespie claimed to have entered every dwelling in Conejos County, meaning he must have visited—and by doing so, infuriated—the dangerous Espinosas of San Rafael. Nor did Carleton immediately recall Gillespie from his census-taking duties after the War Department removed Colorado Territory from his jurisdiction. The diligent major was still performing his incendiary work at the time of the San Rafael outbreak.[45]

Officials such as Deputy Austin, Captain Eaton, Marshal Hunt, Major Gillespie, and even an unidentified tax assessor whose life had been threatened in the Culebra country[46] were trying to do two jobs at once: fashion a new territory along American lines in a region entirely foreign to them and impose Anglo notions of law and order on a resistant native population.

The people of the San Luís Valley were culturally very different from the Anglos concentrated around Denver, Cañon City, Colorado City, South Park, and California Gulch, most of whom had stampeded into these regions during the Pike's Peak gold rush of 1859. The Hispanos had been the first residents of what was now called Colorado but they would always feel they were actually the people of an ancient homeland, New Mexico, whose special character they traced back to medieval Spain. They did not even speak the Spanish spoken in Mexico but a dialect of their own, uniquely New Mexican. "Steeped in Spanish and Catholic tradition and living in communities built in the familiar plaza style," one historian has written, "these Coloradans had little in common" with the Johnny-Come-Latelies above the Arkansas River.[47]

They had settled on *mercedes* (land grants) conferred by the Mexican government before the American conquest and, as grantees who had occupied and improved the land, they considered themselves its absolute owners, owing no payments to any authority in the form of taxes. Furthermore, they knew enough of the Anglo greed for property and mineral resources to dread an influx of Americans that would displace them from their lands and destroy their way of life.[48]

The condescending attitude of Colorado Anglos toward their Hispano fellow citizens, mingled with the inevitable American hunger for new lands and resources belonging to others, persisted even eight years later, when *The Rocky Mountain Directory and Colorado Gazette* of 1871 gave this description of Conejos County:

> This county, lying west of the Rio Grande river, contains a population of over 2,500, chiefly Mexican and half-breeds. Owing to its somewhat isolated position, the resources of this county are comparatively little known. It contains a large area of well watered and arable land, but the class of inhabitants settled within its borders are not particularly noted for enterprise and thrift; hence very little has been accomplished in the way of development. The inhabitants live in *adobe* houses, grouped here and there into little *plazas*, or villages, for purposes of protection from hostile bands of Indians, as well as for social reasons. . . . The time is not far distant when this interesting region, with its beautiful climate and rich grazing lands, will attract more attention than it has yet done.[49]

Historian Eugene H. Berwanger has written:

> Anglo Coloradans seldom encountered Mexican Americans because they did not move north [in substantial numbers] from the southern counties until the

twentieth century. Still, most expressed a dislike for Spanish-speaking people and discriminated against them. White Coloradans assumed that Hispanos were lazy because of their relaxed lifestyle, they considered their eagerness to hold *fandangos* as indicative of a lack of seriousness, and they were suspicious of their Roman Catholicism. Almost without exception English-language newspapers used the phrase "degraded and ignorant" before the word Mexican.[50]

Captain Eaton had been busy trying to bridge this chasm of tradition and culture. Earlier that same fateful January, also at the request of Deputy Austin, the captain had dispatched Lieutenant Hodt with a detail of twenty-five men of the First New Mexico Volunteers to a *plaza* said to be ten miles beyond the town of Conejos—perhaps San Rafael itself—to help the deputy make some arrests, but found "the people in a great state of excitement, holding secret meetings with armed sentinels before the doors" and "the most inflammatory speeches . . . being made, particularly by one Francisco Gallegos, who stated that 'the laws ought not to be obeyed, and shall not be!'" Some arrests were made on that occasion but the voluble Gallegos himself escaped.[51]

Previously, on December 27, 1862, again in response to Austin's reports of unrest in Conejos, Eaton had dispatched Hodt and some troopers there, and Hodt had arrested the same Gallegos, along with Aneseto Martinez, Antonio Gálvez, and Nasario Gallegos for "treason or resisting law by the force of arms."[52] Francisco Gallegos, evidently a slippery customer, escaped that time also,[53] though he was later taken into custody and bound over to the next term of US District Court in Pueblo.[54] At the time of his harangue urging disobedience of the Anglo laws, and again during the San Rafael gunfight (if indeed he was present there), Gallegos was under bond to answer the December charges. Ironically, these charges were later dropped for unknown reasons, probably lack of evidence actually proving treasonous intent.[55]

As early as August 1862, the *Rocky Mountain News Weekly* was reporting from Fort Garland, "We are well informed that the Mexicans of Costilla and Conejos Counties are holding secret meetings and organizing for an armed resistance to the collection of taxes."[56] And again, in September, also from Fort Garland: "Law threatening murmurs still continue to be heard from the Mexicans, and those residents who are best posted think they see some real cause for apprehension. . . . The two great causes of the discontent were first at the Territorial tax, and last but not least the abolition of Peon slavery,"[57] a measure the New Mexico legislature was then currently debating, which Colorado Hispanos feared might be inflicted on them.

The latter was a well-founded concern. The practice of enslaving Indian children was deeply ingrained in the lives of the Hispanos of Costilla and Conejos counties. For generations Indians and Hispanos had carried on a reciprocal process of alternating warfare and trade involving the stealing, buying, and selling of each other's children to serve as slaves. Two years later, when the US superintendent of Indian Affairs required a census of Indian slaves, there were 88 such captives in Conejos County and 61 in Costilla County.[58] In 1863, the prospect of their emancipation represented not simply a domestic inconvenience but also a serious potential loss of capital, adding yet another grievance Hispanos could nurse against Anglos.[59]

It is entirely possible that the fears on both sides were exaggerated. The Hispanos of the San Luís were probably not actually on the brink of a whole-sale insurrection, any more than the Americans were consciously intent on abolishing at one fell swoop every Hispano institution in the valley. But it felt that way to the San Luís Hispanos, and those feelings impelled men to act.

Clearly, General Carleton's order to arrest the Espinosas in Conejos County—evidently an epicenter of Hispano suspicion of everything the Anglos were trying to do—had come at the worst possible time. It did not matter if they were being charged only with robbery; the atmosphere surrounding the attempt to arrest them was rife with American fears of a treasonous Hispano conspiracy. In the prevailing hysteria, one crime blended with the other. For the American army or the authorities of the Territory to lay hands on *any* Hispano, for *any* charge, just then, was to touch fire to the already smoldering embers of revolt. And that was exactly what happened on those two violent January days in San Rafael.

The full account of that incident, as reported in the *Rocky Mountain News Weekly*, deserves to be quoted in its entirety:

THE RECENT DIFFICULTIES IN CONEJOS

FORT GARLAND, C.T., Jan. 25, 1863

EDS. NEWS:—For several days past we have had more than the usual excitement attending our isolated post. The event which I mentioned in one of my letters last summer as most to be feared, viz: an insurrection among the people, has at last made its appearance, and but for the very prompt and efficient measures adopted by Captain Eaton, in command of this post, would have assumed a magnitude quite alarming.

About two weeks since, Deputy US Marshal Austin arrived at the post from Conejos and stated that in attempting to make some arrests he had been resisted and when he asked for assistance it had been refused, and asked for a military detachment to be sent over to compel obedience. Capt. Eaton despatched Lieut. Hodt and twenty-five men who rode to Conejos, fifty miles, and from there to a plaza, ten miles, and made the arrests and back to Conejos that night, making seventy miles and doing his business in nineteen hours from the time of starting. He found the people in a great state of excitement, holding secret meetings with armed sentinels before the doors. Besides, the most inflammatory speeches were made in public, particularly by one Francisco Gallegos, who stated that "the laws ought not to be enforced, and shall not be!" Several of the leaders were arrested and brought back here. Gallegos and others made their escape.

About ten days ago Lieut. Hodt was again sent with ten men to make some arrests, which he had partially succeeded in, having two of them by the name of Espenosa [*sic*] in a room where he left them, placing a sergeant at the door to guard it while he went after the others, whom he succeeded in taking, but when he returned the two Espenosas had broken through the partition and procured arms, guns, pistols and bows and arrows, and commenced firing the arrows from doors and windows. Having but two men and a sergeant with him, and they being obliged to leave their arms to lull suspicion, together with the probability that he was as liable to be attacked from the outside as those from the inside, prevented him from making a rush into the room.

He sent for the balance of his men and armed and ordered the house to be set on fire to compel them to come out. While the latter order was being executed, the men made a rush out of the door, discharging a shower of arrows. The Lieut. fired all the charges from one pistol without any apparent effect, and drawing the other it would not stand cocked, and in throwing it from him on the ground it struck on the hammer and was discharged, the ball striking him in the forehead and glanced up through his hat, wounding him severely. The other men having arrived, he ordered an immediate pursuit and requested Dept. US Marshal Austin, who came with them, to assist. He started with the party, but in crossing the river his horse slipped on the ice and falling on his leg broke it just above the ankle, and he was taken back to the plaza. Part of the men pursued the fugitives to the mountains, where they had taken refuge among the rocks. The Lieut. then sent an express to the fort, detailing the circumstances and asking that Dr. McLain should be sent over.

The express arrived about 9 o'clock in the evening, and at four o'clock the next morning Capt. Eaton and the Dr. arrived there with a detachment of men. They found that the party in pursuit having lost the trail had scattered to search for it, when one Corporal Batea [Abeyta] succeeded in finding it, he turned and called to the men, which was immediately followed by the report of a gun. The men hastened to the spot and found the Corporal shot through the head and quite dead. The pursuit was kept up all the next day, but with no avail. Part of the mountain being covered with snow and part of it bare. Capt. Eaton left two parties in pursuit and returned to the post, bringing the Lieut. and Deputy Marshal.—Nothing has been heard of them since, but that every effort will be made to take them is certain, and it is to be hoped they will succeed, for they are desperate and lawless bravos, known over the entire country.[60]

Tobin recalled:

Captain Eaton sent one Lieutenant Hutt with fifteen Mexican soldiers, one American Sergeant for the purpose of capturing the Espinosas. They were joined at Conejos by a Deputy US Marshal named George Austin, they went and found the Espinosas. Lieut. Hutt told him that they were recruiting soldiers and asked them if they would enlist. They told him they would let him know the next morning. Hutt went to the house the next morning. Vivian Espinosa stepped out and met them. Hutt asked them if they would enlist. Vivian said he would ask his brother. . . . If he was willing to enlist if he was, all right; if not, neither would he. When the brother refused to enlist Vivian also refused. Then Lieut. Hutt made a grab at him and said, you are my prisoner. He answered, "No, I am not," springing into the house where his brother was. They had no weapons on them. The house was a log house. They knocked the chinking out between the logs and the woman passed their weapons to them from the adjoining room. They then sprang out amongst the soldiers, killed one Corporal, scattered the soldiers and made their way to the Mountain and escaped. In pursuing them the Deputy Marshal's horse fell and hurt his leg badly.[61]

If Tobin's reminiscence is correct, and there is little reason to doubt its general substance, Hodt's pretense of recruiting the Espinosas into the American military as a way of securing their arrest seems a clumsy bit of nonsense. The

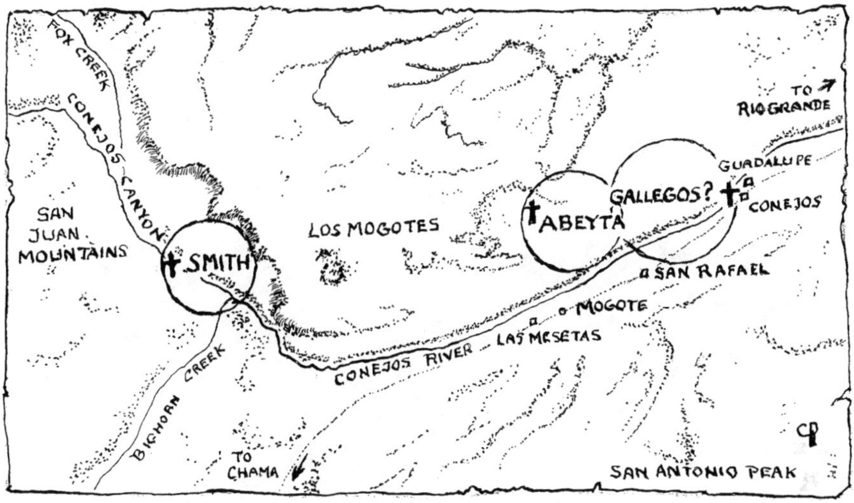

The San Rafael/Los Mogotes area where Corporal Abeyta died at the beginning of the Espinosa outbreak and where, later, Felipe Espinosa murdered William Smith and possibly Francisco Gallegos.

Espinosas should have seen through his mummery, and perhaps they did, for their suggestion that Hodt return the following day smacks of a cynical counterstratagem, perhaps with an eye to laying an ambush. Yet, amazingly, the lieutenant's ploy seems to have worked, at least in part; somehow, according to the newspaper report, he managed to make the arrests and lost his prisoners only after he became embroiled with other attackers "from the outside."[62]

It is worth noting that all these accounts come from Anglo sources; we do not have firsthand reports giving the Hispano points of view.

The Rocky Mountain News Weekly rounded off its coverage of the San Rafael skirmish with a stinging comment on the condition of affairs in the southern part of Colorado Territory:

> It is to be regretted that the interests of this part of the country are seemingly overlooked, and it can only be attributed to the fact that our civil allegiance is due to Colorado, while being attached to the military department of New Mexico, and although the military force stationed at this post [Fort Garland] is sufficient for the purpose intended, still the unsettled state of the country at present renders a larger force very desirable if not absolutely necessary.[63]

This was a stab at General Carleton, whose refusal to bow to War Department orders to relinquish command of southern Colorado had left military affairs in the San Luís Valley in an impossible muddle. Ever since those orders went into effect in November 1862, Colonel John M. Chivington, commander of the Military District of Colorado Territory, had been sending Carleton entreaties, and finally increasingly heated demands, that he cease tampering in the affairs of southern Colorado by demanding reports from Captain Eaton at Fort Garland and issuing him peremptory orders, as in the case of the Espinosas.[64]

In a letter of January 30—the second such message he sent to Carleton that same Friday—Colonel Chivington explicitly blamed the general for the trouble that had come to a head at San Rafael fifteen days before: "[T]he disturbances among our citizens in the San Luís Valley require that we have the means of protecting the citizens and of enforcing our laws at an accessible point. . . . [Y]our regulations at Fort Garland have interfered with our civil officers in the discharge of their duty."[65]

There would be occasions when Carleton would appear to acquiesce in the jurisdictional change. On February 20 the general's adjutant finally forwarded to Gillespie a copy of the order transferring command of Fort Garland to Chivington's district and implicitly instructing Gillespie to suspend his census and return to the Santa Fe headquarters.[66] But Carleton would on some occasions continue to press his case for control of the San Luís and on others would seem to abandon it. As late as December 17, Colorado governor Evans was writing to Secretary of War Edwin M. Stanton asking him to issue an order settling the jurisdictional question once and for all, stating, "It seems to me strange that anyone should propose to place the command of a Post in this Territory, which is maintained alone for the control of the Indians under my care, and for the protection of the citizens of Colorado territory, under the command of a Department so inconvenient and without community of interest as that of New Mexico."[67] It would be over a year after the official transfer of Fort Garland to the District of Colorado before the hardheaded Carleton would acquiesce in the change.

Meanwhile Captain Eaton, the subject of the jurisdictional tug-of-war between rival superiors, was making every effort to track down the fugitive Espinosas while trying to figure out which master he must serve. Dutifully, on February 7, he reported not to his nominal superior Chivington but to Captain Ben C. Cutler, Carleton's adjutant:

> I have the honor to report the return of the two parties left at Conejos to follow up the men I was instructed to arrest at that place. The Sgt. and party was out four days, and the corporal with the Utes Indians was out seven days trailing them—they came back to Conejos again after making a large circle of fifty or sixty miles, but then all trace of them was lost.
>
> They have many friends there that give them information of all that passes—I have since learned that they were seen and followed by some of the citizens of Conejos—but were not caught—they fired at the Constable that was after them.[68]

But the harsh Colorado winter was coming on. The Espinosas disappeared, probably into the fastnesses of the San Juan Mountains behind San Rafael to wait for spring. They would not emerge until early March, when they would ride across the San Luís Valley and over the Sangre de Cristo Mountains into the Arkansas Valley country and find Franklin Bruce working at his new sawmill on Hardscrabble Creek.

NOTES

1. *Rocky Mountain News Weekly*, February 12, 1863.

2. Though the Hispano farmers of the San Luís Valley were often too poor to afford firearms, they remained adept with handmade bows and arrows. Olibama López Tushar, *The People of El Valle: A History of the Spanish Settlers in the San Luís Valley* (Pueblo, CO: El Escritorio, 2007), 79, shows an illustration of a *vaquero* (cattle herder) carrying a bow and quiver of arrows.

3. Casualty Sheet, Corporal Decedero Abaita [*sic*], "killed by a criminal," January 16, 1863; Compiled Service Record, Adjutant General's Office, Record Group 94, National Archives and Records Administration, Washington, DC.

4. *Rocky Mountain News Weekly*, February 5, 1863.

5. Ibid.

6. Ibid.

7. *Rocky Mountain News Weekly*, February 12, 1863.

8. Ibid.

9. Perkins, *Tom Tobin*, 171, note 1, says the census as it applies to the Espinosas dates from 1840 but gives no explanation why this should be so.

10. Frances Leon Quintana, *Pobladores: Hispanic Americans of the Ute Frontier* (South Bend, IN: University of Notre Dame Press, 1991), 15.

11. Christine Trujillo, Director, El Rito Public Library, personal communication with the author April 22, 2009; Robert J. Tórrez and Robert Trapp, *Rio Arriba: A New Mexico*

County (Los Ranchos, NM: Río Grande Books, 2010), 56, assert that in a claims court in 1883 Jesús María Vigil testified that the town of El Rito consisted of five distinct *plazas* located one to three miles from each other along the Río Colorado, and that the *plaza de los Espinosas* was one of these; it is not known if the Espinosas who eventually moved to southern Colorado and launched their career of outlawry there had once resided in this particular *plaza*; George B. Anderson, *History of New Mexico: Its Resources and Its People*, Vol. II (Los Angeles, CA: Pacific States Publishing Company, 1907), 523. It is possible, since the first county boundaries were imprecise, that El Rito may have been a part of the old Santa Ana County, which was abolished in 1876. The 1850 Federal Census (see note 13 below) incorporated southern Río Arriba County into Santa Ana County. For the 1850 Census showing southern Río Arriba as part of Santa Ana, see http://files.usgwarchives.net/nm/santaana/census/1850/pg226b.txt, accessed February 28, 2013.

12. Virginia Langham Olmsted, *New Mexico Spanish and Mexican Colonial Censuses: 1790, 1823, 1845* (Albuquerque: New Mexico Genealogical Society, 1975). See also http://www.nmgs.org/bksB2.htm, accessed January 20, 2013.

13. This count shows the father, Pedro, 56; mother, Gertrudes María [*sic*], 46; Felipe, 23; María Thomas [*sic*], 21; José Vivián, 19; Francisco, 18; and José, 3; 1850 Federal Census of Santa Ana County, NMT, http://files.usgwarchives.net/nm/santaana/census/1850/pg278a.txt (Sheet No. 278B, Reel No. M432–468, Page 555), accessed February 28, 2013. The ages of these family members must have been guesses on the part of the individuals concerned or of the census takers, since only the mother appears to have gained the appropriate five years between 1845 and 1850. Also Juan Antonio, present in the home in 1845, is missing in 1850 and the Francisco and José shown in 1850 do not appear in 1845, though the former may be a mistaken name for Juan Antonio and the latter could have been born during the period between enumerations and does not appear in the family later, though Perkins believes he was an illegitimate child of María Juana. As noted in the text, Perkins, *Tom Tobin*, 299, had access to descendants of Felipe and Vivián and constructed what is probably the definitive genealogy of the Espinosas; it corresponds with the names, if not the ages, in the 1845 Census.

14. 1850 Federal Census of Santa Ana County.

15. Ibid. The enumerator for both the Espinosas and the Hurtados was one J. M. Giddings.

16. Perkins, *Tom Tobin*, 299.

17. 1860 Census of Conejos, Taos County, NMT, cited in Trujullo, "The Espinosa Brothers," 169.

18. Perkins, *Tom Tobin*, 127.

19. Weigle, Marta, *The Penitentes of the Southwest* (Santa Fe, NM: Ancient City Press, 1970), 3.

20. John Ray de Aragón, *Padre Martínez and Bishop Lamy* (Santa Fe, NM: Sunstone Press, 2006), 113–114. Aragón asserts that Martínez was recognized as the *Supremo* or

Superior of the Penitente Brotherhood and may have even founded it in the capacity of *El Conciliador*, unifying various such societies into a single form. Aragón also credits Martínez with having written many of the sermons, dramatizations, and dialogues used by the Brotherhood during Holy Week, as well as developing much of its organizational terminology. No firm evidence is adduced substantiating these assertions, however. Aragón also reports (77) that Lamy, returning from a visit to Rome in 1854, brought orders from the Pope that the Brotherhood be eradicated if "certain abuses practiced by the members in the name of religion were continued," and that Martínez promised to abide by the order. Paul Horgan, *Lamy of Santa Fe* (New York: Farrar, Straus and Giroux, 1975), 241, confirms this but goes on to point out that "folkways persisted, and the Penitentes continued to survive." Marta Weigle, *Brothers of Light, Brothers of Blood: The Penitentes of the Southwest* (Santa Fe, NM: Ancient City Press, 1976), 52–57, discusses rules for the Penitentes that even Lamy is believed to have written over time starting in 1856, though these rules have not survived. Fray Angélico Chávez, *But Time and Chance: The Story of Padre Martínez of Taos, 1793–1867* (Santa Fe, NM: Sunstone Press, 1981), 36–37, working from Hispanic sources, confirms that Martínez wrote a defense of *La Orden de la Santa Hermandad*, a document now lost, but offers the possibility that his defense may have reflected "his confusion of the centuries-old and most venerable Franciscan Third Order" with the Penitentes of his day. A Presbyterian missionary to the Hispanos of southern Colorado, the Rev. Alex M. Darley, cited verbatim what he called a "Constitution" of the Penitentes in his self-published book *The Passionists of the Southwest, or the Holy Brotherhood: A Revelation of the "Penitentes,"* (Pueblo, NM, 1893), 14–18, the text of which he claims to have received from a then-deceased *Hermano Mayor* of the Brotherhood, Bernardo Abeyta, together with an identical copy of the same rules received from a "Brother," Pedro Sánchez, on February 13, 1860. Chávez's and Aragón's books appear to have been inspired by a desire to present Martínez in a more favorable light than has generally been the case in Anglo sources, especially Willa Cather's novel *Death Comes for the Archbishop*.

21. Chávez, *But Time and Chance*, 92–160, gives, from the Hispano point of view, an excellent account of the long and contentious struggle between Lamy and Martínez, who sought to preserve the rights of native priests and resist the "reforms" of the "foreigners," while at the same time relating surprisingly well with the Anglo authorities of the new United States Territory of New Mexico.

22. In his definitive biography, Horgan, *Lamy of Santa Fe*, 149–150 and 230–251, describes the same struggle as the bishop saw it. Assisting Lamy in this conflict were his vicar general and lifelong friend, Joseph Projectus Machebeuf, and Fr. Domaso Taladrid, a Spaniard, with whom Lamy wished to replace Martínez at Taos.

23. Weigle, *Brothers of Light, Brothers of Blood*, 47–49.

24. Perkins, *Tom Tobin*, 127. Horgan, *Lamy of Santa Fe*, 129, says the school was for both boys and girls with an emphasis on preparing the boys for the priesthood. Tórrez and

Trapp, *Rio Arriba*, 182, while acknowledging that little is known of the particulars of Padre Martínez's school, say that he is credited with tutoring "a number of young men with the advanced studies they needed to attend the seminary in Durango," Mexico. It cannot be established with certainty that boys intended for a secular life, such as the Espinosas, were also taught there.

25. T. D. Burns, Letter to Tom Tobin, April 13, 1897, Tom Tobin/Cragin Collection, Box 15, Colorado Springs Pioneers Museum, Starsmore Center for Local History, Colorado Springs, Colorado. Burns says of Felipe's appearance, "He had a big scar I think on his left cheek, and his face was covered with a black griesly [*sic*] beard." Perkins (*Tom Tobin*, 176) quotes a story from the the *Denver Daily News* of March 10, 1899, in which one of the soldiers who saw Felipe said his face "sloped back to the crown of the head and the forehead seemed to be entirely missing." It is worth noting that no likenesses of the Espinosas are extant and that Anglo perceptions may have been biased by prejudice, causing many to regard all Hispanos as repulsive in appearance. Also, the later depredations of the Espinosas may have caused Anglos to view them as appearing inhuman or horrific.

26. Trujillo, "The Espinosa Brothers," 169, quotes an article from the March 18, 1938, *Colorado Springs Gazette Telegraph* announcing the death, at age 106, of Mrs. Eugenia H. Lucero, Secundina's sister, who often told her grandchildren of her abduction by Felipe Espinosa. After Secundina escaped and returned home, Mrs. Lucero recalled, "her back [was] horribly scarred from a lashing."

27. Ibid.

28. Perkins, *Tom Tobin*, 128.

29. Ibid.

30. Quintana, *Pobladores*, 77–79, says, "all the communities southwest of present-day Conejos . . . were Penitente communities." These *plazas* were San Rafael, Mesitas, and Mogote. The settlers brought an image of San Rafael with them; a Penitente *morada* (meetinghouse) has long been associated with the *plaza* of San Rafael.

31. López Tushar, *The People of El Valle*, 51. Manuel Salazar, "José María Jaques," *Colorado Hispanic Genealogist*, Vol. 5, No. 4 (December 2008): 12, notes that Jaques led the first group of settlers into the Guadalupe section of Conejos in October 1854 but these colonists were driven out when Indians stole their stock the following March. They returned to grow the first grain crop in 1855 and Jaques built the first water-powered mill on the Conejos River in 1856.

32. Vivián should have been about twenty-nine years old at this time.

33. Trujillo, "The Espinosa Brothers," 172.

34. Ibid. Henrietta M. Christmas, "Conejos, Colorado: Voting in 1861," *Colorado Hispanic Genealogist*, Vol. 1, No. 2 (June 2004): 27–37, shows that Felipe Espinosa voted in the election for representatives to the first Territorial Assembly of the new Territory of Colorado, mandated by Governor William Gilpin on July 13, 1861. Candidates included

John M. Francisco, R. B. Willis, Querino Maes, Juan Miguel Vigil, W. E. Easterday, H. N. Welton, Victor García, and Jesús M. Barela. Virginia Sánchez, "Colorado's Hispanic Legislator Biographies," *Colorado Hispanic Genealogist*, Vol. 6, No. 2 (June 2009), shows that Barela, a Democrat, was the first representative of Costilla County, and that José Victor García, a Republican, first represented Conejos and Costilla counties. It is unclear whether this is an inconsistency or perhaps a result of a redistricting of the counties that occurred in December 1861 between the first and second sessions of the legislature.

35. The original adobe church was destroyed by fire but a new church, built in 1929, now stands in its place; the *plaza* was sometimes called *Paisaje*, meaning landscape, or *Pasaje*, meaning passage. It was named San Rafael by one of the original settlers, Jesús Velasquez; Frances Harvey Mead, *Conejos Country: The Canyon, the River, the People* (Colorado Springs: Century One Press, 1984), 53.

36. Perkins, *Tom Tobin*, 129.

37. Ibid., 128.

38. Tobin, "The Capture of the Espinosas," *The Colorado Magazine*.

39. Ibid.

40. *Rocky Mountain News Weekly*, February 5, 1863, quotes Marshal Hunt's letter about the clash at San Rafael as saying the "Mexican robbers" with whom the army fought were "the same who waylaid the Catholic priest below Santa Fe last month."

41. Colorado Territory had been formed in 1861 and its southern boundary had severed the upper half of the San Luís Valley from its lower half in New Mexico Territory, where Carleton ruled.

42. Correspondence dealing with Carleton's unwillingness to give up control over Fort Garland and the San Luís Valley exists in Letters Received, Department of New Mexico, Record Group 393, Rolls 16, 18, 19, Adjutant General's Office, National Archives and Records Administration, Washington, DC, and in the Denver newspapers of early 1863. The dispute is covered in some detail in Chapter 9.

43. Ibid.; E. W. Eaton to Assistant Adjutant General, District of Colorado, April 19, 1863, Letters Received, Department of New Mexico.

44. Smith, *The Birth of Colorado*, 106.

45. A voluminous correspondence relating to Major Gillespie's assignment may be found in Letters Received, Department of New Mexico, and in Letters Received by the Commission Branch, Adjutant General's Office, US Army, 1863–1870, M-1064, Roll 91, RG 94, Entry 518, pertaining to Major Archibald H. Gillespie, Additional Aide de Camp to Major General Henry W. Halleck, National Archives and Records Administration, Washington, DC. Chapter 9 examines Gillespie's activities in detail.

46. Major A. H. Gillespie to Captain B. C. Cutler, January 20, 1863, Letters Received, Department of New Mexico, Record Group 393, Rolls 16, 18, 19, Adjutant General's Office, National Archives and Records Administration, Washington, DC.

47. Smith, *The Birth of Colorado*, 59; Berwanger, *Rise of the Centennial State*, 5.

48. Quintana, *Pobladores*, 79.

49. H. S. Wallihan and T. O. Bigney, *The Rocky Mountain Directory and Colorado Gazetteer for 1871* (Denver: S. S. Wallihan and Company, 1871).

50. Berwanger, *The Rise of the Centennial State*, 112–113.

51. Letter Book, Fort Garland, Colorado Territory, 1861–62; National Archives and Records Administration, Washington, DC, 168, Date of July 31, 1862. Even at this early date Major A. H. Mayer, Eaton's predecessor as commander of Fort Garland, reported to Headquarters, Department of New Mexico, "For several days I have had various reports brought to me of disaffection of the People of Culebra and Costilla. This morning I was informed that various secret meetings had been held, that . . . parties had been heard to say, as soon as the American troops left Fort Garland they mean to raise a revolt as they would not have anything to contend with[,] the [New] Mexican troops would join them." Mayer himself distrusted his New Mexican troops. See Chapter 9.

52. Record Group No. 21, Records of the District Courts of the US, Colorado Territory, Bankruptcy, Civil and Criminal Case Files, 1862–1876, Entry 9, Third Judicial District, *US vs. Francisco Gallegos, Aneseto Martine [sic], Antonio Galvez and Nasanio [sic] Gallegos*.

53. *Rocky Mountain News Weekly*, February 12, 1863.

54. *US vs. Francisco Gallegos et al.*; see note 52 above. Parkhill, *The Law Goes West*, 43, notes that Gallegos, living near Guadalupita in Conejos County, was indicted and "a confiscation decree entered against his 220 acres and improvements." Obviously Gallegos was no rebellious *peon* but instead a prosperous landowner. A question exists whether this is the same Francisco Gallegos who was elected as Territorial representative for the 13th Territorial District (Conejos County) in December 1861; see Hubert Howe Bancroft, *History of Nevada, Colorado and Wyoming 1540–1888* (San Francisco, CA: The History Company, 1890), 420, and *Rocky Mountain News Weekly*, April 5, 1862. This Gallegos was reported murdered in the *plaza* of Conejos in the fall of 1863; see Chapter 10.

55. Ibid.

56. *Rocky Mountain News Weekly*, August 21, 1862.

57. *Rocky Mountain News Weekly*, September 4, 1862.

58. D. Gene Combs, "Enslavement of Indians in the San Luís Valley of Colorado," *The San Luís Valley Historian*, Vol. 5, No. 1 (1973): 22–29. See also David M. Brugge, *Navajos in the Catholic Church Records of New Mexico: 1694–1875*, 3rd ed. (Santa Fe, NM: School for Advanced Research Press, 1985), 123–125; Ramón A. Gutiérrez, *When Jesus Came, the Corn Mothers Went Away* (Stanford, CA: Stanford University Press, 1991), 151–156; and James F. Brooks, *Captives and Cousins: Slavery, Kinship, and Community in the Southwest Borderlands* (Chapel Hill: University of North Carolina Press, 2002), 332.

59. Quintana, *Pobladores*, 79, avers that the leading citizen of Conejos at this time—in fact the titular *patrón* of the region—was an Anglo from Missouri named Lafayette Head

who had pioneered the settlement of the *plaza* of Guadalupe in 1854 and by 1863 was serving Colorado Territory as agent for the Tabeguache Utes. Head was so respected by the people of Conejos that he was reputed to have been initiated into the local Penitente Brotherhood, one of the few Anglos ever to be accorded that privilege. Popularly known as "*Tío* [Uncle] Lafe" and recorded in the Conejos Parish records as "Rafael Cabeza," Head was the county's most affluent citizen, himself the owner of Indian slaves, and reportedly had amassed much of his wealth from "ransoms offered by the kinsmen of Indian captives." It was Head who prepared the 1865 Census of Indian captives, significantly excluding himself from the list of slaveowners. Combs, in "Enslavement of Indians in the San Luis Valley of Colorado," cites a letter of army lieutenant colonel Samuel F. Tappan to Michael Steck, superintendent of Indian Affairs for New Mexico, dated January 27, 1866, saying that while in command of Fort Garland in the fall of 1863 he "received information which satisfied me of the complicity of Lafayette Head . . . in the kidnapping and enslaving of Navajo Indian women and children." Most of the Indian captives were from the Ute and Navajo tribes. Brugge, *Navajos in the Catholic Church Records of New Mexico*, 96, quotes a letter of Steck responding to the commissioner of Indian Affairs in Washington who had forwarded Tappan's missive to him. Steck endorsed Tappan's sentiments and wrote in part, "Of the probable number [of slaves], two thousand, now in the hands of the people of New Mexico, many have been captured recently, while others have served from childhood to old age; it is therefore an evil which has existed for many years." Also Laura E. Gomez, "Off-White in an Age of White Supremacy: Mexican Elites and the Rights of Indians and Blacks in Nineteenth-Century New Mexico," *UCLA School of Law Review*, Vol. 25, No. 9 (2005): 52, reports Head justified his slaveholding before a grand jury by saying the slaves "enjoy the full privilege of returning to their people whenever they have the inclination or disposition to do so," but not explaining that they were children taken in raids whose families' whereabouts were both distant and unknown.

60. *Rocky Mountain News Weekly*, February 12, 1863.

61. Tobin, "The Capture of the Espinosas," 59–60.

62. *Rocky Mountain News Weekly*, February 12, 1863.

63. Ibid.

64. Typical are Col. J. M. Chivington to Brig. Gen. J. H. Carleton, December 30, 1862, and Chivington to Carleton, January 30, 1863, Letters Received, Department of New Mexico.

65. Ibid.

66. Cutler to Gillespie, February 20, 1863, Letters Received, Department of New Mexico. This action seems to have been prompted by a letter of February 8 from Gillespie to Cutler describing an express received at Fort Garland from Chivington emphasizing that Garland belonged to the District of Colorado and that the major's

presence there was no longer desired; Gillespie to Cutler, February 8, 1863, Letters Received, Department of New Mexico. In his letter Gillespie had asked for clarification of the jurisdictional issue, but not before complaining of interference by "the clerical [a Methodist parson] Colonel" whom he deemed guilty of "discourtesy" toward Carleton and of "want of knowledge and good breeding."

67. John Evans to Edwin M. Stanton, December 17, 1863, Letters Received, Department of New Mexico.

68. Capt. E. W. Eaton to Capt. B. C. Cutler, February 7, 1863, Letters Received, Department of New Mexico.

"Revenge for the Infamies Committed Against Our Families"

8

Serial Murder as Vendetta

In his abortive attack on the Espinosa home, Lieutenant Hodt had set fire to their dwelling. Tom Tobin remembered it as a house of logs,[1] perhaps a rude affair called a *fuerte* by the inhabitants of the San Luís Valley,[2] but more probably the typical Hispano *jacal* made of adobe mud packed around a frame of *varillas*, or upright cottonwood poles, with a flat or pitched roof consisting of layers of leaves and dirt covering a lathe of wood in a herringbone pattern[3]—a flimsy affair that would have quickly burned. Because of its framing of *varillas*, this type of house was sometimes thought of as constructed of logs, though the logs were vertical rather than horizontal. Or the house might have been a more substantial structure of adobe bricks set on a rock foundation, which usually replaced the *jacal* after a family became more established.[4] But even such a sturdier dwelling would have been vulnerable to fire because of its wooden framing and its roof of *latía* lathing of aspen or cedar.

The house may have been a freestanding structure facing on a central *plaza* or street or possibly one in a joined row of units called a *corrillera*, each living space walled off from its neighbors.[5] In the latter case, a fire in one unit could easily have spread to the adjoining ones; thus, in the case of the Espinosas and Hurtados, whose households seem to have been located next

DOI: 10.5876/9781607322375.c08

Ruined adobe dwelling, village of San Rafael. (Author photo)

door to one another, the dwellings of several members of both families might have been affected.

We do not know whether the home or homes were totally destroyed, but they must have been at least partially consumed, and of course Felipe and Vivián themselves—or perhaps, as Tobin claimed, their womenfolk—had broken through some interior walls to gain possession of the weapons the brothers used to repel the soldiers. Whatever the extent of exterior and interior damage to the living quarters of the families, it is safe to say it was sufficient to inconvenience, if not entirely to dispossess, the occupants.

Whose house was the focus of the attack? The records do not tell us. The 1860 Census suggests there were four households: that of Secundina's parents and siblings, the Hurtados; the home of Felipe and his family; the house where Vivián and his wife and children lived with the Espinosa matriarch; and that of José Ledio Hurtado, probably a kinsman of Secundina, and his wife and six-year-old child.[6]

By 1863 there may also have been a separate dwelling for Secundina's sister Eugenia and her new husband José Francisco Lucero, though it is also possible the couple was living with Eugenia's widowed mother in the home of her father, the late José Salvador Hurtado. But the availability of firearms and bows and arrows suggests the burned home or homes may have been Felipe's and/or Vivián's, the two Espinosas we can be reasonably certain were armed with a variety of weapons other than the odd fowling piece or musket sometimes belonging to poor *peones*.[7]

Nor were the losses of the families limited to destruction by fire. Eventually the army and US Marshal Hunt would return, confiscate, and sell the personal property of the men now referred to as "the Conejos murderers."[8] According to Captain Eaton, the proceeds of the sale were used to "pay expenses incured [*sic*] in hunting for said murderers," including "horse hire[,] Spy and Guide, rations for citizens for the burial of the Corporal Killed."[9] Disposed of in this way were "two cows and one steer[,] four *fanegas*[10] wheat and one ox[;] also one trunk."[11]

Marshal Hunt took possession of other property and stored it at Fort Garland for eventual disposition by the assistant quartermaster there, including "8 cows and oxen, four beds and bedding[,] 1 beaver trap, [and] 2 water Buckets."[12] Eaton also noted that the murderers owned real estate of an undetermined value and implied that this property would also be sold.

Beds and bedding especially would have been a luxury for ordinary farming families in the San Luís Valley at this time, who normally slept on their hard-packed dirt floors on wool-filled *colchónes*, or mattresses, which during the day were stored against the walls on wooden or adobe benches called *tarimas*. Eaton's accounting shows a surprising abundance of possessions in view of the traditional belief that the Espinosas were poor. However, as we have seen, three years earlier Vivián was shown to have possessed unusual amounts of real and personal property.[13] Perhaps some of what the army and the marshal confiscated were the ill-gotten gains of the December robbery of the Mexican teamster, or of other prior crimes that have gone unrecorded.[14]

In any case, from the viewpoint of Felipe and Vivián, they and their relatives had suffered an unforgivable offense. The army had attacked and burned their homes, terrifying and endangering the lives of their elderly widowed mother, their wives, their own six children and other related youngsters, Felipe's in-laws, and possibly additional kinfolk and neighbors. Furthermore, Anglo officials both military and civil had appropriated most, if not all, of their possessions and livestock. Their families were left destitute and possibly homeless.

We do not need to guess how the already volatile Felipe felt about all this. Evidently it did not occur to him, or to Vivián, that their own illegal acts had contributed to the catastrophe. Felipe's rage and hatred against all *gringos*, exacerbated by the treatment of his family, now deepened into a lethal obsession. He put his feelings in writing before he died: "They [the Americans] ruined our families—they took everything in our house; first our beds and blankets, then our provisions. Seeing this we said, 'We would rather be dead than see such infamies committed on our families.' These were the reasons we had to go out and kill Americans—revenge for the infamies committed on our families."[15]

It is often written that the Espinosas promised the Virgin Mary to kill a certain number of Americans, the figures ranging from fifty to a preposterous six hundred.[16] But most of these tales were set down long after the fact. With two doubtful exceptions, the few scraps of the Espinosas' writings that have survived make no mention of such a motive. The words the brothers did leave are chilling enough; the goal they expressed was the ghastly and simple one of killing as many Americans as they could.

Though the Espinosas are usually thought of as religious fanatics dedicating their killing spree to the Mother of God, only two pieces of writing attributed to them explicitly link the murders to their religious faith, and we have no exact copy of what they wrote in either instance, only characterizations, and those by Anglos whose understanding of the Spanish language was limited. Nathan Hurd claimed an inscription scrawled on victim Fred Lehman's paper collar and pinned to a tree in Red Hill Pass said, "vengeance was to be wreaked upon Americans as a sacrifice to the Virgin."[17] We have independent evidence that the collar existed,[18] but no verification of what the exact wording of its message was. In 1901, Colorado historian Frank Hall claimed to have seen the "diary" found on the body of Vivián Espinosa and declared he found it "wholly impossible to gather any rational motive for their deeds except that [the killings] appeared to be given as blood offerings to the Virgin." But a contemporary newspaper summary of the diary's contents makes no such mention of its contents.[19] In any event the diary has disappeared, and until it and another writing said to have been discovered with Felipe at his death[20] are found and examined, it is impossible to declare with certainty that either brother wrote about the killings as sacrificial in a religious sense.

Beyond this, there is a newspaper translation of two letters of Felipe's, one apparently meant for Secundina, found among his effects after he was killed. Secundina's letter invokes the names of Christ, the Virgin, and a number of saints but does not connect these sacred names to his bloody deeds. It is clear from its wording that Felipe was both pious and in an abnormal mental state. A second note, perhaps a copy of a message sent earlier to Colorado governor Evans, is by turns boastful and repentant, threatening and solicitous, suggestive of the ravings of an unbalanced mind.[21] It does make the claim of having killed thirty-two Americans, but says nothing about a religious motive.

We can safely assume that Vivián's faith was as intense as his brother's, since, as we have remarked, both were known among their descendants as practicing Penitentes.[22] Membership in the *Santa Hermandad* almost always denoted a fervent spirituality, though in rare cases individuals could become *hermanos de obscuras* (unknown or hidden brothers), joining for political advancement, hope of gain, or to exploit the benefits of membership without respecting its tenets[23]—shallow reasons that are difficult to reconcile with what we know, from their descendants, of the Espinosas' passionate Catholic beliefs.

Much was made in the press of the time of the mutilations of the Espinosas' victims, rightfully condemned as atrocities. In addition to being shot, the murdered men were viciously slashed with knives or hatchets; often their heads were shattered. In at least one modern account, the butchery of Franklin Bruce was described in a way suggesting religious significance—a crosslike shape cut into his torso[24]—though contemporary newspaper reports do not substantiate this particular wound. Of course the mutilations were inflicted to impose a savage vengeance on the Americans whose army had assaulted them. But nothing in the contemporary record implies a further sacramental or ritualistic purpose in these disfigurements.[25]

In this respect, perhaps it is useful to recall that, as Penitentes, Felipe and Vivián were accustomed by long habit to mutilating themselves and their Brethren in imitation of the sufferings of Christ before and during his crucifixion. As mentioned earlier,[26] these *ejercicios* involved a variety of penitential punishments, including self-flagellation and flagellation by others using whips called *disciplinas* made of yucca fiber or *cuerdas* made of finely knitted wool, the whips dipped in tea to make them heavier and sometimes in vinegar to make them more painful. These floggings caused deep and bloody lacerations and, despite subsequent bathings of the back with silver sage tea as an astringent, the deeply torn flesh they produced resulted in permanent scarring. Obsidian knives, *pedernales* (sharp flints), and cactus spines were also employed to cut the skin. *Hermanos* also abused and abased themselves by dragging about huge wooden crosses called *maderos*, taller than a man, or pulled a cart loaded with heavy stones and carrying an image of Doña

Sebastiana, a female figure reminiscent of the arrow-pierced male Catholic Saint Sebastian, representing *La Muerte*, death.[27]

The apex of Penitente suffering was the reenactment of the Crucifixion itself on Good Friday of Holy Week. It was a high honor for an *Hermano* to be chosen to play the role of the *Cristo*, who had to carry a cumbersome cross from station to station along the Via Crucis and then be bound with ropes to the cross, wearing a crown of cactus thorns. This was an excruciating ordeal but ordinarily did not result in serious injury and perhaps never in actual death, though accidentally fatal crucifixions are said to have occurred on rare occasions.[28] Some Anglos believed, probably without foundation, that nails, not ropes, were routinely used in these reenactments and that the *Cristos* sometimes died as a result.

It is a cliché, but a truth nonetheless, that history is written by the winners—in this case, by the Anglos. There is no Hispano history of the Espinosas, though one is badly needed. And just as the Anglos of nineteenth-century New Mexico and Colorado territories, ignorant of the actual purposes of the *Santa Hermandad*, misunderstood and exaggerated its practices, so it has been easy for Anglo writers then and now to imagine the Espinosas as deranged *Hermanos* deliberately escalating and perverting the penitential exercises of their Brotherhood and turning them outward, in the form of sacramental murder, toward the hated *gringo*. Such an idea may be an oversimplification but also may not be entirely false. The Espinosas may have acted in this way, though perhaps not consciously. For if they were deliberately, volitionally engaged in a faith-based crusade, would they not have made more of it in their writings than they did?

With the possible but equally questionable exceptions of the message on Lehman's paper collar and the sentiment Frank Hall said he remembered from Vivián's "diary," the Espinosas wrote nothing explaining their actions in religious terms. Instead they spoke only of revenge. Is it not possible they exacted that revenge in the manner that came most naturally to them as Penitentes, through mutilation? Perhaps the expression of their revenge indirectly reflected the liturgical mutilations of the *Santa Hermandad* that they had practiced and observed all their adult lives in the *moradas* of El Rito, Cochití, and San Rafael, only surcharged and transformed by a retributive fury. For it cannot be denied that violence was implicit in the *ejercicios* and was therefore a familiar tool that might lie within them, waiting for employment, not only for the purpose of expiating sin but also—in men no longer reasoning normally—

for enacting a savagely damaging personal vengeance. The content of that vengeance, then, would not be sacramental but uniquely and aberrantly personal. And, perhaps, political.

Felipe and Vivián would have been teenagers on August 19, 1846, when General Stephen Watts Kearny of the United States Army of the West, after marching his 1,700-man force of infantry, cavalry, and artillery overland from Fort Leavenworth in what is now Kansas, stood in the *plaza* of Santa Fe and told a gathering of bewildered *nuevomexicanos* that they were no longer subjects of the Republic of Mexico but "American citizens, subject only to the laws of the United States."[29]

Kearny's assignment was the conquest of New Mexico and California, one of the opening moves in President James K. Polk's bold plan to implement the doctrine of Manifest Destiny, which held that it was the fate of the United States to rule the whole of the North American continent below Canada. Kearny had taken New Mexico without firing a shot, thanks to a combination of threats, lies, and bribery that had swept away the administration of Mexican governor Manuel Armijo and his second in command, Colonel Diego Archuleta.

In his address, Kearny promised a golden future for impoverished New Mexico and its people:

> We come as friends, to better your condition. . . . We mean not to murder you or rob you of your property. Your families shall be free from molestation; your women secure from violence. My soldiers shall take nothing from you but what they pay for. In taking possession of New Mexico, we do not mean to take away your religion. Religion and government have no connection in our country. There, all religions are equal; one has no preference over the other; the Catholic and the Protestant are esteemed alike. . . . In our government, all men are equal. We esteem the most peaceable man, the best man. I advise you to attend to your domestic pursuits, cultivate industry, be peaceable and obedient to the laws.[30]

It would not be the last time an American invoked the ideals of democracy as a prelude to sacrificing them on the altar of political expediency. But even had Kearny been sincere, he and his words of conciliation were soon gone. He speedily installed a fresh government for the new American colony of New Mexico, composed of a mixture of Anglos and collaborating Hispanos. This body was headed by Governor Charles Bent, who with his brother, William, had long been a fixture of the Santa Fe trade. Then the general marched off into the sunset to bring California, too, under benevolent rule of the *norteños*.

Three days later, he and his troops were replaced by a volunteer corps of occupation under the command of Colonel Sterling Price of the United States Army. Colonel Price's troops were hard-case Missourians who quickly set about nullifying everything Kearny had promised. In the words of Tobin biographer James E. Perkins:

> The [New] Mexicans, even in their dire poverty, had always prided themselves on their courtesy to others, their polite language, love of family, and love of God and Church. The newcomers[,] by contrast, were uncouth, rough, dirty, and most couldn't utter three words without cursing. They considered [New] Mexicans to be a stupid, inferior race. . . . They belittled and mocked the Church and the holy Catholic faith, and they laughed at the sight of the wooden . . . *Santos*. . . . [T]he people of New Mexico wanted nothing to do with them. They wanted the foreigners to leave, and their country back.[31]

Consequently, on January 18, 1847, four months almost to the day after Kearny's reassuring speech in the Santa Fe *plaza*, a large number of Hispanos and Indians from the Taos Pueblo, enraged by the contemptuous behavior of the Missourians and what seemed the theft of their country's sovereignty by the United States, rose in violent rebellion. The outbreak was significant because it involved New Mexican elites, poor *peones*, mixed-blood *mestizos*, and Pueblo Indians, social and ethnic groups that heretofore had not always seen eye to eye. It was carefully planned by a cabal made up of all these parties and rumor said it was controlled by none other than the Penitente "Superior," Padre Martínez, though his complicity was never proven.[32]

In fact Fray Angélico Chávez, native New Mexican priest, historian, author, and poet who consulted nineteenth-century Hispano biographies of Martínez,[33] has written persuasively that far from fomenting and aiding the plot, Martínez argued against it to the plotters, may have sent Colonel Price advance warning of it, and gave shelter to *Taoseños* innocent of involvement.[34]

In Taos the rebels brutally murdered Governor Bent, other officials of the Anglo government, and any other Americans and collaborating Hispanos they could seek out. Men like Tom Tobin—who had given up his American citizenship, converted to Catholicism, married a New Mexican wife, and been for years an accepted member of the Hispano community—were attacked. Tobin himself was fortunate to escape with his life, though Anglo friends who shared his circumstances did not.[35] The insurrection was brought under control only after Colonel Price organized a volunteer company (including Tobin and his half-brother, Charles Autobees), combined it with his army units, and crushed the rebel forces in a series of engagements ending with the killing of approximately 150 New Mexicans and Indians at the Taos Pueblo—in the process destroying the Pueblo's ancient church of San Gerónimo.[36]

The sudden American occupation, the arrogant and disrespectful demeanor of the occupiers,[37] and the ferocity of the repression of the revolt shocked most New Mexicans, particularly those who, like Felipe and Vivián Espinosa, were young and impressionable. Patriotic sentiments were exacerbated when the Americans publicly tried and hanged the leaders of the uprising in the *plaza* of Taos, using the lariats of some Anglo traders who happened to arrive from the States just in time for the occasion. It did not help that the traders openly laughed and joked while greasing their lariats for the hanging.[38] To his credit, one of the traders, Lewis H. Garrard, attending the trial, felt the essential unfairness of the Anglo notion of justice:

> It certainly did appear to be a great assumption on the part of the Americans to conquer a country and then arraign the revolting inhabitants for treason. American judges sat on the bench, New Mexicans and Americans filled the jury box, and an American soldiery guarded the halls. Verily, a strange mixture of violence and justice—a strange middle ground between the martial and common law.[39]

There is no proof that any member of the Espinosa family participated in or even witnessed the events of the 1847 revolt. But Taos, scene of the massacre of the rebels and the execution of the purported leaders of the revolt, was only about a day's horseback ride eastward from their home in El Rito. The outbreak was an ominous rumble on the edge of their world, bespeaking events to come that were unknowable but surely dire. The old, known, torpid world was ending; a new world was being born in musketry, cannon fire, flames, and blood.

Though the Anglo takeover was, for *nuevomexicanos*, a profound trauma, Laura Gomez has written that, for the United States, New Mexico was "merely an annoying obstacle" to be overcome in the process of reaching the Pacific Coast:

> As is often the case . . . the law of unintended consequences was at work. Unfolding events in the war [with Mexico] and its conclusion in 1848 with

the Treaty of Guadalupe Hidalgo, as well as the unique circumstances of the region, made New Mexico more of a problem . . . than had been anticipated. In particular, the United States, feeling its way as a colonial power for the first time . . . , was unprepared for the relatively unusual dynamics of . . . "double colonization." The US colonization of the nineteenth century was grafted onto a previous European colonization of the region—the Spanish colonization of the seventeenth and eighteenth centuries. . . . American military and civil authorities encountered an entrenched set of European-origin political and social institutions that were operated by a largely non-European population consisting of small, widely dispersed . . . mixed Spanish and indigenous and Pueblo Indian communities. . . . [They] encountered a fully developed Spanish-Mexican legal system, as well as an entrenched system of canon law in the Catholic Church. This was, of course, a new scenario for the Americans.[40]

Under American law New Mexican men could theoretically claim United States citizenship, but the reality was that Anglo prejudice made it difficult for them to avoid being called, and treated as, "greasers" who deserved few if any rights or consideration. Mid-nineteenth-century Americans who customarily saw people either as superior whites or inferior blacks or Indians had a hard time knowing where on the scale of subordination the Hispano population belonged, but all too often their innate bigotry prevailed.

Hispanic elites tended to be granted a degree of respect—indeed, Gomez argues they became a "wedge" racial group that simultaneously buttressed and challenged white supremacy[41]—but *pobres* like the Espinosas could normally expect to be the recipients of *gringo* contempt and derision. Furthermore, the civilian administration of government and law courts—where New Mexican elites could and did serve—was, for three decades, trumped by the fact the Territory was encumbered by American military rule. Especially harsh was the form of martial law imposed by General James H. Carleton, whose arrogance we have previously noticed.[42] He served as commander of the Military Department of New Mexico from 1862 to 1866.[43]

At the local level the Americans imposed changes that would be repeated thirteen years later when the Territory of Colorado was created, much to the confusion of the Hispanos in the San Luís Valley, many of whom had moved into that remote location to escape the exactions and religious prejudice that had become rife in the lower part of the Territory. After 1848 the Anglos abolished a traditional municipal organization that had linked New

Mexican towns together under municipal councils called *ayuntamientos*, under the command of a regional prefect, replacing it with an alien county system, to be governed by county commissioners.[44] Individual land tenure came under question as greedy Americans bilked colonists out of their portions of longstanding Spanish or Mexican land grants, and sometimes the grants themselves were declared invalid or were allowed to be bought up wholesale by American speculators.[45] These and a host of other disruptions of old and comfortably established ways of life deeply troubled most New Mexicans and enraged others, almost certainly including the Espinosas.

But nothing irritated Hispanos as much as the endemic Anglo disrespect for their religious faith. Typical were the sentiments of Ovander Hollister of the First Colorado Cavalry as he toured Santa Fe in early 1862:

> The forms of religion, if not its substance, appear to be generally respected and observed. Doubtless the people are as priest-ridden as the most inveterate lover of that kind of craft could wish. For myself, I never realized the utter blankness and poverty of the Mexican mind till I climbed through a hole in the wall about twelve feet from the ground, the door was fastened, and descending, found myself inside of a [Catholic] church for the first time. The impressions a country smith makes on his shop door with a redhot horseshoe, rings, brands, etc. to signify the nature of his occupation to the public, are incomparably superior to the prints, paints and daubs intended to adorn the church walls. What language can adequately express the simplicity, not to say stupidity of a people who treasure such trash in their sanctuaries! It seemed strange that grown men and women could be so infinitely more childish than children themselves.[46]

Attitudes such as this clashed with the heartfelt piety expressed in a poem "so typical of the Hispanic soul as to be anonymous," quoted by Fray Angélico Chávez: "Neither the promise of heaven nor the threat of hell can make me love you, my God, as much as your cross and sufferings and most especially your love; were there no heaven or hell I would still love you as I love you."[47]

This passionate declaration of love for Christ and his church might well be a distillation of the beliefs of the *Santa Hermandad*, and even in the face of the horrific crimes of the brothers Espinosa, who are we to say that they too did not love their God even beyond hope of heaven or fear of hell? They may have slaughtered Americans in revenge for the attack of the army on their families and not as sacrificial offerings to the Mother of God, but it is conceivable that

Blanca Peak. (Author photo)

while they dealt out that vengeance their hearts were also full of revulsion for the arrant sacrilege and social and political dislocations they had seen the *gringo* conquerors visit on their homeland and their faith for most of their adult lives.

No one knows precisely how the Espinosas made their way from point to point in the course of their vengeance raid. We know the points—the places where they struck. But connecting those points must necessarily be guesswork. We can refine our guesses by studying maps and learning the terrain and tracing out the roads and trails of their day, and by knowing where the settlements were. But our conclusions will always be conjectural.

This would hardly seem a debatable point, but some writers have described precise itineraries with such confidence one would think them gifted with privileged information such as the imaginary Espinosa diary with daily entries that one of them has cited as a reliable source.[48] Another writer, in a voice of

Ruts marking the old route of Sangre de Cristo Pass. (Author photo)

persuasive authority, tells us that "on or about March 10, 1863," the Espinosas "left San Rafael, heading northeast. They skirted Fort Garland, continued towards the northeast, and crossed over the Sangre de Cristo Pass. They then swung almost straight north, and rode about forty miles up the Wet Mountain Valley, soon finding an old Indian trail going northeast through the Wet Mountains where they crossed over a pass to the head of North Hardscrabble Creek."[49]

Well, yes, they might have done that. But why would they have gone anywhere near Fort Garland, even "skirting it," at a time when army patrols based at that post were scouring the whole country between Trinchera Creek and the Conejos in hopes of snaring them? Why would they not instead have bypassed Fort Garland more safely, far to the west, perhaps even along the western bank of the Río Grande, and then turned east and crossed behind Blanca Peak and gone over the Sangre de Cristos at 9,780-foot Mosca Pass? Mosca had been used since the 1840s in the whiskey trade between Taos and the Arkansas Valley settlements.[50] Also, had they crossed the range using Music Pass (11,380 feet), an alternate route out of the upper corner of the San Luís and east of the Great Sand Dunes,[51] it would have brought them down from the mountains much nearer to the head of North Hardscrabble Creek than would the route over Sangre de Cristo Pass by Fort Garland—a crossing that would have debouched onto the plains at least sixty miles too far to the south and east for a convenient approach to Hardscrabble.

True, the Sangre de Cristo route featured an improved road and was the more favored and heavily traveled of the various crossings. Since about 1860 there had been weekly stagecoach service over the pass between Fort Garland and Cañon City, and also possibly "large corrals and a way-station called Summit House."[52] Its very popularity would seem to argue against its use by fugitives with prices on their heads. Would not the Espinosas have sought crossings where the chances of being seen were fewer? Mosca and even Medano[53] Pass were also available and, like Music, would have offered ways to get behind Fort Garland and into the Greenhorn–Hardscrabble country with far fewer prospects of being detected.

Of course no one knows exactly how the Espinosas found their way to Franklin Bruce. What we can say with confidence is that ever since the opening of the Santa Fe Trail, Hispanos in northern New Mexico and, later, southern Colorado were familiar with the various trade routes across the mountains and into the Arkansas Valley. Felipe and Vivián would have known, if not from firsthand experience, then from information given them by Hispano traders and acquaintances who had worked in the Anglo settlements, how best to go, and would have chosen the ways offering them the surest prospects of passing safely. Whatever pass through the Sangres they might have chosen, the canyon of North Hardscrabble Creek had long been a favored route for travelers coming up through the mountains from the San Luís Valley.

As best can be estimated, the Espinosas murdered Bruce at Hardscrabble on Monday, March 16, and Henry Harkens at Saw Mill Gulch on the little Fontaine qui Bouille the following Wednesday, March 18. The date of James Addleman's death near Wilkerson Pass is conjectural since his body was found some indeterminate period of time after his actual slaying. As mentioned earlier, one author puts the Addleman killing about a day after the murders of Binkley and Shoup,[54] but this cannot be correct because internal evidence in contemporary newspapers makes it clear he had to have been killed no earlier than Saturday, March 28, and no later than Tuesday, March 31.[55]

Pursuers tracking the perpetrators from the site of the Harkens murder—probably Fremont County sheriff Egbert Bradley and his deputy[56]—are said to have lost their trail in the vicinity of Ute Pass. We do not know what day they turned back, but the distance they had traveled from Saw Mill Gulch must have required three to four days' riding time at most, allowing for wintry weather in the high country and its effect on the available trails and roads. This would mean they had probably given up their search by Sunday, March 22, at the latest, and probably a day or so sooner.

Addleman was murdered at the lower end of South Park, about twenty miles south and west of Ute Pass. So if the sheriff and his deputy had in fact been following the right tracks from Hardscrabble and Saw Mill Gulch as far as Ute Pass, and it is possible they were not, no one can know the Espinosas' whereabouts or what they were doing during the six to nine days between March 22 and the day they killed Addleman—or, in the event the lawmen had been trailing the wrong parties, during the even longer period since Harkens's death on March 18.

The next victims to die[57] at the hands of the Espinosas were Binkley and Shoup, on Wednesday, April 8, near the Kenosha House at the northeast end of South Park. At least eighteen days had elapsed since the peace officers presumably turned back, twenty-two days since the Harkens murder. This long lull, after the bloody start the brothers had made, seems a conspicuous lacuna. Why a pause? Why would bold and possibly insane men obsessed with a mission of vengeful slaughter suddenly go to ground and hide out for the better part of a month?

The obvious answer, that they were waiting for the furor over the triple killings to die down, does not carry the same weight it might if they were ordinary outlaws; the evidence suggests Felipe and Vivián were bent on spreading an epidemic of terror among the *gringos* of central Colorado, and in their next outburst of slaughter they would show an utter disregard for caution. Yet there would be another, similar hiatus after the murders of Binkley and Shoup—a delay of seventeen days, from April 8 to April 25—before they reappeared in the heart of the South Park gold diggings and made their daylight attack on Carter and Metcalf. For this second disappearance in April there is no certain explanation. For the first, we can at least offer a plausible scenario.

In that year of 1863, Holy Week began with Palm Sunday on March 29 and ended with Easter Sunday on April 5, a period accounting for seven of the eighteen to twenty-two days of their quiescence. This was *La Santa Semana*, the most solemnly powerful week in the sacred calendar of the Penitente Brotherhood.

On *Domingo de Ramos*, Palm Sunday, or perhaps the day before, James Addleman was murdered near Wilkerson Pass. And three days after Holy Week ended at sundown on *Domingo de Resurección*, the day Christ rose from the tomb, Jacob Binkley and Abram Shoup were killed near the Kenosha House. Had the brothers Espinosa spent *La Santa Semana* performing the penitential rites with their brother-members of their *cofradía*?

NOTES

1. Tobin, "The Capture of the Espinosas," 59.

2. Virginia McConnell Simmons, *The San Luís Valley: Land of the Six-Armed Cross*, 2nd ed. (Boulder: University Press of Colorado, 1999), 95.

3. Randall Teeuwen, "La Gente de la Tierra," in *La Cultura Constante de San Luís* (San Luis, CO: The San Luis Museum Cultural and Commercial Center, 1985), 10.

4. Ibid.

5. Olibama López Tushar, *The People of El Valle: A History of the Spanish Settlers in the San Luis Valley* (Pueblo, CO: El Escritorio, 2007), 66–67.

6. See 1860 Census, Taos County, New Mexico Territory; and Chapter 7.

7. The third man initially sought by the authorities, Jesús Sánchez, does not appear again in the records of the time. We do not know if he was a relative, friend, or perhaps a Penitente "brother" of Felipe and Vivián. He may or may not have been the third man at the robbery of the teamster.

8. Letter of Captain E. W. Eaton to Assistant Adjutant General, Headquarters, District of Colorado, April 14, 1863, E. Wayne Eaton Papers, Fray Angélico Chávez History Library/The New Mexico History Museum, Palace of the Governors, Santa Fe.

9. Ibid.

10. 1.575 US bushels.

11. It is intriguing to note that an undated PDF image of a clipping from *The Colorado Magazine* shared with the author by Christie Wright, president of the Park County Archives Board, says an "early Spanish rawhide trunk" believed to have been the property of the Espinosas was donated to the Colorado Historical Society by Adolph Mayer, son of early pioneer Leopold Mayer, along with "a pair of large Spanish spurs, a Navy Colt's revolver, a pair of moccasins and a pair of chappelets," also thought to have belonged to the Espinosas. For the spurs, believed to have been the property of Vivián, see Chapter 6, note 40. Joseph Lamb is said to have taken Vivián's boots and Felipe is known to have

worn moccasins. "Chappelets" seems to refer to a divided, apronlike style of chaps or leggings worn to protect a rider's legs in rough country, called "chinks" by Anglo cowboys; these might have belonged to Vivián, as they would have been a natural accessory to a horseman's boots. The pistols usually attributed to the Espinosas are in the museum of History Colorado, formerly the Colorado Historical Society. They are an 1860 Model Colt Army and an 1858 Model Remington Army, not the 1851 Colt Navy mentioned in the clipping; and Perkins, *Tom Tobin*, 175, note 54, says the serial numbers of both guns indicate they were manufactured in early 1863 and probably would not have been available to the Espinosas except under unlikely circumstances, such as acquiring the weapons from victims who had very recently received them from the East by mail order. The revolver found on Felipe when he died was reported to have been a Colt Navy; *Weekly Commonwealth*, October 28, 1863.

12. Eaton to Assistant Adjutant General, April 14, 1863.

13. See 1860 Census, Taos County, New Mexico Territory; see Chapter 7.

14. Perkins, *Tom Tobin*, 131–132, makes this claim and further quotes a descendant of the Espinosas as saying the soldiers stole everything—clothing, food, even the chickens as a way of punishing the family.

15. See Introduction and the *Weekly Commonwealth*, October 28, 1863, quoting the contents of an undated letter written by Felipe to Colorado governor John Evans, found among his effects at his death.

16. Clark Secrest, "The 'Bloody Espinosas': Avenging Angels of the Conejos," in *Colorado Heritage*, Colorado Historical Society (now History Colorado) (Autumn 2000): 12, asserts that, while Felipe vowed vengeance toward Anglos for the attack on their home, Vivián also felt impelled to expiate his father's sins by killing fifty white men. In Jessen et al., "Colorado's Worst Serial Murders: The Espinosa Story," 26, it is Felipe who vowed to the Virgin he would kill the fifty *gringos*. Bob Scott, in *Tom Tobin and the Bloody Espinosas* (Frederick, MD: PublishAmerica, 2004), 70–71, says both brothers actually composed a fourteen-page document entitled "A Statement of Principles" in which they pledged to kill 600 Americans, 100 for each member of their family reputedly killed in the Mexican War. This assertion is unsubstantiated. Scott, 98, also contends the Espinosas kept a "diary" and implies it carried daily entries tabulating the number of their victims. No such diary is known to have existed.

17. *The Alaska Citizen*, May 8, 1911; see also Chapter 4.

18. Black Hawk *Daily Mining Journal*, July 23, 1864; see also Chapter 4.

19. Secrest, "The 'Bloody Espinosas,'" 15. See also Chapters 6 and 14.

20. See Chapter 6.

21. See Introduction and Chapter 14.

22. Perkins, *Tom Tobin*, 171, note 2.

23. Weigle, *Brothers of Light, Brothers of Blood*, 143.

24. Perkins, *Tom Tobin*, 134, asserts that Bruce, the Espinosas' first victim, had "a large cross" carved into his chest.

25. Scott, *Tom Tobin and the Bloody Espinosas*, 78–106, makes the wholly unsupported claim that the Espinosas habitually inserted tree branches into the wounds of their victims as a kind of hallmark or insignia.

26. See Chapter 7.

27. Weigle, *Brothers of Light, Brothers of Blood*, 159–173.

28. Ibid., 171–173; Virginia McConnell Simmons, "The Penitentes: Remnant of a Vanishing Lifestyle," *The San Luis Valley Historian*, Vol. XXIV, No. 4 (1992), cites a report in 1874 by a Conejos priest that a Penitente had died during a crucifixion reenactment.

29. William A. Keleher, *Turmoil in New Mexico, 1846–1868* (Santa Fe, NM: The Rydal Press, 1962), 15.

30. Ibid.

31. Perkins, *Tom Tobin*, 49–51.

32. Laura E. Gomez, "Off-White in an Age of White Supremacy," 30.

33. Chávez, *But Time and Chance*, 82–83. Chávez refers to Santiago Valdez's *Biografía del Rev. P. Antonio José Martínez, Cura-Parroco del Curaro de Taos, N.M.*, 1877.

34. Chávez, *But Time and Chance*, 84–85.

35. Perkins, *Tom Tobin*, 54–61.

36. Ibid., 50–69; Gomez, "Off-White in an Age of White Supremacy," 29. See also Ralph Emerson Twitchell, *The History of the Military Occupation of the Territory of New Mexico from 1846 to 1851 by the Government of the United States* (Denver, CO: Smith-Brooks Company, 1909), 124–145; Bancroft, *History of Arizona and New Mexico*, 408–437; and Brooks, *Captains and Cousins*, 281–288.

37. Gutiérrez, *When Jesus Came, the Corn Mothers Went Away*, 338–340.

38. Lewis H. Garrard, *Wah-to-yah and the Taos Trail* (Norman: University of Oklahoma Press, 1955), 190–200.

39. Ibid., 172.

40. Gomez, "Off-White in an Age of White Supremacy," 14.

41. Ibid., 58.

42. See Chapter 7.

43. Ibid., 22; Keleher, *Turmoil in New Mexico*, 278–399.

44. Quintana, *Pobladores*, 173.

45. Simmons, *The San Luis Valley*, 143–151.

46. Hollister, *Boldly They Rode*, 157.

47. Fray Angélico Chávez, *My Penitente Land: Reflections on Spanish New Mexico* (Albuquerque: University of New Mexico Press, 1974), 24.

48. Scott, *Tom Tobin and the Bloody Espinosas*, not only claims the Espinosas kept a nonexistent diary (see note 16 above) and cites its contents, he has a Sheriff Hart (?),

while pursuing the Espinosas after the Bruce and Harkens murders, sending a telegram to Fort Garland from a Western Union office in Woodland Park, Colorado, twenty-seven years before the town was founded (Bright, *Place Names in Colorado*, 188) and five years before even Denver had reliable telegraph service from the East, much less branch lines connecting towns and military posts; see Jepson, "The Telegraph Comes to Colorado," 20.

49. Perkins, *Tom Tobin*, 132.

50. Jack Pyle Cooper, "A Rebuttal Concerning Roads, Trails, Traces and Wagons," *The San Luis County Historian*, Vol. XXXIII, No. 3 (2001): 20.

51. Helmuth, *The Passes of Colorado*, 148, 154–155.

52. Nancy Christopherson, "Huerfano County, Colorado History," http://www.kmitch.com/Huerfano/hist.html, accessed January 22, 2013.

53. Ibid., 139.

54. That is, about April 9; Perkins, *Tom Tobin*, 141.

55. See Chapter 1.

56. Ibid.

57. This statement is, of course, provisional. There can be no precise accounting for the numbers and names of those killed by the Espinosas. After the death of Addleman, rumors of murders and disappearances abounded in South Park, and it is entirely possible that Felipe and Vivián killed several men in remote locations where the bodies were never found. At the end Felipe claimed the brothers had killed thirty-two victims; the fact that we know the identities of only a dozen or so is no reason to disbelieve their tally, or to believe it either.

9 "Malicious Interference was the Cause"

The Scapegoating of Captain E. Wayne Eaton

The next victim of the Espinosas wasn't a miner or a sawmill owner or a mail-station operator. Nor was he a mule rancher on his way home from testifying in court. He was a soldier. Though he wasn't a fatality, he did receive a severe wound—not a physical one but an injury to his good name, and because he was an officer in the volunteer service of the United States Army, such a wound could have spelled the end of his military career and dealt a ruinous blow to his life in the postwar world. He was Captain Ethan Wayne Eaton, commander of Fort Garland.

On Thursday, April 9, 1863, one day after the Espinosas murdered Jacob Binkley and Abram Shoup near the Kenosha House in South Park, sixteen hundred miles to the east in a War Department Building in Washington City a clerk in the Adjutant General's Office drew up a document, General Order No. 163, dishonorably discharging Eaton from the Army of the United States.[1]

The dismissal was a conspicuous blot on an otherwise unblemished record both military and private. Eaton had been mustered into the army of the United States on May 29, 1861, as captain of the Second Regiment, New Mexico Volunteers, an infantry unit he had raised at Albuquerque and Santa Fe.[2] He commanded several battalions at Fort Craig and was subsequently assigned command of that post and later of

DOI: 10.5876/9781607322375.c09

the garrison at Albuquerque. He saw action at Peralta and Los Pinos and at a skirmish at Albuquerque during the Texan invasion of New Mexico in the winter of 1861–62. In the summer of the latter year, when the volunteer service was reorganized, he became captain of Company D, First New Mexico Volunteers. Eaton's actions were performed under the eye of Colonel E.R.S. Canby, then commander of the Department of New Mexico,[3] and were favorably noticed by the colonel.[4]

In the summer of 1862 Eaton and his company were transferred to Fort Garland, which had been under the command of Major A. H. Mayer since July 20.[5] The company itself seems to have arrived before Eaton, on July 30, temporarily commanded by Second Lieutenant Nicholas Hodt.[6] As New Mexicans, they do not seem to have been regarded as a welcome addition to the garrison. Mayer, a Colorado officer, observed them with a jaundiced eye, noting "Captain Eaton's Company are nearly in rags, and are suffering from lack of blankets and shoes."[7] Even before their arrival, the new post commander had noted dismissively in Garland's letter book, "I understand most of the men comprising Captain Eaton's Co are by nature very proficient in the art of making adobes"[8]—there were additional barracks to be built and evidently Mayer appeared to see the new troops not as soldiers but as common laborers.

Eaton and his second in command, First Lieutenant John Lewis, reported for duty on August 10. The very next day Mayer saw fit to seek permission from Headquarters, Department of New Mexico, to rid himself of Eaton and of Eaton's New Mexicans, using as his excuse that "in case of trouble with the people[,] the Mexican soldiers will be more of detriment than good."[9] Eaton was not a man to lie quiescent under such treatment, nor was he inclined to tolerate slights against his men. On August 18 he wrote a blistering letter to Headquarters complaining of discrimination against his New Mexican troops "by the officers of this post," obviously including Mayer.[10] The letter had to be endorsed by Mayer, who must have resented this criticism by his newly arrived and very outspoken subordinate. Headquarters took no action on Mayer's request for Eaton's transfer. On November 30 Eaton again wrote Headquarters, asking payment for twenty-five of his men who had been on detached service when the paymaster visited Fort Garland, noting that the men had been "in the service of the United States fifteen months and have not rec'd a cent of pay and most of them have families that are in absolute want."[11] Eaton's defense of his troops was typical of his affinity for New Mexicans

Ethan Wayne Eaton and his wife Marcelina Chávez in later life. (Photo unattributed and undated, courtesy of the Palace of the Governors Photo Archives [NMHM/DCA], neg. nos. 122150 and 122151)

and their culture, a sensitivity most white officers lacked. Both letters demonstrated Eaton's strong convictions and somewhat reckless courage.

In August and September 1862 Eaton led an extended scout in the area between Greenhorn Creek and the Spanish Peaks in search of "a party of armed men," believed to be the Confederate guerrilla gang under Captain George Madison,[12] but while he was unable to track down the Rebels he did report a belief that "thirty or forty men of Mexican Bands are camped in the mountains with a large quantity of Stock."[13] By this time he and Mayer appear to have become officially reconciled, though it is hard to believe their relationship did not remain strained.

Finally, on December 11, Major Mayer was transferred and Eaton, then thirty-five years old, became commander of Fort Garland. In the period between then and the outbreak of the Espinosas at San Rafael he had made a good if not uncontroversial record in that command. His chief difficulty resulted from being caught between dueling superior officers as General Carleton resisted the transfer of Fort Garland from his jurisdiction to that of the District of Colorado.[14]

But Eaton had led a varied life that taught him adaptability, self-assurance, and firm resolve, qualities that had served him well since coming west in 1849 and that he would need in abundance over the coming months. Before the Civil War those traits had earned him a place as one of the most considerable figures in the Territory of New Mexico. A native of Montgomery County, New York, he left home at age sixteen after the accidental death of his father, took a job as a store clerk, administered a wire factory, worked on the Erie Canal, and eventually came to New Mexico during the California Gold Rush but elected to remain there rather than go on to the West Coast goldfields.[15] He clerked and prospected in a mining camp, operated a store, eventually married a Hispanic woman, Marcelina Chávez, and fathered nine children. He learned to speak and write fluent Spanish and, unlike many Anglos, fitted comfortably into the easygoing culture of *Nuevo Mexico*.[16]

In 1851, with a partner, A. W. Raynolds, he bought the 200,000-acre San Cristóbal land grant in the Galisteo Basin from its principal grantee Domingo Fernández.[17] Afterwards he acquired Raynolds's share for $262 and became a prominent farmer and stock raiser. He was known as a man of great "nerve and promptitude of action." Once Apache Indians made off with some of his cattle and he pursued them for a hundred miles with the assistance of only twelve men, engaged the hostiles, and he and his party killed all but one of the Apaches and recovered his stock. "He received a wound in the thigh from an arrowhead two and a half inches long," and it was over two months before he could have it removed.[18]

Clearly Wayne Eaton was someone to be conjured with, both as a man and as a soldier. So why was he dismissed? The answer is simple on the surface but once examined becomes quite complex. The simple reason was that General Carleton in Santa Fe blamed him for the escape of the Espinosas during the mid-January firefight at San Rafael. In the wake of that debacle, Eaton had dutifully sent a frank report of the affair to Headquarters, which Carleton returned bearing a stinging and sarcastic endorsement:

> "The General Commanding Department is not at all satisfied with Lt. Hodt's management of the affair. It is doubtful [from his course of] conduct whether he has not mistaken his profession. Capt. Eaton will himself see that these robbers and murderers are arrested and brought to Fort Garland dead or alive and all those that aid and abet be brought there. These men will be led by Capt. Eaton and the search will not be given up until the prisoners are caught or killed. . . .

> He can take as many men from Fort Garland as may be necessary, such to be in all up to half the effective strength of the garrison. . . . All the property of the Mexicans will be [confiscated] and accounted for at given rates."[19]

The criticism of Hodt was just; the hapless lieutenant[20] had badly botched the job of arresting and holding the Espinosas and Eaton knew it. As Hodt's immediate superior, he also knew he rightly bore final responsibility for the blunder. Naturally he was eager to restore Carleton's confidence in his judgment and skill. On February 16 he assembled a detail of twenty-five troopers on the parade ground at Fort Garland and prepared to set out in search of the fugitives.

Before he could leave, it was necessary for him to turn over temporary command of the post to his ranking subordinate, First Lieutenant Lewis. Unfortunately there was bad blood between the two,[21] and immediately upon assuming command Lewis spitefully refused to allow Eaton to requisition a teamster's horse that the captain wished to take along.

The horse had already been saddled and was ready to go when, at a time when Eaton was briefly absent, Lewis ordered it taken back to the corral and unsaddled. In the circumstances his behavior was petty and meaningless. When Eaton returned to the parade ground, he became irritated, countermanded Lewis's order, and resumed command of the post long enough to direct that the horse be resaddled. But when the animal was brought back to the line, Lewis stripped the gear off again and flung it to the ground with the remark that "he would be God-damned if he would not do something about this."

As Eaton later wrote, "[Lewis's] ungentlemanly language, manner and acts . . . took me wholly by surprise, and so aggravated me, that my next act was rather hasty." While he does not say what that act was, he must have struck Lewis, for the lieutenant then went to his quarters and returned armed with a revolver. Eaton was not carrying a weapon and for a moment the situation looked dangerous, but somehow the dispute passed off without further incident and Eaton again relinquished command to Lewis and proceeded with his scout.[22]

A witness to this altercation was Major Archibald H. Gillespie, the officer Carleton had sent into the San Luís Valley to conduct a military census. Gillespie had been based at Fort Garland since October 21,[23] coming and going between the post and the various Hispano settlements in the valley where he was obliged to count all males of military age and gather information about conditions and natural resources in the region.[24]

Gillespie had also been present during a previous encounter between Eaton and Lewis, only twenty days after Eaton had assumed command. A midnight "frolic" on New Year's Eve 1863, partly instigated by Lewis and post sutler T. W. Posthoff, and perhaps condoned or even ignored by Eaton, got out of hand and caused an unseemly commotion that Eaton later tried to cover up in a way that Lewis and Gillespie thought reflected unfairly on the lieutenant.[25]

Gillespie, for much of his adult life, had struggled with alcoholism. Eaton would later write that the major "scarcely drew a sober breath" the entire time he was based at Garland.[26] It happened that Lieutenant Lewis had a fondness for drink equal to the major's. Gillespie and Eaton did not get along and evidently the major and Lewis formed an alliance based on their common hostility against the post commander.

On Gillespie's side, some of his animosity must have been personal: Eaton was married to a New Mexican woman, was warmly attached to his Hispano troops, and had fitted comfortably into the culture of his adopted New Mexican homeland. These were not qualities the major would have appreciated; it is evident from his writings that he was bitterly prejudiced against Hispanos.[27]

In a letter of December 3, 1862, to Captain Ben C. Cutler, Carleton's assistant adjutant general, Gillespie expressed his strongly negative feelings:

> These New Mexicans have no morale whatever, and, consequently, not the esprit as is always found amongst our own nation's Troops, and they appear to feel that they entered the Service to lead an idle, lazy life, and to do as they please. They have never been fed or clothed so well before in their lives, and never had any money—the most of them having been Peons, who discharged their debt to their masters by enlisting in the Service of the United States—yet they will sell their clothing and rations to gratify their appetites and go in want, rags and dirt if not closely watched. With Non-Commissioned officers, particularly Sergeants of American or European birth, something might be made of these New Mexicans.[28]

Contrast this with Captain Eaton's passionate defense of his New Mexican Volunteers four months earlier, when Major Mayer was still in command and Eaton and his company had only been at Fort Garland a few days. Eaton had complained to the Santa Fe Headquarters of "a feeling of distrust towards my company on account of their being Mexicans" by the officers of Fort Garland:

> The policy generally used towards the Mexican people by Americans in my opinion is wrong and not for the best interest of the Country or government—when New Mexico was made a part of the United States [t]he people were made our people, entitled to the Same privileges and protections as ourselves. They are greatly behind us in civilization and perhaps an inferior race—and it is most certainly for the interests of the Country and Government to advance them in every possible way—This can best be done with a kind but just policy towards them. They have feelings as well as ourselves—and by mistrusting them and underestimating them in [indecipherable], we do nothing but keep them back continually stirring up a feeling of jealousy and animosity between the two people—Never being made soldiers and treated properly and encouraged.[29]

Eaton may have been a man of his time—his phrase "perhaps an inferior race" might seem to indicate he was at least a paternalist—but on the other hand, few Anglos in the nineteenth-century Southwest would have bothered to use the qualifier "perhaps." Nothing in his treatment of New Mexicans suggests he believed them inferior, not least his decision to marry one. He probably used the phrase as a superficial concession to the bigotry of his superiors in hopes of arousing *their* paternalism, the softer side of white supremacy, as a way of gaining better treatment for his soldiers.

Clearly Eaton and Gillespie were worlds apart in their attitudes toward Hispanos. On January 31, 1863, fifteen days after the incident at San Rafael, Gillespie sent to Carleton an abstract of his military census for the vicinity of Fort Garland and took the opportunity to comment on what he believed to be rampant indiscipline at the post, garrisoned entirely by New Mexican troops. He specifically mentioned "occurrences at this Garrison, such as I have never witnessed before, in a long military experience."[30] Though he was careful to condition his criticisms—"mention is now made of [the occurrences] in a spirit entirely free from all personality, but governed by a strict sense of duty to our National Army"[31]—any military man would have concluded he was laying the blame for these conditions on the commander of the post, Captain Eaton.

In a set of "Remarks" appended to the letter, Gillespie went out of his way to stigmatize the New Mexican women—wives of the volunteers, laundresses, and, yes, prostitutes—who lived in and around Fort Garland, as "bad characters" who, "in addition to other bad traits, steal." He went on at enough length to raise questions how an officer of "a long military experience" could have been so naïve and puritanical. Josefa Montoya he described as "insolent, . . . disgraceful in appearance, filthy and the upper portion of her person nude." Ursula Nervares he condemned for having deserted her husband and cohabiting "with another person since that time."[32] In an obscure reference that seemed to question Eaton's personal morals he further remarked, "During the late absence of Capt. Eaton at Conejos a sentry was posted at this woman's door," raising a suspicion that at least one modern historian has interpreted as evidence Eaton kept a mistress,[33] a highly unlikely arrangement since Eaton shared quarters with his wife Marcelina and their children as well as with the post schoolmistress, who even Gillespie wrote was "very respectable."[34]

Eaton and Gillespie openly clashed[35] several times over the number and type of Fort Garland troops the major wanted for his escort, his means of conveyance, and the number of horses or mules required to accompany him to his various destinations in the far-flung San Luís. In the midst of this running quarrel, Carleton wrote Gillespie directing him to undertake an investigation of the New Year's Eve incident. Eaton had sent a report of the affair to Headquarters that underplayed its significance. But Eaton's account aroused Carleton's suspicions and exacerbated his distrust of the captain, which had lingered after the fiasco at San Rafael.

Carleton's choice of Gillespie as his special investigator was an odd one. From their very first encounter, their relationship had been strained and during Gillespie's altercations with Eaton about the composition of his escort, which the major had detailed in several letters of complaint to the General, Carleton had grown impatient with both officers, especially with the major, whose attitude during the dispute had become increasingly petty and sarcastic. Carleton must have known Gillespie would be far from objective in his investigation of the New Year's Eve affair.[36]

Predictably, the result of Gillespie's investigation was a formal report dated February 14 in which the major offered his opinion that Eaton had mishandled the New Year's Eve incident and for this and other reasons was not "a suitable person to command troops."[37] Carleton would eventually use this report to charge Eaton with "neglect of duty, disregard and contempt of the army regulations and conduct unbecoming an officer and a gentleman."[38]

But for the moment he was content to plunge Eaton into hot water with Colonel John M. Chivington, commander of the District of Colorado. On February 28 he wrote Chivington asserting that Eaton "is entirely unworthy of his position" and strongly suggesting that another officer be sent to Fort

Garland "to look after the important interests of the Government."[39] Carleton based his recommendation on "a report which I have received from Major Gillespie."[40]

In writing thus, Carleton appears to have yielded up one of his most jealously held prerogatives: military command over southern Colorado, an area the War Department had transferred from his domain to Chivington's District of Colorado the previous fall, but which he had continued to claim. By writing to Chivington about Eaton, he seemed to be conceding that Chivington, not he, commanded southern Colorado after all. Oddly, later he would revert to his former insistence that the region belonged to him, despite repeated assurances to the contrary from higher-ups.[41]

There is a possible explanation for this temporary easing of the jurisdictional deadlock between the two commanders. Carleton needed reinforcements. He worried that the Confederate Texans driven out of New Mexico the previous spring were now planning a second invasion;[42] also he was planning a campaign against hostile Mescalero Apache and Navajo Indians.[43] To carry out these objectives he would naturally have wanted to concentrate all his New Mexican troops under his own eye, in the forts of the Department of New Mexico. This desire would have dovetailed with Chivington's oft-expressed goal of garrisoning Fort Garland wholly with Colorado troops, something he and Governor Evans had been striving to achieve so as to merge Colorado's military jurisdiction with its superintendency of the Ute Indians, whose agency was based at Conejos under Agent Lafayette Head. The unrest among the Hispanos in the San Luís Valley, culminating in the Espinosa incident in mid-January, had added a special urgency to this need.

Given these complementary concerns, Carleton could withdraw the New Mexicans from Fort Garland to meet the perceived threat from Texas or to chastise the hostile tribes—but without altogether surrendering his claim to command of southern Colorado; while Chivington, in exchange for achieving his immediate goal of getting his own troops into Garland, could tolerate, for the time being, Carleton's stubborn pretense of continuing to command there. Under such a compromise, Eaton and his New Mexicans would doubtless have been expecting, during the early spring of 1863, to be transferred out of Colorado.

Carleton, in his letter to Chivington of January 28, had written, "Should you order Captain Eaton's Company away from Fort Garland, please . . . direct it to proceed without delay to Fort Wingate [New Mexico] in the Navajo

Country."[44] Evidently this troop transfer was well under way by late March, for on the 25th of that month Captain Joseph C. Davidson and Company C, First Colorado Cavalry, started from Denver to join the garrison at Fort Garland and, in time, to replace Eaton's New Mexicans.[45]

On March 31 Chivington had ordered Eaton to travel down to Conejos and settle debts he had incurred in pursuing the Espinosas.[46] As we have seen, Eaton fulfilled this duty, returned to Garland and, on April 11, reported its outcome to Chivington, directing his communication "through Post Comdr," for, by that time, Captain Davidson had arrived and superseded him in command of Fort Garland.[47]

Though Eaton must have been anticipating relief by a Colorado officer at some point, Captain Davidson's sudden assumption of command surprised and angered him, probably because it had occurred during his absence and sooner than expected.[48] He was also highly incensed to learn that while he was in Conejos, his enemy Lieutenant Lewis, to whom he had again been forced to relinquish command while in the south, had falsely reported him absent without leave in musters given to Captain Davidson when the Colorado officer arrived. Because Davidson, not knowing any better, had signed the musters making them official, they could not subsequently be changed despite the fact Eaton could produce Chivington's order showing he had been absent in Conejos on assigned duty.[49]

The next day, April 19, Eaton received formal notice from Chivington's headquarters that he had been removed from command.[50] Either officially or unofficially he learned he was charged with habitual drunkenness and arbitrary treatment of a subordinate officer, Lieutenant Lewis, during the February 16 incident. He either assumed or was told that the accusations had come from Lewis and Gillespie. Eaton could hardly have had time to absorb this staggering blow before learning, to his further dismay, that he had also been dishonorably discharged from the military service of the United States. The two thunderbolts had struck within days of each other.[51]

What makes the action against Captain Eaton so strange—indeed, carries it into a realm of almost inexplicable weirdness—is that by the time of Carleton's February 28 letter citing Gillespie's report as the basis for removing Eaton, Gillespie himself was in such bad odor with Carleton that Carleton would, only a week later, arrest and charge the major himself with disobedience of orders, drunkenness on duty, and conduct unbecoming an officer and a gentleman.[52] By this time Carleton held Gillespie in utmost contempt. Why

Brevet Brigadier General James Henry Carleton, commander of the Military Department of New Mexico during the Espinosa troubles. (Photo unattributed, 1866, courtesy of the Palace of the Governors Photo Archives [NMHM/DCA], neg. no. 022938)

would he have believed anything the major told him?

Perhaps he did *not* believe him but cynically employed him to serve a double purpose. Though he would later undergo a change of heart with regard to Eaton, during this period Carleton nursed an equal contempt for both men. He may have used Gillespie to dispose of Eaton while at the same time setting in motion machinery to get rid of Gillespie, too. In a March 17 letter to the adjutant general of the army he had sought special dismissal authority: "If the authorities in Washington would give the Commander of this distant Department authority to dismiss volunteer officers who, beyond a doubt, are found to be too dissipated and worthless to perform their duty, the efficiency and economy of the service would be greatly promoted."[53]

The War Department granted Carleton this authority on April 14 although he would not receive official notice of it for several more days.[54] Interestingly, though he would successfully use the authority to dismiss Gillespie rather than go through the tedious process of court-martialing him, Gillespie was an officer in the Regular Army, not the volunteer service; technically the special-dismissal authority did not apply to him. Eaton, however, a volunteer officer, *was* subject to the special authority. Carleton seems to have gotten away with killing two very dissimilar birds with one stone, and since he probably did not yet know the War Department had given him the special authority, in Eaton's case he had acted prematurely and without official sanction.

Who were these two men, Carleton and Gillespie, simultaneously enemies and allies, who so improbably conspired to destroy a junior officer with a previously sterling record? Why did they do what they did?

Carleton, a native of Lubec, Maine, was forty-eight years old in the spring of 1863. Commissioned in the Regular Army in 1839, he served with Brigadier General Kearny in the Rocky Mountain Expedition of 1846. In the Mexican War he earned a brevet as a major for gallantry at the battle of Buena Vista. When the Civil War began, he was appointed colonel of the First California Infantry and it was in that capacity that he led a Union force called the California Column from the West Coast to recapture federal posts and frontier settlements in Arizona, New Mexico, and West Texas held by the invading Confederates of Brigadier General Henry H. Sibley's Texas Brigade. After the defeat of the Texans at Glorieta Pass[55] in New Mexico he was promoted brigadier general and assumed command of the Department of New Mexico.[56]

During his tenure in the department Carleton was described by one supportive newspaper as "unsurpassable for energy, intelligence, vigor and integrity."[57] But it is safe to say most New Mexicans in civil life despised him. In some ways warm and winning, in others cold and arrogant, he was, in the words of historian William A. Keleher, "a many-sided man, with puzzling traits of character." "Perhaps," Keleher went on, "the word 'rigid' described him most adequately. There was no indication of flexibility in his makeup. Seemingly, whenever he made up his mind about a man, or a situation, there was no swerving, no deviation."[58]

He deplored drunkenness, a sentiment partially explaining his dislike of Major Gillespie and that, interestingly, Gillespie seems to have manipulated so as to deepen the general's animosity toward Eaton.[59] Carleton was a stickler for rectitude but saw no conflict between these scruples and his own frequent practice of bending the rules and disobeying orders from his superiors when such acts suited his interests, all the while demanding punctilious obedience from his subordinates. He was capable of genuine kindness and solicitude for his soldiers and of shocking cruelties in his treatment of officers and men he disliked, and especially of the Native American tribes he warred against.

Author Hampton Sides has described him thus:

> [He] was a pedant, a prig, a man who thought of everything and whose perfectionism seldom gave him an occasion to apologize. But also an officer of rare excellence, rigid ethics, fine manners, and multi-faceted competence. An officer with a probing but perhaps overly tidy intellect. . . . It would be facile to

Fort Marcy, Santa Fe, New Mexico, General Carleton's headquarters. (Photo by War Department, US National Archives, courtesy of the Palace of the Governors Photo Archives [NMHM/DCA], neg. no. 001714)

call him, as many have, a villain and a fiend and be done with it. But Carleton was a much more nuanced man than he is usually given credit for.[60]

Carleton's misfortune was to have assumed command of New Mexico just as the Texan invasion was turned back by his predecessor colonel, now brigadier general, Canby. Canby, wearing laurels of victory, had gone on to higher fame and larger duties, and Carleton, who had wrought something of a largely unnoticed miracle himself by driving his California Column across burning deserts to take back Arizona from its Confederate occupiers, found himself ruling New Mexico with no Rebel enemies left to fight and little more renown to win.[61]

He could, and did, rattle the saber with repeated warnings that the Texans were scheming to return, but he had to know that was actually a remote prospect; they had been so soundly beaten they lacked the means or the will to essay another invasion. So he turned on the Mescalero Apaches and the Navajos, nomadic raiders who for generations had plagued the Hispano population, and put all his considerable energies into the work of pacifying or exterminating them, utterly indifferent as to which of these outcomes he achieved. It was principally as cannon fodder for his Indian wars that he wanted his New Mexican troops back from Colorado and the Hispanos of the San Luís Valley enrolled as "minute-men" in the course of Gillespie's "military census" there.[62]

Carleton's nearly four-month-long refusal to terminate Gillespie's census in the face of War Department orders revoking his authority to continue such work had contributed directly to the near-revolt of Hispanos in the San Luís; as late as March 19 a Fort Garland correspondent was writing, "[T]he Greasers [have been complaining a good deal more] about the taxes. There will be a good and gay time here for assessors and collectors. It is said that some of them have sworn to pay their taxes with the rifle."[63]

Fears of a military draft aroused by Gillespie at Carleton's behest, together with growing Hispano resentment against the imposition of Territorial taxes, had merged to create dangerously insurgent conditions. By ordering Eaton to arrest the Espinosas at San Rafael, an order he no longer had the authority to issue, Carleton had hurled Eaton and Lieutenant Hodt into a combustible atmosphere of his own making. It follows, then, that the general's narrow-minded obstinacy was a chief cause of the Espinosa raid. But rather than assume any responsibility for these troubles, he had turned on Eaton, a convenient scapegoat for the Espinosas' depredations.

Gillespie, the second of Eaton's pair of nemeses, was fifty-two years old, Carleton's senior in age if not in rank and a man who had, at an earlier period, far exceeded any recognition Carleton would ever enjoy. When a young lieutenant of marines, Gillespie had played a significant if somewhat mysterious role in the American conquest of California, vaulting in a few months' time from obscurity into prominence, winning both promotion and acclaim and basking briefly in the sun glare of national celebrity, only to tumble afterward, Icarus-like, into disgrace, a slave to demon rum.

His was the classic tragedy of golden youth brought low by fate, bad health, the envy of lesser men (in his view), and, most of all, his own flaws of character. Born in New York City to a prosperous merchant family, joining the Marine Corps as an enlisted man at eighteen, he received his commission as a second lieutenant in 1832 and for the next thirteen years enjoyed a successful and rewarding career on land and sea.[64]

For reasons that remain obscure,[65] late in 1845, after completing a two-and-a-half-year cruise on the frigate USS *Brandywine* as commander of marine guards, he was ordered to report to Secretary of the Navy George Bancroft for special duty and, incredibly, Bancroft sent him on to a meeting with President James Knox Polk, who designated the young officer as a confidential agent to carry messages to the newly appointed American consul in Mexican California, merchant Thomas Oliver Larkin.[66]

The exact nature of these messages, which Gillespie had to commit to memory to reduce the risk of discovery while traveling through Mexican territory, remains a secret to this day. We do know that Polk was determined to capture California for the westward expansion of the United States and that Larkin and army captain John C. Frémont, then exploring in northern California, were to play roles in effecting that capture. Gillespie was to communicate on Polk's behalf with both men.[67]

But Gillespie did far more than carry messages. In cooperation with Frémont and other officers of the American military and despite his youth and delicate health, he helped lead the Bear Flag Revolt, which ousted the Mexicans from both northern and southern California, in the process proving himself valiant, resourceful, and diligent but also imprudent, vainglorious, blindly intolerant of the indigenous culture, and much too fond of strong drink. At Los Angeles his despotic behavior as commander incited a revolt by the native Californians.[68]

Though still technically only a marine lieutenant, Gillespie gained promotion first as a captain of the provisional California Battalion and then as an army major in command of two companies of mounted riflemen.[69] After the arrival of General Stephen Kearny from Santa Fe, Gillespie and his mounted riflemen joined that force and Gillespie was severely wounded by Mexican lancers at the battle of San Pascual. Later he was struck in the hip by a musket ball in an engagement on the San Gabriel River. Despite these heroics, somehow Kearny became convinced that Gillespie's high-handed actions in southern California were suggestive of sedition. However, nothing came of this implication, save it added another shadow to the already ambivalent character of Gillespie's performance in California.[70]

Despite the controversy surrounding some of his actions, Gillespie returned to Washington in 1847 riding on clouds of glory briefly more glowing than those of Frémont, Kearny, or the other major players in the affair, all of whom had fallen out over which of them deserved the greatest credit for adding California to the growing Union. His prospects brighter than ever before, in the summer of 1849[71] Gillespie made an enviable marriage, taking as his bride an accomplished and widely admired young lady, Elizabeth Duane, daughter of William J. Duane, former secretary of the Treasury. The new Mrs. Gillespie was also a great-granddaughter of Benjamin Franklin.[72] Not only had he married well, but through his wife Gillespie now made several important political connections, including Francis Preston Blair,[73] father of Montgomery Blair, Lincoln's secretary of the Treasury, and Francis (Frank) Blair, Jr., a brigadier general in the Union Army. The senior Blair had been a close friend of President Andrew Jackson and editor of the powerful Democratic newspaper the Washington *Globe*.[74]

But by the early 1850s, Gillespie's fortunes were in decline owing to his excessive fondness for drink, which may have been worsened by the constant pain of his Mexican War wounds, two severe lance thrusts through his mouth, another through his lung, and the musket wound in his hip, all of this aggravated by the chronic diarrhea he suffered as a result of contracting dysentery in California. In addition, his facial wounds seem to have severely disfigured him, a possible reason we have no likeness of him.[75]

In 1854, after a series of disappointing duty assignments, Gillespie's luck seemed to change for the better when he was given command of the marine guard aboard USS *Independence*; but on the eve of sailing he was forced to resign from the service when his fellow officers accused him of misappropriating mess funds.[76] At about this same time his marriage to Elizabeth Duane broke up, again, it is thought, because of his habitual drunkenness, though Mrs. Gillespie had recently given birth to a daughter, Ellen. The couple were never divorced and frequently corresponded afterward but never reconciled.[77]

His life in shambles, Gillespie wandered out to California where he worked briefly in a business establishment owned by his brother, tried farming and blacksmithing, and battled but could not conquer his drinking problem. Finally, in 1858, he landed a job as personal secretary to California governor John B. Weller, and when Weller was appointed envoy extraordinaire and minister plenipotentiary to Mexico in 1860, Gillespie went with him as secretary of legation.[78]

Almost immediately, however, newly elected president Abraham Lincoln replaced Weller with Kentucky congressman and orator Thomas Corwin,[79] and Gillespie, now unemployed, apparently remained in Mexico City until, in the spring of 1862, he received "from the President, through the Secretary of War, the appointment of Additional Aide-de-Camp upon the staff of Maj. Genl. H.W. Halleck with the rank of Major in the US Army, with orders to report to Brig. Genl. Canby at Santa Fe, New Mexico."[80] This appointment had been made at the instigation of Francis Blair, the highly placed friend of Gillespie and his wife from Washington days.[81]

Eager to reclaim his good name, Gillespie hastened to Washington for an interview with Secretary of War Edwin M. Stanton and "immediately departed for New Mexico."[82] On his way west he attempted to pay a courtesy call on Halleck, the officer to whose staff he was now attached, but the general, who was exercising a field command in the Department of Mississippi at this time,[83] refused to see him, later writing that Gillespie's appointment had been made without his knowledge or recommendation, adding that the major's "previous conduct had been so disgraceful that I refused, when he reported to me, to recognize him as a member of my staff."[84] Halleck was a Californian, had served there during the Mexican War, and had known the major during his days of shame in the late 1850s. Undaunted by this rebuff, Gillespie hurried on toward New Mexico Territory.

Arriving at Fort Union, he reported to General Canby as his orders required; but Canby, who was himself preparing to proceed east to take up a new command, decided the major's orders attached him not to Canby personally but to the new commander of the Department of New Mexico and sent him on to Santa Fe, where the major met a "civil but very cold"[85] reception by General Carleton. Carleton, like Halleck, probably knew Gillespie by reputation if not by name. At any rate, when Gillespie made his introduction Carleton replied with a distinct lack of enthusiasm, "Ah, yes. I've heard of you." The general protested he had not been forewarned of Gillespie's appointment to his staff and that he had no opening for an officer of Gillespie's rank; but then, with evident reluctance, agreed to accept him.[86]

Things went wrong between the two very quickly. Not only was their first meeting an awkward one but that same night, at a *fandango*,[87] something happened. There are two versions and we will never know which is accurate or whether the truth is a mixture of both. Either Gillespie unwisely twitted General Carleton for dancing with a female the major considered to be a prostitute or Gillespie himself, sodden with drink, made a spectacle of himself by trifling with a woman of easy virtue in public. Whatever the facts, from then on Carleton loathed his new staff officer.[88]

On October 7 Carleton gave Gillespie an assignment that would serve a number of his desired ends—especially ridding himself of the unwanted staff officer. He needed to know how many armed men of military age resided in the remote areas of northern New Mexico and the San Luís Valley in case he had to call up reinforcements for his Indian wars or to resist another Texan invasion. Another motive was an economic one, the gathering of data about population, livestock, productivity of the soil, industries, types of crops grown, natural resources—information that Manifest Destiny–era Americans always wanted as they sharpened their eyes on new lands suitable for Anglo settlement and "improvement."[89]

From Carleton's point of view, the hated Gillespie was the ideal choice to perform the census. He spoke Spanish and was presumably well acquainted with the culture.[90] The task would remove him from headquarters for an indefinite period, and though Carleton must have hoped the census would be completed and prove useful to him, he may have also seen it as a convenient pretext for testing Gillespie with a duty so menial for an officer of his rank that the major would become disillusioned and seek a transfer.

But what Carleton could not know was that even in his fallen state, Archibald Gillespie still owned a will of iron and the stubbornness of a bulldog. Give him a degrading task and he would do the opposite of what was expected. He would not resign or risk a court-martial by refusing the duty. He would not shun or shirk; he would not complain the work was beneath him. Instead, he would perform it with scrupulous excellence. He would do the work so well that no one, not even his fiercest critic, could find in it the slightest flaw or omission.

Based at Fort Garland, where first Major Mayer and then Captain Eaton commanded, Gillespie traveled long distances over hard country as winter came on, and suffered terrible hardships[91] but meticulously and single-mindedly carried on his census, fueling himself all the while with alcohol. He must have been a highly functioning alcoholic,[92] for even as he drank copious amounts of liquor he was able to conduct his interviews, draw up sheaves of census abstracts, and send them back to Santa Fe complete with highly detailed cover letters.

If he was aware that his work was contributing to serious unrest among the Hispanos of the San Luís, he seemed at first to misinterpret the reaction as the simple disinclination on the part of an alien population to cooperate with an occupier, though after the Espinosa episode he did come to see it differently and in a much more ominous light. In a letter to headquarters written only four days after the fight at San Rafael, he declared "a feeling of disloyalty exists to a very great extent in this territory, which is constantly shown by an indisposition to pay proper respect to US officers, and a total disregard of the Civil Authorities of the Territory [and] is a spirit of lawless recklessness which requires the strong arm of the military power to punish and destroy without delay."

It is clear he saw no connection between his own inflammatory actions and the growing unrest among the Hispanos of the San Luís. Anglo intrusions were not the problem; instead, he asserted, the Conejos Valley was filled with "renegade Peons from New Mexico . . . disaffected, disloyal wretches, who are ever more ready to kill and rob an inoffensive, unarmed white, than the worst Indians of the most hostile tribes."[93] This indictment was a far cry indeed from the mild assessment he had made near the beginning of his census that "the people have been found to be very well disposed and are desirous to be enrolled; they appear to be gratified that the Commanding General has thought them worthy of protection."[94]

Now that blood had been shed in San Rafael, Gillespie had no need to toady to Carleton and could give free rein to his prejudice against Hispanos, which was always straining for release. "It is disagreeable to report so very unfavorably respecting this small population," he went on in his January letter, "but a true one, confirmed in opinion and belief more and more . . . in all and every part of the valley, and proved to be correct by occurrences which have since taken place in open deadly resistance to officers of the United States and the Civil Authorities of Colorado Territory."[95]

Yet despite the violence in San Rafael that his census had helped to provoke, Gillespie would persist in it for another month and Carleton would make no move to suspend it. No more than Gillespie did Carleton see a link between the intrusive census and the rising resentment of the people being counted. One might think the general wished the project completed because he set a high value on the information being collected. Apart from the unrest it caused, the census information might have proved quite useful,[96] but Carleton never seems to have paid it much heed or even to have acknowledged the major's diligent labors; nor did he bother to respond on the frequent occasions when the major asked him by mail for clarifications or instructions.

Between them, Carleton and Gillespie, mismatched and distrustful conspirators, each bearing grudges of his own, had done their best, with the help of Lieutenant Lewis, to discredit Wayne Eaton for the Espinosa affair that they had helped incite. But Eaton was not the kind of man to take such behindhand punishment without a fight. His first action on the same day he

Colonel John M. Chivington, commander of the Military District of Colorado. (Photo courtesy of History Colorado, scan no. 10047783)

learned of his dismissal from command of Fort Garland was to scribble a blistering rebuttal to Colonel Chivington:

> During my absence on duty at Conejos settling debts contracted by me while in pursuit of the Conejos murderers . . . Captain Davidson arrived here and assumed command. Since I returned, I have learned that reports unfavorable to me have been made to you unofficially from this Post [referring] to matters here. This is both unfair and unjust[,] much more so when you, as commander of the [District] let such [illegible] reports affect any person officially.
>
> If you considered those reports true, it is in your power to investigate them. The worst criminal is allowed to defend himself—and officers in the service can be [maligned] by designing and unscrupulous scoundrels that are afraid to act openly—When they must obtain any other clap in life should be allowed a hearing. I must say I am disappointed in the justice of the military. I understand that one of the reports is that I am continually drunk. This charge upon its face shows to all men its falsity. . . . I scarcely taste liquor much less get drunk.

Eaton then referred to Carleton's dissatisfaction with his and Lieutenant Hodt's handling of the Espinosa arrests and the general's express order that Eaton, in person, take the field to pursue, capture, or kill the fugitives. Concerning his February 16 altercation with Lewis, Eaton wrote:

> I prepared to scout [when] Lt. Lewis being then in command of the Post threw every obstacle in the way of getting what was requisite for the scout that I was obliged again to assume command in order to get what was needed and get the detachment away that evening. I did. When I completed my arrangements I again resigned the command. No person was drunk.

> Malicious interference was the cause of my assuming command & after having once resigned it—This was a whining sniveling coward that resorts to means that are dishonorable to obtain his ends. If there were any acts of mine that were wrong he [did] not report officially through propper [*sic*] channels. But no. If he done that, official note must be taken of it and he would be exposed—I consider the order for Captain Davidson to take command of the Post illegal and a direct insult to me.
>
> While I remain at the Post and respectfully ask that the matter may be investigated, which [illegible] should have been made and reported upon before I was relieved of Command & I am entitled to, allowing the [illegible] to be legal. I respectfully refer the Cmd of Dist to 62 Art. Of War and Par > Revised regulations in relation to the duty I was on when Captain Davidson [illegible] when I was reported absent without leave without cause[;] I was to report by mail.[97]

Eaton subsequently preferred charges against Lewis, accusing him of violating the Articles of War by falsely reporting him absent without leave and of being guilty of conduct unbecoming an officer and a gentleman, citing several specific violations.[98] Predictably, Lewis filed countercharges[99] but his action seems to have gone nowhere. A court-martial at Fort Garland on May 30 found Lewis guilty of the charge of falsely reporting Eaton and his men absent without leave and guilty of "conduct unbecoming" except for two of the minor specifications. The court recommended that Lewis be cashiered from the service and the findings were submitted up the chain of command for review.[100]

After dealing with Lewis, Eaton made his way down to Santa Fe and in late June seems to have personally confronted Carleton in the next stage of his effort to rehabilitate himself. While there he wrote two letters to the general on June 22, the first concerning the charge of arbitrary conduct toward Lieutenant Lewis on January 16 and the second dealing with the incident on New Year's Eve. Both were more restrained in tone and more closely reasoned than his intemperate message to Chivington of April 19 but each still smarted with righteous indignation.

In the first, Eaton explained how Lewis's conduct had provoked his "perhaps rather hasty" act and manfully added, "I respectfully submit the foregoing statement to the Genl Cmd Dptmt of New Mexico as a true version of the arbitrary conduct towards Lt. Lewis by me, which I believe to be the only act of mine since I have been in the service that can in any manner be viewed in that light."[101] He supported this assertion with statements from officers and citizens residing at and near Fort Garland approving his overall conduct.

In the second, more heated letter Eaton began with the startling observation that "there is nothing retained in your office from Major A. H. Gillespie except his report, and remarks, upon the investigation made by him in relation to the occurrences of New Years Eve." In other words, somehow Gillespie's full report or reports that had been used to dismiss Eaton for several specific delinquencies had disappeared from the files of the Department of New Mexico, with the single exception of the one relating to the New Year's Eve incident in which, Eaton wrote, "All the conclusions drawn by [Gillespie] . . . show upon their face a malicious and studied intent to throw all the blame of the affair . . . upon me and make Lt. Lewis to be a model of Military discipline and attention to duty."

He refuted Gillespie's account of that incident point by point and concluded, "As to my being a suitable person to command a company of troops, let the Condition of my old Company, and officers and citizens that are not continually under the influence of liquor, and that are unprejudiced, and that have had ample opportunity to form an opinion, decide. I do not fear the decision of honest men."[102]

By this time Gillespie had been dismissed from the service much as Eaton had, without an inquiry or hearing of any kind, effective June 4[103] in accordance with the special authority granted Carleton by the adjutant general. By the time of Eaton's June 22 letter, Carleton would have been uncomfortably aware that Gillespie's military career had come to a messy end only after a public airing that did not reflect well on his own behavior,[104] and that Lieutenant Lewis, chief source of most of the allegations against Eaton, had been court-martialed, cashiered, and also discredited. It is no surprise that most of the paperwork Gillespie had submitted, and that Carleton had used to bring Eaton down, had vanished, probably by Carleton's order.

Eaton's robust defense began to turn the tide in his favor. On June 27, at Eaton's request, Colonel Chivington reversed his previous course and offered a written statement of support saying he "saw nothing wrong that Capt. Eaton had done but on the contrary found that he had administered the affairs of [Fort Garland] much more satisfactorily than his predecessor had done."[105] By this time Carleton had acquiesced in his loss of command over southern Colorado, emboldening Chivington to speak up on Eaton's behalf without risking further jurisdictional interference from Santa Fe.

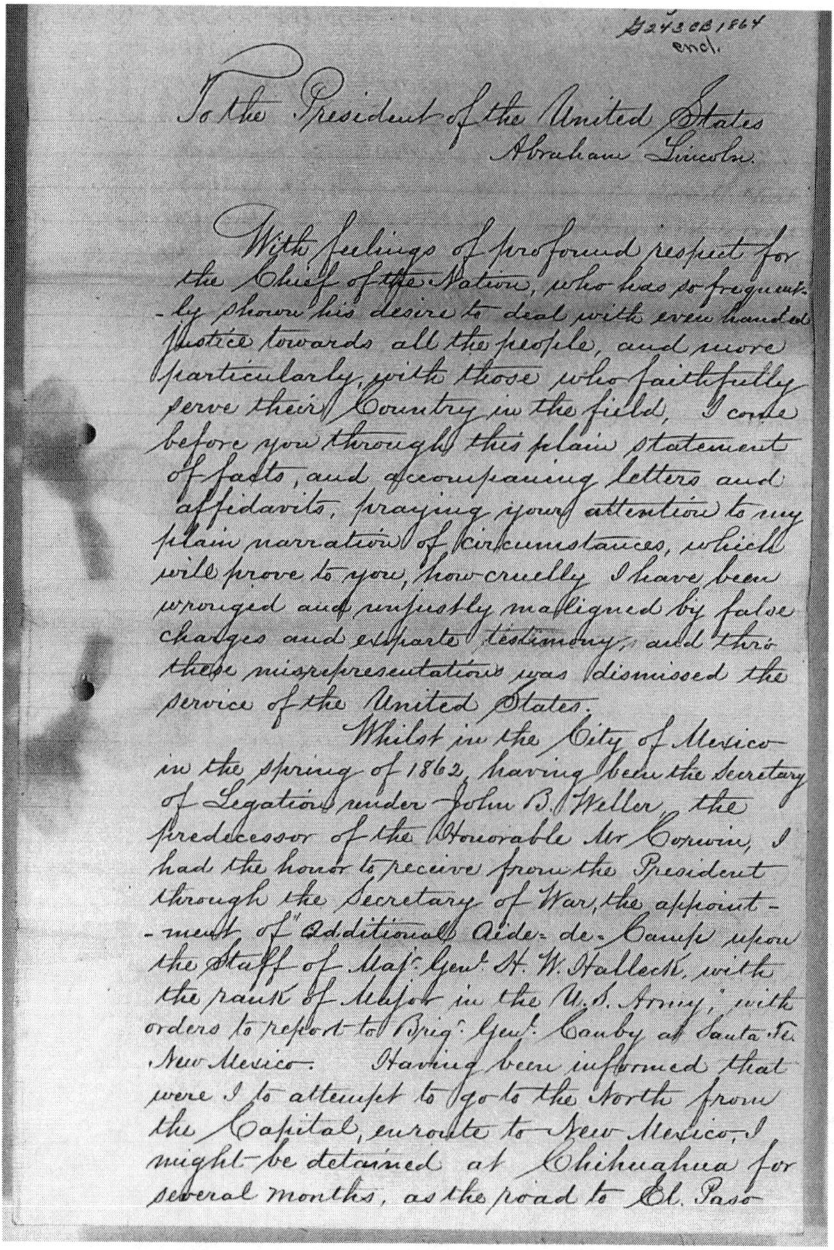

G243 CB 1864
encl.

To the President of the United States
Abraham Lincoln.

With feelings of profound respect for the Chief of the Nation, who has so frequently shown his desire to deal with even handed justice towards all the people, and more particularly with those who faithfully serve their Country in the field, I come before you through this plain statement of facts, and accompanying letters and affidavits, praying your attention to my plain narration of circumstances, which will prove to you, how cruelly I have been wronged and unjustly maligned by false charges and exparte testimony, and thro' these misrepresentations was dismissed the service of the United States.

Whilst in the City of Mexico in the spring of 1862, having been the Secretary of Legation under John B. Weller, the predecessor of the Honorable Mr Corwin, I had the honor to receive from the President through the Secretary of War, the appointment of "Additional Aide-de-Camp upon the Staff of Majr. Genl. H. W. Halleck, with the rank of Major in the U.S. Army," with orders to report to Brig. Genl. Canby at Santa Fe New Mexico. Having been informed that were I to attempt to go to the North from the Capital, en route to New Mexico, I might be detained at Chihuahua for several months, as the road to El Paso

First page of Major Archibald H. Gillespie's memorial to President Abraham Lincoln protesting his discharge from the United States Army. (Author photo, Letters Received by the Commission Branch, Adjutant General's Office, US Army, 1863–1870, M-1064, Roll 91, RG 94, Entry 518, courtesy of National Archives and Records Administration)

Carleton, too, began to relent, for when Eaton traveled to New York to seek a revocation of his dismissal from his former commander, Brigadier General Canby, it was, he wrote, at Carleton's recommendation.[106] In a letter to Canby, Eaton asked for a court-martial or other hearing to clear his name and insisted he had done nothing to deserve "the dishonorable dismissal that I have received which not only disgraces [me but also] my family after me." Noting that Gillespie had been dismissed and Lewis court-martialed, Eaton contended, "the character of the persons making the report [against me] should have some weight in the matter." He went on:

> I am dismissed, as the order States, for "neglect of duty," "Disregard and contempt of the Army regulations," and "conduct unbecoming an officer and a gentleman." What the Specifications are to sustain the above I am entirely ignorant Except what I learn from Genl Carleton's recollection of the report, no copy having been retained in the AAA [Acting Assistant Adjutant] General's Office at Santa Fe.[107]

Canby obliged Eaton by endorsing a letter from Judge John S. Watts, lately New Mexico's delegate to Congress and a friend of Eaton's, asking President Lincoln and Secretary of War Stanton to revoke the dismissal. In a final irony Carleton, too, endorsed the recommendation. In the face of these high-powered appeals, Lincoln and Stanton revoked the dismissal. But reinstatement to his former rank proved impossible because Eaton's old vacancy in the volunteer service of New Mexico had already been filled. In a letter of September 29 to a subdued Carleton, Eaton, back in Santa Fe, coolly suggested he be promoted major in place of a retiring officer of that rank. It wasn't long before Carleton and the governor of New Mexico obliged him.[108]

In fact, according to a statement Eaton made near the end of his long life, in a quirk of fortune he became such a favorite of Carleton's that at war's end the general offered him Colonel Kit Carson's rank and command as an inducement to keep him in the army.[109] On November 23, 1863, Eaton was commissioned a major and by January 31, 1864, was in command of Fort Wingate, where he served brilliantly, if reluctantly because of his sympathy to the Indians' plight, in Carleton's campaigns against the Navajo. By February 1865, again moved up in grade, he was a lieutenant colonel, still commanding at Wingate.[110]

Gillespie, despite Herculean efforts to regain his rank and reputation, returned to California a defeated man and continued his dissipated ways. Though he had briefly reunited with his wife while in Washington in the spring of 1864, their separation from then on became permanent and in her memoirs Mrs. Gillespie would refer to her daughter Ellen as "for many years an orphan."[111] Gillespie faded from the light of history and died in obscurity on August 14, 1874, a forgotten figure.[112] The ultimate fate of Lieutenant Lewis is not known.

General Carleton was removed as commander of the Department of New Mexico by order of the secretary of war on September 19, 1866,[113] principally because of the disastrous failure of his experiment confining the defeated Navajo and Mescalero Indians to the Bosque Redondo Reservation in southeastern New Mexico where hundreds had died of starvation and disease. A contributing cause was his despotic rule over the Territory, which one newspaper, hailing his removal, said had gained him "the detestation and contempt of almost the entire population."[114] He died in San Antonio, Texas, on January 7, 1873.[115]

On April 10, 1865, with the Civil War drawing near its close, Ethan Wayne Eaton's request to resign from the service was granted.[116] He returned to Galisteo, operated one of the great ranches of New Mexico, and raised his large family. In 1880 he relocated to Socorro to engage in mining and smelting. Lawlessness broke out there and when the constituted officers proved unwilling or unable to act, Eaton formed and led a vigilance committee that enforced lynch law until peace was restored.[117] He later became deputy sheriff of Socorro County and then a deputy US marshal.[118]

When one of the Socorro outlaws threatened his life, Eaton marched into a saloon where the fellow waited and braced him in a stand-up, Wild West–style gunfight. The outlaw beat the nearly sixty-year-old Eaton to the draw and with his first bullet broke Eaton's right arm in two places. But Eaton shifted his own weapon to his left hand and coolly shot the man dead.

In 1882, during a raid by hostile Indians, Eaton took command of a volunteer unit called the Socorro Rangers, helping quell that incident. In 1889 he was named to the Board of Trustees of the New Mexico School of Mines (now the New Mexico Institute of Mining and Technology).[119] He passed away in 1916[120] at the age of eighty-nine, "as a result of injuries sustained by being drawn into a gasoline engine," an implausible end to a life of adventure and accomplishment but one consistent with what seems to have been his active and inquiring nature.

But a mystery remains. In the file of Eaton's personal papers at the Fray Angélico Chávez History Library of the New Mexico History Museum at Santa Fe the following letter can be found:

Sir:

Not knowing whether I will ever rise off my sick bed, I hope whatever I have done by word or deed, you will except [*sic*] my humble apology, and if the Almighty allows me to return to my duty once more, I hope it will be as brothers.

I am, Captain
With much Respect

John Lewis
N.M. Vols[121]

The letter is addressed to "Captain E. W. Eaton, Co. 'D,' 1st N.M. Vols., Comm'g Post," and seems to be dated February 12, 1867, at Fort Garland. It appears to be genuine; the handwriting strongly resembles that of Lewis's other correspondence. But by 1867 Eaton had been out of the army for almost two years and Fort Garland was commanded by Lieutenant Colonel Kit Carson. Though the "7" in "1867" is somewhat scrawled and could conceivably be interpreted as a "2," the year 1862 doesn't fit either, because both Eaton and Lewis were in New Mexico then.

A final possibility is that Lewis misdated the letter and meant to write "February 12, 1863." But this is hardly credible; that would place the letter amid the whitest heat of their dispute, only days before they came to blows—and perhaps close to shooting—in their argument over the teamster's horse.

When did Lewis write? Why? Did he recover from the sickness he feared would be his last? What eventually happened to him?

We don't know. What we do know is that Eaton kept the letter to the end of his long life. It had significance for him. Perhaps, whenever it was written and whenever it was received and read, for him it had healed many an old wound.

In a way it was fortuitous for Wayne Eaton that the imbroglio over his dismissal diverted everyone's attention away from the initial cause of General Carleton's ire: the bungled arrest of the Espinosas. For while the officers of the army wrangled among themselves through the spring of 1863, Felipe and Vivián Espinosa left the San Juans and began murdering their way across the Pike's Peak country and into South Park. It was not until May 21, in reporting the death of Vivián Espinosa at the hands of John McCannon's possemen, that the *Weekly Commonwealth* linked the string of previously mysterious killings to the Espinosas of San Rafael.[122]

By then few if any officers in the army—with the possible exceptions of Lieutenants Shoup, Wilson, and Oster of the First Colorado Cavalry, and perhaps John M. Chivington—might have remembered that the Espinosas had broken loose on Eaton's watch, or that Carleton's policy of conducting a military census in a volatile region he no longer rightfully commanded may have helped incite their murder spree.

At least in the army hierarchy, pursuing the rivalries of rank and reputation had seemed more important than capturing or killing the worst serial murderers in the history of the American West.

NOTES

1. Officer's Casualty Sheet, Captain E. Wayne Eaton, Compiled Service Record, Adjutant General's Office, Record Group 94, National Archives, Washington, DC.

2. E. W. Eaton to Brigadier General E.R.S. Canby, July 26, 1863; E. W. Eaton Papers; Eaton, Compiled Service Record.

3. Ibid.; E. W. Eaton to Lieutenant L. G. Murphy, March 9, 1864; Jerry D. Thompson, *New Mexico Territory During the Civil War: Wallen and Davis Inspection Reports, 1862–1863* (Santa Fe: University of New Mexico Press, 2008), 204, note 4.

4. E. W. Eaton to Brigadier General E.R.S. Canby, July 26, 1863.

5. *Rocky Mountain News Weekly*, August 21, 1862. Mayer had arrived at Garland on July 17 but did not assume command until the 20th; Letter Book, Fort Garland, 164, Date of July 27, 1862.

6. Ibid., 168, Date of July 31, 1862.

7. Ibid., 175, Date of August 4, 1862.

8. Ibid., 166, Date of July 27, 1862.

9. Ibid., 178, Date of August 11, 1862. Mayer was concerned about disaffection among the Hispanos of the San Luís Valley. See Chapter 7.

10. E. W. Eaton to Captain [Illegible] Chaplin, Assistant Adjutant General, Department of New Mexico, August 18, 1862; Letters Received, Department of New Mexico, Record Group 393, Rolls 16, 18, 19, Adjutant General's Office, National Archives, Washington, DC.

11. E. W. Eaton to Captain B. C. Cutler, November 30, 1862; Letters Received, Department of New Mexico.

12. See Chapter 3; E. W. Eaton to Major A. H. Mayer, September 5, 1863; Letters Received, Department of New Mexico.

13. Letter Book, Fort Garland, 184, date in September unclear. In ibid., 184, date of September 29, 1862, Major Mayer forwarded to headquarters a report of Lieutenant Hodt "detailed on Spy Service by . . . Capt. Eaton," which "fully satisfies me that the marauding bands who have been infesting this section, have sought another locality."

14. See Chapter 7. War Department General Order No. 155 in the fall of 1862 reorganized the US Army's military departments and districts; under its provisions, Colorado Territory was transferred out of Carleton's Department of New Mexico and into the Department of Missouri, commanded by Major General Samuel Curtis, which encompassed Chivington's Eleventh Military District of Colorado. General Curtis implemented this change from his St. Louis headquarters by means of General Order No. 11 on November 2, 1862; US Army Adjutant General's Office and US War Department, *War of the Rebellion: A Compilation of the Official Records of the Union and Confederate Armies*, Series I, Vol. 13, Serial No. 19 (Wilmington, NC: Broadfoot Publishing Company), CD-ROM. Chivington in turn published General Order No. 1 on November 13, 1862, assuming command of the District of Colorado, including Fort Garland, a copy of which, along with a copy of G.O. 11, was published in the *Rocky Mountain News Weekly* of November 20, 1862. Carleton probably took the position that Fort Garland had not been included in this transfer, since the post, under a previous organizational scheme, had belonged to the Department of Kansas and then to the Department of New Mexico; John H. Eicher and David J. Eicher, *Civil War High Commands* (Stanford, CA: Stanford University Press, 2001), 836. Fort Garland had been transferred to the Department of New Mexico from Kansas as recently as February 14, 1862; *Official Records*, Series I, Vol. 9, Serial No. 9. But despite all this, Carleton had not a leg to stand on in disregarding his loss of command over Fort Garland. Although telegraphic communication between Washington and Santa Fe was a good deal slower than between Washington and Denver (see Keleher, *Turmoil in New Mexico*, 386), Carleton should have been aware of the change at least by early December 1862, and probably well before then, and should have conformed to it. See also Chivington to Carleton, December 30, 1862; Chivington to Carleton, January 30, 1863; second letter, Chivington to Carleton, January 30, 1863; Letters Received, Department of New Mexico. The jurisdictional dispute was also the subject of editorial comment in the *Rocky Mountain News Weekly* of February 12 and March 19, 1863. Originally an editorialist had complained that the conflict over command of the San Luís Valley was the fault of Eaton and his predecessor, Major Mayer, who were supposedly reluctant for their troops to come under the control of Colorado. It is true that Mayer refused to acknowledge the transfer (see Letter Book, Fort Garland, 209, date of November 23, 1862). However, it is clear from Eaton's correspondence (see E. W. Eaton to Captain B. C. Cutler, January 10, 1863; Letters Received, Department of New Mexico) and from a defense of his conduct written to the *News Weekly* by a Fort Garland correspondent, that Eaton had conscientiously tried to do his proper duty while caught in the vise of conflicting orders from competing commanders. A particularly sore spot

was Carleton's standing order that no official person be allowed to travel in the San Luís without a pass, a requirement he had no authority to impose and that Lafayette Head, agent for the Utes, found ridiculous when applied to him in his frequent travels to and from Denver and other places as a public officer. Eaton had briefly detained Head for traveling without a pass and then released him.

15. Autobiographical sketch in Chester D. Potter, edited by Paige W. Christiansen, "Reminiscences of the Socorro Vigilantes," *New Mexico Historical Review*, Vol. XL, No. 1 (January 1965): 46–47.

16. Christina Singleton Mednick, *San Cristóbal: Voices and Vision of the Galisteo Basin* (Santa Fe: Museum of New Mexico, 1996), 157.

17. Ralph Emerson Twitchell, *The Spanish Archives of New Mexico*, Vol. 1 (Cedar Rapids, IA: The Torch Press, 1914), 96.

18. Mednick, *San Cristóbal*, 157.

19. Carleton's endorsement is quoted by Eaton in his letter of April 19, 1863, to Assistant Adjutant General, District of Colorado; Letters Received, Department of New Mexico.

20. Hodt seems to have been accident-prone. Not only did he accidentally shoot himself in the head after throwing away his supposedly empty revolver at San Rafael, but he was killed on May 16, 1866, "by the accidental discharge of his own pistol"; Keleher, *Turmoil in New Mexico*, 487, note 32.

21. Proceedings of a General Court Martial Convened at Fort Garland C.T. on the 15th Day of May 1863; First Lieutenant John Lewis, Compiled Service Record, Adjutant General's Office; Charges and Specifications; Court Martial Transcript, Record Group 94, National Archives, Washington, DC, 17ff; Testimony of Lieutenant Nicholas Hodt to the effect that Lewis told him in December 1862 or January 1863 that he would not blame men for deserting from the Fort Garland garrison because they were "ill treated" and "lived in a meager manner" under Eaton's command.

22. This account of the incident of February 16 is in E. W. Eaton to Brigadier General James H. Carleton, June 22, 1863; E. W. Eaton Papers.

23. Letter Book, Fort Garland, 199, Date of October 27, 1862; Gillespie did not report his arrival at the post until two days later; Gillespie to Captain B. C. Cutler (Carleton's assistant adjutant general), October 29, 1863; Letters Received, Department of New Mexico.

24. Letter Book, Fort Garland, 201, Date of November 27, 1862. Mayer wrote, "I would respectfully state Major A. H. Gillespie is now over in (Conejos). I have advised him on the subject requesting him to use every exertion to have the General Commanding's Order complied with."

25. Second Letter of E. W. Eaton to Carleton, June 22, 1863; E. W. Eaton Papers; E. W. Eaton to Colonel John M. Chivington, April 19, 1863, Letters Received, Department of New Mexico.

26. First Letter of E. W. Eaton to Carleton, June 22, 1863; E. W. Eaton Papers.

27. Dorrance, "Archibald H. Gillespie in the Department of New Mexico," 1987, unpublished thesis, Special Collections, University of Arizona Library, Tucson. 6, 18, 25.

28. A. H. Gillespie to Cutler, December 3, 1862; Letters Received, Department of New Mexico (underlining in original).

29. E. W. Eaton to Captain [illegible] Chaplin, August 18, 1862. Historian Darlis A. Miller wrote a penetrating and insightful analysis of New Mexican and American attitudes during this period; see Darlis E. Miller, "Hispanos and the Civil War in New Mexico: A Reconsideration," *New Mexico Historical Review*, Vol. 54. No. 2 (1979): 105–123.

30. A. H. Gillespie to Captain B. C. Cutler, January 31, 1863; Letters Received, Department of New Mexico.

31. Ibid.

32. "Remarks" appended to Gillespie's letter of January 31, 1863, to Captain B. C. Cutler; Letters Received, Department of New Mexico.

33. One historian, in an essay on Hispanic women in the military, seems to draw on Gillespie's ambiguous comment in writing that "one prominent New Mexican officer kept a mistress at Fort Garland during the Civil War, next to quarters inhabited by his wife. When he left the post for a trip to Conejos, he posted a sentinel at night outside his mistress's quarters"; Darlis E. Miller, "Foragers, Army Women, Prostitutes," in Joan M. Jensen and Darlis A. Miller, *New Mexican Women: Intercultural Perspectives* (Santa Fe: University of New Mexico Press, 1986), 161. Anyone visiting the commandant's quarters at Fort Garland, where all the inside doors open off a single corridor, would recognize the implausibility of such an arrangement.

34. "Remarks" appended to Gillespie's letter of January 31, 1863, to Captain B. C. Cutler; Letters Received, Department of New Mexico.

35. E. W. Eaton to Major Archibald H. Gillespie, February 3, 1863, E. W. Eaton Papers; E. W. Eaton to Captain B. C. Cutler, February 8, 1863, Letters Received, Department of New Mexico.

36. A. H. Gillespie to Cutler, January 19, 1863; A. H. Gillespie to Eaton, February 2, 1863; Eaton to Gillespie, February 2, 1863; Gillespie to Eaton, February 3, 1863; Gillespie to Cutler, February 7, 1863; Eaton to Cutler, February 8, 1863; Letters Received, Department of New Mexico; Eaton to Gillespie, February 3, 1863, E. W. Eaton Papers. In an endorsement on Gillespie's February 7 letter to Cutler, Carleton curtly noted, "File this. By all means let this quarrel subside by having no attention paid to this correspondence. [signed] C. Feb. 16 63."

37. A. H. Gillespie to Cutler, February 14, 1863, Letters Received, Department of New Mexico.

38. E. W. Eaton to Brigadier General E.R.S. Canby, July 26, 1863, E. W. Eaton Papers.

39. J. H. Carleton to Chivington, February 28, 1863, E. W. Eaton Papers.

40. Ibid.

41. Letter of March 3, 1863, from Assistant Adjutant General Thomas M. Vincent, War Department, Washington, DC, to Carleton, in reply to an inquiry from Carleton dated January 29, 1863, definitively informing him Fort Garland belonged not to the Department of New Mexico but to that of Missouri; Letters Received, Department of New Mexico.

42. *Rocky Mountain News Weekly*, December 18, 1862; January 8, 1863; January 15, 1863.

43. Keleher, *Turmoil in New Mexico*, 278–279; Hampton Sides, *Blood and Thunder: The Epic Story of Kit Carson and the Conquest of the American West* (New York: Anchor Books, 2007), 325–482.

44. J. H. Carleton to Chivington, February 28, 1863, E. W. Eaton Papers.

45. *Rocky Mountain News Weekly*, March 26, 1863.

46. E. W. Eaton to Assistant Adjutant General, Headquarters, District of Colorado, April 14, 1863, E. W. Eaton Papers; see Chapter 8.

47. Ibid.

48. E. W. Eaton to Assistant Adjutant General, District of Colorado, April 19, 1863, Letters Received, Department of New Mexico.

49. Proceedings of a General Court Martial Convened at Fort Garland C.T. on the 15th Day of May 1863; First Lieutenant John Lewis, Compiled Service Record, Adjutant General's Office; E. W. Eaton to Assistant Adjutant General, District of Colorado, April 19, 1863; E. W. Eaton to Carleton, June 22, 1863, and E. W. Eaton to Brigadier General E.R.S. Canby, July 26, 1863, E. W. Eaton Letters; Thompson, *New Mexico Territory During the Civil War*, 204–205, 209, 211. Lewis seems also to have been involved in misappropriating quartermaster stores and other misdeeds.

50. This order has not been found but its receipt is verified by a letter Eaton wrote on that date to Chivington. See note 48 above.

51. Eaton's Compiled Service Record at the National Archives does not contain a copy of the order, only a Casualty Sheet showing him dishonorably discharged.

52. Major A. H. Gillespie to President of the United States, April 15, 1863; Letters Received by the Commission Branch, Adjutant General's Office, US Army, 1863–1870, M-1064, Roll 91, RG 94, Entry 518, pertaining to Major Archibald H. Gillespie, Additional Aide de Camp to Major General Henry W. Halleck, National Archives, Washington, DC; Dorrance, "Archibald H. Gillespie in the Department of New Mexico," 38–47. Dorrance is to be congratulated for being the first researcher to write that the Gillespie of Mexican War fame was the same officer who served in New Mexico during the Civil War. The author made this connection independently and became aware of Dorrance's work subsequent to his own discovery.

53. J. H. Carleton to Brigadier General Lorenzo Thomas, Adjutant General, US Army, March 17, 1863; Letters Received by the Commission Branch.

54. Dorrance, "Archibald Gillespie in New Mexico," 36; Letters Received by the Commission Branch.

55. Ray C. Colton, *The Civil War in the Western Territories: Arizona, Colorado, New Mexico and Utah* (Norman: University of Oklahoma Press, 1959), 49–80; Donald S. Frazier, *Blood & Treasure: Confederate Empire in the Southwest* (College Station: Texas A&M University Press, 1995), 157–230. Coloradans held the view that the Union army commanded by Colonel E.R.S. Canby during the Texan invasion, made up largely of New Mexican volunteers, was being badly beaten in the campaign until the First Colorado Cavalry under the command of Colonel John P. Slough made an epic march through winter weather from Fort Lyon, Colorado, and brought about the defeat of the Texans at Glorieta Pass. Chivington succeeded Slough in command of the regiment. He was widely perceived as the hero of the engagement by gaining the Confederate rear and destroying the Rebels' baggage train, forcing them to retreat.

56. Patricia L. Faust, *Historical Times Illustrated Encyclopedia of the Civil War* (New York: Harper & Row, 1986), 113; Keleher, *Turmoil in New Mexico*, note 2, 481–482.

57. *Santa Fe Gazette*, August 13, quoted in Keleher, *Turmoil in New Mexico*, 280.

58. Keleher, *Turmoil in New Mexico*, 279.

59. Gillespie, either directly or through an intermediary, convinced Carleton that Eaton was "continually drunk"; E. W. Eaton to Assistant Adjutant General; "Comdg Gen. Dist. Col," April 19, 1863; Letters Received, Department of New Mexico.

60. Sides, *Blood and Thunder*, 381.

61. Keleher, *Turmoil in New Mexico*, 213–259.

62. Special Order No. 180, Headquarters, Department of New Mexico, addressed to Maj. A. H. Gillespie, Additional Aide-de-Camp, Etc., October 7, 1862, included in Gillespie's memorial to President Lincoln; Letters Received by the Commission Branch. The order instructed Gillespie that all males he enrolls are to be "known and considered 'Minute-Men' liable to be called up for the defense of New Mexico Territory at a moment's notice" (underline in original). This provision played straight into the fears of the Hispanos of the San Luís Valley that they were to be drafted into the American military, at a time when they were already uneasy about taxation and the enactment of new Anglo laws.

63. *Rocky Mountain News Weekly*, March 19, 1863.

64. Dorrance, "Archibald Gillespie in the Department of New Mexico," 2–3; Werner H. Marti, *Messenger of Destiny: The California Adventures, 1846–1847 of Archibald H. Gillespie, U.S. Marine Corps* (San Francisco, CA: John Howell Books, 1960), 6–7.

65. Marti, *Messenger of Destiny*, 7, believes Gillespie was chosen in part because of his record for "carrying out his duties faithfully and well" and possibly also owing to the influence of his guardian, Joseph Reckless, a prominent New Jersey politician who had the ear of President Polk.

66. Dorrance, "Archibald H. Gillespie in the Department of New Mexico," 4.

67. The full incredible story of Gillespie's involvement in the Bear Flag Revolt and the conquest of California cannot be recited here. Gillespie's own quite thorough and

well-written account is in his forty-four-page Memorial to President Lincoln, April 15, 1864, Letters Received by the Commission Branch; Marti, *Messenger of Destiny*, 3–107, also covers this period in detail; and Dorrance, "Archibald Gillespie in the Department of New Mexico," 4–7, offers a brief summary. Sides, *Blood and Thunder*, 89–91, 97, 110, 122, 184–186, 188, 196, also provides good coverage of this period in Gillespie's life.

68. Marcus Benjamin, *John Bidwell, Pioneer: A Sketch of his Career* (Washington, DC: National Tribune, 1907), 15; Bidwell characterized this revolt as due to "the intolerant and exasperating administration of affairs" by Gillespie.

69. Compiled Service Record, Archibald H. Gillespie, Mexican War; Adjutant General's Office, National Archives and Records Administration, Washington, DC.

70. Marti, *Messenger of Destiny*, 115.

71. Ibid., 119–120; Marti says the marriage occurred in the spring of 1848; Dorrance, "Archibald H. Gillespie in the Department of New Mexico," 7, says it occurred in the summer of 1849.

72. Marti, *Messenger of Destiny*, 119–120.

73. Elizabeth Duane Gillespie, *A Book of Remembrance* (Philadelphia, PA: J. B. Lippincott Company, 1901), 72.

74. Faust, *Historical Times Illustrated Encyclopedia of the Civil War*, 64–65.

75. At the author's request, the National Archives and Records Administration searched all the images in NARA custody and found no likeness of Gillespie; letter to the author dated May 15, 2012, from the Still Picture Reference Team, Special Media Archives Services Division, NARA.

76. Dorrance, "Archibald H. Gillespie in the Department New Mexico," 8; Secretary of the Navy, *Navy Register of the United States for the Year 1855*, Resignations and Casualties, 107: Brevet Major A. H. Gillespie, October 14, 1854.

77. Ibid. Elizabeth Gillespie wrote an engaging memoir, *A Book of Remembrance* (note 73 above), in which her husband appears by name or reference only twice.

78. Dorrance, "Archibald H. Gillespie in the Department of New Mexico," 9.

79. Alexander H. McClure and Byron Andrews, eds., *Famous American Statesmen and Orators*, Vol. VI (New York: F. F. Lovell Publishing Company, 1902), 43.

80. Gillespie, Memorial to the President, April 15, 1864, Letters Received by the Commission Branch; *General Orders of the War Department, Embracing the Years 1861, 1862 & 1863, Adapted Specially for the Army and Navy of the United States* (New York: Derby & Miller, 1864), 274; *New York Times*, July 19, 1862; Compiled Service Record, A. H. Gillespie, Return of Fort Craig, NMT, "Official Communication Rec'd, G.O. 90 dted Oct. 2, 1862, Dept Dd Qtrs Oct 7 62, Maj. A. H. Gillespie assigned for Duty at the Hd Qrs at Santa Fe, N.M."

81. Virginia Jeans Laas, *Wartime Washington: The Civil War Letters of Elizabeth Blair Lee* (Urbana: University of Illinois Press, 1991), 112: Mrs. Lee was the daughter of Blair. She was married to Samuel Phillips Lee, a Union navy officer and relative of Confederate

general Robert E. Lee. In a letter dated March 18, 1862, Mrs. Lee wrote her husband, "Father got Gillespie a Lt. [*sic*] place in New Mexico under Canby—so he has a chance to fight himself up in life again." By the time Gillespie reported to New Mexico, Canby had been replaced by Carleton.

82. A. H. Gillespie, Memorial to the President, April 15, 1864, Letters Received by the Commission Branch.

83. Faust, *Historical Times Illustrated Encyclopedia of the Civil War*, 332.

84. Endorsement dated April 14, 1863, by Halleck on a March 17 letter of Brigadier General James H. Carleton to Brigadier General Lorenzo Thomas, Adjutant General of the US Army, Letters Received by the Commission Branch.

85. A. H. Gillespie, Memorial to the President, April 15, 1864, Letters Received by the Commission Branch; Dorrance, "Archibald H. Gillespie in the Department of New Mexico," 11–50. Dorrance has an excellent summary of Gillespie's subsequent experiences. Unless otherwise noted, these two documents are the sources for what follows pertaining to Gillespie.

86. The quote by Carleton is cited by Gillespie in his Memorial to the President.

87. A New Mexican dance, or *baile*, a popular off-duty pastime for American officers.

88. Prostitutes sometimes attended these affairs but women of good reputation might also be present. Gillespie claims he saw Carleton dancing with a woman of easy virtue and reproved the general good-naturedly, only to incur his wrath. Others claimed it was Gillespie who, under the influence of alcohol, publicly misbehaved with a prostitute.

89. See note 14 above. While the San Luís Valley remained within Carleton's jurisdiction on October 7, 1862, the date of Gillespie's order, within another month it was transferred to the District of Colorado, Department of Missouri, under Chivington. After that transfer, Carleton no longer had authority to proceed with the census unless Chivington approved it, and there is no written evidence that Chivington did so.

90. Actually, due to his prejudice, Gillespie badly misunderstood the culture by confusing it with that of Mexico and Mexican California, which he abhorred; the Hispanos of northern New Mexico and the San Luís were, as we have seen, unique.

91. In addition to his war wounds and chronic diarrhea, he suffered from an agonizing swelling on his neck and severely chapped and cracked hands.

92. Subsequently several officers and civilians would offer affidavits confirming that Gillespie was often drunk on duty.

93. A. H. Gillespie to Captain B. C. Butler, January 20, 1863; Letters Received, Department of New Mexico.

94. A. H. Gillespie to Captain B. C. Cutler, October 29, 1862; Letters Received, Department of New Mexico.

95. A. H. Gillespie to Captain B. C. Butler, January 20, 1863; Letters Received, Department of New Mexico.

96. Letters Received, Department of New Mexico. Written across the top of Gillespie's report of January 20, 1863, are the words "The following very interesting letter from Major Gillespie . . . gives a very graphic idea of the District of Conejos in Colorado Territory. We have been authorized to publish it for general information." In a letter of August 21, 1863, to Carleton, Gillespie wrote that he had seen the material in an edition of the *Santa Fe Gazette*, date not known, but complained that he had never received "any acknowledgement [from Headquarters] of the various documents I had sent forward." We do not know if any use was ever made of Gillespie's census, which was, however unwisely timed, remarkably detailed and gives a fascinating glimpse of a people and place theretofore virtually unknown. It is worth noting that this particular letter was written after the Espinosa outbreak and mentions that affair indirectly. It also paints an extremely negative opinion of the Hispanos of the San Luís Valley, whereas in earlier communications Gillespie had mostly striven for objectivity even if he failed to achieve it.

97. E. W. Eaton to Assistant Adjutant General, District of Colorado, April 19, 1863; Letters Received, Department of New Mexico (underline in original). Eaton's rage is evident in the scrawled script of this letter. Further, the National Archives microfilm copy is severely underexposed and very hard to read; some words and phrases are completely illegible.

98. E. W. Eaton to Brigadier General E.R.S. Canby, July 26, 1863, E. W. Eaton Papers.

99. Ibid.

100. Proceedings of a General Court Martial Convened at Fort Garland C.T. on the 15th Day of May 1863; First Lieutenant John Lewis, Compiled Service Record, Adjutant General's Office, 38–39. Also Thompson, *New Mexico Territory During the Civil War*, 209. The Fort Garland verdict was approved by Chivington on June 18 and forwarded for review by the commander, Department of Missouri, Major General John Schofield, who on July 25 found fault with the manner in which the charges and specifications were drawn, disapproved the sentence, and ordered Lewis released from arrest. At the outbreak of the war Lewis, formerly a member of the Regular Army, had been commissioned a first lieutenant in Company C, First New Mexico Volunteers, then transferred to Company D and in June 1862 was under arrest on unspecified charges at Peralta. He had resigned his commission at the time the Fort Garland court-martial found against him, but after his sentence was reversed by General Schofield he joined the First New Mexico Infantry but was again court-martialed in early 1865 at Fort Union for embezzlement and cashiered. He then joined the First New Mexico Cavalry as a private on May 18, 1865, and served his full enlistment, separating from the service in May 1866.

101. E. W. Eaton to Carleton, June 22, 1863; E. W. Eaton papers.

102. Second Letter, E. W. Eaton to Carleton, June 22, 1863, E. W. Eaton Letters (underline in original).

103. *General Orders*, Adjutant General's Office for 1863, with an Index, Government Printing Office, Washington, DC, 1864, 84; F. B. Heitman, *Historical Register of the United States from Its Organization September 29, 1789 to September 29, 1889* (Washington, DC: The National Tribune, 1890), 291.

104. Gillespie mounted a spirited defense of his conduct, blaming all his misfortunes on the animosity of Carleton, and in the process appealed for redress of his grievances to Canby, Halleck, Secretary of War Stanton, numerous congressmen and influential citizens, and finally President Lincoln. This airing of departmental dirty laundry would have been an embarrassment to Carleton despite the fact he achieved his aim of ridding himself of the troublesome major; Letters Received by the Commission Branch.

105. Endorsement by Chivington, June 27, 1863, on Carleton's letter of February 24; E. W. Eaton Papers.

106. E. W. Eaton to Brigadier General E.R.S. Canby, July 26, 1863; E. W. Eaton Papers.

107. Ibid. (underline in original).

108. E. W. Eaton to Carleton, September 29, 1863; Letters Received, Department of New Mexico.

109. Potter, "Reminiscences of the Socorro Vigilantes," 48–49.

110. E. W. Eaton, Compiled Service Record.

111. Gillespie, *A Book of Remembrance*, 382.

112. Dorrance, "Archibald H. Gillespie in the Department of New Mexico," 50.

113. Keleher, *Turmoil in New Mexico*, 457.

114. Santa Fe *New Mexican*, October 27, 1866.

115. Faust, *Historical Times Illustrated Encyclopedia of the Civil War*, 113.

116. Officers Casualty Sheet, April 10, 1865; E. W. Eaton Compiled Service Record.

117. Potter, "Reminiscences of the Socorro Vigilantes," 25ff.

118. Bob L'Aloge, *The Incident of New Mexico's Nightriders: A True Account of the Socorro Vigilantes* (Sunnyside, WA: BJS Brand Books, 1992), 50, 72.

119. Paige W. Christiansen, *College on the Rio Grande: The Story of a Small School*, web edition, http://books.google.com/books/about/College_on_the_Rio_Grande.html?id=QRjFtgAACAAJ, accessed March 4, 2013.

120. Undated newspaper clipping, September 15, 1916; Mednick, *San Cristóbal*, 157; FindAGrave.com, accessed April 11, 2012. For grave information, see http://www.findagrave.com/cgi-bin/fg.cgi?page=gr&GSln=Eaton&GSfn=E&GSmn=W&GSbyrel=all&GSdy=1916&GSdyrel=in&GScntry=4&GSob=n&GRid=44369868&df=all&, accessed March 3, 2013. Newspaper article appears on this link but does not identify source.

121. Letter of Lieutenant John Lewis to Captain E. W. Eaton, date uncertain; E. W. Eaton Papers.

122. See Chapter 6.

"Times Have Become Quiet Again"

Panic Recedes in South Park but Murder Moves Elsewhere

10

Euphoria spread throughout central Colorado in the wake of the killing of Vivián Espinosa. John McCannon's possemen basked in a general glow of gratitude. Wrote an editorialist of the *Rocky Mountain News Weekly*:

> The people of California Gulch are entitled to a great deal of credit for the zeal they displayed in ridding the country of a desperado, and having performed the labor and spent the time necessary for that object it is no more than fair that other localities should stand the expense incurred. California gulch was not more directly interested than Denver or any other locality—not nearly so much so as some places—yet her people shouldered the main burden of the undertaking. Let Denver respond by paying a portion at least of the expenses incurred.[1]

As in the case of the Oro City committee's call for reimbursement of McCannon's volunteers, it is unknown whether the *News*' solicitation produced a monetary outpouring equal to the enthusiasm of its appeal. Whether or not McCannon, Joseph Lamb, and Charles Carter received rewards, all three would long be remembered for the roles they played in ending at least part of the Espinosas' reign of terror.

In South Park, matters gradually returned to normal. Nearly contemporaneous with the death of Vivián

DOI: 10.5876/9781607322375.c10

Espinosa there was one more brief flurry of excitement on the northern verge of the Park when a party of men from Gold Run in the Blue River country were assaulted by five "guerrillas" on the same route Lehman and Seyga had traveled, the Denver, Bradford, and Blue River toll road. According to the May 9 edition of Central City's *Miner's Register*, the attack resulted in "a terrible fight" after which four of the ruffians were taken, the fifth escaping.

The *Register*'s informant reported the not unfamiliar news that two of the miscreants were "hung to make them reveal the whereabouts of their accomplices—one of these died in the operation, and the other was so nearly killed as to render him unable to travel. The other two are said to have been sent to Denver." Evidently not yet aware of the activities of "Commandant" Wilson's mob and John McCannon's posse, the *Register*'s editorialist declared, "it is high time the bands which infest some portions of our Territory were exterminated," though of course he was at pains to explain, "we are not in favor of mob law as a general rule." However, the people, he insisted, should "take the law into their own hands, so far as to preserve their lives and remove the danger of constant attacks."[2]

Meanwhile, a private named John T. McGahey in Lieutenant Wilson's Company F, First Colorado Cavalry,[3] sent a reassuring bulletin to the *Weekly Commonwealth and Republican* from Fairplay: "Times have become quiet in the Park again, and we poor soldiers are beginning to have it easier; citizens are traveling unmolested and it is hoped the country is rid of the robbers and murderers infesting it for the last two or three months."[4] Mining activity had resumed and wages were good, the only drawback being "the want of water, the ditch not being large enough to supply the demand." However, business was falling off dramatically in Cañon City, ninety miles away. McGahey and some friends had visited there recently, only to find the place "almost entirely deserted, without trade or travel." Only a single inhabited ranch existed between Cañon City and South Park.[5] Clearly the Territory's population drain was being felt.

However, the *Weekly Commonwealth*'s "Dornick" agreed the Park was enjoying its interlude of peace, writing from Pueblo on May 23 where he was again attending a term of US District Court, this time for the Third Judicial District. "All is quiet throughout the country in regard to jayhawkers, and murders especially," he reported, "since the capture and summary execution of the Mexican Espinosa near Canon City. . . . The one who escaped has not yet been taken or heard of."[6]

The Third District, by far the largest in the Territory, encompassed Lake, Fremont, Pueblo, Huerfano, Conejos, and Costilla counties. Originally based in Cañon City, the court had recently moved to Pueblo,[7] doubtless another reflection on the decrepitude of the once bustling mining supply town farther up the Arkansas.

The presiding judge of the Third District was Allen E. Bradford, a former prospector, thought to be a competent jurist—a rarity among the presidential appointments to the Territorial bench[8]—but he was also a notable eccentric. He was accustomed to appearing in court with unlaced shoes, fly and coat unbuttoned, and clothes covered with food droppings. He sometimes wore a Mexican serape or a tobacco-stained linen duster.[9] Obese and clumsy, he spoke in a shrill falsetto voice. The Mexicans who came before him called him *el juez gordo*, the fat judge.[10]

The court itself was as colorful as Bradford. Historian Forbes Parkhill described it: "Sometimes Mexican spectators squatted on the dirt floor of the courtroom, playing Spanish monte and smoking cornshuck cigarettes during the judicial proceedings. Everyone else, including the judge, smoked pipes." Judge Bradford occupied a sheepskin-covered soapbox, using a larger box for a desk. Lawyers sat on boards laid across logs. The court building itself was a mud-roofed shack.[11] "Dornick" mentioned that the judge, whom he misnamed Howard, was accompanied in court by his dog.[12]

It was in these rustic and bizarre surroundings that the Third District grand jury, on June 9, returned an indictment for murder in the Espinosa killings. For some reason, however, it was believed that Vivián, not Felipe, had escaped the McCannon ambush, so the indictment was drawn against "Bivian Espenosa." The indictment commanded Marshal Hunt to arrest Vivián "and him safely keep, so that you have his body before the . . . Court . . . at the next term thereof to be held in the town of Pueblo . . . on the first Monday of September A.D. 1863, then and there to answer . . . upon an indictment for wilfil [*sic*] murder."[13]

"Dornick" noted the grand jury action in his *Weekly Commonwealth* story, perpetuating the mistake that Vivián was "the Mexican who escaped when his brother, Felipe Espenosa, was shot above Canon City." Directly contradicting his own earlier assertion that the murderer had "not been heard of," he stated, "This escaped one has been heard of lately and seen within a few days, and Marshal Hunt has taken prompt measures to capture him, and has hopes of corralling him in a short time."[14] This was wishful thinking. Hunt proved unable to make the arrest. The writ attached to the indictment in the records of the court bears Hunt's laconic undated scribble, "Can't find Him, is dead."[15]

After "Dornick" returned to Montgomery he engaged in another instance of wishful thinking, writing on June 19, "A report has come in that the Mexican, Bivian Espinosa, has been taken by Lieut. Shoup and hung."[16] Accepting the report for gospel, an editorialist for the *Weekly Commonwealth* later wrote, "now that Lt. Shoup is reported to have caught and hung Bivian Espinosa, and the terror caused by the assassinations of the Espinosa fiends has subsided, we opine there is little necessity for a home police, and extensive scouting after Indians will occupy the First Cavalry in future. A service combining all the pleasures of soldiering, with very few of its disagreeables."[17]

For Private Romine Ostrander, like McGahey a member of Company F of the First, the pleasures of soldiering in early July included the staging of two dramatic productions, *The Golden Farmer* and *Love in a Cottage*. But even dramaturgy was not easy for the horny-fisted Firsters. "We have built a stage today which will do very well by carpeting it with blankets," Ostrander confided to his diary on July 11. "We also have painted some of the scenery, all of which we had intended should be the best, had it not been for an order we got today to march to Denver next Tuesday. When we heard it after working hard two days, we were on the point of tearing our work in piece[s] but the citizens told us to fix it as well as we could and give them one performance any way."[18]

With this encouragement from the citizens, the show "went off first rate." "[A]ll expressed themselves well satisfied," Ostrander wrote the day after the performance, July 14. "I went to a dance after the Theatre and did not go to bed at all. We got started about nine this morning[;] all the stores in Fairplay treated till all hands were drunk. The people seemed sorry to have us leave, and I am sure the boys were sorry to leave for we have been treated as gentlemen here and behaved as such."[19] Evidently no one regarded as ungentlemanly in the least the part the Firsters—or some of the citizens themselves, for that matter—had played in the lynching of Baxter, the torturing of Snyder, or the hanging of the unidentified "horse thief."

The *Rocky Mountain News Weekly* confirmed the sadness felt by the people of Park County at the departure of the First Colorados. In its edition of July 23 appeared this item: "RETURNING—The troops in the South Park, under Lieuts. Wilson and Oster, are on their way back here, all being quiet in 'Skinbuck Joe' and surroundings. Residents in those mines, Mosquito,

Conejos Canyon. Felipe Espinosa murdered William Smith at some unknown location within the canyon. (Photo by Ruth Ellen Price)

Montgomery, Fairplay and beyond the range, in California gulch and Cash [*sic*] Creek, express much dissatisfaction on account of the troops being called away." The complaint was that withdrawal of the troops would leave the "citizens, miners and prospectors" unprotected against "white guerrillas or disaffected Utes, whenever and wherever the two dangerous forces may choose to spring up and hold them at their savage mercies. Wilson's boys were well liked by the miners up there."[20]

The people of South Park need not have worried. For them the Espinosa terror was gone for good even if its dark memory would linger for a time. But the death terror was not over; it had merely relocated. Twenty-two days after the killing of Vivián in Oil Creek Canyon, Felipe Espinosa committed another murder a little less than two hundred miles southwest on the Conejos River, not far from the village of San Rafael where the brothers' bloodbath had begun. The victim was a lone fisherman, an Anglo named William Smith.[21] The details of Smith's identity and the circumstances of his murder are shrouded in mystery; the only other detail we have is the fact, stated in an indictment handed up by the Third District Court grand jury against Felipe four months afterward, that he used a rifle to commit the crime.[22]

After murdering Smith, Felipe is said to have composed a *pasquinade*, a song celebrating his vendetta against the Americans, which he liked to sing to himself. The words were a play on his name: *"Felipe le dice a Nerio, vamos matando este gringo"* ("Felipe tells Nerio, let us kill this *gringo*").[23]

The surviving Espinosa's actions and whereabouts between May 8, when Vivián died, and May 30, when Smith was killed, cannot be fully documented. But it is obvious that, after fleeing Oil Creek Canyon, Felipe somehow made his way back to Conejos County. The commonly accepted account is that he escaped from McCannon's posse "with only a rifle, a pistol, and the clothes he was wearing . . . afoot without food or blankets."[24] He probably stole a horse[25] and according to one source, he also killed two other men in the Cañon City area, though if this happened, the press failed to report it.[26] He would have been able to shoot game for food but must have moved very circumspectly in order to make his way home undetected over a stretch of country whose people had been alerted to be on the lookout for a solitary Mexican whose name and crimes, and perhaps even his description, were known.

James Perkins, Tom Tobin's able biographer, convincingly speculates about this period: "Whatever [Felipe] had to do to survive, he did; and in a few days he was back in San Rafael. But the situation at home was now much worse. . . .

His family was still destitute, and it was only through the kindness of relatives and friends that they were kept fed and clothed."[27] It is also probable that the *Hermanos* of the Penitente *morada* in San Rafael, following the longstanding philanthropic tradition of the *Santa Hermandad*, had contributed to the support of the impoverished Espinosas and Hurtados in the brothers' absence.[28]

Perkins goes on to imagine that Felipe built a hut "hidden in the willows and cottonwoods along the Conejos River, and a short distance from where his family lived. Here he remained most of the time."[29] This seems unlikely given the fact the army and the Territorial authorities were still on the lookout for him and troops stationed in the *plaza* of Conejos routinely patrolled the San Rafael area. More probably Felipe hid out in the rocky outcroppings of the heights of Los Mogotes,[30] where he and Vivián had fought off the soldiers back in January, or even more distantly, in the inaccessible defiles of the San Juan Mountains.

Perkins lost his bearings, however, in supposing that Felipe hid for several months and even helped out with planting the family fields the following spring. That would have put him in San Rafael in March or April 1864,[31] a patent impossibility.

What Felipe did do, though, sounds even more improbable but can actually be verified: he traveled back to Oil Creek Canyon, located Vivián's skeletal remains where McCannon's posse had left them and buried them, but not before cutting off one of his brother's mummified feet for a keepsake.[32] The *Colorado Springs Telegraph* of March 18, 1938, in its obituary of Secundina's sister Eugenia H. Lucero at age 106, said Eugenia remembered that "Felipe, on his infrequent visits [to Secundina] always carried a blackened, shrunken foot of [his] brother," the rest of whose body he had found and interred after Americans killed him.[33] Eugenia said Secundina "occasionally received a precious stone or money from her notorious husband" but always returned the valuables, knowing they had been stolen.[34]

It is undisputed that at some point in mid- to late 1863 Felipe recruited an enthusiastic young nephew to take Vivián's place in the work of exterminating *gringos*. Perkins identifies the nephew as José Vincente Espinosa, sixteen-year-old son of Felipe's unmarried sister María Tomasa.[35] Other sources say the boy, "still in his teens," was called Julio or Julián.[36] The 1850 New Mexico Territorial Census shows a three-month-old child, José, in the same household with the Espinosas, including Felipe, Vivián, and María Tomasa. The Espinosas were counted in January 1850, meaning the child would have been

Huerfano Butte, near the supposed site of the killing of Leon Constantine by Felipe and José Vincente Espinosa; mountains of the Sierra Blanca in the background. (Photo by Ruth Ellen Price)

born in 1849. Assuming this was Tomasa's son, he would have been fourteen years of age in 1863.[37]

It may have been with José Vincente's help that Felipe killed again, at least once and possibly several more times. Tom Tobin believed one of their victims was a young French-Canadian named Leon Constantine, who with three partners was farming corn and wheat on the Huerfano River near Huerfano Butte. Tobin also believed the Espinosas killed another, nameless man in the Sangre de Cristo Mountains.[38] One San Luís Valley history claims Felipe and his nephew had killed eleven more times by early September 1863.[39]

An intriguing item appeared in the *Rocky Mountain News Daily* of September 3:

> INTERESTING FROM CONEJOS—From Daniel Witter, Esq., who returned yesterday from Conejos and southern Colorado, we learn that Espinosas [*sic*], the villainous murderer of South Park notoriety, drove into Conejos last night a fortnight, and delivered five letters at the office of Major Head, Indian

Agent, addressed respectively to Mr. Head, Lieut. Moore, of Fort Garland, Col. Chivington, Governor Evans and the judge of Conejos County. After visiting two sisters who live in that town, he mounted his fast mustang, fired off six shots from his revolver, and made for the mountains, fifty or sixty miles westward. The citizens and a portion of a military company from Fort Garland, then stationed in the plaza, upon hearing of the bold advent of the notorious Mexican, started after him next morning, but were unable to find track of him. The substance of the letters left by him was this: he wanted the Governor to give him pardon and restore the amount of property lost by himself and brother, or that in less than a month he would come down out of his mountain strongholds and commence a war of extermination against Mexican and American citizens of that section of the Territory, wherever he could strike them: that he had killed in all twenty-two men, and thought his "bravery" deserved an "honorable amnesty." Great excitement prevailed in that part of the country. . . . Espinosa stated he lived eight days in the San Juan mountains without eating any but berries. He is either constitutionally crazy, or a second Quantrell,[40] and in either case should be immediately hunted down and hung on the highest limb in the Sangre de Cristo ranges. Mr. Witter also informed us that Hon. Mr. Gallegos, formerly member of our Legislature, was found dead, with a rope around his neck, in the plaza of Conejos a couple of weeks ago. Particulars of his murder are not known.[41]

More mysteries than the immediate one of the supposed murder of Gallegos are raised by the last two sentences of this article. José Francisco Gallegos, a Democrat, had been chosen representative for the Thirteenth Territorial District (Conejos County) at the general election of December 1861 when the first legislative body of Colorado was expanded for its second session into thirteen councilmen and twenty-six representatives. The expanded legislature convened on the first Monday of June 1862 and adjourned on November 8. Gallegos served as chair of the Elections and Apportionment Committee and a member of the Territorial Affairs Committee.[42] Due to a shortage of appropriations by July 1862, the election of legislators for 1863 was postponed to that year.[43] Evidently Gallegos did not serve out his full term, for José Victor García is shown as representative for Conejos County later in 1862.[44]

However, it will be recalled that a man named Francisco Gallegos was a prominent leader of the Hispano unrest in Conejos County at the time the army raided the Espinosa home in San Rafael,[45] and was arrested at least twice by Lieutenant Hodt for resisting the laws of the United States by force of arms. This Gallegos repeatedly escaped from custody and finally forfeited his bonds upon rearrest, and the government ended by confiscating his 220 acres of lands and improvements when he failed to appear for trial.[46]

Except for the fact that this Gallegos was a substantial landowner, one would be tempted to believe from the court records citing his involvement in the civil disobedience during the winter of 1862–63 that the rebellious Gallegos was a simple rabble-rouser of the *peon* class and that he and the legislator were two different persons. But given the insurgent Gallegos's extensive land holdings and the fact that Gallegos the public servant was apparently no longer a legislator by the time of the Conejos disorders, it is at least possible that the two were in fact one and the same. Perhaps Gallegos was a politician who had been radicalized during his legislative service by the hubris of the Anglo masters of southern Colorado.[47]

On its face the Rocky *Mountain News Daily* report seems to imply that Felipe Espinosa may have had a hand in the reputed murder of Gallegos. It says Felipe delivered his letters in the *plaza* of Conejos "last night a fortnight" and that Gallegos was found dead in the same *plaza* "a couple of weeks ago"; in other word, both events are said to have occurred at approximately the same time. Compounding the puzzle, however, is the fact that the death of Gallegos is reported nowhere else in the contemporary press, as would be expected if he were, indeed, a former legislator; nor did the *News* follow up Witter's story with subsequent reporting, or with a correction if the piece turned out to be based on rumor.

The *Weekly Commonwealth* had a correspondent pen-named "Battery," a member of Lieutenant Horace W. Baldwin's Right Section of McLain's Colorado Battery, posted at Fort Garland, who provided regular reports from the south. On the very day the *News* printed its piece on the supposed murder of Gallegos, "Battery" wrote that while there had indeed been "considerable trouble at Conejos," it involved the killing of one Philippe [*sic*] Anarza by three soldiers of Company E of the First Colorado and a citizen by the name of Canadray. Anarza was "suspected of being a confederate of Espinosa."

"Battery" further confided that "late arrivals from [Conejos] agree in representing the worst of feeling between the citizens and soldiers. Soldiers walking the streets at night are expected to have a loaded pistol in their hand at all times."[48] By this time troops seem to have been permanently stationed in

Conejos to maintain order among the restive Hispanos. In an earlier bulletin "Battery" had remarked, "There is no trouble here at present, but it is anticipated in case of collection of taxes or carrying out of the draft."[49]

Assuming the unsubstantiated *News* report of the killing of Gallegos to have been true,[50] and further assuming that Felipe may have committed the crime, the question arises what his motive might have been. Presumably he and Gallegos had been allies, or at least fellow participants, in the Hispano revolt in the Conejos during the winter of 1862–63, though we cannot know whether they were personally acquainted.

Why would Felipe have turned on a politician, or even if the slain Gallegos was *not* the former legislator, who likely held anti-Anglo views similar to his own? Of course one answer has to be that by this period in his life Felipe was not acting rationally, if he ever had. Another clue may be embedded in the content of the letters he is said to have delivered to Lafayette Head's office. According to Witter, Felipe wrote that if he were not pardoned, he would "in less than a month, come down out of his mountain strongholds and commence a war of extermination against *Mexican* [emphasis added] and American citizens of that section of the Territory."

If that is the case, Felipe Espinosa, by the late summer of 1863, had become more dangerous than ever.

NOTES

1. *Rocky Mountain News Weekly*, May 28, 1863.

2. *Miner's Register*, Central City, Colorado, May 9, 1863; account provided by Christie Wright.

3. Hollister, *Boldly They Rode*, 177.

4. *Weekly Commonwealth*, May 28, 1863.

5. Ibid.

6. Ibid.

7. Parkhill, *The Law Goes West*, 21.

8. Ibid., 20.

9. Leonard, *Lynching in Colorado*, 42.

10. Parkhill, *The Law Goes West*, 22.

11. Ibid., 23.

12. *Weekly Commonwealth*, May 28, 1863.

13. *United States vs. Bivian Espenosa* [*sic*], Indictment, US Court for the Third Judicial District, Territory of Colorado, June 9, 1863; Record Group 21, Records of the District

Court of the US Territory of Colorado; Bankruptcy, Civil and Criminal Case Files, 1862–74, National Archives and Records Administration, Rocky Mountain Division, Denver, Colorado.

14. *Weekly Commonwealth*, May 28, 1863.

15. *United States vs. Bivian Espenosa*, Indictment.

16. *Weekly Commonwealth*, June 25, 1863.

17. Ibid., July 2, 1863.

18. Ostrander, *This Soldier Life*, 32.

19. Ibid. Ostrander, uncharacteristically upset by the Baxter lynching, had recovered his customary disengagement by May 15 when he recorded his reaction to the news of Vivián Espinosa's death: "The stage came along about eleven o'clock. We saddled up and ready to go with it. It was full of passengers. We heard the California gulch boys had killed a mexican supposed to be one of the murderers. He had a companion who has escaped. We came to the Talbut house kept by Mr. McLaughlin."

20. *Rocky Mountain News Weekly*, July 23, 1863.

21. Jessen et al., "Colorado's Worst Serial Murders," 21; Indictment of Jose Felipe Enorio [*sic*] Espinosa, September 7, 1863; Record Group 21, Records of the District Courts of the US, Territory of Colorado.

22. Ibid. Somehow Tom Tobin knew of this murder but gave no details: "[Felipe] then came to Conejos and there killed a man, Bill Smith"; Tobin, "The Capture of the Espinosas," 61.

23. Jessen et al., "Colorado's Worst Serial Murders," 21. The same source says Felipe left a message bearing the words of his *pasquinade* at the door of Lafayette Head, who mistakenly thought a Conejos resident named Felipe Nerio de Herrera was the composer. Head had troops dispatched from Fort Garland who executed Herrera in his own house. This story is not otherwise confirmed.

24. Perkins, *Tom Tobin*, 155.

25. Ibid.

26. Jessen et al., "Colorado's Worst Serial Murders," 21.

27. Perkins, *Tom Tobin*, 155.

28. Weigle, *Brothers of Light, Brothers of Blood*, 151–153; Quintana, *Pobladores*, 77; Simmons, "The Penitentes," 19–25.

29. Perkins, *Tom Tobin*, 156.

30. Jessen et al., "Colorado's Worst Serial Murders," 14.

31. That is, four or five months after he was dead.

32. It is also possible that Felipe, as a devout Penitente, wished to give Vivián the funeral rites of the *Santa Hermandad* called the *velorio de defuntos* (wake for the dead), a ceremony involving the preparation of the body, the singing of *alabados* (hymns), the wrapping of the corpse with a *mortaja* (shroud) for burial, and other solemn rituals; Weigle, *Brothers of Light, Brothers of Blood*, 175–178.

33. Quoted in Trujillo, "The Espinoza Brothers," 169.

34. Ibid.

35. Perkins, *Tom Tobin*, 157 and 175, note 44. Perkins writes that José Vincente's father was named Romero and was a cousin to Jacinta Romero, the wife of Tobin's brother-in-law, Juan de Jesús Bernal; he was also a cousin to José Mateo Romero, husband of Tobin's sister-in-law, Soledad Bernal.

36. Jessen et al., "Colorado's Worst Serial Murders," 21. Ruth M. Colville, ed., "Time-Event Chart of the San Luis Valley," *The San Luis Valley Historian*, Vol. I, No. 2 (April 1969), and Parkhill, *The Law Goes West*, 53, also say the nephew's name was Julián, but neither gives an attribution.

37. See Chapter 7.

38. Perkins, *Tom Tobin*, 161; Tobin, "The Capture of the Espinosas," 61.

39. Jessen et al., "Colorado's Worst Serial Murders," 22.

40. The reference is to Confederate guerrilla commander William Clarke Quantrill, whose bloody raid on Lawrence, Kansas, on August 31 was much in the news at the time.

41. *Rocky Mountain News Daily*, September 5, 1863.

42. *Rocky Mountain News Weekly*, April 5, 1862; Colorado Joint Legislative Library: *Colorado Legislators Past and Present*, http://www.leg.state.co.us/lcs/leghist.nsf/736b5262efff1c5087257751006d4155/705d04c0a23ee71c872578e2005df9a3?OpenDocument, accessed March 3, 2013; see also *Supplemental Guide to Shaping the Law of the Land: Hispanics in the Colorado Legislature*, 9.

43. Bancroft, *History of Nevada, Colorado and Wyoming*, 428.

44. Hall, *History of the State of Colorado*, 536. By then Conejos County was the Eleventh Territorial District, no longer the Thirteenth. Interestingly, on August 8, 1862, the legislature approved a private act granting Gallegos, Francisco Ruibar, and Juan Bautista Jacquez a power of incorporation to create a twenty-five-acre private cemetery in Conejos County; see *General Laws and Joint Resolutions, Memorials and Private Acts Passed at the Second Session of the Legislative Assembly of the Territory of Colorado* (Denver: Rocky Mountain News Printing Company, 1863), 125.

45. See Chapter 7, and Parkhill, *The Law Goes West*, 43.

46. Parkhill, *The Law Goes West*, 43.

47. For instance, the legislative session in which Gallegos seems to have served enacted a measure requiring that the laws of the Territory be translated into Spanish so the Hispano population of the Territory could understand them, yet as late as October 1863 no such translation had ever occurred. See Bancroft, *History of Nevada, Colorado and Wyoming*, 428. The *Weekly Commonwealth*, November 11, 1863, discussing the bad blood between Hispanos and Anglos in the San Luís, reported, "It seems that . . . an almost interminable series of difficulties had arisen, all of which can be traced, in greater or less degree, to the fact that the laws of the Territory are not printed in the Mexican [*sic*] language."

48. *Weekly Commonwealth*, September 17, 1863.

49. Ibid., September 3, 1863.

50. It should be noted that while most nineteenth-century directories show Gallegos as serving part of a term in 1862, at least one modern directory suggests he served until 1864; see Colorado Joint Legislative Library: *Colorado Legislators Past and Present*. If this is correct, obviously Gallegos was not killed in 1863. But nineteenth-century directories show his service as portrayed in the text. Another difference between modern and contemporary sources is that some modern sources (see Note 42, "Colorado Legislators Past and Present.") show Gallegos as a representative of Costilla County while authoritative nineteenth-century sources show him as representing Conejos County.

"Ready for Any Duty, Untiring, and Full of Energy"

11

Samuel F. Tappan Takes Up the Hunt for the Espinosas

"The summer of 1863," wrote Frank Hall, early Colorado legislator and later historian, "was marked by a protracted drouth which dried up the streams, and prevented growth of crops in the limited area then cultivated." Then, "[e]arlier than usual, about the middle of October, one of the severest winters ever known in this latitude set in, with frequent heavy snows and very cold weather."[1]

The extremes were indeed remarkable, since the winter of 1862–63 had been unusually mild and spring had come delightfully early.[2] But by the beginning of August the scorch of summer was so severe it had begun to wear down the spirits of many, including an editorialist for the *Weekly Commonwealth*:

> Saturday morning came in close and murky as usual for the last few days. Before 9 o'clock the mercury was at 94. A few dark clouds casting heavy shadows towards the mountains and some bilious looking thunderheads peeping from behind the range, gave a slight promise of the long wished rain. About noon, the clouds dripped a little, just enough to wet a handkerchief, and then the rainy season passed inconveniently over. We resigned ourself [*sic*] to our fate in a very melancholy mood.[3]

Yet, before that month was out, signs of wintry weather were already showing themselves around

DOI: 10.5876/9781607322375.c011

Lieutenant Colonel Samuel F. Tappan, commandant of Fort Garland at the time of the Espinosas' attack on Philbrook and Dolores Sánches. (Photo courtesy of History Colorado, scan no. 10035782)

the Front Range. "There was frost night before last on Clear Creek, six miles west of here," reported the *Rocky Mountain News Daily* on August 26, "and several inches of snow fell on the nearer mountains."[4] We do not know what conditions were like in the remote San Luís Valley where, two days before the *News* spoke of frost and snow, Lieutenant Colonel Samuel F. Tappan rode into Fort Garland to assume command.[5] Tappan was relieving First Lieutenant William B. Moore, who had taken temporary charge of the post after Captain Davidson, of the E. Wayne Eaton affair, relinquished it twelve days previously, pending Tappan's arrival.[6]

The onset of winter was always unpredictable in the San Luís. Frost was common in September and October and heavy snowfalls were erratic, sometimes holding off till December and on other occasions coming in early October, at times whitening the mountains while leaving the valley floor untouched. Sometimes snows were very light or even nonexistent until January, and then they could persist far into the spring months. The winters were almost always cold and blustery.[7] But nothing in the records suggests anything but a sunny and agreeable clime on the day Samuel Tappan came to Garland.

Tappan was not the kind of man to shrink from wind, weather, or hard duty. He was a slight but still imposing figure of medium size, and with a penetrating gaze. A heavy mane of dark hair swept up like wings from a part low on the left side of his head, complemented by a thick mustache and a rounded chin that was somewhat withdrawn but strengthened nonetheless by a firm, full-lipped mouth and evenly trimmed chin-whiskers. His manner conveyed an impression of coolness and composure, touched perhaps with a faint suggestion of superiority.

Technically the San Luís was part of the Eastern Ute Indian Reservation, whose agency, under Lafayette Head, was located at Conejos. Fort Garland had originally been built in 1858, successor to Fort Massachusetts, the first military post in what was to become Colorado. The purpose of Massachusetts was to protect the largely Hispano inhabitants of the valley from the Utes and to guard the passes through the Sangres. But Massachusetts had turned out to be badly placed in a swampy, unhealthy area and six years later was abandoned in favor of Garland—though some would question whether the change was beneficial. With its short summers and long winters, Garland was generally considered the least desirable post in the entire Southwest.[8]

After initially resisting encroachment by Hispanos from northern New Mexico,[9] the Utes had by 1863 begun grudgingly to accept the inevitable, that with increasing immigration from the south by Hispanos and from the north and east by Americans, they would eventually lose control of the San Luís. As a matter of fact, the authorities of Colorado Territory in 1863 were already laying plans for a treaty with the Utes that would push them westward into the San Juan Mountains.

Providing military protection for an upcoming treaty conference with the Eastern bands of Utes[10] at the Conejos agency was one of the assignments Tappan had been sent to Fort Garland to carry out.[11] Another was to end what he termed "*La Penitente* . . . self torturing of Mexicans."[12] Near the top of the list,[13] however, was "Capturing Espanosas [*sic*] who had murdered 32 persons."[14] Presumably these orders had been given him by Colonel Chivington, commander of the Colorado District, in consultation with Governor Evans. Capturing or killing the Espinosas had now become one of the highest priorities of the Territorial government.

Tappan and Chivington were bitter enemies at this time and it is not difficult to glimpse a measure of spite in Chivington's selection of his second in command, a highly accomplished and well-regarded officer carrying the rank of lieutenant colonel, to take charge of the worst post in the Southwest usually commanded by a captain, a rank two grades inferior to Tappan's. But on the other hand, the Espinosas were now big game—the biggest in Colorado—and perhaps Evans, if not Chivington, thought Tappan the officer best equipped to bring them down.

Samuel Tappan is an unjustly neglected figure in the history of the American West, but in his own time was widely respected, and as cordially disliked, as a military officer, journalist, antislavery activist, and advocate for the rights of

Native Americans. This item from the *Weekly Commonwealth*, published a little over a year before he arrived at Fort Garland, expresses the positive opinion many of his contemporaries held of him:

> Lieut.-Colonel S. F. Tappan.
>
> We are very highly gratified to hear from both officers and men of the First Regiment, the highest ecomiums [*sic*] upon the character and conduct of this most excellent officer.
>
> Col. Tappan entered the service as a Captain, at a time when the services of true men were greatly needed. He entered it with great diffidence, modestly doubting his own ability to do his full duty as an officer, on account of his previous ignorance of military affairs.
>
> But from the moment he entered the service, he applied himself diligently to the work of mastering his profession.—Ready for any duty, untiring, and full of energy, he has been steadily growing in ability, and in the affection of both officers and men of his command.
>
> The testimony of those of the Regiment whom we have seen is unanimous in his praise as an officer and a gentleman.
>
> At the battles in which the Regiment was engaged, he exhibited great coolness and bravery, and proved himself to be the right man in the right place.
>
> Upon the resignation of Col. . . . Slough [first commander of the regiment] Col. Tappan modestly refused the appointment tendered him of the Colonelcy of the regiment—his right according to his rank—and himself urged the appointment of Major Chivington to the place. . . . He is beloved and honored by his . . . Regiment.[15]

Ovando Hollister, who served under Tappan during the Texan invasion and observed him at the battle of Pigeon's Ranch on March 28, 1862, wrote of the man's courage under fire, "Lieut. Colonel Tappan sat his horse during the [enemy] charge, leisurely loading and firing his pistols as if rabbit hunting."[16]

But John Chivington was not among Tappan's admirers. Though Tappan had performed well during the 1862 battles, Chivington had emerged as Colorado's greatest hero. Before Colonel Slough's resignation he had ached to command the regiment and then, gaining that position owing to Tappan's deference, had longed to control the District of Colorado. No sooner did he reach that goal than he hankered to be promoted general. Though a Methodist minister, Chivington was a rough, burly, belligerent character whose ambition knew no bounds—just the sort of fellow the ruffians of the First Colorado preferred.[17]

Chivington's animus toward Tappan probably stemmed from the fact he owed Tappan his place at the head of the regiment. By stepping aside and permitting Chivington to assume a command that was justly his, Tappan had forced Chivington into an obligation, and had also, perhaps not unintentionally, come off looking like a man of high character while exposing Chivington's unseemly greed for advancement. Nothing annoys a swaggerer like owing a favor to someone, especially if that someone is seen as conniving and perhaps disingenuous. Perhaps the act Tappan had meant to be interpreted as self-abnegation had looked to Chivington more like hypocrisy and a case of invidious comparison. Whatever the reasons, the two were now enemies, and Tappan, however modest, was not above spitting venom at his superior. Historian Duane Smith quoted the following letter Tappan wrote to Chivington:

> I understand that you have in the presence of several [people] threatened if the officers of our regiment meet together to take into consideration the affairs of the regiment and I am among them I shall be put in irons. . . . I confess that I am exceedingly annoyed and excited to anger when I hear that you in my absence threatened me with this and that you speak of me with contempt. I most earnestly and sincerely protest against such proceedings. . . . Do not exercise the power conferred upon you to gratify your personal spite and sacrifice the interests of our country for the gratification of your political ambitions.[18]

Tappan came by his lofty principles honestly; he was a Yankee abolitionist, born at Manchester, Massachusetts, in 1831.[19] The Tappans were a prominent New England clan, counting among their ranks clergymen, politicians, inventors, writers, poets, philanthropists, educators, and businessmen. Despite these impressive connections, young Sam Tappan of Manchester received a common school education and afterward took up the lowly cabinet-making trade.

But in 1848 he entered a mercantile house in Boston and while there came under the influence of such abolitionists as William Lloyd Garrison and Wendell Phillips. Galvanized by these mentors against the institution of slavery and appalled by enforcement of the Fugitive Slave Act, a radicalized Tappan emigrated to Kansas in 1854, where he became one of the founders of the Free State settlement of Lawrence. There he involved himself in the Underground Railroad, helping runaway slaves pass through Kansas into the Northern states. It was not long before he came into conflict with proslavery Border Ruffians from

Missouri, with whom Free Soilers were contending for supremacy in Kansas Territory.[20] During this period Tappan also became a correspondent for Horace Greeley's *New York Tribune*, reporting on the struggles in "Bleeding Kansas."

Tappan associated himself with the Emigrant Aid Society and helped smuggle Sharps rifles (named Beecher's Bibles for the prominent abolitionist Henry Ward Beecher) to Free Soil settlers. He performed a number of duties in the various legislative bodies associated with the forging of a Free State constitution for Kansas and contributed materially to the eventual overthrow of the proslavery faction and the admission of Kansas to the Union as a state where slavery was prohibited.

In July 1860, Tappan, infected with Pike's Peak gold fever, left Kansas for Colorado. "Arriving in Denver I found the city actually ruled by desperate characters and murders of frequent occurrence," Tappan wrote in an 1895 autobiographical sketch. "Becoming connected with the *Daily Herald*[21] I antagonized the rowdy element by advocating the organization of a city government, and late in Dec. 1860, was mobbed by them, cut with bowie knives, a crowd gathered and the mob dispersed."[22]

After this temporary diversion into investigative journalism and the establishment of law and order, Tappan finally went looking for gold in the Central City diggings.[23] His cousins Lewis and George Tappan came to Denver, too, and, electing to supply miners rather than try mining themselves, soon established one of the city's best-known general stores; Lewis was also one of the founders of El Paso County.[24]

With the coming of the Civil War, Sam Tappan found himself "commissioned to enlist a company of infantry volunteers for the war," which he succeeded in doing, only to run afoul of Denver's lawless element once again, this time a gang led by gambler and Rebel sympathizer Charley Harrison, who would one day perish at the hands of Osage Indians while trying to conquer Colorado for the Confederacy.[25] In August 1861, Tappan was commissioned lieutenant colonel of the First Regiment of Colorado Volunteers in which Chivington held the rank of major.

After the defeat of the Texans, Tappan was assigned to Fort Scott[26] in Kansas and then to command of Fort Lyon[27] on the Arkansas River in the plains country of Colorado Territory. When the Firsters were officially designated a cavalry unit, Tappan returned to Denver to mount and drill them; he was engaged in that duty when he was ordered to assume command of Garland. He marched to Garland "with 400 cavalry, 200 infantry and a Battery."[28]

While Tappan was settling in at Garland, Governor Evans was finalizing arrangements for the upcoming treaty conference with the Utes at the Conejos agency. The council was set for October 1 and much of Tappan's attention during September must have been devoted to planning military security for the conclave; in mid-September he was also forced to make a "flying visit" to Conejos to prevent "a big fight . . . between several hundred Kiowas and a large body of Utes" evidently beginning to gather for the conference;[29] he would have had little time to devote to his mission of hunting down the Espinosas. Set to attend the treaty-making were Evans, Chivington, and Lafayette Head; Simeon Whiteley, agent for the Ute Western bands; Michael Steck, New Mexico's superintendent of Indian Affairs; and John Nicolay, President Lincoln's secretary—quite a collection of luminaries. They had gathered at Fort Garland by September 28 and on the morning of September 30, left the post for the conference, with Tappan in command of Companies D, E, and I of the First Colorado and the Right Section of McClain's Colorado Battery.[30]

An unverified rumor has persisted over the years that the Espinosas, angered by Evans's refusal to pardon them as Felipe's recent letter[31] had demanded, hoped somehow to penetrate the Conejos treaty conference in order to assassinate the governor or, failing that, to ambush him on the road.[32] If indeed they formed such plans, Felipe and his nephew failed to carry them out and the treaty conference proceeded without interruption, though a Mexican was murdered the day before the council opened, apparently by a soldier.[33]

Reporting from the treaty-making site, "Battery" described the tense scene at the beginning of the conference:

> The governor, Col. Chivington, Lieut. Col. Tappan, and other prominent officers of the Colorado troops are here.
>
> It is the current belief of those who ought to know, that the Utes will make no acceptable treaty unless force be used to compel them to; and is equally the general opinion that force will be used. So the prospect for a fight is good.
>
> There are but few Indians to be seen in or about town as yet, although it is said there are not less than five or six thousand encamped on the creeks and in the canyons not many miles off. Major Head, Indian Agent, has stated there would be twenty-five thousand on hand on the day appointed for the treaty.
>
> We are expecting six companies of cavalry and a battery of artillery from Fort Union, which, added to the troops already here, will make a force capable of whipping two Ute nations.[34]

Nothing so dramatic transpired, however. Of all the Indian bands invited, Agent Whiteley's Western Utes remained in the mountains; some Capotes and Weenuches started for Conejos but then changed their minds and returned home; and fifteen hundred Tabeguaches attended, along with one Capote chief and three Muache chiefs who, because their bands had not appeared in numbers, could not become parties to any agreement made.

A treaty was successfully negotiated and signing occurred on October 7.[35] Signatories included Governor Evans, Steck, Head, and Whitely, and Ute chiefs Red Color, Blue Flower, Colorow, Arrow (Ouray), One That Slides Under the Snow, Blue River, Red Wind, Lock of Hair, White Warm, and Left Hand. Witnessing the signing were Nicolay and Charles E. Phillips, assistant secretary to the treaty commission; Chivington, Tappan, and two captains of the First Colorado; and interpreters Juan V. Valdez, Bernardo Sánchez, and Amador Sánchez.[36]

By the terms of the treaty the Tabeguaches relinquished all their lands east of the Continental Divide plus Middle Park. In exchange for their new, more restricted western reservation the Utes received annuities, provisions, and livestock. Essentially the ceded lands were those already occupied by Anglo and Hispano settlers and miners and their towns.[37]

An editorialist for the *Weekly Commonwealth* lauded the work of the treaty commissioners, noting with enthusiasm that the ceded lands amounted to an area equal to one-third of Colorado Territory and that "the lower part of the San Luís valley will be surveyed as soon as possible and opened to settlement,"[38] a consummation long devoutly wished by land-hungry Anglos and one certain to visit even more grief on Hispano colonists already bedeviled by Territorial taxes, fears of military conscription, and the threatened loss of their Indian slaves.

Tappan attracted favorable notice throughout the proceedings. "Typo" wrote that the lieutenant colonel drilled the military units "about every day" during the week and at one point caused six rounds each of shell and canister to be fired by the Battery in the presence of the Indians, the sights and sounds of which "completely astonished" the Utes. He further confided the firing was "indeed splendid, considering that it was the first time . . . the boys had practiced" with either type of projectile.[39]

"Typo's" rival, "Battery," agreed that Tappan "kept [the troops] pretty busily drilling most of the time, a part of the military science he thoroughly understands."[40] It would be interesting to know how he and Chivington, given their differences, managed to get along, but perhaps, surrounded by dignitaries both white and red, they contrived to offer an appearance of congeniality. "Typo" offered a counterintuitive glimpse of a festive sing-along by the famously truculent Chivington and others "at Major Head's Plaza," but Tappan's name is conspicuously missing from the list of genial choristers. "The welkin was made to ring in the chorus of 'Rally Round the Flag, Boys,'" the correspondent exulted.[41]

In their respective articles both reporters confessed they had looked forward to the Conejos visit hoping to enjoy the region's famous *fandangos* and pretty *señoritas*—hopes that were dashed when they learned the bad conduct of the troops stationed there over the previous weeks had left all Americans in bad odor with the local population. "Thus it is," lamented "Typo," "that the sins of the few are visited upon the many."[42]

"Battery's" article, filed on October 12 after the troops had returned to Fort Garland, covered a number of other incidents of the conference, ending with the observation, "We have been favored with a little excitement,"[43] a remark that would prove a considerable understatement once the nature of the excitement revealed itself. "Typo," also filing on the twelfth, elucidated: "For the past ten days there has [*sic*] been several rumors floating around about one or two persons having been shot at in the neighborhood of Sangre de Cristo Creek."[44]

In fact the Espinosas had struck again, this time only a few miles from Fort Garland itself, and now Sam Tappan would turn his whole attention back to the most vital task he had been sent to the San Luís to perform: hunting down the renegades and bringing an end to their campaign of terror.

NOTES

1. Hall, *History of the State of Colorado*, I: 306.

2. See Chapter 1.

3. *Weekly Commonwealth,* August 6, 1863.

4. *Rocky Mountain News Daily*, August 26, 1863.

5. *Weekly Commonwealth*, September 3, 1863.

6. Fort Garland Commanders by Dates in Command, http://www.fortgarlandmuseumfriends.com/Officers.htm, accessed May 18, 2008 (no longer available as of March 3, 2013).

7. Walter Clemmons, Mrs. Walter Clemmons et al., "Winter in the San Luis Valley," *The San Luis Valley Historian*, Vol. II, No. 1 (Winter 1970): 34–38.

8. Thompson, *New Mexico Territory During the Civil War*, 39.

9. Pauline S. Sharp, "Kit Carson at Fort Garland, C.T.," *The San Luis Valley Historian*, Vol. II, No. 2 (Spring 1970): 12: "By the 1850's New Mexican settlers . . . were moving up the well-traveled trails from Santa Fe and Taos, Ojo Caliente and El Rito, even Abiquiú, into the land ceded to the United States by the Treaty of Guadalupe Hidalgo. . . . Many had come before them as settlers on the two large land grants [the Sangre de Cristo and Conejos grants] given to wealthy, influential citizens who, in order to validate the grants, were to have settlers on them within ten years. Thus were the northern frontiers of New Mexico to be colonized." As we saw in Chapter 7, the Espinosas of El Rito were among those settlers. The *plaza* of San Luís, fifteen miles south of Garland, was the earliest Hispano settlement. Many followed, including the Espinosas' *plaza* of San Rafael. The residents of all these communities, together with the few Anglo settlers in the area—especially the ranchers on the eastern side of the Sangre de Cristos along the Culebra and Huerfano rivers and in the Spanish Peaks country—relied on the protection afforded by Fort Garland.

10. Virginia McConnell Simmons, *The Ute Indians Indians of Utah, Colorado and New Mexico* (Boulder: University Press of Colorado, 2000), 18, 112. Technically the post served only the Muache Utes but many Tabeguaches used it also. There were thirteen Ute bands. Other than the two mentioned, these were the Pahvant, Moanunt, Sanpits, Timpagonots, Uintah, Seuvarits, Yampa, Parianuche, Sabuagana, Weenuche, and Capote.

11. Negative copy of holograph of note of Tappan headed, "Six Months at Fort Garland," MSS 667, FF2, Stephen H. Hart Library, Colorado Historical Society.

12. Ibid. This attempt to prevent the ceremonial mutilations practiced by the *Santa Hermandad* does not seem to have produced much in the way of results. Quintana, *Pobladores*, 75, recounts an undated occasion when, one Good Friday, a cavalry troop sent from Fort Garland attempted to break up a Penitente crucifixion reenactment. The soldiers arrived at the point in the ceremony when the *Hermanos*, representing their anguish over the "death" of the "crucified" and perhaps also the earthquake and storm said to have followed the passion of Christ on the cross, performed the *tinieblas*, a loud outcry and rattling of chains and wooden noisemakers called *matracas*. The tumult frightened the troop horses, which became unmanageable and unseated many of their riders. Simmons, "The Penitentes," 17, relates the same incident. It is a measure of Anglo misunderstanding of the practices of the Penitentes that the Territorial government thought it best to try to put an end to them. Another item on Tappan's list was "securing release of Navajo Indians held as slaves," also an Anglo move to wipe out a traditional Hispano practice. There is no evidence Tappan attempted to carry out this order.

13. Ibid. Dealing with the Espinosas was the second task on Tappan's list. The first was to "execute a Mexican soldier for murder." However, Tappan, a man of firm principles, believed the soldier charged with murder had not been legally tried and refused to

execute him on grounds the act would have been unconstitutional. He claimed his decision was later upheld by the US Supreme Court after Secretary of War Stanton repealed the order of execution and two acts of Congress sustained Stanton's position. It is interesting that Tappan, like Eaton before him, believed Hispanos were American citizens who deserved equal protection under the laws.

14. Tappan, "Six Months at Fort Garland."

15. *Weekly Commonwealth*, September 25, 1862.

16. Hollister, *Boldly They Rode*, 70.

17. Smith, *The Birth of Colorado*, 113. Keleher, *Turmoil in New Mexico*, 205, note 45, gives this biographical portrait of Chivington: "John Milton Chivington, who left his pulpit to take up the sword during the Civil War, was born near Lebanon, Ohio, on January 27, 1821. He died in Denver . . . October 4, 1894. [He] joined the conference of the Methodist Episcopal Church at Pleasant Green, Cooper County, Missouri, and was ordained a preacher in 1848. A powerful and persuasive personality in camp meetings in Illinois, Missouri and Nebraska, [he] moved to Denver in 1860 and became presiding elder of the Rocky Mountain conference. Opposed to slavery on principle, [he] joined the army at the outbreak of the war." Keleher quotes a historian of the Colorado Volunteers, Dr. William Clarke Whitford: "Chivington developed extraordinary military ability, although he had had no military training before he abandoned the pulpit for the battlefield. In action he became the incarnation of war. The bravest of the brave, a giant in stature and a whirlwind in strife, he had, also, the rather unusual qualities that go to make soldiers personally love such a leader, and eager to follow him into the jaws of death." Chivington would, on November 29, 1864, lead the infamous attack on the camp of peaceful Cheyenne Indians at Sand Creek, Colorado, a controversial act he defended to his dying day as a heroic battle with dangerous hostiles. Other men who had been involved in the Espinosa affair were also present at Sand Creek, including George L. Shoup, by then a colonel; Lieutenant Luther Wilson; Captain John McCannon; and Joseph Lamb. Tappan had argued with Chivington against the attack and later was appointed head of a military commission investigating the colonel's conduct. Chivington was condemned for the Sand Creek Massacre but resigned from the army and, thanks to a general amnesty at war's end, suffered no penalty. He died admired and respected by many white Coloradans.

18. Ibid. Regrettably Smith does not give the date of this letter or describe the particular circumstances that occasioned it. From internal evidence it was penned some time after the date when Tappan deferred to Chivington, yielding command of the regiment to the latter.

19. Tappan, Samuel F., unpublished autobiography, Kansas State Historical Society, Manuscript Department, Misc. Tap–Tra; also http://www.arlingtoncemetery.net/sftappan.html, accessed March 15, 2010 (no longer available as of March 3, 2013).

20. Ibid.

21. Evidently the *Daily Herald* of New York City.

22. Ibid.

23. Smith, *The Birth of Colorado*, 113.

24. See Chapter 1, note 39.

25. Ibid. Tappan wrote that he had brought his company into Denver and encamped them when "the roughs made an attack upon my sentinel but were soon arrested, and released upon their paroles. I then disarmed the city taking all the rifles and muskets, also ammunition, I could find[,] giving receipts for them. That night [the] sentry [was] again attacked and [the] shot came from the rear of Charles Harrison's saloon gambling hall and theatre. I immediately entered the hall and ordered the crowd to disperse, about 500, disarming all I did not know as loyal and arresting Harrison . . . and others, taking them to camp, there keeping them for about a month and then surrendering them to the US Marshall [*sic*]." This account contains so much one-man derring-do as to raise suspicions about its veracity. No other source mentions such a showdown with Harrison. Hollister, *Boldly They Rode*, 4, says, "collisions" with the "town secesh" sometimes occurred, "but they never resulted in anything serious." Hollister, 6, quotes an undated newspaper report that "Capt. S.F. Tappan" and his 101 men of Company B had arrived in Denver "from the mountains." For Harrison's fate see Chapter 3.

26. Ibid.

27. *Weekly Commonwealth*, July 30, 1863.

28. Tappan, "Six Months at Fort Garland."

29. *Weekly Commonwealth*, September 17, 1863.

30. *Rocky Mountain News Weekly*, October 21, 1863.

31. See Chapter 10.

32. Simmons, *The San Luís Valley*, 142; Secrest, "The 'Bloody Espinosas,'" 13; Taylor, *Colorado South of the Border*, 213, says Evans and Chivington came into the San Luís not for the Ute conference but to "facilitate the hunt" for the Espinosas and that Felipe and his nephew planned to grab Evans "between Greenhorn and the Sangre de Cristo Mountains," demand that he pardon them, and kill him if he refused. Secrest writes that Chivington and Evans "attempted to salve the growing fears over the ongoing murders" and transferred Company I of the Second Colorado Volunteers, which had been ordered to protect the Cañon City vicinity from the Espinosas in April, to Conejos "to protect Evans and Chivington, there to remain all winter to calm the populace and try to catch the Espinosas." Newspaper accounts of the time, however, show that elements of the First Colorado Cavalry had been stationed in Conejos for some time (see Chapter 10, this volume) and that army elements also remained in the area after the treaty conference. Scott, *Tom Tobin and the Bloody Espinosas*, 122–124, again quoting from an "Espinosa diary" that is not known to exist, gives an extensive and detailed description of how the two

supposedly plotted to kill the governor. Tobin, "The Capture of the Espinosas," 61, says, "While the Governor was at Major Head's [for the Ute conference], [the Espinosas] saw him through the window at Major Head's but did not know the Governor [by sight]. [They] came to the Sangre de Christo [*sic*] Mountains to head off the Governor and see if he would pardon [them], and, if not, kill him."

33. *Weekly Commonwealth*, October 28, 1863, story dated October 12. Was this the soldier Tappan mentioned as accused of murder in his note "Six Months at Fort Garland"? Tappan referred to this soldier as a Mexican, and "Battery," in mentioning the incident in his October 28 bulletin to the newspaper, makes it clear the killer was supposed to be an Anglo: "I know that there are soldiers mean enough to do almost anything, but I believe they study their own interests too much to be committing the murders . . . that are charged to them.—While they behave themselves they can have all the fun they want, and be on good terms with the inhabitants, have no privilege denied them, and have every desire gratified. On the contrary, they make themselves a terror to the people; the women leave or hide, their men are [surly?], and the 'fandangos' broken up. It seems to me that Colorado soldiers appreciate this, and are not such fools as to cut short their only fun and frolic merely from an ambition to cut a 'greaser's' throat." If indeed there were mysterious murders roundabout Conejos at this time, it is not beyond the realm of possibility that the culprits were the Espinosas, who had promised to "commence a war of extermination against Mexicans and Americans" if they were not pardoned (see Chapter 10).

34. *Weekly Commonwealth*, October 15, 1863.

35. The text of the treaty may be found online at http://digital.library.okstate.edu/kappler/vol2/treaties/uta0856.htm, accessed March 3, 2013. It was ratified March 25, 1864, and proclaimed December 14, 1864.

36. Ibid.

37. Simmons, *The Ute Indians*, 117–118.

38. *Weekly Commonwealth*, October 22, 1863.

39. *Rocky Mountain News Weekly*, October 21, 1863.

40. *Weekly Commonwealth*, October 28, 1863.

41. *Rocky Mountain News Weekly*, October 21, 1863.

42. Ibid.

43. *Weekly Commonwealth*, October 28, 1863.

44. *Rocky Mountain News Weekly*, October 21, 1863.

"If This Woman Is Found Dead, Tell the People the Espinosas of the Conejos Killed Her"

The Attack on Philbrook and Dolores Sánches

12

In 1863 the settlement of Trinidad in vast Huerfano County on the plains east of the Sangre de Cristo Mountains was only about three years old.[1] It consisted of a huddle of adobes and picket houses[2] mainly on the south bank of a stream French trappers called the Purgatoire (Purgatory) and Hispanos had earlier named *El Río de Las Animas Perdidos en Purgatorio,* or the River of Lost Souls in Purgatory.[3] A wooden bridge crossed the river connecting the dusty village to a few other structures on the north bank and to a large grove of cottonwoods and willows. The surrounding bottomlands were hospitable to both grazing and irrigated cultivation, and a number of small farms and ranches had already been established by the scattered Hispano and Anglo settlers. Trees, wild plums, and tangled undergrowth grew thickly on undeveloped ground.[4]

The Purgatoire takes its rise in the Sangres and wends its way for 150 miles through a fertile valley surrounded by "hills covered with *piñon* and *sabina* [a species of juniper], relieving somewhat the hard gray aspect of the bold cliffs beyond,"[5] eventually emptying into the Arkansas River far out on the flats of eastern Colorado. An early directory mentions "inexhaustible beds of coal" underlying the town, with "outcrops of the same . . . visible in all the surrounding ravines."[6] The day would come when exploitation of this visible

DOI: 10.5876/9781607322375.c12

Main Street, Trinidad, Colorado Territory, home of the Philbrook brothers and Dolores Sánches. (Photo courtesy of History Colorado, scan no. 10034750)

resource would make a boomtown of sleepy Trinidad and an expansive coalfield of the area around it, leading eventually to bloody labor unrest and the infamous Ludlow Massacre. But in 1863 the town and county were not yet widely settled; the few ranches and farms were strewn sparsely along the river and settlements of any size were few and far between.

Though Trinidad had not been an actual town until 1860 or 1861, for over twenty years the river crossing at that point had been familiar to traders using the Mountain Branch of the Santa Fe Trail leading from Bent's Fort on the Arkansas and over the Raton Mountains south of the river into New Mexico. In fact, the cottonwood grove on the north bank had been a favorite stopping place for traders, emigrants, and freighters, as well as for mountain men who also used this route to enter the ranges to the west hunting for pelts.[7]

Trinidad was, and is, dominated to the south by a rugged, square-topped basaltic mesa some have called Raton Peak and others Fisher's Peak[8] and on the north by the smaller, buttelike Simpson's Rest, though the latter name did not come into use until later.[9] The setting is quite agreeable, not at all suggestive of the gloomy appellation of the stream on which the village sat.[10]

In fact, the name of the town by the River of Lost Souls ironically invokes the redemptive trinity of Father, Son, and Holy Ghost. But reputedly it honors not the *Santissima Trinidad* but a woman called Trinidad, daughter of a Hispano founder of the town, Don Felipe Baca.[11]

Technically, of course, souls in Purgatory are not lost but are only waiting to be purified before ascending into Heaven, so to that extent the river's name is something of a non sequitur.[12] But then the notion of Purgatory does imply some degree of suffering for those who, though in a state of grace, yet remain in need of forgiveness for certain sins. It might be said that the Philbrook brothers, Leander D. and Henry Clay, two of the earliest occupants of Trinidad,[13] were spiritual sufferers indeed, not necessarily because they themselves had committed sins yet to be expiated but because a third brother, Darius, had recently been executed for the crime of attempted murder, and that blow must have afflicted the surviving two with personal torments.

The Philbrook line from which the brothers descended was a long-established Maine family, respectable and law-abiding as far as we know. The father, Samuel, and the mother, Emily Twitchell, were natives of Gilead in Oxford County.[14] At some point before 1830 the family moved from Gilead to Rushville, Yates County, New York, where the three brothers destined to go to Colorado were born. The oldest of these was Leander; Henry was the youngest, and Darius, the ill-fated middle brother. They had one older brother, Samuel, born in Maine; an older sister, Hannah; two younger sisters, Emma and Lucy; and a younger brother, Orin, all born in Rushville.[15]

Darius had enlisted in the US Army in 1851, and sometime in the late 1850s, while he was serving a second five-year enlistment, the rest of the family moved to Brookfield, Wisconsin, a suburb of Milwaukee, where Leander and Henry worked for a time as farm laborers. In the spring of 1861 the brothers evidently caught Colorado gold fever and emigrated to Breckenridge beyond the northern rim of South Park, but instead of striking it rich in the diggings, Leander worked as a sawyer and Henry as a mason. That summer Darius, finally mustered out of the army, came to Breckenridge to join them.

With the outbreak of the Civil War, all three brothers rallied to the Union cause. Darius and Leander, also in Denver, enlisted in Company K of the First Colorado Regiment of Volunteers on September 1. Darius, apparently owing to his previous military experience, became a sergeant; Leander, a private.[16] Henry joined the Denver Home Guard on September 12.

The following spring, tragedy struck. On the evening of March 12, 1862, during the march of the First Colorado into New Mexico Territory to resist the invasion of the Texan army under Confederate brigadier general Henry Hopkins Sibley, Darius became drunk and provoked an incident that Ovando Hollister of Company F declared "distressing [but] is the natural consequence of the lawless tone of public sentiment prevalent in the regiment."[17]

> Lieut. [Isaac] Gray of B Company was shot in the act of arresting Sergeant Philbrook . . . for drunkenness and noise. There are fifty different stories about it, but as near as I can judge the Sergeant had little provocation. He shot five times at Gray, and hit him once. The ball struck on the bridge of the nose between the eyes, and glancing down lodged in the lower part of the face. It did not seriously injure him. Other officers near by emptied their revolvers at Philbrook, but he escaped their shots and was finally confined to the guard house.
>
> At first there was much excitement, B Company demanding instant justice by lynch process—K extenuating their sergeant's case by circulating various versions of the affair favorable to him. By the firmness of Capt. [George L.] Sanborn, officer of the day, the prisoner was saved from Judge Lynch, locked up, and the excited passions of all parties allowed to cool. Doubtless, Gray was peremptory in the discharge of his duty, but no one in his senses will say that his conduct justified the attempt of the Sergeant to kill him.
>
> It is too much the impression among us that whiskey justifies anything, and that a free use of it is a necessary qualification of a gentleman. The present is likely to prove an occasion for a severe lesson on this and kindred topics. We have played soldier a good long time and with a high hand. It would not surprise me if things were to take a different aspect. Surely a change cannot come too soon. Such scenes as this, and others that could be easily pointed out in our history, are ruinous and disgraceful to the perpetrators not only as soldiers but as men.[18]

Darius was later tried by court-martial and found guilty of attempting to kill Lieutenant Gray. Nothing is known of his natural temperament; he seems to have had an honorable record over his two enlistments in the Regular Army, and Leander and Henry appear to have been inoffensive men, suggesting a family trait of mildness. But at his court-martial Darius testified he was addicted to alcohol and as a result could remember nothing of the shooting incident. The pre–Civil War army, with its often remote stations and duties that were frequently long and monotonous, was a notorious breeding ground for alcoholics, and Darius had spent ten years in that dreary environment. If we can credit Hollister's remark that drinking had become a sort of badge of honor among the men of the First Regiment, the riotous nature of that unit can hardly have been good for a veteran already far too fond of his dram.

The unfortunate Darius was shot to death by firing squad at Fort Union, New Mexico Territory, on April 8, 1862.[19] It is not known whether Leander had any part in this affair but his complicity seems unlikely. His health had already suffered severely during the arduous winter campaign.[20] Now his weakened constitution sustained another shock because of the fate of Darius. In June 1862 he was discharged from the First Colorado as unfit for duty.

Henry's six-month enlistment in the Denver Home Guard had expired on April 1, seven days before Darius's execution, and he quickly came south to care for Leander, who now was thought nearly incapable of physical labor. The brothers settled in Trinidad late that same year and on January 14, 1863, Leander received a license to operate a grocery store in his home—the first in the tiny village.[21] Six days later, Henry and one W. R. Walker[22] signed as securities for Leander's bond.[23] For the whole of 1863 they seem to have been moderately successful; they paid federal taxes of $13.33 on their retail business and $26.67 for the liquor they sold, a total of $40.[24]

The story of Darius's execution was well-known throughout Colorado Territory and, having occurred but eighteen months previously, must have still, in October 1863, caused the two surviving brothers anguish and perhaps shame. Leander, though, despite his supposed physical limitations, had somewhat eased any discomfort he may have felt by traveling to Ottawa, Illinois, the previous April to marry a young lady named Nancy J. Graham.[25] He is believed to have returned with her to Trinidad, as she appears a few years later living with Leander and the bachelor Henry in the Montana goldfields.

Leander and Henry couldn't be blamed if they felt the fates had dealt harshly with them during their time in the West. But the fates were not done with them yet. Another trauma remained to be visited on one of them; he would be the next *gringo* to confront the Espinosas. We cannot say with absolute certainty which brother this was, for the free and easy frontier journalism of the time only gives the last name Philbrook and a diligent search of the records of Huerfano County has uncovered no mention of the encounter with the serial killers; but a historian who has done research on the Philbrooks is convinced that it was Leander who ran afoul of the outlaws.[26]

The Espinosa attack occurred while Philbrook was driving a mule-drawn buggy over the western descent of Sangre de Cristo Pass during a trip from Trinidad to Costilla, New Mexico Territory.[27] His passenger was a Hispanic woman, María Dolores Sánches, who was traveling to Costilla to visit her family.[28] Nothing else is known of Dolores Sánches except that in the trials she was about to endure she behaved with extraordinary courage, fortitude, and grace.

The same would prove true of Philbrook, and if this indeed was Leander, his courage and stamina must be considered nothing short of phenomenal in view of his documented frailties—unless they were far less severe than originally thought.[29]

The record does not tell us whether Dolores was a friend of Philbrook's, an employee of the grocery, a housekeeper, or perhaps someone with a more intimate connection. Obviously Leander thought well enough of Dolores to go to the trouble of escorting her on a trip of some distance and difficulty. In either case, the journey to Costilla in an open buggy could hardly have been a secret, so it seems unlikely there was anything indiscreet in the relationship, especially if the driver was Leander, married but five months previously. Furthering this belief in Dolores's good character is the fact that one of the correspondents who covered the attack refers to her as "a lady,"[30] a term of respect not often used by Anglo reporters in reference to a Hispanic female, much less one who could possibly have been suspected of concubinage.

The pair must have left Trinidad about Thursday, October 8, 1863.[31] They may have followed the valley of the Purgatoire, ascended its North Fork, passed through Cucharas Pass[32] behind West Spanish Peak, and dropped down to Francisco Plaza,[33] now La Veta, just then being transformed from a ranch and farm into an adobe fort by its joint owners John M. Francisco, Henry Daigre, and Hiram W. Vásquez. But as far as we know this was not a well-traveled trail at the time and certainly not an improved road. A somewhat more likely, better-traveled, and easier itinerary would have taken them over the plains north along the Mountain Branch of the Santa Fe Trail[34] to a point near the future site of Walsenburg,[35] then west up the Cucharas River to Francisco Plaza.

A buggy trip of that length, about sixty miles either way, would have required an overnight stay before reaching Francisco Plaza, possibly at a ranch somewhere in the Guajatoya or upper Cucharas Valley if they took the Purgatoire route or at a way station along the Mountain Branch of the Santa Fe Trail, if they passed that way. Leaving from Francisco Plaza on the morning of Saturday, October 10,[36] Leander and Dolores followed the steep, coiling pass later known as La Veta[37] over the Sangre de Cristos. Just past the summit, their trail met the graded wagon road of Sangre de Cristo Pass sloping down along the broad drainage of Sangre de Cristo Creek toward the San Luís Valley.

At some point that day, the travelers met a large official party returning from the Conejos treaty conference, including Governor Evans and John Nicolay, President Lincoln's secretary, accompanied by a military guard.[38] Presumably the travelers exchanged greetings and each group passed on, the governor and his escort toward the summit and Philbrook and Dolores Sánches toward the valley floor. About two hours before sunset, time enough for them to cover the last downhill miles[39] to Fort Garland, Philbrook's buggy entered a defile then called the Canyon of the Sangre de Cristo.[40]

Here, north and south walls of dark red stone drew close to the trail, perhaps only twenty-five yards apart.[41] Suddenly four shots were fired at the travelers "from the side of the mountain and a little to their rear,"[42] presumably from the north rim of the canyon, since three shots missed but the fourth bullet struck the offside, or right-hand, mule. Philbrook whipped up the team and drove "as fast as [he] could"[43] in an attempt to escape but the wounded animal soon fell dead near a pond formed by a beaver dam across Sangre de Cristo Creek.[44]

Philbrook was armed with a revolver but decided it would be best to continue the attempt to flee; he jumped from the buggy, cut the traces to free it from the dead mule, and was preparing to drive away with the remaining animal when, wrote "Battery" for the *Weekly Commonwealth*, "the robbers coming nearer[,] he helped the woman out of the carriage and they both made for the mountains."[45] "Battery" continued:

> The robbers came down, shot the remaining mule, took the baggage out of the carriage and set it on fire. Five shots were fired at the man and two at the woman. Mr. Philbrook . . . made his way up the mountain, keeping behind trees and rocks, and out of sight of his enemies for some distance, then taking the road made his way [as] rapidly as possible to the fort, while the lady, too weak to bear the fatigue of such a tramp, concealed herself in the mountains.[46]

Tom Tobin, who was acquainted with Dolores Sánches and spoke with her the day after the attack, reported: "Philbrook ran up the side of the mountain and the assassins after him. The woman went up the side of the mountain and hid herself behind a big rock."[47] The account in the *Rocky Mountain News*

Weekly confirms this. "After going some distance," "Typo" wrote, Dolores "became so tired that she could not proceed any further. She advised Mr. P. to try and make his escape while she hid herself."[48] "Battery," for the opposition paper, either purposely or inadvertently implied that Philbrook's next move was a good deal less than chivalric, reporting that he hastened on to Fort Garland, "leaving the woman in the hands of the high waymen [*sic*]."[49] Some secondary sources claim that in their panic Philbrook ran up one side of the canyon and Dolores climbed the opposite side and that Philbrook, with the outlaws on the canyon floor between him and Dolores, had no choice but to leave her and seek help.[50]

"Typo" gives a version that both clarifies the sequence of events and casts Philbrook in a far better light. After the two started up the mountain, he wrote, the pair of attackers separated and one "came up and killed the other mule and set fire to the carriage," while the other "stood on an elevated point on the opposite side of the gulch." Philbrook shouted to them in Spanish demanding to know what they wanted. The outlaw on the eminence responded by firing at Philbrook with a rifle; the shot missed. Philbrook, armed only with his pistol and knowing the rifleman was out of range for a sidearm, coolly ignored him and opened fire on the outlaw who was igniting the carriage. He fired two rounds but without effect. Dolores then appealed to him to "make his escape, as she was too tired to proceed any further." Reluctantly, Philbrook complied and started off for Fort Garland.[51]

Then began Dolores's ordeal, as described by "Typo":

> She states that shortly after her companion left her the man who had been standing on the point came down and joined the other one in gathering up the baggage that had been removed from the carriage before it was fired, and carried it off up a hollow. She then got up to start off, thinking they had gone, but on looking around, the two men were about half way up the mountain, and a little behind her. She started to run when two shots were fired at her, neither of which took effect. One of the pursuers kept on after her, while the other went down towards the creek to cut off her retreat in that direction. She managed, however, to find another hiding place. After remaining here for some time she concluded they had gone, and hearing the noise of a wagon on the road, ran down towards it, and so soon as in sight called out to the men in it to stop, which they did.[52]

Tom Tobin tells what happened next:

> One of the Mexicans was named Pedro García and could speak good English. The woman told Pedro what had happened; he told her to get in his wagon and he would try to save her. The Espinosas came running down to where he had the woman in the wagon. They called out, "What people? Answer quick or we will fire on you. We are the Espinosas." Pedro answered, "Mexicans." Espinosa asked, "Did you meet or see a Gringo running down the road?" He answered that he saw a man running down the mountain and he motioned him to go back. They said that was the Gringo they were after; they could run him down before he got to Fort Garland and kill him. They asked, "Did you see a woman about here?" Pedro denied the woman to them, when she poked her head out of the wagon. Espinosa said, "Put that prostitute of the American out of the wagon or we will fire on you." He refused to put her out although he had no weapons. The woman cried, "Don Pedro, don't perish for me; they are Christians and won't hurt me," and got down from the wagon. They told Pedro to drive off. They took the lines off the harness and tied the woman hand and foot and abused her disgracefully according to her own testimony.[53]

"Typo's" account added a chilling detail. Before driving on, García left some bread for the Espinosas, probably as a proffered propitiation, and begged the outlaws, "Don't shoot the poor woman." The reply, no doubt from Felipe, was, "Go ahead, and if this woman is found dead, you can tell the people that the Espinosas of the Conejos killed her!"[54]

García described the two as "a man and a boy, were both barefooted, and called each other brother." One of them, again probably Felipe, boasted that "they had made a campaign in the morning, killing two soldiers, whose horses they had at their camp."[55] This must have been wishful thinking, prompted by their having missed kidnapping the well-guarded Governor Evans earlier in the day.

There can be little doubt that one or both of the Espinosas raped Dolores Sánches after Garcia and the other man left; Tobin's language makes this tragic fact plain, though "Typo" makes no such assertion and "Battery" dances around the subject with typical nineteenth-century restraint: "Her story . . . is very clear, and bears the marks of truth. I will not intrude it upon your readers, but a few facts may not be without interest." He simply goes on to say the Espinosas tied Dolores up and then "went in search of Philbrook." After they had gone, the dauntless woman chewed through her bonds and escaped, "wending her way toward Fort Garland." "Typo" stated the outlaws "took some straps from the harness of the mules[,] . . . tied her hands and feet and went off in search of Mr. Philbrook." No sooner had they left on their quest than Dolores managed to work herself free of her restraints and climb farther up the mountain. By now night had fallen. After Dolores reached the ridgetop the attackers returned and found to their chagrin that she had escaped.[56]

Tobin said she could hear the two complaining about her escape: "They were saying to one another, where could that huzzy [*sic*] have gone to—they would get her again in the morning."[57]

Reconciled to having lost their captive, the outlaws collected their plunder and withdrew into the mountains. "After they had gone," wrote "Typo," "the poor woman started for [Fort Garland], but after walking around for a long time and becoming very tired and thirsty, went down to the creek to get some water. On reaching the road she found she was at the same place from where she first started after getting out of the buggy." One can only imagine her frustration and fear. However, she happened to find one of her shawls that the robbers had dropped and, thus somewhat heartened, wrapped herself in its folds and "again went up the mountain and sat down to wait for daylight."[58]

But dawn did not bring her long-wished-for safety. Instead she spied one of the outlaws coming down the mountain opposite to where the dead mules were lying. His companion appeared on the ridge above him, keeping watch, while he removed some of the harness from the mule carcasses and once more climbed the slope to join the lookout. "They then went in the direction where she last saw them the evening before." Dolores waited for some time before deciding to resume her effort to reach Fort Garland. But her ordeal was not quite over. "After proceeding some two miles, having kept out of sight as much as possible, she espied three Mexicans coming along with two animals. She told what had happened and offered the one that was mounted four dollars to take her to Fort Garland." Here she encountered the dread that the Espinosas inspired all over southern Colorado among Anglos and Hispanos alike. The horseman refused, "saying that if he did, Espinosa would kill him." Dolores resumed her weary, painful trudge toward the distant fort.[59]

> Earlier in the night Philbrook had reached that place, where, in Tobin's words, he stated the case to Colonel Sam Tappan. . . . This being the third or fourth [occasion] of people being fired on in the mountains, he sent about twenty soldiers to find out what they could of Pedro García and to see if they could

> find the woman. They crossed the mountains and . . . overhauled Pedro García and learned from him that the bandits were Espinosa and companion, but García did not know what had become of the woman. The soldiers on the road back overtook the woman and brought her to Fort Garland.[60]

It is worth noting that Philbrook, fatigued and footsore as he must have been, accompanied the military search party,[61] an act of endurance and concern that speaks volumes about his determination to rescue Dolores Sánches. This act meant that in the long hours between late afternoon and sometime early the following morning he had endured the shock and fear of the Espinosas' attack, managed an escape, negotiated a difficult descent of twelve miles over rough country in the dark, given an interview to Tappan, and then volunteered to join a nearly nightlong ride with the soldiers. Thus the two disheveled travelers were finally reunited when the search party from the fort[62] caught up with Dolores about eight miles from Fort Garland.[63]

It is not hard to see a kind of redemptive symbolism in this story of two extraordinary persons, a Hispanic woman and an Anglo man, whom the Espinosas damaged—the woman, their own kind, most foully—but who refused to submit to the injuries they sustained and persisted against odds to make their way to the fort and tell Colonel Tappan the whereabouts of their abusers. A white man and a New Mexican woman had worked together to initiate the downfall of the Hispano killers who professed to hate all *gringos* but in the end had turned on one of their own to show that it was hate itself—not patriotism or religion or even revenge for the wrongs done them—that was the actual cause they served.

For Leander Philbrook, perhaps his actions that day and over that long night and morning in October 1863 helped somehow to dispel the clouds that had gathered over him and Henry when Darius was executed. Maybe the brothers found release from Purgatory after all.[64]

Samuel Tappan had just returned from the treaty conference with the Utes in Conejos, an occasion that had placed him unwillingly under the immediate and no doubt heavy-handed supervision of his bitter enemy and commander, Colonel John M. Chivington. Given the friction between them, there is every possibility Chivington had used the conference as an opportunity to demean, in large ways and small, and before an audience of eminent men, the officer to whom he grudgingly owed his present position at the head of the First Colorado Cavalry.

Tappan had come to Fort Garland a little more than a month before with high-priority orders from Chivington to capture or kill the Espinosas, but arranging for the treaty conference had consumed most of his attention since assuming command. In the time since, the Espinosas were thought to have murdered Francisco Gallegos and perhaps another Mexican in Conejos on the very eve of the conference and almost under the eyes of Governor Evans and the other luminaries of the commission. Chivington was not the kind of man to pass up a chance to blame Tappan for these embarrassing events, probably in public; nor was Tappan, with his high sense of rectitude, the sort to crouch and cringe under the scorn of a person he despised as much as he did Chivington. We can believe he returned to Fort Garland fired with a renewed determination to put an end to the Espinosa rampage and silence, at least for a while, the complaints of his superior.

So the news Philbrook and Dolores Sánches brought him between midnight and dawn of Sunday, October 11, must have seemed providential. At last the Espinosas—until now as elusive as phantoms slipping in and out of the distant mountains—had ventured near and struck almost within the shadow of Fort Garland, as if daring him to come out and take them.

And Tappan knew just how to meet that dare. He sent for Tom Tobin.

NOTES

1. Wallihan, *The Rocky Mountain Directory and Colorado Gazetteer for 1871*, 397.

2. Otherwise known as *jacales*, rude structures made of upright poles plastered with mud.

3. Bright, *Colorado Place Names*, 144.

4. Taylor, Morris L., *Trinidad, Colorado Territory*, Trinidad State College, 1966, 20–23.

5. Wallihan, *The Rocky Mountain Directory and Colorado Gazetteer for 1871*, 397.

6. Ibid.

7. Taylor, *Trinidad, Colorado Territory*, 23.

8. Ibid., 8–13, discusses the origin and provenance of these names.

9. Taylor, *Colorado South of the Border*, 293, 295.

10. Ibid., 281; Taylor says an early Spanish party of exploration, accompanied by a priest, entering what is now Colorado in search of the illusory Seven Cities of Gold, fell apart when its leaders quarreled and one murdered the other, causing the priest to turn back in disgust. Dr. David Sandoval of Colorado State University in Pueblo has pointed out to the author that this first expedition was an unauthorized one and I am obliged to him for this information. A later expedition found the "parched bones and equipment" of

the earlier group beside a river; decided the group, cursed by murder and the departure of the priest, had died in sin and unshriven; and gave the river its somber name. Bright, *Colorado Place Names*, 144, agrees, saying French hunters in the eighteenth century translated the older Spanish name. However, Taylor, *Trinidad, Colorado Territory*, 1–7, asserts the full Spanish name did not begin to appear on maps until the late nineteenth century.

11. Ibid., 284. Taylor, *Trinidad, Colorado Territory*, 24–25, dismisses this theory "since it appears that Baca never had a daughter named Trinidad." Instead, he writes, Trinidad was the name of a fondly remembered "affinity" of an early settler named Gabriel Gutiérrez, who suggested it at a public meeting called expressly for the purpose of naming the town. Taylor admits there are also other versions of the naming.

12. Taylor, *Trinidad, Colorado Territory*, 1–2.

13. Karen Mitchell, *Huerfano County, Colorado, Index to Book 1*, 10; http://www.kmitch.com/Huerfano/book1.html, accessed January 24, 2013; Wallihan, *The Rocky Mountain Directory and Gazetteer for 1871*, 397–398. The author is indebted to Ms. Mitchell for her permission to quote the material from her website.

14. Descendant List of Sergeant Thomas Philbrick, http://homepages.rootsweb.ancestry.com/~nvjack/fylbrigg/pdfs/descendants_of_sgt_thomas_philbrick.pdf, 93–94, accessed March 4, 2013.

15. Ibid.

16. Dr. Jeffrey Safford, professor emeritus of history, Montana State University, personal communication with the author March 22, 2010, March 25, 2010, March 26, 2010, April 2, 2010, October 19, 2012, and October 24, 2012. Dr. Safford has researched the Philbooks as part of his study identifying the backgrounds of the men and women—including Leander and Henry—who settled in Hot Springs Mining District, Madison County, Montana, between 1864 and 1868. He has studied the military records of the three brothers who came west, and the information they gave upon enlistment regarding birth dates varies in some instances from that found in the genealogical sources the author has consulted. Dr. Safford and the author have chosen to treat the ages the brothers offered to the enlisting officers as authoritative. The author is deeply indebted to Dr. Safford for providing nearly all the personal information about the Philbrook brothers appearing here.

17. Hollister, *Boldly They Rode*, 53.

18. Ibid., 53–54.

19. Philbrook, Robert, *The Execution of Sgt. Darius Philbrook, 1st Colorado Volunteers*, http://www.philbrick-genealogy.org/Civil%20War/Darius_Philbrook_story.htm, accessed January 24, 2013.

20. Colton, *The Civil War in the Western Territories*, 44–46, describes the "dreary march in freezing weather" of the First Colorado, leaving in two detachments, one from

Camp Weld near Denver and another from Fort Wise two hundred miles southeast, and marching a "phenomenal" four hundred miles in thirteen days to reach the army of Col. E.R.S. Canby in New Mexico. Only one or two companies—including Ovando Hollister's Company F—were mounted for scouting purposes. "Most . . . walked the entire distance" over broken country using rough trails or wagons roads and spending one "strenuous day of toilsome climbing" over Raton Pass. Leander Philbrook would not have been the only man to have broken down under these conditions. Interestingly, during the march, the two columns rendezvoused on the Purgatoire River near Trinidad. This may have been the occasion when Leander first became interested in the area where he and Henry would later settle.

21. Wallihan, *The Rocky Mountain Directory and Gazetteer for 1871*, 397–398; Mitchell, *Huerfano County, Colorado, Index to Book* 1, 10.

22. Taylor, *Trinidad, Colorado Territory*, 27, identified William R. Walker as one of the earliest settlers of Trinidad. A former soldier, he first saw the town in 1861 when it had but four or five log cabins; he returned the following spring with his family, finding that Trinidad had more than doubled its size during his absence. Walker would be a dominant figure throughout Trinidad's Territorial days.

23. Mitchell, *Huerfano County, Colorado, Index to Book 1*, 10.

24. US IRS Tax Assessment Lists, 1862–1918. The author expresses his gratitude to Christie Wright, president, Park County Local History Archives Board, for locating and sharing this information.

25. See note 16 above.

26. Dr. Jeffrey Safford, personal communication with the author, October 19, 2012. Dr. Safford mentioned above in note 16 that the Philbrook who accompanied Dolores Sánches must have been Leander, despite the frailties attributed to him. Dr. Safford's study shows Leander traveling extensively in Utah, Nevada, Montana, and back to Utah between 1864 and 1879.

27. Tobin, "The Capture of the Espinosas," 61.

28. Ibid. Jessen et al., "Colorado's Worst Serial Murders," 22, refers to this woman as Lola Sánches. So does the *Rocky Mountain News Weekly* of October 21, 1863. Tobin, who knew her, calls her Dolores Sánchez. So do most other sources. But in Spanish, Lola is a recognized diminutive of Dolores, a name derived from *María de Dolores*, or Mary of the Sorrows, the Mother of Christ.

29. See note 26.

30. "Battery" of the *Weekly Commonwealth*, October 28, 1863, terms her "a very intelligent Mexican lady."

31. Ibid. Tobin dictated his account of the killing of the Espinosas late in life and misremembered the dates involved, stating the month of the attack as September when it was actually October.

32. Helmuth, *The Passes of Colorado*, 59, says the first known use of this pass was in 1706 by Juan de Ulibarri but that regular use by travelers did not begin until 1877. If Philbrook followed this route, he must have used an old Indian trail.

33. Raymond Wilson, *Biographical Sketches: Colonel John M. Francisco, Hiram Vasquez, Henry Daigre* (LaVeta, CO: Huerfano County Historical Society, 1970), 2. Francisco, former sutler at both Fort Massachusetts and its successor, Fort Garland, purchased this property from the original Mexican land grant of Cornelio Vigil and Ceran St. Vrain. According to Wilson, "The fort served as a trading post, a protective shelter, and a stopping place for scouts, trappers and pioneers." It could also provide shelter for travelers like Philbrook and Dolores Sánches.

34. Taylor, *Trinidad, Colorado Territory*, 21.

35. Bright, *Colorado Place Names*, 183. Walsenburg was not settled until about 1873.

36. Jessen et al., "Colorado's Worst Serial Murders," 22, gives the date of October 12 but the date of the 10th is clear in the *Weekly Commonwealth* of October 28, 1862.

37. Kit Carson III, "The Lives of Two Great Scouts," *The Westerner's Brand Book* (Denver, CO: Art Craft Press, 1946), 198; Carson, the grandson of both Tobin and the famous scout Kit Carson, said Tobin told him Philbrook and Sánches used La Veta Pass. Karen Mitchell, webmaster of the Huerfano County website http://www.kmitch.com (site remains under construction as of March 4, 2013), in personal communication with the author April 1, 2010, confirmed that this pass would have been the most convenient.

38. *Weekly Commonwealth*, October 28, 1863: "It is a noteworthy fact that Gov. Evans and Mr. Nicolay met Philbrook and his lady companion only a few miles from the place of attack. Happily the Governor was escorted by a number of soldiers thoughtfully detached by Col. Chivington, in view of the danger." This information lends some credence to Tobin's idea (this volume, Chapter 11, note 32) that the Espinosas hoped to encounter Evans in the mountains and extract a pardon from him or kill him, and that the authorities feared just this possibility.

39. "Battery," reporting for the *Weekly Commonwealth*, October 28, 1863, as well as Lt. H. W. Baldwin, who commanded both the search for Dolores Sánches and the subsequent hunt for the Espinosas (Report of October 16, 1863, "Scout from Fort Garland, Colo., and killing of the outlaw Espinoza [*sic*]," *Official Records of the Union and Confederate Armies*, Series I, Vol. 22, Reports, Serial No. 32, 704) mentions the distance as seventeen or eighteen miles. Perkins, *Tom Tobin*, 158, gives the distance as twelve miles.

40. This "Canyon of Sangre de Cristo" does not appear on modern maps. The only terrain on the western end of Sangre de Cristo Pass road resembling anything like canyon topography lies to the south of the present Highway 160, which roughly follows the route of the old pass road. James E. Perkins, Tom Tobin's biographer, in personal communication with the author March 31, 2010, expressed the belief the old trail

followed Sangre de Cristo Creek south of the present Highway 160. The author partially agrees but has seen the ruts of the old trail in various places nearer the summit north of Highway 160 and the creek, and believes that at some point, now indeterminable, it crossed the line of the present highway from north to south and again followed the creek. Helmuth, *The Passes of Colorado*, 193, agrees: "The pass is visible from US160, about one-half mile down the west side from the North La Veta Pass summit. Ruts, which run off the pass down to the highway and then below the highway going west, show best when a little snow is on the ground. All these ruts are on private property." Below this point of crossing, two parallel formations south of the creek, called Black Canyon and Blind Canyon on today's maps, lie on a line running generally northeast to southwest and are located between eleven and twelve miles above Fort Garland, measuring by today's highway distances—a distance corresponding to Perkins's estimate and in his communication to the author. Though both canyons are to the *south* of Sangre de Cristo Creek, one of them may be the location of the Espinosas' attack. Repeated inquiries by the author locally and among regional historians have not resulted in a positive identification of the site. Nor did an inquiry to the Historical Topographic Map Collection of the US Geological Survey in Denver, which found no such place-name in the US Board on Geographic Names database (personal communication to author, July 9, 2012).

41. This is Perkins's estimate.

42. *Weekly Commonwealth*, October 28, 1863. The *Rocky Mountain News Weekly*, October 21, 1863, says three shots were fired, two bullets "passing through the carriage" and a fourth striking one of the mules after the team was "hurried up."

43. Tobin, "The Capture of the Espinosas," 61.

44. Ibid.

45. *Weekly Commonwealth*, October 28, 1863.

46. Ibid.

47. Tobin, "The Capture of the Espinosas," 61.

48. *Rocky Mountain News Weekly*, October 21, 1863.

49. *Weekly Commonwealth*, October 28, 1863.

50. Secrest, "The Bloody Espinosas," 13, shares this interpretation, stating, "Philbrook and Sanchez [*sic*] fled in opposite directions." Perkins, *Tom Tobin*, 158, agrees.

51. *Rocky Mountain News Weekly*, October 21, 1863.

52. Ibid.

53. Tobin, "The Capture of the Espinosas," 61–62.

54. *Rocky Mountain News Weekly*, October 21, 1863.

55. *Weekly Commonwealth*, October 28, 1863.

56. *Rocky Mountain News Weekly*, October 21, 1863.

57. Tobin, "The Capture of the Espinosas," 62.

58. *Rocky Mountain News Weekly*, October 21, 1863.

59. Ibid.

60. Tobin, "The Capture of the Espinosas," 62.

61. *Weekly Commonwealth*, October 28, 1863.

62. A detail of soldiers from Company E of the First Colorado and McClain's Battery, under the command of First Lieutenant Samuel N. Crane of the First; *Weekly Commonwealth*, October 28, 1863.

63. Perkins, *Tom Tobin*, 159.

64. Dr. Jeffrey Safford, personal communication with the author April 1, 2010, and October 19, 2012. Based on a study of Leander Philbrook's pension deposition made before officials at Salt Lake City in 1879, Dr. Safford notes that Henry remained with Leander for at least ten or fifteen years. After leaving Trinidad the brothers relocated to Madison County, Montana, to work gold claims. Dr. Safford's later research shows Leander living back in Brookfield, Wisconsin, at the time of the 1880 Census and remaining there for a decade. In 1892 he is reported to have traveled to Hot Springs, Arkansas, for unspecified "treatment." The Census of 1900 finds him in Bidwell Township, Butte County, California, a gold-mining ghost town. His reason for settling there is unknown. Eventually he returned home to Brookfield and entered the National Home for Disabled Volunteer Soldiers there. He died December 5, 1906, and is buried in the Pioneer Cemetery in Brookfield; Henry's death date and burial site are unknown. Leander may have died a widower, as no record of Nancy's death has been found in Wisconsin records. "Frankly," Dr. Safford wrote the author, "Leanders's peripatetic wanderings, so often difficult, increase my wonderment at the state of his health. Or was it desperation? His longevity . . . , unusual for his alleged precious state of health, needs thought."

13 "I Drew His Head Back over a Fallen Tree and Cut It Off"

Tom Tobin Ends the Terror

Tom Tobin was a man in the mythic mold of his friend Kit Carson, a frontier type even then beginning to pass from the scene. Mountain man, trapper, whiskey trader, and Indian scout, Tobin, like Carson, was a living legend if on a smaller scale than the universally famed and beloved Carson. Few outside northern New Mexico and southern Colorado had ever heard of him, though within that compass he was widely known, respected, feared, and even disliked. An acquaintance wrote that he was "hard and gruff and taciturn and fearless . . . [and] was never too well thought of by his neighbors."[1]

In 1863 he even looked the part of a frontiersman of twenty years earlier, often wearing a fringed buckskin coat, a bead-worked waistcoat and moccasins, and a feathered cap of bear fur. He carried a .53-caliber Hawken rifle—the old-time plainsman's preferred hunting piece—and wore an 1851 Navy Colt revolver in a holster made from the rump and tail of a buffalo.[2]

Hanging from his neck was a leather disc edged with pips to which were attached percussion caps for the Hawken, allowing him to load, cap, and fire the single-shot rifle in seconds.[3] And he was a dead shot.[4] In October 1863 when Colonel Tappan summoned him, the big four-and-a-half-foot-long, sixteen-pound Hawken had ten notches filed into the barrel just in front of the caplock, one for each man—red, white,

DOI: 10.5876/9781607322375.c13

and Hispano—whom Tobin had killed.[5] In those days, the notching of a gun to record one's kills was thought to bespeak a certain vicious indifference to human life, but in Tobin's case, though he certainly could kill quickly and without evident thought, the practice seems to have been a simple matter of accounting; he was known for his bad memory.

Dr. Edgar Hewett, an archaeologist who knew the scout in the late 1890s, wrote, "Tobin gained his great reputation as a trail man by his uncanny ability to detect and follow 'sign.' He 'could track a grasshopper through sagebrush.' Those who had seen him trailing told me that he always took the most likely starting point, swung round and round in ever widening circles until he 'cut sign,' then clung to his 'sign' until his quarry was overtaken."[6] It was a technique he had learned from the Indians with whom he had often fought and, in better times, traded. When tracking, he often got down on all fours with his face close to the ground, "following 'sign' that was imperceptible to less acute eyes."[7]

According to contemporary historian Frank Hall, John M. Francisco, who knew Tobin both as a friend and as a contractor supplying Fort Garland with provisions and horses, said the scout's "only fault was his recklessness in an Indian fight. While the enemy was in view he seemed to regard the battle as individually his own."[8] It was a paradox that Tobin, by all accounts capable of a cold-blooded ferocity in conflict and in ordinary discourse reticent to the point of rudeness,[9] was in fact, in Dr. Hewett's words, "golden hearted."

A dedicated family man, he sired six living children by his wives and a Navajo mistress, adopted a seventh, an Indian girl, and married again as a widower in his middle sixties. He was remembered as a warm and loving father and grandfather, especially by his grandson, Kit Carson III, whose reminiscences of Tobin are tinged with a deep fondness and admiration. In a domestic setting Tobin was always gentle and expressive, even with animals in a time and place when many men were inclined to thoughtless cruelty to beasts. Among friends he could be gregarious and even enjoyed a good joke and a laugh, and was capable of telling entertaining "stretchers," or tall tales, often at his own expense.

James Perkins, Tobin's biographer, describes the scout as standing about five feet seven inches tall and weighing 140 pounds—not at all a prepossessing figure even in a period when men tended to be smaller than now—with coal-black hair, blue eyes, and a natural complexion that was rather odd-looking—

Tom Tobin (ca. 1893) holding the Hawken rifle with which he killed Felipe and José Vincente Espinosa. (Photo courtesy of History Colorado, no scan number)

an ash-gray paleness, often overlain by sun- and windburn from long exposure to the elements, lending him a swarthy appearance.[10]

His photographs show him to have been markedly unhandsome, even homely, and his heavily modeled features had a somewhat Indian cast, causing many to believe he was a half-breed, which in fact he was, though his blood was not mixed with that of Native Americans. His father, Bartholomew Tobin, was an illiterate Irish immigrant; his mother, Sarah Tate Autobees, was a light-skinned mulatto thought to have been a native of Nova Scotia.

While his intermingled ethnic heritage was evident in his features, it also resisted easy classification—he might as easily have been part Hispano, part Indian, or part African American. All that could be said for certain was that he did not look to be entirely white, and this may have partially explained why Dr. Hewett said he was "never too well thought of" by his neighbors—prejudiced Anglo neighbors, most likely, for Tobin was highly regarded by Hispanos, whose ways he genuinely admired.

Thomas Tate Tobin was born to Bartholomew and Sarah in St. Louis, Missouri, perhaps in March or maybe in May, either in 1823 or 1824; Tom didn't know for sure because he himself was not only illiterate but would always suffer from an inability correctly to remember dates.[11] He had an older half-brother, Charles Autobees, who had emigrated west before him to become one of the notable pioneers of the Southwest, founding the settlement of Autobees Plaza on the Huerfano River about two miles above its mouth on the Arkansas;[12] and a sister who may have been named Caroline, of whom all record has been lost.[13]

Tobin, when about fifteen years old, had come west in 1837, joining Charles, known on the frontier as Charley, eventually finding work with a man named Simeon Turley who operated a general store at a place in northern New Mexico near Taos called Arroyo Hondo. Charley and Tom made deliveries of flour, other provisions, and whiskey—the renowned "Taos Lightning," which Turley manufactured—to the northern trading posts on the Santa Fe Trail and the Arkansas River and made annual trips back and forth between Arroyo Hondo and Independence, Missouri, for supplies.

Tobin fitted effortlessly into the New Mexican lifestyle. He learned to speak fluent Spanish and, much as Captain Wayne Eaton would a few years later, gained a deep respect for the Hispano people and their traditions. In 1844, at the age of twenty-one, he became a naturalized Mexican citizen and joined the Roman Catholic Church in order to marry a Hispano girl, fifteen-year-old

María Pascuala Bernal. Padre José Martínez officiated.[14] It will be remembered that Martínez, former *cura* of the Catholic Church in New Mexico, was also reputed to be the "Superior" of the *Santa Hermandad* and may have been, if not a mentor of Felipe and Vivián Espinosa, then perhaps an indirect influence on their early lives.[15]

Nor was this the only intriguing connection between Tobin and the men Colonel Tappan would later ask him to hunt down and exterminate. María Pascuala was the daughter of Felipe Espinosa y Bernal and María Candelaria de Herrera, and through her father, Tom's new bride was distantly related to the Espinosas of El Rito, Cochití, and San Rafael.[16]

As Frances León Quintana has pointed out, the term *cousin* in New Mexico "is used among near and distant cousins and among people whose relationship is unknown if they share a surname, always in a context of friendliness and egalitarianism."[17] So it is entirely possible that María Pascuala knew of her Espinosa relatives, and possibly had feelings for them, especially since she and Tom would eventually find a home in the *plaza* of Costilla just below the border of what would become Colorado Territory, only about a day's horseback ride from where the Espinosas lived in San Rafael.

Soon after his marriage Tobin barely survived the great Pueblo revolt of 1847 and he and Charley joined a force of volunteers that helped to suppress it.[18] Subsequently he lived the life of a trader, buffalo hunter, and mountain man; became an intimate and admirer of Carson; earned fame as a remorseless Indian fighter, most notably at the battle of El Cerro de Olla against the Utes in 1849; and in 1853 guided a grueling trek to California for Edward F. Beale's exploration party.

Tobin was about forty years old in 1863; he seems to have settled down after 1854, the last season when he is known to have gone trading with the Cheyenne and Arapaho Indians on the eastern plains. In 1852 he and half-brother Charley Autobees helped build first Fort Massachusetts in the upper San Luís and then, in 1858, its successor, Fort Garland. After Garland was completed, Tobin founded a ranch on Trinchera Creek nearby, arranging contracts with then–post sutler John Francisco to provide the garrison with grain, vegetables, and horses.

By this time he was a prosperous rancher. The 1860 Census showed he owned real estate worth $2,000 and personal property valued at $3,000. Presumably the latter figure included the worth of his seventeen-year-old male Indian slave, Dario Mondragón. Sometime in early 1863 he also acquired a female Navajo slave called Dominga,[19] ostensibly to serve as a housekeeper at the Trinchera ranch, but soon Dominga would be pregnant with his baby—awkwardly, at the same time Pascuala was carrying his sixth child.[20] Tom Tobin was as rough and ready in his love life as he was in other ways.

On the morning of October 11 Tobin was in the process of closing down the ranch, as he did every fall, preparing to travel south to Costilla where he would spend the winter months with Pascuala and the children. He had harvested and sold his crops, finished off some adobe buildings that needed repairs, and readied his horse herd for the bitter cold of a San Luís winter. But then Colonel Tappan's messenger arrived with a request to come immediately, "prepared to go for a trip in the mountains,"[21] and soon Tom was in the saddle on his way to Fort Garland.

In his account he does not say whether Tappan's message mentioned the Espinosas, but if it did, or if the galloper who brought it told him Dolores Sánches had identified her abusers by name, one wonders what thoughts the scout might have pondered during the brief, two-and-a-half-mile ride to the post. As had everybody else in Colorado Territory, he had followed the Espinosas' exploits over the months, but his own interest must have been sharper and more personal than anyone's, for the outlaws were kin to his pregnant wife and he must have known that Tappan wanted him to track them down—that, after all, was his special skill.

But then Tom Tobin does not seem to have been a reflective man. He would later say he went after the Espinosas only because "I . . . thought it the duty of all citizens to rid the country of all such characters as quick as possible."[22] The Espinosas needed to be liquidated and it would be his job to do it. In this reasoning he resembled his compatriot Carson, whom historian Hampton Sides has called "a natural born killer"[23] whose inability to read and write made him feel inferior to men of authority and education, so that he tended to obey the orders of such men, like John C. Frémont and James H. Carleton, without question, even when they were atrocious. As Sides put it, Carson's "trigger finger did not communicate with his conscience."[24]

Yet Carson, whose manner was mild and modest, was greatly loved despite his bursts of violence. Tom Tobin, also illiterate, did not enjoy the advantage of being lovable save within his own circle of family and friends; but, like Carson, neither did he dither over troubling questions of right and wrong. In the life he had lived, to dither was to invite sudden death. Furthermore, Samuel Tappan was a compelling figure—clearly the highest-ranked, most intelligent and accomplished officer yet to command in the San Luís—and

Tobin probably felt obliged to do whatever the colonel said and was no more inclined than Carson to inquire too deeply into the matter.

So he probably rode to Fort Garland that morning without a single worry or mental reservation, even knowing he might soon have to track down and kill his wife's kinsmen.

He told of his meeting with Tappan:

> He stated to me what he had been informed [by Dolores Sánches], he told me to go and see the woman, she had told him she had known me for some years. I went by Col. Tappan's orders and questioned the woman carefully. She said she knew they were Espinosas because she heard them tell Pedro García who they were and how they had maltreated her at the time.
>
> Col. Tappan then told me he wanted me to go after them. I then told him I would go. He said if I would go capture them and bring their heads to him, he would see I was recompensed for it, for me to be careful and not make a mistake and bring other parties. He asked me how many soldiers I wanted to go with me. I was then called aside by Captain [W. A.] Van Vliet, who was then acting Quarter Master at Fort Garland, who asked me if I knew them soldiers; if I did not, he would advise me not to go with them unless somebody went in command; they were all brave fighting men, if they should become dissatisfied, they would be as apt to kill me as Espinosa. I went to where Col. Tappan was. I told him I would go, but not with the soldiers. He said he wanted me to go but not without protection. I told him a citizen I would like to have with me was away from home. He said I must have soldiers with me for my protection. Lieut. H[orace] W. Baldwin, who was then Adjutant for Col. Tappan, said he would like to go if the Col. Would let him. The Col. Told him he could go, that he was a man he could depend on.[25]

It is difficult to know what to make of this back-and-forth about dissatisfied soldiers, whether or not Tobin should make the search alone, and his desire to take along an unnamed "citizen." One suspects Tobin's strongest desire was to travel and hunt in solitude; the clatter and clangor of a detachment of cavalry would not only be certain to alert the Espinosas, it would also complicate the business of cutting sign and, probably most important of all, would simply annoy and distract the scout. The absent "citizen" was likely just a dodge Tobin used to try to free himself of army interference.

Why the soldiers might have become "dissatisfied" with Tobin, as Captain Van Vliet warned him, is a mystery. We have already seen that the "Pet Lambs" tended to be a rum lot, but nothing appears in the record suggesting any friction between them and the fort's longtime contractor for provender, forage, and horseflesh.

One faint possibility does arise. During the 1862 campaign against the Texans, the Firsters had come to nourish a cordial dislike for all "Greasers." Their prejudices had only been exacerbated by their recent experience with the people of Conejos during the time some of them had been stationed there and then during the recent treaty conference.[26] If they somehow knew that Tobin's wife was Hispanic or, even less probable, had they known she was related, even remotely, to the very Hispanos they were hunting, they might have suspected Tobin of being in secret sympathy with the outlaws.

But none of this seems very likely. As far as can be established, Pascuala had yet to visit the ranch on the Trinchera or Fort Garland itself to be seen by the rank and file, and even if Tappan and Van Vliet knew she was Hispanic, this was hardly news they, as officers, would have shared with the rankers of the regiment.

It is probably best to regard these matters as detritus from an unrecoverable past that can never be assembled into an intelligible pattern. Our narrator is a man of few words and less introspection trying in old age to recall a complex event from long ago; nuances have gone unexpressed, explanations have been left out, facts have been forgotten or conflated.

If we need further proof that the past is a foreign country where things are done differently and beyond our complete comprehension, consider what Tom Tobin did next. He chose a Mexican boy, Juan Montoya, sometimes reported to have been as young as eleven or twelve,[27] to accompany him on the hunt for the most feared murderers in the Territory. Montoya worked for Captain Van Vliet. Tobin's reason? "I asked the Quarter Master to let me take the boy so he could lead my horse while I tracked the assassins."[28]

Beyond offering a tantalizing glimpse into Tobin's trailing methods—obviously he spent much of his scouting time afoot—the selection of Montoya makes little sense to the modern mind, which conceives of youths in their preteens as children to be protected and not as companions to manhunters trailing serial murderers across a pitiless frontier wilderness. But the world of Tobin and Montoya was not a world we can finally know. It is sufficient that the two of them were content with the arrangement, which to them was not at all remarkable. Were Tobin and the boy acquainted before the day he picked him, and if they were, what qualities had the lad shown that prompted Tobin's choice? There is no way of telling. But as we shall see, when the time came to spill blood, Montoya would prove equal to the challenge, so obviously Tobin had good reasons for bringing him along. We just don't know what they were.

At eleven o'clock in the morning of Monday, October 12,[29] Tobin left Fort Garland together with Lieutenant Baldwin and fifteen soldiers,[30] Montoya, and a citizen named Loren Jenks,[31] possibly a regularly employed army scout. Tappan also ordered other details out "in every direction where a spot likely to be made a rendezvous by the Espinosas was to be found."[32]

"Typo" wrote that Baldwin's detachment rode out with six days' rations and remarked that if Baldwin were to find any sign of "the villains," he would "follow as long as there is any prospect whatever of catching them."[33] The correspondent does not mention Tobin's presence, though "Battery," reporting for the rival newspaper, says, "A gentleman . . . who knows the mountains well, and who has no equal in following a trail, attends the [Baldwin] scout."[34] Oddly, "Battery" refers to Tobin as "Mr. Ottot," perhaps an awkward phonetic rendering of Autobees, a name Tom sometimes used.

Evidently the Espinosas had not been idle since their attack on Philbrook and Dolores Sánches. "Typo" wrote that two men came into the fort on the evening of the day the scouting detachments left, "stating that they had been shot at twice in the same vicinity that the other shooting took place, but who did it they did not know."[35] Far from being driven away from Sangre de Cristo Canyon by the realization that Philbrook and the woman had successfully made their way to Fort Garland to alert the authorities, it appears the Espinosas were remaining defiantly in place, waiting for the soldiers to come after them. This may have been braggadocio or it may have been insanity, but one fact seemed evident: Felipe and José Vincente were as dangerous as ever.

Their recklessness may have brought about an early clash with the searchers, for, shockingly, Tobin later claimed he "found the assassins the first day out."

> Me and four soldiers chased them through heavy pine and quaking aspen but they got away from us. I then went and took their pony tracks, and followed to a branch that was full of pebbles. They took up this branch. I told Lieut. Baldwin to go down this branch till he came to the Valley and then stop till I came to him. The Mexican boy discovered the two assassins and told Lieut. Baldwin, there goes two men on horseback, but he could not make the Lieut.

> understand until he showed him the pony track. They were then just going out of sight over the ridge, were out of sight too quick for the soldier to shoot. We then struck down the canon towards Fort Garland and camped that night.[36]

Lieutenant Baldwin's report, found in *The Official Records of the Union and Confederate Armies*, mentions no such encounter. Instead, in the flat bureaucratic language of all military correspondence, he only says the detachment "proceeded up the road toward the Sangre de Cristo Pass, to a spot in the road where a man, supposed to be Espanoza [*sic*] had committed certain outrages a day or two previous. Camped near this spot the first night."[37]

There is a languid, dismissive tone to these words, especially the reference to "a man, supposed to be Espanoza," since the ravaged but nonetheless clear-headed Dolores Sánches had given Tobin and Tappan a positive identification of the attackers that they had undoubtedly passed on to the lieutenant. If Baldwin was, as Colonel Tappan assured Tobin back at the fort, "a man he could depend on," his demeanor on the first day had done little to justify Tappan's, or Tobin's, confidence. Even the boy Montoya had shown himself more vigilant and capable—that is, if Tobin's discovery and chase of the Espinosas happened at all. Baldwin's failure to allude to the incident is hardly consistent with the scout's reminiscence.

That said, Tobin's description of the day is itself well nigh incomprehensible owing to its nearly total lack of detail. Where was he when he "found the assassins," and how did he do it? In what direction did the Espinosas flee and how far did he and the four soldiers chase them? Evidently, at some point, Tobin came across a stream with pebbles in it that descended back toward the valley. Why did he tell Lieutenant Baldwin to go down it "till he came to the Valley and then stop till I came to him?" What was the plan—to somehow catch the fugitives between them? On what ridge did Montoya see the Espinosas?

None of these questions can be answered and, surprisingly for an old mountain man, Tobin gives us no topographical information enabling us to place these activities on the ground. The only clue he gives us is that, at the end of the day, he and the soldiers "struck down the canon towards Fort Garland," implying that all the day's events had happened somewhere between the upper mouth of Sangre de Cristo Canyon and the summit of the pass. But according to Lieutenant Baldwin, the detachment had done no more that day than ride to the spot in the canyon where Philbrook and Dolores Sánches were ambushed and pitch camp.

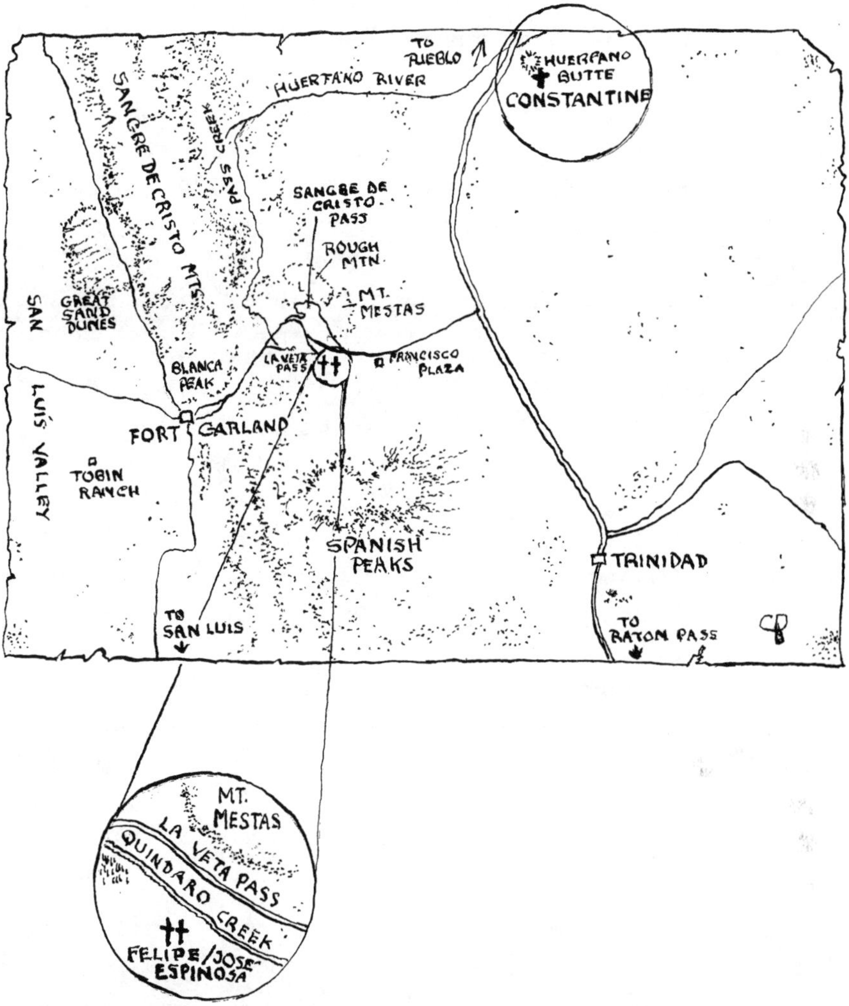

The Sangre de Cristo Pass/Huerfano River area where Felipe and José Vincente Espinosa killed Leon Constantine and where, later, Tom Tobin killed the murderers on Quindaro Creek.

The two widely divergent stories cannot be brought into conformity. Perhaps one fact deserves to be emphasized: Baldwin wrote his report on October 16, four days after the events he describes, and Tobin dictated his version on March 23, 1895,[38] thirty-two years later, when he was in his seventies. In Tobin's memory, the whole hunt for the Espinosas transpired from September 7 to September 11, evidence of his lifelong confusion about dates, and also a possible indicator that the events he recounts as happening on the first day, if they occurred at all, may have actually happened on the second, on Tuesday, October 13.

Tobin concluded his description of the first day's hunt by saying the party "camped that night with Tom Barns," illustrating he was no better with names than he was with dates. The person he refers to here is Thomas D. Burns, a young freighter then two days away from his nineteenth birthday,[39] carrying a load of goods from Denver to Fort Garland. In a letter he wrote to Tobin in 1897—doubtless in response to a request by Tom to refresh his failing recollections—Burns told what happened on the night of the encampment and the following day:

> [I]n the Cañon of Sangre de Cristo I met Lt Baldwin . . . and yourself and about fifteen men. [W]e camped together that night. [Y]ou told me that the Espanosas [*sic*] had killed two mules and burnt a buggy of an American a few days before. [T]hat the day before he had fired at the two men from behind a large rock in the Cañon. . . . Lt Baldwin and yourself thot [*sic*] the best way would be to put seven men in my wagon. I was to drive down the Cañon until we passed the rock from which he fired the day before. [I]f he fired at me then the soldiers were to jump out and go after him. The Lt and yourself with the balance of the men were to come along behind but out of sight with the rest of the men and the horses of the men who were in my wagon. I passed the rock about half a mile. The Espanosa [*sic*] did not take a shot at me, so I stopped the wagon. [T]he men got out, in a few minutes you came up to where I was. [T]he soldiers mounted your horses and you all went up the Cañon again.[40]

Interestingly, neither Baldwin nor Tobin tells of Burns's assistance in this unsuccessful ruse, perhaps because in retrospect it looked a little silly; if the Espinosas were at all vigilant, they must have been aware of the commotion it entailed and known better than to take the bait. Though Tobin fails to describe Burns's help, he does say that on the second morning "we came down the Canon until we came in sight of a peak, from which [the Espinosas] watched the road."[41] This may have been the point when the ploy was recognized as having failed.

The plucky Burns went on toward Fort Garland, presumably with the thanks of Tobin and Baldwin, and the detachment resumed its search, going up a branch, in Tobin's words, "on the left side of the Sangre de Christo [*sic*] until we got up in the mountains."[42] Evidently the party explored the timbered

Typical terrain in the Sangre de Cristo Range over which Tobin and the army detail trailed the Espinosas. (Author photos)

heights along the north side of the pass road below the summit, and this may have been the occasion when Tobin spotted and chased the Espinosas with four soldiers as recounted earlier—he speaks of having ridden through pines and quaking aspen, which stood, and still stand, in thick groves on that terrain—though, again, Baldwin says nothing of such a pursuit.

At some point on this second day, according to Tobin, "we found a lot of pony tracks where the Ute Indians had been. The soldiers scattered in all directions following up the pony tracks"; the implication is that Tobin knew the sign had been made by Indians[43] but the troopers believed it belonged to the Espinosas. The confusion chagrined Tobin. "Baldwin and some half dozen soldiers followed me. The balance of the soldiers and [Loren Jenks] got lost from us."[44] That portion of the detachment would not rejoin.[45] The reduced search party camped that night somewhere near the summit of the pass, perhaps on the western side of today's Sheep Mountain.

Next morning they made a descent, possibly from the headwaters of a creek now called Spring Branch and over the low divide to what is known on our maps as Pass Creek. From here they seem to have turned upstream, mounting toward the summit of the modern Pass Creek Pass, which crosses the Sangres between the Wet Mountain Valley and the San Luís.[46] Nearby, multiple passes offer ways over the range: Abeyta or La Veta Pass, following the old Quindaro Creek[47] down to Francisco Plaza; Pass Creek Pass; North La Veta Pass, which now accommodates US Highway 160 toward Walsenburg; the Sangre de Cristo Pass proper; and others. Tobin said, "We came down out of the mountain on to what is now called Pass Creek. We went around the dividing ridge and camped on the Veta Mountain," which is now called Mount Mestas.[48]

The next morning, Thursday, October 15, would be the last day. The diminished detachment followed Quindaro Creek downstream through thick stands of pine, willow, aspen, and cane, probably along the south-facing slope of Veta Mountain. About nine or ten o'clock they came across the tracks of two oxen.

> I got down [Tobin wrote] and examined the trail and found the two assassins were driving them. I tracked them around through the thick groves of pine and quaking asp[en], soon found they had let one of the oxen go. I knew then they had taken the other ox to their camp to butcher him. It was only by the broken twigs that I could follow them by. Lieut. Baldwin could not follow me with the horses. I told him to go to a certain point we had passed and wait for me there

Reputed location where Tobin killed and beheaded Felipe and José Vincente Espinosa. The actual site may have been destroyed by the construction of the modern highway but was more likely in the ravine at the bottom of the photograph. (Author photo)

> till he heard from me. A soldier named Joe Smith said, "What does this mean? I will go with you." Another said, "So will I." The two soldiers and the Mexican boy went with me.[49]

Now at last Tobin's account and Lieutenant Baldwin's begin to coincide—somewhat. The officer of artillery, finally abandoning the monotonous official writing style of the earlier sections of his report, used language that captured the suspense and urgency of the moment:

> Following this trail through an almost impossible fall of dead timber a distance of about 5 miles, a number of crows were seen flying over a spot on the side of, and near the top of, a lofty mountain,[50] indicating a camp or carrion near; two magpies were also seen flying about near this spot. Being convinced that a camp was near, I sent a few men with the horses which were being led . . . to the rear and behind a hill, that they might not be seen, or their heavy tread over the dead timber not be heard, in case the object of our search should be near at hand. Thomas Tobin (guide) and 4 soldiers were in advance.[51]

This was the first mention of Tobin's presence in Baldwin's report.

> Many places [Tobin recalled] I would crawl under the fallen timber to keep the direction they were driving the ox, till I got out of the timber into a clear space where I could see their tracks again. I saw some crows flying around in a circle. . . . [A] soldier that went with Baldwin came to us. I sent him to tell Baldwin to be sure and wait for me, as I thought I was close to their camps. A third soldier came to me. I went on about a hundred yards further. I discovered some magpies flying around. I watched carefully and soon located their camp. I told the soldiers not to speak, if I raised my hand to squat down and cock their guns but not to fire unless I told them to.

The encampment, according to the *Weekly Commonwealth*, probably based on interviews with one or more of the soldiers, was "in a spot almost inaccessible from all sides and commanding a view of the entire surrounding country." From this height it may have been possible to glimpse the plains to the east, perhaps even one of the rugged crowns of the Spanish Peaks above Francisco Plaza. The site was described as lying "at the head of Quindaro Creek," "about six miles from the road, and about two miles South of the summit of the range"; that is, presumably, the summit of Veta Mountain. The road referred to here may have been the Veta Pass road but, given the specified

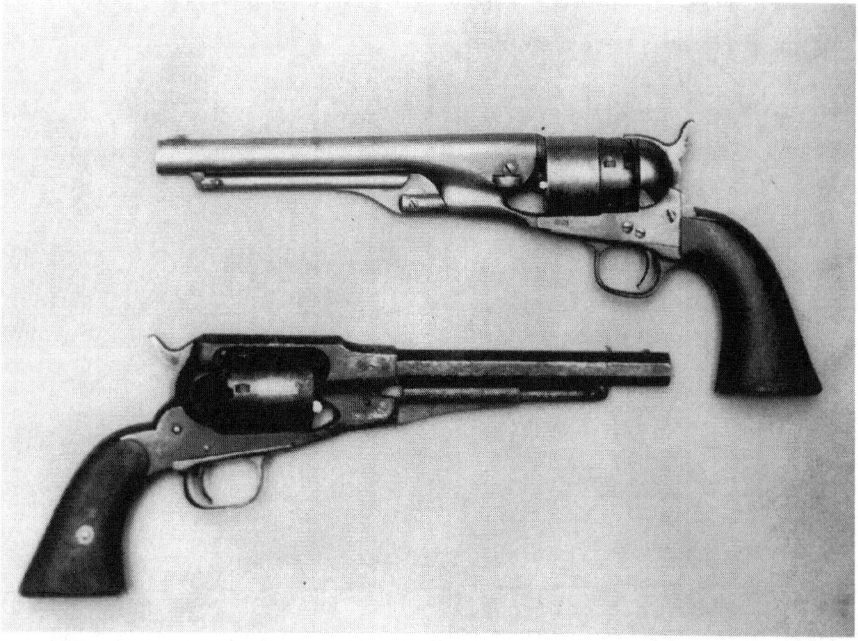

The pistols taken from the bodies of Felipe and José Vincente Espinosa. At the top is an 1860 Model Colt Army revolver, caliber .44; at the bottom is an 1858 Remington Army revolver, also caliber .44. (Photo courtesy of History Colorado, scan no. 10034565)

six-mile distance, was more likely the Sangre de Cristo Pass road. Fort Garland lay twenty-five miles distant on the west side of the mountains.[52]

Tobin advanced slowly through the tangle of fallen timber, planting each step with scrupulous care. In his mouth were two .53-caliber rifle balls, each somewhat more than half an inch through, weighing nearly an ounce apiece. These were for quick reloading—it was faster to spit a lead ball straight down the barrel of the rifle than to fumble for one in a shot pouch and then insert it through the muzzle by hand and seat it with a ramrod; also, saliva on the ball helped the powder in the chamber to adhere. Hanging around his neck was his leather disc edged with pips, to which were attached a dozen copper percussion caps, each ready to be plucked off its pip at speed and thumbed onto the nipple of the rifle cock. All his faculties were tuned for action both quick and exact as he approached the campsite, which was in a ravine just below him, the pungent smoke of its cookfire drifting upward, the carcass of the ox dangling from a tree, crows and magpies wheeling above.

"I took a step or two . . . and saw the head of one of the assassins," Tobin said.[53] It was Felipe, resting with his back against a log; the nephew sat nearby, the campfire burning between them. As Tobin watched, Felipe rose, crossed to the tree, carved a steak out of the hanging carcass of the ox, returned to the fire, and once more reclined.[54] It is not known for certain whether Tobin knew Felipe by sight, though something he would say in another moment suggests that he did. If he did, the ghastly appearance of his wife's distant kinsman may have given even the taciturn old scout a turn. Felipe's face sloped back to the crown of his skull so that he appeared to have no forehead;[55] he had a deep scar along his left cheek and wore a black, bristling beard;[56] his fingernails were long and curled inward like talons—he resembled a wild animal more than a man.[57]

Tobin may have inadvertently stepped back from this inhuman vision, for with uncharacteristic carelessness he trod on a dry stick and it broke with a snap; Felipe flinched with surprise and snatched up a pistol. "Before he turned around fairly I fired and hit him in the side; he bellowed like a bull and cried out, 'Jesus favor me,' and cried to his companion, 'Escape. I am killed.'" Tobin's bullet struck about four inches below the heart; Felipe fell but began to crawl on his hands and knees, still holding his pistol.

The young nephew, José Vincente, darted from the ravine and ran toward an undergrowth of aspen. "I sung out, 'Shoot, boys.' The three fired [two soldiers and the Mexican] and missed him. I tipped my powder horn into my rifle, dropped a bullet from my mouth into the muzzle . . . while I was capping it. I drew my gun up and fired at first sight and broke his back above his hips." The boy pitched forward. According to the *Weekly Commonwealth*, he "commenced to pray most vigorously, but soon breathed his last."[58]

Tobin knelt over Felipe, who had ceased crawling but still clutched his revolver. "Do you know me?" Tobin asked, and identified himself. Why did he do this? Did he boastfully want Felipe to know the identity of his killer as he died? Or was this a last wistful exchange between two men who knew one another, between two men who acknowledged they were related by marriage? But Felipe only swore, and when a soldier drew near, fired at him with the pistol but missed. The others riddled him with bullets. "I then caught him by the hair," said Tobin, "drew his head back over a fallen tree and cut it off. I sent [Montoya] to cut off the head of the other fellow; he cut it off and brought it to me." Clearly, Juan Montoya was no child.

It should be noted that in Lieutenant Baldwin's report Tom Tobin's leading part in this action is nearly indistinguishable; instead, the whole affair appears to have been a successful military operation. While Baldwin does identify Tobin as the search party's guide, and admits it was Tobin who led the soldiers to the camp and fired the first shot, wounding Felipe, after that the scout fades from sight:

> A boy at this time was seen to run from a spot near where the man was sitting. He was instantly shot. The man, Espanoza [*sic*], had dodged behind a log or logs, which had been thrown up as a sort of defense. While lying in this position behind the logs he was fired at several times by advancing party [soldiers]. From this sort of defense Espanoza [*sic*] fired two shots at soldiers, but without effect. He then raised his body enough to be visible, when he was pierced by many bullets, killing him instantly. The heads of the two dead persons were severed and taken to our first night's camp.[59]

It will be remembered that in Tobin's version, as the searchers approached the vicinity of what he believed was the Espinosa camp, Tom had instructed Lieutenant Baldwin to "go to a certain point and wait for me," and that as soon as the position of the camp was verified, he sent a soldier back "to tell Baldwin to be sure and wait for me, as I thought I was close to their camps." Baldwin himself admitted in his own report that "Thomas Tobin (guide) and 4 soldiers were in advance" just before the Espinosas were taken under fire.[60]

The lieutenant, then, must have been waiting some distance from the actual scene of the fight, perhaps too far in the rear for him to have seen what transpired in any detail. This, together with his natural desire to make himself and his troops appear to have been the heroes of the affair, may have prompted him to downplay Tobin's role. On the other hand, it may have been Tobin who was giving himself the best of a good story. Even if this were so, history has passed judgment in his favor. In every reliable account but Baldwin's it is Tobin, not the army, who receives credit for dispatching the Espinosas.

In his reminiscences, Tobin continued: "We rushed into their camp, the soldiers gathered their baggage and the woman's dresses and a side saddle she had with her. I took a diary and all the letters and papers I could find in the camp and the rifles, pistols and butcher knives. . . . I put their heads in a sack, came and camped on the Sangre de Cristo that night."

One cannot resist wondering whether the dresses and sidesaddle stolen from Dolores Sánches were meant to be Felipe's gifts to his wife Secundina, evidence that perhaps even in the depths of his madness and brutality, Felipe could still feel, if dimly, a tenderness for the mother of his children.

His decapitated body and that of José Vincente were left where they fell. Later Denver storekeeper George Tappan, the colonel's brother, gave the *Weekly Commonwealth* an extract from a letter in which Sam Tappan enumerated the "articles found in Espinosa's camp," including "one Colt's revolver, Navy size, a Hawkin's [*sic*] rifle, one doubled-barrelled rifle, one side-saddle, one pair of small shoes, one memorandum book, several letters, a pocket book, pen holder, and one case knife."[61] Among the writings discovered at the campsite was a request for a pardon from Governor Evans, weirdly coupled with a threat to keep killing Anglos if the pardon were denied, "for, also in killing, one gains his liberty."[62]

Another was an unfinished letter Felipe may have been writing to Secundina just before Tobin killed him: "I, Felipe, on this the forty-third night of my company with the angels. I am blessed with the milk from the breast of the Holy Mother Mary! I am covered with the cloak of the Holy San Salvador! I am defended by the sword of Holy St. Paul!"

> I am looking after animals and my enemies.
> They have hands and cannot touch me;
> They have feet and cannot catch me;
> They have eyes and cannot see me;
> They have ears and cannot hear me.
>
> I am as free as Our Lord was originally. Amen—Jesus! Flying along a narrow path, I met Jesus Christ. Jesus Christ be my father; Mother Mary be my mother; Holy St. Clement be my sponsor, so that the devil may not meet me by day or night.
>
> I will be sitting on the lap of the Virgin Mary, until I die in her arms.
> Amen—Jesus.[63]

NOTES

1. Edgar L. Hewett, "Tom Tobin," *The Colorado Magazine*, Vol. 23, No. 5 (September 1946): 211.

2. Several photographs of Tobin, taken in later life, show him wearing an elaborate costume including a long fringed buckskin coat and leggings, a highly decorated vest, and moccasins. These garments are presently on display in the San Luís Valley Museum of Alamosa, Colorado. However, researchers there have determined that much of this finery, except perhaps the moccasins, was manufactured not by Native Americans, as

often supposed, but rather by the Frontier Costuming Company of Las Vegas, New Mexico. The outfit was allegedly given to Tobin by Colorado governor Alexander Cummings, who served from 1865 to 1867, but the museum believes the outfit dates from 1886, long after Cummings's time in office. While Cummings may have gifted Tobin with the clothing during his gubernatorial tenure and thus closer to the time of Tobin's encounter with the Espinosas, he may also have done so at the later time while in private life. Further research may clear up this mystery. However, the moccasins are thought to have been of legitimate Native American provenance, probably Kiowa. The author is indebted to Captain John Brandt of Alamosa for the latter information. Tobin's Hawken rifle is now in a private collection.

3. The description is from Perkins, *Tom Tobin*, 271–285.

4. Gerald C. Smith, "The Adventures of Three Fort Garland Heroes: Tom Tobin's Great Exploit," *The San Luís Valley Historian*, Vol. II, No. 2 (Spring 1970): 3; Smith, who spoke with Tobin's grandson Kit Carson III, said Tobin "could hit a half dollar consistently at 200 yards" with the Hawken "and reload in twenty seconds." He would better that speed when he encountered the Espinosas. The Hawken had double set triggers for greater accuracy and ease of firing.

5. Perkins, *Tom Tobin*, 282, has a photograph of the rifle with the notches. The gun itself is described on page 272.

6. Hewett, "Tom Tobin," 211.

7. Ibid.

8. Hall, *History of the State of Colorado*, II: 256.

9. Smith, "The Adventures of Three Fort Garland Heroes," 2; Kit Carson III believed Tobin "was incommunicative [especially] in the presence of educated people as he could neither read nor write."

10. Perkins, *Tom Tobin*, 1–2.

11. Ibid., 7.

12. Ibid., 8, 100.

13. Ibid., 8.

14. This and all previous biographical information is drawn from Perkins, *Tom Tobin*, 7–33.

15. See Chapter 7.

16. Perkins, *Tom Tobin*, 10.

17. Quintana, *Pobladores*, 193.

18. See Chapter 7.

19. Combs, "Enslavement of Indians in the San Luis Valley of Colorado." On Lafayette Head's "List of Indians acquired by purchase and now in the service of citizens of Costilla County, C.T.," July 1865, T. T. Tobin is shown as the owner of a twenty-five-year-old Navajo slave named Domingo [*sic*] purchased from Mexicans and unwilling to

return to the tribe. Head's own Indian slaves are not listed. See also Brugge, *Navajos in the Catholic Church Records of New Mexico*, 124–125.

20. Perkins, *Tom Tobin*, 34–123. The children would be born within two months of each other, Pascuala's daughter, María Pascuala, on October 23 and Dominga's on December 31. Dominga's daughter would be christened María Catarina Tobin and Dominga herself would be baptized a Christian with the name of María Dominga Tobin.

21. Tobin, "The Capture of the Espinosas," 62.

22. Ibid., 65.

23. Sides, *Blood and Thunder*, 10.

24. Ibid., 121.

25. Tobin, "The Capture of the Espinosas," 62–63.

26. See Chapter 11.

27. Scott, *Tom Tobin and the Bloody Espinosas*, 144. Scott cites no evidence for the boy's age. Tobin, in his account, simply refers to "one Mexican boy." Smith, "The Adventures of Three Fort Garland Heroes," who got the story from Kit Carson III, says the boy was fourteen.

28. Tobin, "The Capture of the Espinosas," 63. Tobin's amanuensis, perhaps Charles John of Fort Garland, spelled the name Montolly, but Montoya or Montolla would be the preferred Spanish spelling.

29. Baldwin, "Scout from Fort Garland," 704.

30. *Weekly Commonwealth*, October 28, 1863; the soldiers were from Company C, First Colorado Cavalry. The soldiers of Company C "present at the taking of Espinosa" were Corporal Joseph B. Crickson and Privates James C. Morrison, Joseph Smith, John G. Bradley, Timothy K. Graham, William Baldwin, and Francis R. King. Also present, from Lieutenant Baldwin's command, McClain's First Battery, was Corporal William B. Waddell.

31. Hall, *History of the State of Colorado*, IV: 304; Simmons, *The San Luís Valley*, 132; R. Laurie Simmons and Thomas H. Simmons, *Town of Saguache and Cochetopa Corridor Historic Resources Survey, 2000* (Denver: Front Range Associates, 2001), available online at http://scseed.org/wb/media/RPTSAGUWP51.pdf, accessed March 6, 2013. Tobin calls this man Loring Jinks but the author gives his name as found in the sources. Jenks and his family, former residents of the Fontaine qui Bouille north of Pueblo, were among the earliest Anglo residents of the upper San Luís Valley near present Saguache. They settled about 1865 on Kerber Creek above Villa Grove along with Captain Charles Kerber, Lieutenant Albert Walters, George Neihardt, and others—ex-members of Company I, First Colorado Cavalry, formerly stationed at Fort Garland. Hispano families had already settled in the area when the veterans came. Jenks does not seem to have been a member of Company I but was evidently employed at the post in October 1863, perhaps in the capacity of a scout, when he accompanied the hunt for the Espinosas.

32. *Weekly Commonwealth*, October 28, 1861.

33. *Rocky Mountain News Weekly*, October 21, 1863.

34. *Weekly Commonwealth*, October 28, 1863.

35. *Rocky Mountain News Weekly*, October 21, 1863.

36. Tobin, "The Capture of the Espinosas," 63.

37. *The War of the Rebellion: A Compilation of the Official Records of the Union and Confederate Armies*, Series I, Vol. 22, Part I, Reports, Serial No. 32, 704–705.

38. The date of his statement, given at Fort Garland, perhaps to Charles John, who later, at Tobin's request, gave the manuscript to the Colorado Historical Society, now History Colorado.

39. Robert J. Torrez, "'El Bornes': La Tierra Amarilla and T. D. Burns," *New Mexico Historical Review*, Vol. 56, No. 2 (1981): 161–163; Burns was born October 15, 1844, in County Waterford, Ireland. When he was ten years old his family emigrated to the United States and lived in New York until moving to Whitewater, Wisconsin, in 1859. The next year Burns ran away from home to join the Pike's Peak gold rush. Soon tiring of prospecting, he found work in Denver with J. Jackson and Company, a wholesale grocery supply house. Despite his youth he seems to have been appointed a United States marshal and assigned to Fort Lyon, Colorado, where he operated a sutler's store and examined passing caravans for Confederate contraband. He then went into the freighting business, and was so engaged at the time he appears in the Espinosa story. About 1866 Burns settled in the section of northern New Mexico known as La Tierra Amarilla and, "for nearly half a century held sway" over the region as a powerful political figure and landowner. Quintana, *Pobladores*, 85–91, discusses the business methods there of Burns and other Anglos engaged in the alienation of Mexican land grants. Hispanos believed Burns and others assembled vast tracts of land by swindling the rightful owners.

40. T. D. Burns, Letter to T. T. Tobin, April 13, 1897; Tom Tobin/Cragin Collection, Box 15, Colorado Springs Museum, 215 South Tejon Street, Colorado Springs, CO 80903.

41. Tobin, "The Capture of the Espinosas," 63.

42. Ibid.

43. Patricia Richmond, "Map of the Southeastern San Luís Valley," front endpaper, *The San Luís Valley Historian*, Vol. II, No. 2 (Spring 1970), shows an old Ute trail in this vicinity, following what is now Placer Creek upstream north and west from modern Russell, then heading northwest through the mountains in the general direction of the western outlet of Mosca Pass.

44. Ibid.

45. Baldwin's report says nothing of the Indian tracks or the dividing of the detachment. From this point on his account fails to make clear what happened on which day of the pursuit and in fact becomes quite garbled, implying the party went toward the summit "on the main traveled road," then for some reason returned to the site of the

Philbrook–Sánches ambush where the dead mules and burned buggy still lay, then "took a new direction, entirely opposite to the one we had taken the day before," which sounds as if they explored the south side of the pass road until, Baldwin writes, "We followed the mountains on the *north side of the road* [emphasis added] until we struck the range of the Sierra Madre Mountains." Since there are no Sierra Madre Mountains in this area, Baldwin must have meant the Sangre de Cristo Range. But then he says, "we followed the range in a southern direction, entering the Great Cañon at its mouth, near the main road." Here he says they found a moccasin track but it was old and "of no importance to us." Was this moccasin track his equivalent of the Ute pony sign that caused the detachment to divide? From this point Baldwin writes that the party rode back up the pass road about five miles from the upper mouth of the Sangre de Cristo Canyon. Here his account and Tobin's finally appear to converge.

46. Helmuth, *The Passes of Colorado*, 163–164.

47. Richmond, "Map of the Southeastern San Luis Valley."

48. Perkins, *Tom Tobin*, 162; Bright, *Colorado Place Names*, 116.

49. Tobin, "The Capture of the Espinosas," 64.

50. This must have been Mount Mestas, or what was then called Veta Mountain.

51. Baldwin, "Scout from Fort Garland," 705.

52. *Weekly Commonwealth*, October 28, 1863.

53. Tobin, "The Capture of the Espinosas," 64ff. All the following quotations of Tobin relating to the encounter with the Espinosas are from the scout's recollections.

54. *Weekly Commonwealth*, October 28, 1863. There were four articles about the killing of the Espinosas in this one edition of the paper, some written before and some after the event. Two were offered by the regular correspondent "Battery," one evidently by an editorialist, and one, quoted here, by a reporter based on an interview with "Mr. Cuppy, of Company C, 1st Colorado Cavalry, who arrived [in Denver] from Fort Garland with dispatches to Col. Chivington." Cuppy identified the expedition's guide as Thomas Andebeau, evidently another unsuccessful phonetic spelling of Autobees. In the days of hand-setting of metal type in newspapers, the lowercase letter "u" could easily be "turned." It would be harder to catch as an error than most other letters because, at a glance at the backward lettering in the printer's slug, this turned letter would not stand out as an upside-down letter. Instead, it would "hide" as a right-side-up letter "n." Thus, "Andebeau" might have been intended as "Audebeau," which is an even closer approximation to "Autobees" (or "Autobee"). The soldier appears on a February 28, 1863, roster of Company C as Fourth Corporal Thomas W. Cuppy; Hollister, *Boldly They Rode*, 174.

55. Perkins, *Tom Tobin*, 176, note 75, quoting J. S. Sanderson, supposedly one of the soldiers who accompanied Tobin and Baldwin on the hunt. But it will be noted Sanderson's name does not appear in the *Weekly Commonwealth*'s list of the soldiers

"present at the taking of Espinosa." Nor does it appear on a roster of Company C as it existed February 28, 1863; Hollister, *Boldly They Rode*, 174.

56. Burns, Letter to T. T. Tobin; Burns saw the head when Tobin delivered it to Colonel Tappan.

57. Smith, "The Adventures of Three Fort Garland Heroes," 5; information apparently to Smith given by Kit Carson III based on his grandfather's description.

58. *Weekly Commonwealth*, October 28, 1863.

59. Baldwin, "Scout from Fort Garland," 705.

60. Ibid.

61. Ibid.

62. Ibid.

63. Ibid.

"The Brightest Success Rewarded Them for Their Toils"
Tobin Brings in the Heads

14

There are almost as many accounts of the delivery of the Espinosas' heads to Colonel Tappan as there were people who participated in the event or claimed to have witnessed it. A point of general agreement, with one exception, was that Tom Tobin and Lieutenant Baldwin's reduced detachment[1] returned to Fort Garland on the morning of Friday, October 16; Tobin himself, always befuddled about dates, says this happened on the eleventh of September.[2] They arrived "just after guard mounting,"[3] that is, about nine o'clock.[4]

Tobin, in relating his story later published in *The Colorado Magazine*, described what transpired;

> I rode up in front of the Commanding Officer's quarters and called for Col. Tappan. I rolled the assassins [*sic*] heads out of the sack at Col. Tappan's feet. I said, "Here, Col., I have accomplished what you wished. This head is Espinosa's. This other is his companion's head and there is no mistake made." Lieut. Baldwin spoke, "Yes, Col., there is no mistake, for we have this diary and letters and papers to show that they were the assassins. The diary showed that they had killed twenty-two up to the date the first Espinosa was killed, not counting the Mexican Corporal, the first killed. . . . There was about thirty killed altogether."[5]

DOI: 10.5876/9781607322375.c14

The post commandant's headquarters, Fort Garland, where Tobin delivered the Espinosas' heads to Colonel Tappan. (Author photo)

Given Tobin's discomfort with the spoken word, the speech he gives himself in this version is unconvincing to say the least. His grandson, Kit Carson III, in his reminiscences, may have better preserved both the old scout's terseness and the actual circumstances of the exposure of the grisly trophies:

> When grandpa got back to fort Garland he found that Colonel Tappan and some other officers were out horseback riding with their wives. He didn't say anything; just stood around with his gunnysack, waiting.
>
> After a while the riding party came back and somebody told the colonel Tom Tobin was waiting to see him. So he sent for grandpa, and when he came into the room, he asked, "Any luck, Tom?" Grandpa said, "So-so," and he held the gunnysack upside down and rolled the two heads out on the floor and the ladies screamed and grandpa said the colonel himself turned kind of green.
>
> For a good many years we lived at Fort Garland in the same room where Grandpa had rolled the heads out on the floor, but it didn't bother anybody.[6]

Another eyewitness was Tom Burns, the young freighter who had concealed soldiers in his wagon in hopes of tempting the Espinosas to attack on the second day of the scout. In his 1897 letter to Tobin he recalled the scene:

> I was in Col Tappan's office at the Fort. . . . [Y]ou came into the office with a flour sac [*sic*] in your hand and told Col Tappan "I have got them" he said got what, when you put your hand in the sack and pulled out the head of Espinosa. [I]t was a horrible sight . . . then you took out the head of the boy, he must have been about eighteen years old.
>
> Lt Baldwin and the men said that you had killed both of them, and I saw you take their heads out of the sack. Mr. C.F. Stallsteimer who was at Ft Garland at the time says he had the heads in his hands.[7]

At least by Burns's account Baldwin was gracious enough in Tappan's presence to give Tobin credit for bringing down both Espinosas, an accomplishment he denied the scout later that day when writing his report. As for his own description of the transfer of the heads, Baldwin's, addressed to Tappan, is the briefest on record: "We delivered to you the heads of the two persons as soon as we arrived."[8]

Perhaps the least plausible of the stories, though supposedly gained from Kit Carson III, says Tobin and Montoya arrived at dusk, without any soldiers, and found that Tappan was out walking with his wife—a highly unlikely prospect since Tappan was then a bachelor. The heads, tied in a buckskin bag, were temporarily stashed behind an office door. "In a few minutes Tappan came in, and after hearing Tobin's short report and examining the evidence he directed the orderly to bury it behind the stables"[9]

The tracking and killing of the Espinosas were hailed by "Battery":

> Lt. Baldwin's party was out four days, and traversed some of the ruggedest portions of the mountains to be found in these parts; yet the party with the most determined perseverance, followed the lead of their heroic guide—Thomas T. Tobens [*sic*]—until the brightest success rewarded them for their toils. From the first, no precaution was omitted, which could in any way add a chance of final success. Perfect silence was enjoined and maintained, and for three days these man-hunters said not a word. The one absorbing idea was of the Espinosas. The thought of their name, and the hope of their capture, that burned in every breast, stilled every tongue! At night, no more fire was made than absolutely necessary, and that, so concealed as to avoid discovery.[10]

In the happy circumstances the hyperbole was justified. Nor was Colonel Tappan any more restrained in the congratulatory order he issued on Saturday,

October 17. He began by praising the efforts of the officers and men who had sought and rescued Dolores Sánches on the night after the attack. Then he extended his "admiration and thanks" to Baldwin and the men of his detachment "and to Thomas T. Tobins [*sic*], Esq., who accompanied Lieut. Baldwin as their guide, for their energy and activity in the pursuit, the patience and perseverance of their march, the success of their efforts in the capture and beheading of the assassins, Espinosas; and thus ridding the country of these dreaded murderers and highwaymen." He continued:

> Therefore, in behalf of the men, women and children of this Territory; in behalf of the friends of those whom Espinosa has assassinated, and in my own behalf, I thank you and congratulate you upon the final success of your efforts in the capture of those who for a long time have evaded pursuit, and whose knowledge of the country and skill in covering their trail and hiding, have for so long a time enabled them to escape capture and the death their manifold crimes merited.
>
> I congratulate you, heroic soldiers of Colorado upon being instrumental in the saving of many valuable lives, or had these assassins (who only a few hours before their death placed upon paper a statement that they had already murdered thirty two Americans and intended to assassinate many more) been allowed to continue in their course of blood we know not how many or who would have fallen victims.
>
> The success which has attended your efforts is the result of your energy, courage and perseverance. Not intimidated by the difficulties and dangers which beset you, you continued to support and follow your brave guide and accomplished the object for which you were sent.
>
> Again I thank you, and hope that an honorable course in the service of your country and immortal renown awaits you.[11]

It is both agreeable and somewhat surprising to note the prominence awarded Tobin both in the newspaper account and by Tappan, especially in circumstances where the temptation to attribute all success to the military must have been very great. After all, Tappan's highest-priority assignment—given him by Chivington, no doubt, in hopes his detested subordinate would fail—had been accomplished against odds and Tappan, in his order, could have been excused for grabbing all the glory for himself and his troops, as indeed Baldwin had already done in his report. Still, it is fairly obvious that without Tom Tobin's tracking skills the army would never have cornered and killed the

The breechlock of Tobin's Hawken rifle, showing twelve notches filed into the barrel, two denoting Felipe and José Vincente Espinosa. (Photo courtesy of James E. Perkins)

Espinosas, and that the scout actually deserved an even larger share of praise than he received.

But to his credit Tappan was not content with a mere expression of thanks; he also told Tobin he had seen a report in the *Rocky Mountain News* that Governor Evans had offered a reward of $2,500 for the capture of the Espinosas. Tappan, Baldwin, and others at the post urged Tom to apply for it.[12] Tobin, quite well off at the time,[13] had undertaken the duty without any thought of payment or reward, but upon the advice of the officers and his friends he eventually put in a claim for it. His repeated attempts to secure the reward as his material circumstances deteriorated and age and ill health beset him would form a melancholy chapter of his later life.

The ultimate disposition of the Espinosas' heads has remained a mystery. For a time they were on display in the adjutant's office at Fort Garland, which was located in the same building as Tappan's quarters.[14] After that, their fate is uncertain. Perhaps they were simply buried behind the stables at Fort Garland after all. They were now useless as evidence; the materials found in the Espinosas' camp had removed any doubt about the identities of the dead.

But nineteenth-century America was fascinated, if not infatuated, with death and with the relics of death.[15] While the photographs Mathew Brady took of dead soldiers at Antietam are often truthfully cited as first acquainting Americans with the ghoulish spectacle of mass death,[16] it should also be remembered that likenesses of deceased infants, wives, husbands, and other loved ones were cherished mementos in the homes of bereaved families throughout the late Victorian age. Equally as compelling and popular, if much more lurid, were the preserved physical remains of infamous persons, especially heads.[17] The taking of heads and other body parts as proof of death was actually not uncommon on the frontier. Consequently the heads of the terrible Espinosas took on a morbid significance among the citizens of Colorado Territory who had lived in fear of the rampaging outlaws for six long months. Stories about them have abounded throughout the ensuing years.

The heads are sometimes said to have been stored in a hidden recess of the Colorado Historical Society (now History Colorado) or in the basement of the State Capitol. But perhaps the most bizarre theory of all tells that Tobin put Felipe's head in a crock of alcohol to preserve it until he could carry it to Denver to claim the reward, only to learn that the post doctor had stolen it and started for Pueblo. However, the doctor happened to drop the crock on the way, breaking it. Tobin, following the doctor to recapture the purloined head, found it lying by the roadside, retrieved it, and hurried on into Pueblo in search of more alcohol with which to repickle the now much bedraggled trophy. There was momentary confusion when it was discovered that for the first and possibly last time in its history Pueblo lacked a sufficiency of alcohol to preserve the head; but before day's end a supply train arrived and relieved the shortage.[18]

Unfortunately for the veracity of this entertaining account, Fort Garland's physician, Dr. L. B. McLain, was considered an officer of high reputation, "competent and attentive to his duties,"[19] and thus most unlikely to have made off with the pickled head. It may be worth noting that in 1920, in a piece about Tom Tobin, a Colorado Springs newspaper stated that the head of Espinosa "is reported to have been preserved in alcohol, and afterward taken to Pueblo, where it is now said to occupy a place in a collection of skulls of notorious murderers."[20]

There is also a stubbornly unverifiable story that when Chivington assigned Tappan to Fort Garland in August with orders to capture or kill the Espinosas, he insisted that the heads be obtained as proof positive of the outlaws' demise; but when Tappan obediently shipped the trophies to headquarters in Denver, Chivington publicly condemned him for having committed an "unchristian" act, a strangely finicky reaction for the perpetrator of the Sand Creek Massacre, where Colorado troops under his personal command gleefully slashed body parts from the slaughtered Cheyenne, including female genitalia that they draped over their hats and saddle horns.[21] One cannot help wishing this particular tale might be substantiated, if only in order to savor its black irony.

Mystery also surrounds the writings found in the camp of the Espinosas: the "memorandum book, several letters" and the strangely worded request for a pardon from Governor Evans.[22] The memorandum book, also referred to in some sources as a diary, may have been the item Kit Carson III said Tom Tobin found while searching the bodies of the Espinosas. "Grandpa told me he . . . found a little book listing all the people they had killed. He thought it listed twenty-five killings. I don't know whatever became of the little book. I think grandpa turned it over to the colonel [Tappan]."[23] On the other hand, Frank Hall, historian and former legislator, wrote in his *History of the State of Colorado*, "By a memorandum book taken from one of the Espinosas, for a long time in my possession, it was found that they had killed thirty-two Americans in the course of their different raids."[24]

It will be recalled that Felipe had ridden into Conejos in September, delivering a letter to the home of Lafayette Head and also addressed to Governor Evans, claiming he had killed twenty-two men in all and thought his "bravery" deserved an "honorable amnesty,"[25] wording similar to the writings found in the camp on Quindaro Creek, which the *Weekly Commonwealth* said was also addressed to the governor, translating it as follows:

> They [the Anglos] ruined our families—they took everything in our house; first our beds and blankets, then our provisions. Seeing this we said, "We would rather be dead than see such infamies committed on our families. These were the reasons we had to go out and kill Americans—revenge for the infamies committed on our families. But we have repented of killing. Pardon us for what we have done and give us our liberty, so that no officer will have anything to do with us, for also in killing, one gains his liberty. I am aware that you know of some I have killed, but of others you don't know. It is a sufficient number,

however. Ask in New Mexico if any other two men have killed as many men as the Espinosas. We have killed thirty-two.[26]

Here the translation falters, though the writer, "Battery," says Espinosa seemed to acknowledge burning the Philbrook carriage and killing the mules; he also called Americans "*gringos* and cowards" and "ridiculed the idea of their taking him."[27] So reminiscent are these sentiments of the purported content of the September letter left at Major Head's that the possibility arises it might have been a copy of the previous missive, which Felipe had retained, or perhaps a more recent document in which he feverishly repeated his earlier rants. However, "Battery" writes that all the papers found in the camp "are of a late date," but also says a second letter, "which seems to have been written to his wife," seems "particularly" so.[28] If Felipe did mention killing the mules and burning the buggy, the letter found on him must have been written within a day or two of his death.

To confuse matters further, the reader will remember that the McCannon posse found what was called a "memorandum book" on the body of Vivián Espinosa at Oil Springs Canyon, dated "Plaza de Conejos, 1863," also addressed to Governor Evans, alluding to the reward posted against the brothers by Marshal Hunt after the fight at San Rafael in January. This message, as translated by the correspondent "Dornick," stated that the Espinosas were "sworn to exterminate Americans" and would "kill Americans while they live."[29]

None of these documents is known to have survived in the original. We have their fragmentary texts only in imperfect newspaper translations or in the form of characterizations by persons, all Anglos as far as we know, who saw them. The apparent similarity of their content makes it impossible to judge when they were written, and over the years the particular provenance of each has been lost. Clark Secrest, in attempting to sort out the confusion for an article about the Espinosas in the magazine *Colorado Heritage*, noted the remarks of Kit Carson III and "Dornick" and stated there appeared to have been two separate "diaries," one taken off Vivián's body and one reclaimed from Felipe's camp, but Secrest concluded both are lost.

In December 1895 [Secrest wrote], Colorado US Senator Henry Teller wrote to John McCannon . . . stating that he (Teller) recalled McCannon having taken a diary from Vivián's body. Teller adds that he and lawyer Wilbur Fiske Stone . . . translated the diary from the Spanish and that it contained a "record of their bloody deeds." Frank Hall . . . wrote to *The Denver Post* of October

20, 1901, that Stone showed him the diary, from which, in Hall's words, "it was wholly impossible to gather any rational motive for their deeds except that [the killings] appeared to be given as blood offerings to the Virgin.[30]

This 1901 statement by Hall would seem to contradict his assertion in his *History of the State of Colorado* that Vivián's memorandum book had been "for a long time in my possession." Regrettably the matter must be left here. One can only hope that the "diary," the "memorandum book," and the "letters" are sequestered somewhere in private hands, and will one day be released for public scrutiny. Only then can we speak knowledgably about the true intentions and feelings of the Espinosas—or know for certain just how many Americans they claimed to have murdered.

Tobin returned to his ranch on Trinchera Creek and took up his annual routine, completing preparations for the move to his winter home in Costilla. But before he was able to depart, a messenger arrived from Costilla to tell him Pascuala, whose kinsman he had just killed, had given birth to a baby girl on October 23. At this same time his Navajo slave girl Dominga was in her seventh month of pregnancy. At the center of this combination of circumstances, any ordinary man might have set out for Costilla with mixed feelings, but somehow one suspects that Tom Tobin left unvexed. He probably rode south in complete serenity. He was who he was, and it was up to others to adjust to that reality. He took Dominga with him.[31]

NOTES

1. Tobin recalled that the party consisted of himself, Baldwin, and six soldiers. The troopers who had broken off earlier with Loren Jenks had never rejoined.

2. Tobin, "The Capture of the Espinosas," 65.

3. *Weekly Commonwealth*, October 28, 1863.

4. Baldwin, "Scout from Fort Garland," 705.

5. Tobin, "The Capture of the Espinosas," 65.

6. Carson, "The Lives of Two Great Scouts," 200. Carson was the grandson of both Tobin on his mother's side and the famed scout and Indian fighter Kit Carson on his father's side; he lived at Fort Garland when his paternal grandfather commanded there after the Civil War.

7. Letter of T. D. Burns to T. T. Tobin.

8. Baldwin, "Scout from Fort Garland," 705.

9. Smith, "The Adventures of Three Fort Garland Heroes," 6.

10. *Weekly Commonwealth*, October 28, 1863.

11. Ibid.

12. Tobin, "The Capture of the Espinosas," 65. Tobin went on to say no copy of that edition of the newspaper could be found because of the flood that carried away the *News* printing office, but the great Cherry Creek flood did not occur until May 20, 1864; see Smith, *The Birth of Colorado*, 192, and Berwanger, *The Rise of the Centennial State*, 14. To the author's knowledge no such reward notice has been found in editions of the *Rocky Mountain News* during the spring and summer of 1863; though its existence is commonly referred to in secondary sources, the actual date of its publication is not given. There can be little doubt such a notice was published, as both Tom Tobin and John McCannon eventually filed claims for it. See Secrest, "The 'Bloody Espinosas,'" 16. See also Appendix B.

13. Carson, "The Lives of Two Great Scouts," 200; "Grandpa was doing pretty well at the time, so he didn't try to collect the reward money. But when he got to be an old man and wasn't doing so well he put in a claim for the reward." See Appendix B.

14. *Weekly Commonwealth*, October 28, 1863.

15. For instance, see Michael Lesy, *Wisconsin Death Trip* (Albuquerque: University of New Mexico Press, 1973), 2000.

16. William A. Frassanito, *Antietam: The Photographic Legacy of America's Bloodiest Day* (New York: Charles Scribner's Sons, 1978), 16; Frassanito quotes the *New York Times* of October 20, 1862: "Mr. Brady has done something to bring home to us the terrible reality and earnestness of war. If he has not brought the bodies and laid them in our door-yards and along streets, he has done something very like it."

17. Frontier annals are rife with what we would consider ghoulish examples, especially pickled heads. James D. Horan and Paul Sann, *Pictorial History of the Wild West* (New York: Crown Publishers, 1954), 24, show a carnival advertisement announcing the exhibition of the head of California outlaw Joaquín Murieta and the deformed hand of his compatriot, Three-Fingered Jack; Edward E. Leslie, *The Devil Knows How to Ride: The True Story of William Clarke Quantrill and His Confederate Raiders* (New York: Random House, 1996), xxi, tells of the preservation of the skull of the celebrated guerrilla chieftain, to which artificial flesh and features were later applied. Whole corpses, after public examination, often ended up in anatomy labs, as described by Ted Yeatman, *Frank and Jesse James: The Story behind the Legend* (Nashville, TN: Cumberland House, 2000), for the cases of Clell Miller, Bill Stiles, and Charley Pitts of the James–Younger gang, killed in their raid on a bank in Northfield, Minnesota; Pitts's corpse was later submerged in a lake by a physician so as to reduce it by decomposition to a skeleton. Horan and Sann, *Pictorial History of the Wild West*, 210, tell how strips of skin from the body of outlaw Big Nose George Curry were tanned and made into pocketbooks and moccasins. Photographs of dead outlaws were all the rage; Glenn Shirley, *West of Hell's Fringe*

(Norman: University of Oklahoma Press, 1978), offers a gallery of such likenesses (the Dalton brothers, Bill Doolin, Tulsa Jack Blake, Little Dick West, Ned Christie, and many more).

18. Taylor, *Colorado South of the Border*, 216.

19. Thompson, *New Mexico Territory during the Civil War*, 44.

20. *Colorado Springs Gazette*, July 11, 1920.

21. There is an extensive literature dealing with the Sand Creek Massacre, but Perkins, *Tom Tobin*, 183–187, gives some of the most graphic testimony offered before the 1865 military commission charged with investigating the affair. Ironically, the chairman of this body was Lieutenant Colonel Samuel Tappan, Chivington's old enemy and an advocate of Indian rights.

22. See Chapter 13.

23. Carson, "The Lives of Two Great Scouts," 200.

24. Hall, *History of the State of Colorado*, IV: 381.

25. See Chapter 10.

26. *Weekly Commonwealth*, October 28, 1863.

27. Ibid.

28. Ibid. For the letter to Secundina, see Chapter 13.

29. *Weekly Commonwealth*, May 21, 1863. See Chapter 6.

30. Secrest, "The 'Bloody Espinosas,'" 15. This secondhand recollection by Hall is the only piece of evidence supposedly from the hand of an Espinosa, other than the bloody paper collar pinned to the tree in Red Hill Pass (see Chapter 4), which explicitly gives a religious motive for the killings.

31. Perkins, *Tom Tobin*, 170.

"Who Is There to Gather the History of This Wretch?" *The Espinosas Remembered* 15

The "Terrible Espinosas" were not soon forgotten. Like a recurring nightmare, the memory of their bloody onslaught came back again and again to the people of Colorado Territory who had suffered the contagion of dread the brothers and their nephew had unleashed.

But fear of one sort or another was not an unfamiliar sensation on the frontier—danger was endemic to the lives all frontiersmen led—and they had learned to combat it with a dry and quirky humor, as this item in the same edition of the *Rocky Mountain News Weekly* that reported the Espinosas' attack on Philbrook and Dolores Sánches illustrates:

> A little guerrilla excitement obtained here a week or two ago, occasioned by some persons shooting rabbits near the place where Carter was killed last April, just as a timid gentleman from Mosquito was passing. He supposed the shots were fired at him, and ran to Fairplay, a distance of three miles, in about twenty minutes, where he reported having been fired at several times by a party of ten or fifteen guerrillas. All Fairplay patriotically turned out to exterminate the assassins, and a rather awkward explanation ensued on meeting the rabbit hunters, persons well known in the country. If you want a fight on your hands, say guerrilla to any one living in Fairplay.[1]

DOI: 10.5876/9781607322375.c15

Even at the height of terror in South Park, a Montgomery correspondent could submit the following item to the same newspaper shortly after Metcalf was providentially saved from death when a packet of papers in his breast pocket, including President Lincoln's Emancipation Proclamation and some announcements by Congressional Delegate Hiram Pitt Bennett, turned away an Espinosa bullet:

> None stir abroad out of sight of their respective habitations, except in parties of three or more, and armed with double-barreled shot-guns, double shotted with "FFF Hazard" and No. 1 buck-shot. In addition to this, it is thought by many a matter of prudence to carry Bennett's documents neatly folded in the breast pocket of his coat—as the latest "improved patent life preserver." "Greenbacks" carried in the same manner would doubtless be as effective in checking the force of a bullet, and I would recommend all strangers desiring to visit this part of the mountains, to wear them in preference to the documents, as they could readily be made available for other purposes in case they were not needed as "breast-plates."[2]

At nearly the same time, the *Weekly Commonwealth* described a humorous encounter also rooted in "the terror occasioned by the late murders," this time at a ranch on the Platte River where two wayward Mormon travelers, hoping for a drink and directions to their destination, approached the front door, only to awaken an occupant who "hastily dressed, yelling at the top of his voice—'Robbers, robbers; John, John, get your gun, there's robbers around the house!'"

> Our Provos somewhat taken aback by this unlooked for reception, told him to shut up and give them a drink, to no purpose. Insider had got dressed and got his gun by this time and swore he would shoot the Provos if they attempted to open the door, sending John upstairs at the same time to fire out of the window. After another unsuccessful attempt to convince them of their peaceful intentions the Provos mounted their horses and proceeded up the road. They stopped a short distance from the house to fix their saddles, when our courageous ranchmen left the house and after warning them away fired their guns at them. Of course the shots went wide of the mark, and the Provos concluding it was a rather disagreeable vicinity left as soon as they could, amused, yet mad at their adventure.[3]

But with the passage of time the ravaging of the Espinosas began to take on a less risible aspect and dark thoughts of the season of dread the killers had inflicted on the country prevailed. In the summer of 1864 a traveler in South Park found lurid reminders of "the horrid scenes enacted here by Espinosa, during the months of March, April and May, 1863" on all sides:

> We passed by the spot where Brinkley and Shoup were inhumanly butchered by this devilish Greaser, Espinosa. Saw the place where they camped, and where the awful struggle took place. Again, as we enter the Mountain Pass, where the celebrated Red Hills rise grandly beside us another repetition of this awful massacre is brought home more forcibly than pleasantly; for here Layman [*sic*] and Vinton were shot down, and horribly mangled by Espinosa. The shirt collar which Layman wore when killed was nailed to a Poplar sapling, and there remains to the present day.[4]

Almost exactly a month later, the *Daily Mining Journal* of Black Hawk gave additional evidence that the Espinosa terror could still be inflamed. "Reports of trouble in the South Park arising from the re-appearance of the friends or relatives of the defunct Espinosas are rife. Would it not be a pious idea to establish a permanent Post [there], that the inhabitants of that exposed and thinly settled region might have some protection from Texan guerrillas, thieving Indians and Greaser desperadoes?"[5]

An editorialist for the *Weekly Commonwealth*, writing in the same edition that reported Tobin's slaying of the outlaws, spoke of Felipe as "one of the most fiendish desperadoes of modern times" and posed a question that would assume more and more significance as time passed and vivid recollections of the slaughters began to fade: "Who is there to gather the history of this wretch . . . with his hands dipped in blood [?] . . . We doubt not there is enough of the spirit of the evil one penetrating his career, which if brought to light would be a mine of wealth to any publisher of 'yellow-covered' literature."[6]

Yet such has not been the case. Yes, today the Espinosas are remembered, but not widely or very well. Their monstrous depredations remained sufficiently fresh in the minds of the generation who endured their atrocities to be fairly accurately rehearsed in the early histories of the time, such as Frank Hall's *History of the State of Colorado* (1889, 1890, 1895) and O. H. Baskin's *History of the Arkansas River Valley, Colorado* (1881), and in memoirs like Father J. L. Dyer's *The Snow-Shoe Itinerant* (1890) and newspaper interviews with old-timers like Joseph Lamb (1894, 1897). Later, in the early decades of the twentieth century, other relatively reliable firsthand accounts such as Tom Tobin's and Henry Priest's appeared in periodicals such as *The Colorado Magazine*.

But within twenty years of the killing of Vivián, Felipe, and José Vincente, sensation, myth, and legend had already begun to overtake the factual telling of the Espinosa story, and not by writers of "yellow-covered" literature as the editorialist had predicted, who with very few exceptions strangely ignored the worst instance of serial murder in the history of the American West. It was instead journalists of the Hearst stripe who endowed the saga with all the gaudy trappings of melodrama.

Let one example suffice, a retrospective appearing in the *New York Times*, of all places. Published in 1884, the piece was headlined "The Terrible Espinosas: A Memory of Early Days in Colorado: The Mysterious Murders Which Caused a Reign of Terror in the Mining Camps of 21 Years Ago":

> During [the] troublous days of 1863 an unknown danger came. So mysteriously did it work that for the time it fairly paralyzed the mountain communities. In March nine men had been found along the trails near Cañon City. Each man had a bullet in his head. So nearly similar were the death wounds that these mysterious assassinations naturally gave rise to much speculation. And this was increased when it was learned that three weeks before two men had been similarly killed in Santa Fé and also a soldier in Conejos. . . . Along the mountain roads dead bodies were found, each with the fatal bullet in its skull. . . . One singular fact appeared to be this, that all were killed on the wagon roads or on the trails; none were ever found off the beaten paths. . . . [The murderers] were the notorious Espinosas, outlaws from Mexico, two cousins. [The leader] had begun as a religious monomaniac . . . impelled by his patron saint to commit these deeds for the purpose of expiating his father's sins. . . . With this task before him, he enlisted a cousin in his cause, and together they started north from Chihuahua. It was a trail of blood they left behind them. . . . It was evident that gain had played no part in this mission of the elder Espinosa. None of the bodies of his victims had been robbed.[7]

Though the article gives a more or less accurate description of Tobin's taking of Felipe and his nephew, otherwise its multiple exaggerations are so obvious that they need not be enumerated here. Sensationalism only proliferated in years to come.[8] One of the more amusing of these anecdotes, appearing in an Albuquerque newspaper of 1953, not only identified the murdering Espinosa chief as a wealthy young aristocratic rancher wronged by the Americans after their takeover of New Mexico but, in telling of his death at the hands of Tom Tobin, unearthed the recollections of Loren Jenks, the civilian scout who accompanied the Tobin–Baldwin expedition but got separated from the detachment by mistakenly following the tracks of some Ute Indians.[9]

Identified as "a pioneer prospector," Jenks claimed "he organized in 1863 a party of trappers and frontiersmen to hunt down Espinosa 'and his band of ruffians' and selected Tom Tobin, an Irish trapper then living at Taos, as his chief lieutenant. Jenks said his group came upon the tracks of the outlaw in a mountain pass near Fort Garland, Colorado, and he divided his force, Tobin leading one party and he the other."[10] Though awarding himself an imaginary leading role in organizing and leading the expedition, Jenks was at least generous enough to grant Tobin credit for killing the Espinosas.[11]

More recently, books and magazine articles have, from time to time, summarized the exploits of the Espinosas, but as this is written, no reliable, fully researched book-length treatment of their terror raid has yet appeared. The fullest account is in James E. Perkins's fine biography of Tom Tobin, and even there the Espinosa outbreak is confined to a single chapter. The present work is an attempt to fill this gap in the historiography of perhaps the most singular criminal event in the annals of nineteenth-century Colorado, if not of the entire West.

There is a poignant example of how, by as early as the 1930s, memories of the bloody days of 1863 had almost completely disappeared even in South Park, the Espinosas' most prolific killing ground. In 1939 Laura Shoup of Boise, Idaho, daughter of George L. Shoup,[12] former officer of the First Colorado Cavalry, whose brother Abram Nelson Shoup was murdered by the Espinosas, set out by automobile with some friends and relatives to travel to South Park in an effort to find the grave of her uncle. Stopping at the village of Hartsel on the southern edge of the Park, she could find no one who had ever heard of the Espinosas, but a woman identified as a longtime resident suggested she go on to Fairplay, the county seat, and inquire there.

This she and her party did, and after the county clerk told them of an old graveyard on a hilltop nearby, they found the spot and were thrilled and moved to locate the grave of Abram Nelson Shoup, marked by a headstone that his brother George had arranged to be placed there. The stone was found to be broken and some men were hired to mend it, and while this work was being done, one of the party chanced to meet a man named Fisher who turned out to be "the one man in Fairplay who knew the story of the killing of Uncle Nelson and his young mining partner."[13] Ms. Shoup continued:

> This Mr. Fisher went to Park County in 1876; there he had mined, driven freight teams and had been marshal at one time. He knew Tom Paine Kennedy, who had been acquainted with Uncle Nelson, and from him heard the story of the murder, and he was able to take us to the spot where the cabin had stood. He said the two young men were mining near there and were occupying a cabin, which was about three miles from Fairplay. Espenosa [*sic*] and another Mexican had a grudge against the Americans and left a trail of blood on their way toward Mexico, killing twenty-six men as they went. Mr. Fisher . . . had . . . heard that Espenosa ha[d] finally been killed by the scout Tom Tobin.[14]

How should the Espinosas be remembered? Or perhaps the better question is, should they be remembered at all? In the Introduction we saw how *Movimiento* activists are ready with answers to both these questions arising from radical politics. Yes, they will say, the Espinosas are rightly remembered as Chicano patriots who resisted Anglo oppression and, in consequence, deserve a place in the first rank among icons of Hispanic resistance.

Perhaps anti-imperialists will say the Espinosas were first victims of, and then rebels against, colonial conquest by a foreign power that contemptuously insisted on replacing valued traditional institutions and practices with alien ones. Therefore, this rationale might go, the Espinosas are a deterrent example worthy of study by the leaders of any great power seeking to control a weaker, especially when the conquering power exerts destructive force and expropriation, as the American army did in its attack on the Espinosas in San Rafael, an act that provoked an appalling vengeance.

Exponents of liberation theology may offer an argument that, to the extent the Espinosas can be considered religiously motivated—a premise far from certain—the acquiescence of the Vatican in the nearly forcible replacement of Padre José Martínez with Bishop Jean Baptiste Lamy at the head of the church in New Mexico contributed to the alienation of many devout Hispanos like the Espinosas and their Penitente *hermanos*, whose forms of worship had evolved over time in ways the central church condemned as unorthodox and wished to eradicate. That some of these changes were imposed in part at the behest of the mainly Protestant American conquerors must have helped incite a radical religious resistance and caused it to mix with the already simmering anti-imperialist sentiment among New Mexicans. This view would seem to regard the Espinosas as worthy of remembrance, again, as cautionary examples. Without endorsing their bloody acts, such a view can at least partially explain the outbreak and argue that religious hierarchies, when under the influence of secular powers, meddle with indigenous forms of worship only at their peril.

Finally there is the view that the Espinosas were "social bandits," Robin Hood–like figures plaguing a corrupt establishment, espousing the grievances and earning the acclaim and support of the downtrodden underclass.

All these points of view are deserving of study. But whatever the Espinosas' provocations, grievances, or mental states, their reign of terror was in no sense justifiable and may have been inspired by no motive more complicated than criminal insanity.

But we would do well to remember not just the slaughters perpetrated by the Espinosas but also the deeds of "Commandant" Wilson's faction of John McCannon's posse: the lynching of Baxter and perhaps a second man, both innocent of the killings for which they died, and the torturing of Snyder by repeated hanging, as well as the ambushing of Vivián Espinosa by McCannon's own party, which historian Stephen J. Leonard implies may have qualified as a lynching, since Vivián was given no opportunity to surrender.[15] The same may even be said of Tobin's stalking and slaying of Felipe and José Vincente. In the end, if the imposition of terror is an evil deserving of study, then the response to terror is an equally instructive phenomenon.

NOTES

1. *Rocky Mountain News Weekly*, October 21, 1863.
2. Ibid., May 16, 1863.
3. *Weekly Commonwealth*, May 14, 1863.
4. Black Hawk *Daily Mining Journal*, July 23, 1864.
5. Ibid., August 22, 1864.
6. *Weekly Commonwealth*, October 28, 1863.
7. *New York Times*, February 24, 1884.
8. See the Introduction for some of the more preposterous versions of the story.
9. See Chapter 13.
10. *Albuquerque Tribune*, November 27, 1953.
11. Ibid.
12. Shoup had served as governor of Idaho and one of the state's first senators.
13. Letter of Laura Shoup to Walter C. Shoup, August 20, 1939; University of Idaho Library, Special Collections and Archives.
14. Ibid.
15. Leonard, *Lynching in Colorado*, 4.

"Times with Me Have Sadly Changed"
Destinies

16

On the day after Christmas in the first year of the twentieth century, an elderly Tom Tobin persuaded a friend[1] to write a letter for him to the Honorable George L. Shoup, senator from Idaho, in Washington, DC.

It will be remembered that Senator Shoup, once a lieutenant in the First Colorado Cavalry, had lost a brother during the Espinosas' murder raid through South Park. A few years earlier, upon hearing that Tobin had fallen on hard times, Shoup had sent the old scout, through an intermediary, $200 as an expression of "warm gratitude for his bravery and for his noble work in disposing of that arch-fiend and desperado, Espinosa."[2]

By now Tobin, in better days a noted scout whose deadly skills lesser men had often called upon to sweep away dangers that impeded settlement of an unforgiving frontier, found himself beset by illness, poverty, and old age, bereft at last of his old-time stubborn self-sufficiency and silent pride.

He expressed himself as "an humble petitioner" and admitted that "[t]imes with me have sadly changed." He was, he said, "78 years old, very feeble, always bedridden and almost blind," and completely unable to earn even the meager living to which he had been reduced in recent years. "You," he told Shoup, "are one of the many who know what I have done . . . and

DOI: 10.5876/9781607322375.c16

The last image of Tom Tobin, 1902, at seventy-nine years of age. (Photo courtesy of History Colorado, scan no. 10047139)

that I have never received anything from the Government by way of acknowledgement of services during nearly fifty years."

Governor Evans and others, he complained, had from time to time promised to pay him $2,500 "for the killing of the Mexican bandits, the Espinosas." But only after "much petitioning and wrangling in several Colorado Legislatures" had he received but a portion of the full reward, amounting in all to $1,500.[3] "I would ask you now," Tobin entreated, "in these the hours of deepest misery after a long and eventful life, to help a deserving old and broken-down man."[4]

Upon receiving the letter, Shoup generously endorsed it to Colorado senator Edward M. Teller, saying, "if you will introduce a Bill for the relief of Mr. Tobens [*sic*] I will render all the assistance in my power to secure favorable action in the Committee on Pensions, of which I am a member." He noted that Tobin was "undoubtedly very deserving of a pension."[5] But for unexplained reasons nothing came of this effort.

This was only the latest of a series of appeals for assistance Tobin had attempted since falling on hard times in the late 1870s and 1880s. In July of the same year he wrote to Shoup saying he had applied to the federal government for a monthly pension of a meager eight dollars based on his service as a volunteer during the Pueblo Revolt of 1847, but his application was rejected because official records showed he had not served in a regularly constituted military unit.[6]

Tobin's descent into penury had not been swift, but it had been sure. In 1863, the year of his greatest achievement, he had enjoyed affluence, owning properties both in the *plaza* of Costilla in New Mexico Territory and at his ranch on Trinchera Creek near Fort Garland, and he was doing a thriving business as a provision contractor for the post. Though he had already entered his middle years, his constitution was sturdy, as his stamina during the hunt for the Espinosas had shown. His wife had just given birth to a daughter, and after delivering the heads of the Espinosas to Colonel Tappan he had closed down his ranch for the winter and hastened home to his family in Costilla. On November 9 the proud parents traveled to Conejos for the baptism of the infant who, like her mother, was christened María Pascuala; the new child soon came to be called Pascualita, or "Little Pascuala." Soon Tom's wife became pregnant again, but in the meantime, on December 31, Dominga, Tobin's Navajo mistress, also gave birth to a daughter. This child was baptized María Catarina Tobin and her birth was recorded as "natural," a term denoting an unknown father. Tom was listed as the child's godfather.

The newly pregnant María Pascuala pointedly did not attend the ceremony of baptism for Dominga's child. There can be little doubt either that she disapproved of the relationship with Dominga and the illegitimate child or that Tobin, for his part, remained unperturbed by her feelings or by the feelings of anyone else. He was, as always, content within himself even if his behavior inflicted pain on those he loved, and that he did love Pascuala is beyond question. She gave premature birth to a son on May 28, 1864. The child was baptized José Cristóbal Tobin but, to the distress of both Tobin and Pascuala, he died about June 5.

Dominga herself was baptized as a Christian and given the name María Dominga Tobin. In the summer of 1868, after the government required all Navajo slaves to be returned to their natural families, Dominga and three-year-old Catarina were compelled to join the Navajos, then returning to their homeland after their disastrous starving time at the Bosque Redondo Reservation in New Mexico. The fates of Dominga and Catarina after leaving the Tobins are unknown, though James Perkins believes both mother and child perished in a freak blizzard while being transported to the new Navajo Reservation in western New Mexico and eastern Arizona. It is difficult to imagine what their lives must have been like there, given the inevitable stresses and jealousies of the situation, but we can be certain Dominga did not wish to return to her tribe, for in 1865 when Lafayette Head prepared his census of Indian slaves being held in Costilla County, he noted that she had expressed a desire to remain with the Tobins. Eventually Tobin sold his holdings in Costilla and moved María Pascuala and the family to Trinchera Ranch, where he would live for the rest of his long life.

Tobin, who could inflict shame on his beloved wife by openly fathering a child with another woman, who could kill without thought or hesitation even when his victims were his own relatives by marriage, whom life on the raw edge of the frontier had hardened to an implacable toughness—this same man was also capable of such a tender sensitivity that as long as he was financially able, in fact for many years, he secretly contributed to the welfare of Felipe Espinosa's destitute widow, María Secundina, and her children, María Vincenta, José Domingo, and María Manuela.

There is even a persistent story that in the immediate wake of the deaths of Felipe and José Vincente, Tobin secretly rode out to the death site, recovered the headless bodies, and returned them to the family for Christian burial in an undisclosed location.[7] Kit Carson III also said that his grandfather, whenever questioned about the location of the killings, intentionally misidentified the site, naming the ravine on Quindaro Creek when in fact it was in another place, which he never revealed.[8]

While the first act can easily be interpreted as a charitable one, meant to ease the anguish of Felipe's surviving loved ones, the second one is harder to explain. At first blush it would seem to imply not so much concern for the feelings of Felipe's family as some degree of respect for Felipe himself. While knowledge of the whereabouts of the death site might have caused Secundina and the children some discomfort that Tobin might have hoped to avoid, the more common reason for concealing such a location has to do with considerations of public notoriety. Tobin may have kept the real location secret as a way of fending off the morbidly curious or to prevent some kind of desecration of the spot by vengeful survivors of Felipe's victims, or even to keep it from becoming a shrine for Hispanos regarding Felipe as a patriot saint fighting against Anglo oppression. Even if they were distantly related, it is difficult to believe Tobin could have felt any degree of respect for the murderous Felipe. In the end, as is true for much of what we know of Tobin, his real intentions must remain a mystery.

What is certain is that his generosity improved the circumstances of Secundina and her family. As long as his own resources permitted, he sent food and money not only to Secundina and the children but also to the other members of the Hurtado family. In time Secundina remarried. And on May 23, 1872, Tom attended, by special invitation, the wedding of seventeen-year-old María Vincenta Espinosa, Felipe's daughter. He signed the wedding book as one of the honored witnesses. Clearly there was far more to Tom Tobin than the ruthless self-absorption and saturnine reticence many observers saw.

But by 1876 Tom Tobin's luck had begun to turn bad. In that year, while hunting, he was severely mauled by a sow bear protecting her cub. Twelve years later, at the age of sixty-four, he was shot in the groin and pelvis by his son-in-law William Carson in a violent argument over the hard-drinking Carson's treatment of his wife, Tobin's cherished daughter Pascualita.[9] Tobin had actually attempted to kill Carson, attacking him with a knife and a pistol in one of the mindless frenzies of savagery that John Francisco said often consumed him in a fight.

Shortly before this, María Pascuala had died at the age of fifty-seven, and her loss had devastated the old scout. His serious wounds and the passing of his wife caused a swift deterioration of Tobin's health and spirits. Seven months later he rallied briefly to marry a second time, taking to wife a forty-year-old widow, María Rosa Quintana. About this time, though illiterate himself, Tobin developed an interest in education, established schools for poor Hispano children, and even, improbably, became president of a school board.

In his declining years Tobin loved to dress up in his old scouting finery and pose for photographs, holding the big Hawken rifle with which he had once been so expert. It was a spectacular buckskin outfit covered with beadwork and purple-dyed decorative patterns—a full-length fringed coat, pants, vest, leggings, and moccasins. Sometimes he also wore his feathered bear-fur cap and sometimes a broad-brimmed plainsman's sombrero. His buffalo-tail holster was buckled about his waist, on some occasions holding his old cap-and-ball Navy Colt and on others a nickel-plated, ivory-gripped Colt double-action revolver, Model 1878, presented to him in 1883 by an admirer and engraved with his name. For Tom was famous, even if he was poor. He was the man who killed the Espinosas. The old Hawken had twelve notches on it now.

Tom died virtually penniless on May 15, 1904, still hoping to receive the balance of his reward for ridding Colorado Territory of its most horrific marauders. Sadly, despite his charity toward Secundina, he was troubled in his last days by fears that relatives of Felipe Espinosa would seek him out and murder him. He was eighty-one years old, a weak and querulous old man living his last days amid the crumbling adobes of the ranch he no longer could afford to own. At the moment of his passing, all the dogs for miles around began to howl and continued to do so for hours. Next day the then-owner of Trinchera Ranch churlishly turned Tom's surviving family members off the place.[10]

Tom and Pascuala Tobin now lie buried side by side near Fort Garland, in the shadow of Blanca Peak.[11]

NOTES

1. Ferdinand Meyer, a longtime acquaintance who had been one of the earliest merchants in the *plaza* of Costilla and later served as sutler of Fort Garland; Simmons, *The San Luís Valley*, 85.

2. Perkins, *Tom Tobin*, 240–241.

3. On April 3, 1893, the Colorado General Assembly appropriated $1,000 "for the relief of Thomas T. Tobens [*sic*]" and "in full payment for the killing of the Espinosa Brothers"; State of Colorado, *Laws Passed at the Ninth Session of the General Assembly of the State of Colorado, Convened at Denver on the Third Day of January, A.D. 1893* (Denver, CO: Smith-

Brooks Printing Co., 1893), 62. Secrest, "The 'Bloody Espinosas,'" says Tobin received $500 in state money in 1872 under the administration of Governor Edward McCook, an old friend. Interestingly, Secrest notes that John McCannon, leader of the California Gulch posse that killed Vivián Espinosa, also sought unsuccessfully to claim the reward, writing Senator Teller with typical effrontery, "I never received or claimed the reward, as I don't think the State is under any obligation to pay a reward offered by a territorial Governor, but I need it now." Senator Teller replied that he saw no way for McCannon to receive the reward "unless you apply to the Legislature." McCannon followed through in typical blustering fashion, as recounted in Appendix B.

4. Perkins, *Tom Tobin*, 249–250.

5. Ibid., 250.

6. Ibid., 248.

7. Personal discussion by the author with Joey Gallegos, staff assistant, Fort Garland Museum, December 4, 2009.

8. Carson, "The Lives of Two Great Scouts," 198.

9. William (Billy) Carson was the eldest son of Tobin's old partner Kit Carson. He later died of an accidentally self-inflicted gunshot wound and Tobin took in and raised his children, including Kit Carson III.

10. Over the years Tobin had gradually sold off all his Trinchera holdings to William H. Meyer (no relation to Tom's old friend Ferdinand Meyer) and others; after Tobin's resources were completely exhausted, Meyer permitted Tobin and his family to remain on the property until the old scout's death, agreeing to provide a casket and a suit of clothes for the destitute Tobin's funeral. The day after the burial, Meyer sent his foreman to displace Tobin's survivors.

11. All the information above, relating to Tom Tobin's private life, is taken from Perkins, *Tom Tobin*, 177–263.

Appendix

A

Location of the Death Site of Vivián Espinosa

Alternative Theories

While the exact spot where Tom Tobin killed Felipe and José Vincente Espinosa may have been intentionally obscured by Tobin as explained in the text, the location of that site has not been such a subject of dispute as has the place where Vivián Espinosa was killed by members of John McCannon's California Gulch posse on May 8, 1863, somewhere in the canyon lands of Fremont County north of Cañon City. The purpose of this appendix is to explore theories advanced on this subject by James E. Perkins in his biography *Tom Tobin: Frontiersman* and by Nelson D. Walker, a retired Forest Service and Bureau of Land Management forester who enjoys exploring the Colorado backcountry and discovering its history. Over many years both Perkins and Walker have personally tramped through the rugged terrain concerned. Their arguments are presented below.

THE PERKINS THEORY

In his book, referring to the written reports of Joseph Lamb and John McCannon, Perkins believes the posse, after striking Fourmile Creek, continued on for about a mile before halting for supper. "The country to the south was high barren mountains and the Espinosas' trail led right across them," toward Cañon City and the Arkansas River. As the full moon rose

McCannon called for volunteers and he and the smaller group of seven men followed the trail on foot, "leading their horses,"[1] coming out "on a high shale ridge three miles later." Here they were unable to track farther and waited in a nearby gulch for daylight. At dawn they "led their horses down the trail and came out into a large valley shaped like a bowl, with a circle of hills to the east, north and west. To the south it was open all the way to the Arkansas." They followed the trail to "the western side of the valley about a quarter of a mile then turned west into a small gulch near the base of a red rock bluff. Dismounting and carefully following the tracks, the men soon came upon a dense thicket of willows and cattails, all watered by a small spring," with a "little meadow hidden among the willows." This, writes Perkins, was the Espinosas' hideout and the death scene of Vivián (*Tom Tobin*, 148–149). The red bluff "offered protection on the north and west sides from the cold winds. The southern side of the gulch was open to the warm sun" (*Tom Tobin*, 137).

Perkins identifies the site as Grape Spring, located about thirteen miles north of Cañon City in Sec. 33, T 16S, R 70W, NE ¼, NW ¼, in an area ranched for many years by the family of A. W. Dilley (*Tom Tobin*, 172, note 26). In 1900, E. C. "Woody" Higgins, who also had a ranch in the area, found an old rifle missing its lock plate about a quarter of a mile south of Grape Spring. Perkins believes this rifle belonged to Vivián Espinosa, who he says had removed the lock plate for cleaning before the ambush. According to Perkins, the McCannon posse found a lock plate in the Espinosa camp (*Tom Tobin*, 174, note 41).

In emails to the author on March 15 and March 31, 2010, Mr. Perkins elaborated on his reasoning. Below are his comments:

> I had copies of newspapers printed just days after Vivián Espinosa was killed; and I had copies of reports by members of the posse that tracked the brothers down. I carefully followed these reports with my Jeep and my walking boots, and went over every foot of their death trek. I talked to rancher Dilly—and he confirmed the Grape Spring site, which is on his property. I even got down on hands and knees and drank from the spring to confirm that it was good water—it was. I checked out Espinosa Gulch to see if it was possible to travel up or down it. You can't! The canyon is full of boulders the size of a Greyhound bus. It's so rough a person simply couldn't—or wouldn't try it (I did). No horse or mule could make the trip. Nash Spring [Walker's preferred location] is close to the summit of this gulch, and due to the wall-of-mountain between the spring and the valley floor, you can't get there from up high. You have to make a long,

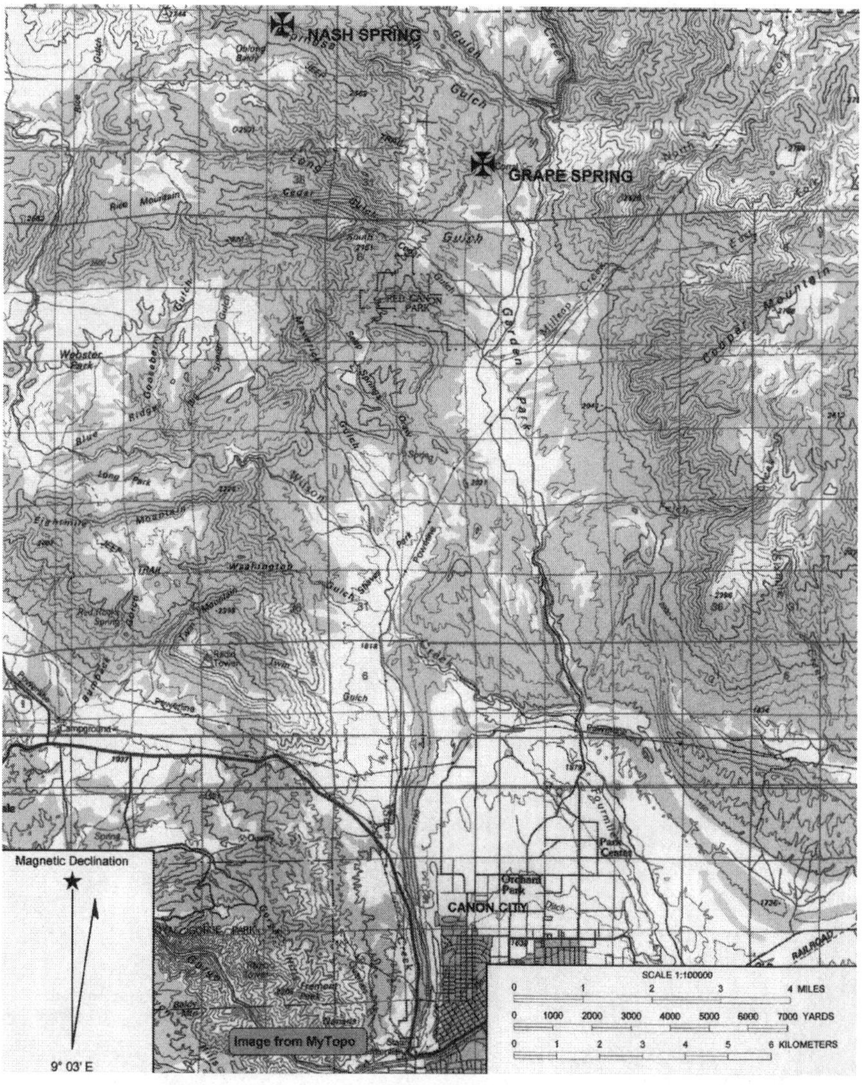

Locations of alternative ambush sites. (Image provided by MyTopo, courtesy of P.N.D. Walker)

circular trip of many, many miles. Yet it is a matter of record that members of the posse, after killing Vivián, went to a ranch house in the valley for something to eat. If they had been at Nash Spring they would have had to go almost to Cañon City and then turn north (and away from the town) to get to that ranch house.

Grape Spring. (Photo courtesy of James E. Perkins)

The posse went by the Oil Springs on their way into Cañon City, following the killing of Vivián. Oil Springs are in the valley that Four-Mile Creek runs through—and only a few miles below Grape Spring. You can't get to the springs from Nash Spring without going down to Cañon City first, and then travel back up the Four-Mile creek valley.

After the author alerted him to the 1897 newspaper interview with Joseph Lamb and the contemporary report in the *Weekly Commonwealth* confirming that the McCannon posse was on foot all the way from California Gulch to the ambush site, Perkins wrote:

> I believe [the confusion about whether the McCannon posse was mounted or afoot] starts with Lamb talking about California Gulch—that is now called Leadville. Then he tells about Espinosa murders in the Fairplay area. Then he mentions going on foot with pack animals due to the rough terrain. Well, between Leadville and Fairplay the road/trail was right over the top of the mountain that both "camps" were on each side of. It's a steep mountain—really steep, and really rough!—and I can see where it might be best to walk over it. But, once in Fairplay it just wouldn't make sense to travel on without horses, owing to the wide open spaces and great distances needed to travel.

THE WALKER THEORY

On March 1, 2010, Nelson Walker generously furnished the author this condensed account of the reasoning that leads him to believe Perkins is mistaken about the Grape Spring site and that it is more likely Vivián was killed at Nash Spring, about four miles west of Grape Spring:

> In his excellent biography, *Tom Tobin: Frontiersman*, James Perkins places the killing of Vivián Espinosa at Grape Spring, which is located about 10 miles north of Cañon City near the lower end of Espinosa Gulch. I do not agree with this conclusion but believe that the killing site is located much higher up Espinosa Gulch at a place called Nash Spring. Evidence supporting my theory includes:
>
> 1. The testimony of several long-time area residents;
> 2. A newspaper article published in the *Pueblo Star-Journal* and *Sunday Chieftain*;
> 3. A letter from Joseph Lamb to Mr. J. A. Israel, dated March 9, 1897;
> 4. Personal knowledge of the local terrain and locations of early travel routes.
>
> While investigating the Espinosa incident I talked to five different ranchers whose families had been ranching in the local area since the early 1900's. I

asked these individuals if they were familiar with the incident and if they had any knowledge of where the ambush occurred. Two of the individuals had heard about the incident but had no knowledge of where the ambush occurred. Three individuals, however, were very familiar with the incident and expressed certainty that the ambush site was located near the top end of Espinosa Gulch. Two of the individuals were specific in describing the site at Nash Spring, just east of Big Baldy. The third individual, who wasn't able to describe the exact location of the site, remembered that his father showed it to him when he was a boy while they were rounding up cattle in the Bare Hills near Big Baldy.

A man named Victor Miller wrote an article about the Espinosa incident for the *Pueblo Star-Journal* and *Sunday Chieftain*, dated March 9, 1969. Miller was a rancher and part-time writer who specialized in the history of the Old West and wrote numerous non-fictional and fictional stories for newspapers and magazines. Miller did much of his writing between 1940 and 1975. He resided on his ranch near Cotapaxi, about 30 miles west of Cañon City, where he and his mother established a homestead in 1922. Miller had a keen interest in the Espinosa incident and would have had the opportunity to interview local ranchers and residents to locate where the killing of Vivián Espinosa occurred. During the time that Miller was conducting his research there would have been many more people alive who would have known about the Espinosa incident and where it occurred. This information would have enabled him to discover the site of the ambush.

Besides providing a summary of the murderous attacks and the subsequent manhunts that ended the Espinosas' lives, Miller's article included a good quality photograph taken at the site where Vivián Espinosa was supposedly shot and killed by Joseph Lamb and Charles Carter. Two men are shown standing in the foreground of the photograph and are identified as Frank Lamb (Joseph Lamb's son), and Victor W. Miller (writer for the *Pueblo Chieftain* and *Pueblo Star-Journal*). According to the article, Frank Lamb had never been to the site until Victor Miller invited him to visit it. Both can be seen standing in a flat clearing in front of a tall rock outcrop with very distinctive fractures in the face of the rock. After obtaining a photocopy of this photograph, I was able to hike to the exact location where Miller and Frank Lamb were standing by using the photograph to find the distinctive rock outcrop. I can say with certainty that the spot where Miller and Lamb were standing is located near the upper end of Espinosa Gulch at Nash Spring.

Frank Lamb and Victor Miller at Nash Spring. (Photo courtesy of the Royal Gorge Regional Museum and History Center, photo no. 1985.106.518 and P.N.D. Walker)

Further evidence supporting the Nash Spring site includes a letter from Joseph Lamb to Mr. J. A. Israel, dated March 9, 1897, in which Joseph Lamb describes the pursuit by the posse and the eventual shooting of Vivián Espinosa. Joseph Lamb, who was a member of the posse and only 19 years old at the time, made the first shot that hit Vivián Espinosa in the chest. Charles Carter made the second shot that hit Espinosa in the head and instantly killed him.

According to Joseph Lamb's description, the ambush occurred very early in the morning. Shortly after Vivián was killed, his brother Felipe appeared on top of a rock outcrop and fired several shots at the posse before escaping. The posse made a brief pursuit after Felipe, but due to the difficult terrain and the danger posed to the individual posse members of being ambushed themselves or mistakenly shooting at each other, the pursuit was quickly called off by Captain McCannon. Lamb then goes on to explain that the posse spent an hour or two gathering items from the outlaws' camp before heading for Cañon City. This is the part of Lamb's testimony that casts doubt on the theory that the ambush occurred at Grape Spring, because according to Lamb's account the posse did not arrive at Garden Park until 9 o'clock in the evening, where they spent the night at the McFarlin ranch.

According to the timeline presented in Lamb's letter, the posse most likely departed the ambush site around 12 o'clock noon. If the ambush site was at Grape Spring, and even if the posse didn't depart the ambush site until 2 or 3 o'clock in the afternoon, they should have easily reached the south end of Garden Park before 9 o'clock. I do not know where the McFarlin ranch was located, but when you consider that the entire length of Garden Park is only about 4 miles long and that Grape Spring is only 2 miles from the north end of the Park, it raises questions about why it took the posse such a long time to travel from the ambush site to the ranch; at most a distance of only 6 miles over easy terrain.

On the other hand, the Nash Spring location fits very well with the 6 to 9 hours of travel time that it took the posse to reach McFarlin's ranch. Although the map distance between Nash Spring and Grape Spring is only 4 miles, it should be understood that this is the straight-line, "as the crow flies" distance. Because of the rugged terrain, it is not possible even today to take pack animals between the two springs by following a direct route through Espinosa Gulch. [It is possible to negotiate the entire length of Espinosa Gulch on foot but there are numerous areas where large boulders and other natural obstacles prevent travel with horses or mules. Thus, it could have been possible for Felipe Espinosa to have made his escape by descending directly down the gulch towards Garden Park, but not a feasible route for the posse to follow with their pack animals.]

For the posse to travel from Nash Spring to Garden Park would have required a more circuitous route. Under the Nash Spring scenario, the posse would have had to backtrack 7 miles from Nash Spring to Fourmile Creek to the place where they separated the day before from the members of the posse who had gone directly to Cañon City. From here they would have traveled another 9 miles via an established trail down Fourmile Creek to Garden Park. Thus, the posse would have traveled a total of 16 miles, or 8 hours, to reach the north end of Garden Park. This fits very closely to the timeline described in Joseph Lamb's letter.

To summarize, I cannot know for certain that Vivián Espinosa was killed at Nash Spring any more than James Perkins can know for sure that he was killed at Grape Spring. In the big scheme of things it probably doesn't really matter where it happened, but my only hope is that future historians will take my theory into account before automatically defaulting to what is presented in Mr. Perkins' book.

NOTE

1. As noted above, Perkins does not believe the posse traveled the whole distance from California Gulch on foot, despite the evidence of Lamb and Lieutenant Wilson that they did. But it is clear that until they separated the night before the ambush, the possemen were leading pack animals, identified by McCannon as "jacks."

Appendix

B

John McCannon's Attempt to Claim the Espinosa Reward

The following is a portion of an article found in the February 25, 1897, edition of the *Rocky Mountain News* in 2012 by Christie Wright, president of the Park County Local History Archives Board, and very generously shared with the author. It has been lightly edited. The author believes it sheds a good deal of light on the character of John McCannon, mistakenly called "McCammon" by the writer of the account.

ESPINOSAS WERE FIENDS
So Say Those Who Saw
Their Bloody Deeds

RECALLING THE HORRORS
John McCammon of Leadville
An Applicant for the Reward
Claims That It Was Through His Efforts
That the Gang was Finally Broken Up, and that Tom Tobin
Is Not Entitled to Any Reward—
Judge Wilbur F. Stone Remembers the Case,
And Says That Tom Tobin Did Kill Old Man Espinosa
In the San Luis Valley . . .

The dispute over the man entitled to the reward offered by Governor Evans for the killing of the Espinosas recurs every legislature and each time recalls stories of the most cold-blooded and daring of the outlaws of the early sixties. . . . While the reign of terror existed Governor Evans offered a large reward for the capture or death of the bandits. After the death of both of the Espinosas an effort was made to find the paper in which the reward had been offered, but every copy was destroyed. Those kept in The News office were carried away by the flood of Cherry Creek in 1863, which buried from sight so many other records. Every legislature for many years has been appealed to for an appropriation to pay this reward, which was supposed to be $2,500, but as the document is destroyed the amount is not certain.

Another Reward Wanted

A bill for the relief of John McCammon was introduced in the lower house of the present legislature by A. E. Whitney of Lake, but was reported adversely by the appropriations committee. The reasons given were the long time that had intervened since the events mentioned and the difficulty in the way of securing reliable data. When Mr. McCammon sent in his claim he sent also a letter from himself and enclosed one from Judge Wilbur F. Stone. Mr. McCammon's letter was:

> GRANITE, Colo., Jan. 15, 1897
> Alex E.J. Whitney:
>
> Dear Sir—As there is likely to be a bill bob up to pay Tom Tobin for something he did not do, I write you the details of the matter.
>
> In 1863 there were a large number of mysterious murders committed in the then territory of Colorado. Governor Evans offered a reward of $2,500 for the discovery or arrest of the murderers. I organized a company of men in California gulch and hunted them down at Saddle Mountain in Fremont county in April, 1863. We made the discovery, killed the principal one and captured all their plunder. In a memorandum they claimed to have killed twenty-two men. I have Espinosa's medal that I took off his neck at my house in Leadville. Colonel Tappan, in his report to Colonel Chivington, says the smaller one returned to the San Luis valley after his escape from Saddle Mountain and took a boy with him. They stole a steer, drove it up into a canon and butchered it. The Mexican herder trailed it to their camp. He reported his discovery to Colonel Tappan at Fort Garland. Tappan sent a squad of soldiers and he says the soldiers fired on them, killing both man and boy. Tobin cut their heads off, he says, and brought them to Fort Garland, and he says he has got $1,500 of the reward and expects to get the other $1,000. I never put in a claim yet, but I do now. I don't want such men

as Tom Tobin paid for my work. I spent $125 of my own money in fitting out the expedition.

Correcting History

Tom S. Wells has been trying to get another man to put in a claim. I expect him to do me all the dirt he can, as he is well aware that I understood his treachery when he deserted me on the trail.[1] I send you Judge Stone's letter and refer you to Senator Teller, General Sam Browne and Judge Weston. They all know I did the work. A report of it was published in an early history of the Arkansas valley in the Fremont county part of the book [Author's note: "An Account by a Participant" in O. H. Baskin's *History of the Arkansas Valley*, cited herein]. It is well to correct some of the Colorado history now. See Judge Stone. Judge Stone is one of the judges of the private claims court. The Rocky Mountain News has always been in the habit of making a great hero of Tom Tobin. It might have been a good idea to have one of the reporters interview Judge Stone so as to get the facts of the case. Tobin has no more right to that reward than you have. Show Stone's letter to the delegation, General McNeely or anyone.

"JOHN M'CAMMON"

Judge Stone's letter to Mr. McCammon reads:

In reply to your letter I will say that I remember very well the part you took in the hunt for the Espinosas and also what Tom Tobin did, and the history of the whole affair. I came down from the park to Canon City and was there the night your party got in there after the encounter up Four-Mile Creek. I do not remember Senator Teller being there at all at that time, though it may be possible that he was. Captain Kerber[2] was there in command of a squad of soldiers at the time, and the memorandum book you refer to was taken by him with other captured plunder, and he brought the memorandum to me and Mr. Hinsdale to translate, as we were the only persons there at that time who knew any Spanish, and we sat up nearly half the night translating it. I made a copy, which I kept for my own interest, but I do not know what became of the original. I knew Tom Tobin well, and I have been over the ground where he killed the last of the Espinosas, and I saw the head which was cut off and carried to Fort Garland and preserved in alcohol by the post surgeon. From various Americans and Mexicans then living in the San Luis valley I got from time to time the whole history of the

Espinosas, and I knew personally every one they murdered. Without your organizing the Lake County expedition and your skillful trailing and finding the principal one, they never would have been taken and Tobin never would have found the other one if it had not been for the nephew boy.

Last summer while at Garland I found from a granddaughter of Tom Tobin, who is also a granddaughter of Kit Carson, that her mother married an Espinosa and is living over there now, which is an odd coincidence. Very truly yours,

WILBUR F. STONE

Says Tobin Killed Them.

Judge Stone has been seen by a *News* reporter and gives it as his firm belief that the Espinosas were killed by Tom Tobin and no one else. Judge Stone was a resident of South park at the time of the murders and well remembers the reign of terror that the atrocities produced. He recounted the incidents relative to the killing of the Espinosas. Tobin, he said, was with a squad of soldiers and it was he who discovered the camp of the renegades when the soldiers, weary with an extended search, were about to turn back, Tobin noticed several buzzards circling in the air at a certain point over the mountain side, and his trained mountaineer's instinct taught him that there was a camp directly below the buzzards and the creatures were waiting their chance to seize some offal probably cast out by the campers. He also noticed a thin column of smoke. Telling the soldiers that he had discovered the camp of the outlaws, he took two companions and went forth to reconnoiter. Coming upon the camp with the utmost precaution he succeeded in killing the desperadoes. The three men then beat a retreat to the home camp and the entire squad marched to the spot and found the bodies of the slain men. There was no doubt, says the judge, that Tobin was the slayer, for his shots were heard by the two companions, and it was in the presence of the whole squad that the two bodies were beheaded.

Judge Stone, it will be remembered, was the Montgomery correspondent for the *Weekly Commonwealth* known as "Dornick" who was so often in the thick of the Espinosa developments in South Park. While his letter to McCannon is carefully worded, crediting the California Gulch posse with beginning a process that eventually ended the Espinosa terror, in his discussion with the *News* reporter Stone gives an account of Tobin's killing of Felipe and José Vincente that is virtually identical to that of Tobin himself, ending by saying, "there was no doubt . . . that Tobin was the slayer." This is a far cry from McCannon's crass assertion that Tobin was being praised "for something he did not do."

An intriguing and so-far-unanswered question is whether Governor John Evans ever officially offered a $2,500 reward for the Espinosas. Even if the published report of it in the *Rocky Mountain News* was washed away in the flood, it would seem that some official evidence of it might be found in the governor's official papers. In May 2012, at the request of this author, Elena Cline of the Department of Personnel and Administration, Colorado State Archives, searched Evans's Executive Orders for the period April to October 1863 and found no document offering a reward for the Espinosas.[3] Pending further study, the documentary source of the reward notice remains a mystery.

NOTES

1. Thomas S. Wells was a member of McCannon's California Gulch posse. The author has found no independent evidence that Wells deserted the posse on the trail. It is not known why he and McCannon might have fallen out.

2. Captain Charles Kerber, commander, Company I, First Colorado Cavalry.

3. Personal communication by email from Elena Cline, May 8, 2012.

Bibliography

PRIMARY SOURCES

Manuscripts and Archives

Captain E. Wayne Eaton, Compiled Service Record, Adjutant General's Office, Record Group 94, National Archives, Washington, DC.

Colonel John M. Chivington, "The First Colorado Regiment," unpublished reminiscence, Archives, Hubert Howe Bancroft Collection, University of Colorado at Boulder, CO.

Corporal Decedero Abaita, Compiled Service Record, Adjutant General's Office, Record Group 94, National Archives, Washington, DC.

Dorrance, David L. *Archibald H. Gillespie in the Department of New Mexico*, 1987, unpublished thesis, Special Collections, University of Arizona Library, Tucson, AZ.

E. Wayne Eaton Papers, Fray Angélico Chávez History Library / The New Mexico History Museum, Palace of the Governors, Santa Fe, NM.

First Lieutenant George L. Shoup, First Colorado Volunteer Cavalry, Diary 1862–1863, typescript, MG 8, Box 3FFDiary, University of Idaho Library Special Collections and Archives, Moscow, ID.

First Lieutenant John Lewis, Compiled Service Record, Adjutant General's Office; Charges and Specifications; Court Martial Transcript, Record Group 94, National Archives, Washington, DC.

Letter Book, Fort Garland, Colorado Territory, 1861–1862; National Archives and Records Administration, Washington, DC.

Letter of John McCannon to J. B. Abbott, July 24, 1858, Item No. 6975, Box 2, Folder 11; letters of John McCannon to James Montgomery, December 24, 1859, and May 1860, Item No. 100320, #446 Folder 2, Kansas Historical Society, Topeka, KS.

Letter of Joseph M. Lamb to J. A. Israel, March 9, 1897, MSS 224, FF3, Tom Tobin File, Stephen H. Hart Library, Colorado Historical Society, Denver, CO.

Letter of T. D. Burns to T. T. Tobin, April 13, 1897, typescript copy, Tom Tobin/Cragin Collection, Box 15, Colorado Springs Pioneers Museum, Starsmore Center for Local History, Colorado Springs, CO.

Letter, Laura Shoup to Walter C. Shoup, August 20, 1939, typescript, MG 8, Box 3FFLetter, University of Idaho Library Special Collections and Archives, Moscow, ID.

Letters and Telegrams Received, Fort Garland, C.T., 1862–1863, RG 393, Pt. 5, 1863–1864, Adjutant General's Office, National Archives and Records Administration, Washington, DC.

Letters Received by the Commission Branch, Adjutant General's Office, US Army, 1863–1870, M-1064, Roll 91, RG 94, Entry 518, pertaining to Major Archibald H. Gillespie, Additional Aide de Camp to Major General Henry W. Halleck, National Archives, Washington, DC.

Letters Received, Department of New Mexico, Record Group 393, Rolls 16, 18, 19, Adjutant General's Office, National Archives, Washington, DC.

Lieutenant-Colonel Samuel F. Tappan, unpublished autobiography (manuscript dated March 12, 1895), Kansas State Historical Society, Manuscript Department, Misc. Tap–Tra; Topeka, KS.

Major Archibald H. Gillespie, Compiled Service Record, Adjutant General's Office, Record Group 94, National Archives, Washington, DC.

Record Group 21, Records of the District Court of the US Territory of Colorado; Bankruptcy, Civil and Criminal Case Files, 1862–74; Entry 6, Case #54, *United States of America vs. George W. Brown, Isaac Roberts, Jonathan Leeper, Slatten and Harrison*, April 1863, National Archives and Records Administration, Rocky Mountain Division, Denver, CO.

Record Group No. 21, Records of the District Courts of the US, Colorado Territory, Bankruptcy, Civil and Criminal Case Files, 1862–1876, Entry 9, Third Judicial District, *U.S. vs. Francisco Gallegos, Aneseto Martine, Antonio Galvez and Nasanio Gallegos*.

Reminiscences of Joseph D. Hutchinson, August 13, 1983, typescript, Hutchinson Homestead Ranch and Learning Center, National Register of Historic Places, Poncha Springs, CO.

Samuel F. Tappan, holograph note "Six Months at Fort Garland, Oct. 3, 1863," negative photocopy, MSS 667, FF2, Stephen H. Hart Library, Colorado Historical Society, Denver, CO.

US Marshal's Files, Records of the US District Court for the Third District of Colorado, National Archives, Rocky Mountain Division, Denver, CO.

Books

Conner, Daniel Ellis. *A Confederate in the Colorado Gold Fields*. Ed. Donald J. Berthrong and Odessa Davenport. Norman: University of Oklahoma Press, 1970.

Darley, Alex M., Rev. *The Passionists of the Southwest, or the Holy Brotherhood: A Revelation of the "Penitentes."* Pueblo, CO: N.p., 1893.

Dyer, J. L. *The Snow-Shoe Itinerant*. Cincinnati: Cranston & Stowe, 1890. (Reprint by Father Dyer Methodist Church, 1975.)

Everett, G. G., and W. F. Hutchinson. *Under the Angel of Shavano*. Denver: Golden Bell Press, 1963.

General Laws and Joint Resolutions, Memorials and Private Acts, Passed at the Second Session of the Legislative Assembly of the Territory of Colorado. Denver: Rocky Mountain News Printing Company, 1863.

Gillespie, E. D., Mrs. *A Book of Remembrance*. Philadelphia: J. B. Lippincott Company, 1901.

Gutiérrez, Ramón A. *When Jesus Came, the Corn Mothers Went Away: Marriage, Sexuality, and Power in New Mexico, 1500–1846*. Stanford, CA: Stanford University Press, 1991.

Hollister, Ovando J. *Boldly They Rode: A History of the First Colorado Regiment of Volunteers*. Lakewood, CO: The Golden Press, 1949.

O'Brien, Thomas M., and Oliver Diefendorf. *General Orders of the War Department Embracing the Years 1861, 1862 and 1863*. Washington, DC: Government Printing Office, 1864.

Ostrander, Romine H. *This Soldier Life: The Diaries of Romine H. Ostrander, 1863 and 1865, in Colorado Territory*. Denver: Colorado Historical Society, 2006.

The Rocky Mountain Directory and Colorado Gazetteer for 1871. Denver: S. S. Wallihan & Company, 1871.

Secretary of the Navy. *Navy Register of the United States for the Year 1855*. Washington, DC, 1855.

Secretary of the Navy. *Register of the Commissioned and Warrant Officers of the Navy of the United States including Officers of the Marine Corps and Others for the Year 1848*. Washington, DC: C. Alexander, 1848.

Slatta, Richard W., ed. *Bandidos: The Varieties of Latin American Banditry*. Westport, CT: Greenwood Press, 1987.

US Army Adjutant General's Office and US War Department. *War of the Rebellion: A Compilation of the Official Records of the Union and Confederate Armies*. CD-ROM. Wilmington, NC: Broadfoot Publishing Company.

US Navy Department. *General Orders, Adjutant General's Office, for 1863, with an Index*. Washington, DC: Government Printing Office, 1864.

Newspapers

The Alaska Citizen, Fairbanks, 1911.

Albuquerque Tribune, 1938.

The Colorado Springs Gazette, 1920.

The Daily Mining Journal, Black Hawk, CO, 1864.

The Denver Daily News, 1894.

The Denver Post, 1901, 1960.

The Denver Republican, 1886.

The Fairplay Flume, 1863, 1908, 1983, 1990.

The Los Angeles Times, 2007.

The Newark Daily Advocate, Newark, NJ, 1896.

The New York Times, 1862.

The Ogden-Examiner, Ogden, UT, 1913.

The Rocky Mountain News Daily, 1863.

The Rocky Mountain News Weekly, 1862, 1863, 1872, and 1881.

Weekly Commonwealth, 1862, 1863.

SECONDARY SOURCES

Books and Articles

Abeyta, Aaron A. *Rise, Do Not Be Afraid*. Denver: Ghost Road Press, 2007.

Anderson, George B. *History of New Mexico: Its Resources and People*, vol. 2. Los Angeles: Pacific States Publishing Company, 1907.

Aragón, Ray John de. *Padre Martínez and Bishop Lamy*. Santa Fe, NM: Sunstone Press, 2006.

Aragón, Ray John de. *The Penitentes of New Mexico: Hermanos de la Luz/Brothers of the Light*. Santa Fe, NM: Sunstone Press, 2006.

Archuleta, Ruben E. *Land of the Penitentes, Land of Tradition*. Pueblo, CO: Schuster's Printing, 2003.

Bancroft, Hubert Howe. *History of Arizona and New Mexico: 1530–1888*, vol. 17. San Francisco: History Company, 1889.

Bancroft, Hubert Howe. *History of Nevada, Colorado, and Wyoming: 1540–1888*, vol. 25. San Francisco: History Company Publishers, 1890.

Baskin, O. L., and Company. *History of the Arkansas Valley, Colorado*. Chicago: O. L. Baskin and Company Publishers, 1881.

Bean, Luther E. *Land of the Blue Sky People*. Alamosa, CO: Q&V Printing, 1962.

Beck, Warren A., and Ynez D. Haase. *Historical Atlas of New Mexico*. Norman: University of Oklahoma Press, 1979.

Benjamin, Marcus. *John Bidwell, Pioneer: A Sketch of His Career*. Washington, DC: National Tribune Co., 1907.

Berwanger, Eugene H. *The Rise of the Centennial State: Colorado Territory, 1861–1876*. Urbana: University of Illinois Press, 2007.

Boessenecker, John. *Bandido: The Life and Times of Tiburcio Vasquez*. Norman: University of Oklahoma Press, 2010.

Bohning, Larry. "Six of the Greatest: Wilbur Fisk Stone." *Colorado Lawyer* 31, no. 7 (July 2002): 23–30.

Bright, William. *Colorado Place Names*. 3rd ed. Boulder, CO: Johnson Books, 2004.

Brooks, James F. *Captives and Cousins: Slavery, Kinship, and Community in the Southwest Borderlands*. Chapel Hill: University of North Carolina Press, 2002.

Brugge, David M. *Navajos in the Catholic Church Records of New Mexico, 1694–1875*. Santa Fe, NM: School for Advanced Research Press, 1985. (Original work published 1968.)

Carroll, Michael P. *The Penitente Brotherhood: Patriarchy and Hispano-Catholicism*. Baltimore: Johns Hopkins University Press, 2002.

Carson, Kit, III. Introduction by Forbes Parkhill. "The Lives of Two Great Scouts." *The Westerner's Brand Book*. Denver: Artcraft Press, 1946.

Cather, Willa. *Death Comes for the Archbishop*. New York: Vintage Books, 1990.

Chávez, Fray Angélico. *But Time and Chance: The Story of Padre Martínez of Taos, 1793–1867*. Santa Fe, NM: Sunstone Press, 1981.

Chávez, Fray Angélico. *My Penitente Land: Reflections on Spanish New Mexico*. Albuquerque: University of New Mexico Press, 1974.

Christmas, Henrietta M. "Conejos, Colorado: Voting in 1861." *Colorado Hispanic Genealogist* 1, no. 2 (June 2004): 27–37.

Clemmons, Walter, Mrs. Walter Clemmons et al. "Winter in the San Luis Valley." *The San Luis Valley Historian* 2, no. 1 (Winter 1970): 34–38.

Cobos, Rubén. *A Dictionary of New Mexico and Southern Colorado Spanish*. Santa Fe, NM: Museum of New Mexico Press, 1983.

Colorado Legislators Past and Present. Denver: Colorado Joint Legislative Library, n.d.

Colton, Ray R. *The Civil War in the Western Territories: Arizona, New Mexico and Utah.* Norman: University of Oklahoma Press, 1959.

Colville, Ruth M., ed. "Time-Event Chart of the San Luis Valley." *The San Luis Valley Historian* 1, no. 2 (April 1969): 1–30.

Combs, D. Gene. "Enslavement of Indians in the San Luis Valley of Colorado." *The San Luis Valley Historian* 5, no. 1 (1973): 1–28.

Cooper, Jack Pyle. "A Rebuttal Concerning Roads, Trails, Traces and Wagons." *The San Luis Valley Historian* 33, no. 3 (2001): 5–41.

Darly, Alex M. *The Passionists of the Southwest, or the Holy Brotherhood: A Revelation of the "Penitentes."* Pueblo, NM: Self-published, 1983.

DeArment, Robert K. *Knights of the Green Cloth: The Saga of Frontier Gamblers*. Norman: University of Oklahoma Press, 1982.

Denver Public Schools. *Supplemental Guide to Shaping the Law of the Land: Hispanics in the Colorado Legislature*. Denver, 2003.

Dill, R. G. "History of Lake County." In *History of the Arkansas Valley, Colorado*, ed. O. L. Baskin. Chicago: O. L. Baskin & Co., 1881.

Egan, Martha. *Milagros: Votive Offerings from the Americas*. Santa Fe, NM: Museum of New Mexico Press, 1991.

Eggenhoffer, Nick. *Wagons, Mules and Men: How the Frontier Moved West*. New York: Hastings House Publishers, 1961.

Eicher, John H., and David J. Eicher. *Civil War High Commands*. Stanford, CA: Stanford University Press, 2001.

Espinosa, Aurelio M., and J. Manuel Espinosa, eds. *The Folklore of Spain in the American Southwest: Traditional Spanish Folk Literature in Northern New Mexico and Southern Colorado*. Norman: University of Oklahoma Press, 1985.

Everett, George G., and Wendell F. Hutchinson. *Under the Angel of Shavano*. Denver: Golden Bell Press, 1863.

Faust, Patricia L., ed. *Historical Times Illustrated Encyclopedia of the Civil War*. New York: Harper & Row, 1986.

Fellman, Michael. *Inside War: The Guerrilla Conflict in Missouri during the American Civil War*. Oxford: Oxford University Press, 1989.

Frassanito, William A. *Antietam: The Photographic Legacy of America's Bloodiest Day*. New York: Charles Scribner's Sons, 1978.

Frazier, Donald S. *Blood and Treasure: Confederate Empire in the Southwest*. College Station: Texas A&M University Press, 1995.

Garrard, Louis H. *Wah-to-yah and the Taos Trail*. Reprint. Norman: University of Oklahoma Press, 1955.

Giffords, Gloria Fraser. *Mexican Folk Retablos*. Rev. ed. Albuquerque: University of New Mexico Press, 1992. (Original work published 1974.)

Gillespie, Elizabeth Duane. *A Book of Remembrance*. Philadelphia, PA: J. B. Lippincott Company, 1901.

Gomez, Laura E. "Off-White in an Age of White Supremacy: Mexican Elites and the Rights of Indians and Blacks in Nineteenth-Century New Mexico." *Chicano-Latino Law Review* 25, no. 9 (2005): 9–59.

Gutiérrez, Ramón A. *When Jesus Came, the Corn Mothers Went Away*. Stanford, CA: Stanford University Press, 1991.

Haley, J. Evetts. *Charles Goodnight: Cowman and Plainsman*. Norman: University of Oklahoma Press, 1936.

Hall, Frank. *History of the State of Colorado*, vol. 1. Chicago: Blakely Printing Company, 1889.

Hall, Frank. *History of the State of Colorado*, vol. 2. Chicago: Blakely Printing Company, 1889.

Hall, Frank. *History of the State of Colorado*, vol. 3. Chicago: Blakely Printing Company, 1890.

Hall, Frank. *History of the State of Colorado*, vol. 4. Chicago: Blakely Printing Company, 1895.

Harbour, Midge. *The Tarryall Mountains and the Puma Hills: A History*. Colorado Springs: Century One Press, 1982.

Heitman, F. B. *Historical Register of the United States Army from Its Organization September 29, 1789, to September 29, 1889*. Washington, DC: The National Tribune, 1890.

Helmuth, Ed, and Gloria Helmuth. *The Passes of Colorado: An Encyclopedia of Watershed Divides*. Boulder, CO: Pruett Publishing Company, 1994.

Hewett, Edgar L. "Tom Tobin." *Colorado Magazine* 23, no. 5 (September 1946): 210–211.

Hobsbawm, Eric. *Primitive Rebels: Studies in Archaic Forms of Social Movement in the 19th and 20th Centuries*. New York: Norton, 1965.

Hodge, Betty L. "Fort Garland: A Window onto Southwest History." *The San Luis Valley Historian* 24, no. 2 (1992): 5–48.

Horan, James D., and Paul Sann. *Pictorial History of the Wild West*. New York: Crown Publishers, 1954.

Horgan, Paul. *Lamy of Santa Fe*. New York: Farrar, Straus and Giroux, 1975.

Jensen, Joan M., and Darlis A. Miller, eds. *New Mexico Women: Intercultural Perspectives*. Albuquerque: University of New Mexico Press, 1986.

Jepson, Thomas C. *The Telegraph Comes to Colorado: A New Technology and Its Consequences.* Essays and Monographs in Colorado History, No. 7. Denver: Historical Society of Colorado, 1987.

Jessen, Ken. *Colorado Gunsmoke: True Stories of Outlaws and Lawmen on the Colorado Frontier.* Loveland, CO: J. V. Publications, 1986.

Jessen, Kenneth, John Lamb, and Dr. David Sandoval. "Colorado's Worst Serial Murders: The Espinosa Story." *The San Luis Valley Historian* 27, no. 4 (1995): 13–29.

Josephy, Alvin M., Jr. *The Civil War in the American West.* New York: Alfred A. Knopf, 1991.

Julian, Robert. *The Place Names of New Mexico.* Rev. ed. Albuquerque: University of New Mexico Press, 1998.

Keleher, William A. *Turmoil in New Mexico, 1846–1868.* Santa Fe, NM: Rydal Press, 1952.

Kessler, Ron. *San Luís Valley Place Names.* Monte Vista, CO: Adobe Village Press, 2002.

Laas, Virginia Jeans. *Wartime Washington: The Civil War Letters of Elizabeth Blair Lee.* Urbana: University of Illinois Press, 1991.

L'Aloge, Bob. *The Incident of New Mexico's Nightriders: A True Account of the Socorro Vigilantes.* Las Cruces, NM: Yucca Tree Press, 1992.

La Plata County Government Records, Collection M-028, Series 18.5. "A History of the District Courts of the San Luis Valley." Durango, CO: Center for Southwest Studies, Fort Lewis College, n.d.

Lass, Virginia Jeans. *Wartime Washington: The Civil War Letters of Elizabeth Blair Lee.* Urbana: University of Illinois Press, 1999.

Leach, Josiah Granville. *Genealogical and Biographical Memorials of the Reading, Howell, Verkes, Watts, Latham, and Elkins Families.* Philadelphia: J. B. Lippincott, 1898.

LeCompte, Janet. *Pueblo, Hardscrabble and Greenhorn: The Upper Arkansas, 1832–1856.* Norman: University of Oklahoma Press, 1978.

Leonard, Stephen J. *Lynching in Colorado, 1859–1919.* Boulder: University Press of Colorado, 2002.

Leslie, Edward E. *The Devil Knows How to Ride: The True Story of William Clarke Quantrill and His Confederate Raiders.* New York: Random House, 1996.

Lesy, Michael. *Wisconsin Death Trip.* Albuquerque: University of New Mexico Press, 1973.

López Tushar, Olibama. *The People of El Valle: A History of the Spanish Settlers in the San Luis Valley.* Pueblo, CO: El Escritorio, 2007.

Marti, Werner H. *Messenger of Destiny: The California Adventures, 1846–1847 of Archibald H. Gillespie, U.S. Marine Corps.* San Francisco: John Howell Books, 1960.

Martin, Craig, Tom Knopick, and John Flick. *Fly Fishing Southern Colorado: An Angler's Guide.* 2nd ed. Boulder, CO: Pruett, 2007.

Martinez, Eluid Levi. *What Is a New Mexican Santo?* Rev. ed. Santa Fe, NM: Sunstone Press, 1978.

McCannon, John. "An Account by a Participant." In *History of the Arkansas Valley, Colorado*. Chicago: O. L. Baskin & Co., 1881.

McClure, Alexander, and Byron Andrews, eds. *Famous American Statesmen and Orators*, vol. 6. New York: F. F. Lovell Publishing Company, 1902.

McCullough, Frances. "The Barlow and Sanderson Stage Line in the San Luis Valley." *The San Luis Valley Historian* 30, no. 3 (1998): 5–62.

Mead, Frances Harvey. *Conejos Country: The Canyon, the River, the People*. Colorado Springs: Century One Press, 1984.

Mednick, Christina Singleton. *San Cristóbal: Voices and Visions of the Galisteo Basin*. Santa Fe, NM: Office of Archaeological Studies, Museum of Santa Fe, 1996.

Miller, Darlis E. "Hispanos and the Civil War in New Mexico." *New Mexico Historical Review* 54, no. 2 (1979): 105–123.

Monaghan, Jay. *Civil War on the Western Border, 1855–1865*. New York: Bonanza Books, 1955.

Moon, Sarah J. "Recollections of Fort Garland and Southern Colorado." *The Colorado Magazine* 24, no. 2 (March 1947): 73–79.

Nankivel, Maj, and H. John. "Fort Garland, Colorado." *The Colorado Magazine* 16, no. 1 (January 1939): 13–28.

Noel, Thomas J., Paul F. Mahoney, and Richard E. Stevens. *Historical Atlas of Colorado*. Norman: University of Oklahoma Press, 1993.

O'Brien, Christopher. *Secrets of the Mysterious Valley*. Kempton, IL: Adventures Unlimited Press, 2007.

Oldham, Ann. *Albert H. Pfeiffer: Indian Agent, Soldier and Mountain Man*. Instantpublisher .com, 2003.

Olmstead, Virginia Langham. G.R.S. translator and compiler. *New Mexico Spanish and Mexican Colonial Censuses: 1790, 1823, 1845*. Albuquerque: New Mexico Genealogical Society, 1975.

Pacific States Publishing Company. *History of New Mexico: Its Resources and Its People*, vol. 2. Los Angeles: Pacific States Publishing Company, 1907.

Parkhill, Forbes. *The Law Goes West*. Denver: Sage Books, 1956.

Perkins, James E. *Tom Tobin, Frontiersman*. Monte Vista, CO: Adobe Village Press, 2005.

Potter, Chester W., and Paige W. Christiansen, eds. "Reminiscences of the Socorro Vigilantes." *New Mexico Historical Review* 40, no. 1 (January 1965): 23–54.

Price, Charles F. "Espinosa Scapegoating Goes Awry: The Strange Case of Capt. E. Wayne Eaton." *Colorado Central Magazine* (April–May 2009).

Price, Charles F. "The Rampage of the Espinosas." *Colorado Central Magazine* (October–November 2008).

Priest, Henry, as told to Elsie Keeton. "The Story of Dead Man's Canyon and of the Espinosas." *The Colorado Magazine* 8, no. 1 (January 1931): 34–38.

Quintana, Frances Leon. *Pobladores: Hispanic Americans of the Ute Frontier*. 2nd rev. ed. Notre Dame, IN: University of Notre Dame Press, 1991.

Rebolledo, Tey Diana, and María Teresa Márquez. *Women's Tales from the New Mexico WPA: La Diabla a Pie*. Houston: Arte Público Press, 2000.

Richmond, Patricia. "Map of the Southeastern San Luís Valley." *The San Luís Valley Historian* 2, no. 2 (Spring 1970): front endpaper.

Rockafellow, B. F. "History of Fremont County." In *History of the Arkansas Valley, Colorado*, ed. O. L. Baskin. Chicago: O. L. Baskin & Co., 1881.

Salazar, Manuel. "José María Jaques." *Colorado Hispanic Genealogist* 5, no. 4 (Winter 2008): 12–22.

Sánchez, Virginia. "Colorado's Hispanic Legislator Biographies." *Colorado Hispanic Genealogist* 6, no. 2 (June 2009): 17–21.

Sanford, Albert B. "Mountain Staging in Colorado." *The Colorado Magazine* 9, no. 2 (March 1932): 66–71.

Schwarz, Maureen Trudelle. *Navajo Lifeways: Contemporary Issues, Ancient Knowledge*. Norman: University of Oklahoma Press, 2001.

Scott, Bob. *Tom Tobin and the Bloody Espinosas*. Baltimore: Publishamerica, 2004.

Secrest, Clark. "The Bloody Espinosas: Avenging Angels of the Conejos." *Colorado Heritage* (Autumn 2000): 11–17.

Sharp, Pauline S. "Kit Carson at Fort Garland, C.T." *The San Luis Valley Historian* 2, no. 2 (Spring 1970).

Shawcroft, Gladys. "A Brief History of the Alamosa River and the La Jara River Valley." *The San Luis Valley Historian* 2, no. 1 (1970): 4–12.

Shawcroft, Gladys. "Biographical Sketches of Early Conejos County Settlers." *The San Luis Valley Historian* 2, no. 1 (1970): 28–30.

Sheldon, A. Z. "History of El Paso County." In *History of the Arkansas Valley, Colorado*, ed. O. L. Baskin. Chicago: O. L. Baskin & Co., 1881.

Shirley, Glenn. *West of Hell's Fringe*. Norman: University of Oklahoma Press, 1978.

Sides, Hampton. *Blood and Thunder: The Epic Story of Kit Carson and the Conquest of the American West*. New York: Anchor Books, 2007.

Simmons, R. Laurie, and Thomas H. Simmons. *The History of Ranching in South Park, Colorado, 1859–1950*. Washington, DC: United States Department of the Interior, National Park Service, 1999.

Simmons, R. Laurie, and Thomas H. Simmons. *Town of Saguache and Cochetopa Corridor Historic Resources Survey, 2000*. Denver: Front Range Research Associates, 2001. http://scseed.org/wb/media/RPTSAGUWP51.pdf.

Simmons, Virginia McConnell. "Ft. Garland Turns 150." *Colorado Central Magazine* (June 2008).

Simmons, Virginia McConnell. "Re-enactors Bring Past Alive at Fort Garland." *Colorado Central Magazine* (June 2008).

Simmons, Virginia McConnell. "The Penitentes: Remnant of a Vanishing Lifestyle." *The San Luis Valley Historian* 24, no. 4 (1992).

Simmons, Virginia McConnell. *Bayou Salado: The Story of South Park*. Rev. ed. Boulder: University Press of Colorado, 2002.

Simmons, Virginia McConnell. *The San Luis Valley: Land of the Six-Armed Cross*. 2nd ed. Niwot: University Press of Colorado, 1999.

Simmons, Virginia McConnell. *The Ute Indians of Utah, Colorado, and New Mexico*. Boulder: University Press of Colorado, 2000.

Slatta, Richard W., ed. *Bandidos: The Varieties of Latin American Banditry*. Westport, CT: Greenwood Press, 1987.

Smith, Duane A. *The Birth of Colorado: A Civil War Perspective*. Norman: University of Oklahoma Press, 1989.

Smith, Gerald C. "The Adventures of Three Fort Garland Heroes." *The San Luis Valley Historian* 2, no. 2 (1970): 1–20.

Snyder, John. "The Bloody Espinosas." Supplement, *Sunday Empire Magazine, The Denver Post*, January 17, 23, and 31, 1960.

Sprague, Marshall. *The Great Gates: The Story of the Rocky Mountain Passes*. Boston: Little, Brown and Company, 1964.

State of Colorado. *Laws Passed at the Ninth Session of the General Assembly of the State of Colorado: Convened at Denver on the Third Day of January, A.D. 1893*. Denver: Smith-Brooks Printing, 1893.

Stiles, T. J. *Jesse James: Last Rebel of the Civil War*. New York: Alfred A. Knopf, 2002.

Stoller, Marianne, Maclovio Martinez, Ron Sandoval, and Randall Teeuwen. *La Cultura Constante de San Luis*. San Luis, CO: San Luis Museum Cultural and Commercial Center, 1985.

Stone, Wilbur Fisk. *History of Colorado*, vols. 1 and 2. Chicago: S. J. Clarke Publishing, 1918. (Original work published 1890.)

Taylor, Morris F. *Trinidad, Colorado Territory*. Trinidad, CO: Trinidad State Junior College, 1966.

Taylor, Ralph C. *Colorado South of the Border*. Denver: Sage Books, 1963.

Thompson, Jerry D. *Texas and New Mexico on the Eve of the Civil War: The Mansfield and Johnston Inspections, 1859–1861*. Albuquerque: University of New Mexico Press, 2001.

Thompson, Jerry D., ed. *New Mexico Territory during the Civil War: Wallen and Evans Inspection Reports, 1862–1863*. Albuquerque: University of New Mexico Press, 2008.

Tobin, Thomas T. "The Capture of the Espinosas." *The Colorado Magazine* 9, no. 2 (March 1932): 59–66.

Tórrez, Robert J. "El Bornes: La Tierra Amarilla and T. D. Burns." *New Mexico Historical Review* 56, no. 2 (1981): 161–175.

Tórrez, Robert J., and Robert Trapp, eds. *Rio Arriba: A New Mexico County*. Los Ranchos, NM: Río Grande Books, 2010.

Trujillo, Will. "The Espinoza Brothers." *Raíces y Ramas* 1, no. 5 (Winter 1999): 167–172.

Trujillo, Will. The Espinoza Brothers, Part Two." *Raíces y Ramas* 1, no. 5 (Winter 1999): 172–175.

Twitchell, Ralph Emerson. *The History of the Occupation of the Territory of New Mexico from 1846 to 1851 by the Government of the United States, Together with Biographical Sketches of Men Prominent in the Conduct of the Government by that Period*. Denver: Smith-Brooks Company, 1909.

Twitchell, Ralph Emerson. *The Leading Facts of New Mexican History*. Cedar Rapids, IA: Torch Press, 1917.

Twitchell, Ralph Emerson. *The Spanish Archives of New Mexico*, vol. 1. Cedar Rapids, IA: Torch Press, 1914.

Vandenbusche, Duane. "Life at a Frontier Post: Fort Garland." *The Colorado Magazine* 42, no. 2 (1966): 13–28.

Wallihan, H. S., and T. O. Bigney. *The Rocky Mountain Directory and Colorado Gazetteer for 1871*. Denver: S. S. Wallihan & Company, 1871.

Warren, Nancy Hunter. *Villages of Hispanic New Mexico*. Santa Fe, NM: School of American Research Press, 1987.

Weber, David J. *Foreigners in Their Native Land: Historical Roots of the Mexican American; Historical Roots of the Mexican Americans*. Rev. ed. Albuquerque: University of New Mexico Press, 2004.

Weigle, Marta. "The Penitente Brotherhood in Northern New Mexico in the Late Nineteenth and Early Twentieth Centuries." In *Images of Penance, Images of Mercy: Southwestern Santos in the Late Nineteenth Century*, by William Wroth, 55–62. Norman: University of Oklahoma Press, 1991.

Weigle, Marta. *Brothers of Light, Brothers of Blood: The Penitentes of the Southwest*. Santa Fe, NM: Ancient City Press, 1976.

Weigle, Marta. *The Penitentes of the Southwest*. Santa Fe, NM: Ancient City Press, 1970.

Wilson, Raymond. *Biographical Sketches: Colonel John M. Francisco, Hiram Vasquez, Henry Daigre*. Walsenburg, CO: Huerfano County Historical Society, 1970.

Witherspoon, Gary. *Navajo Kinship and Marriage*. Chicago: University of Chicago Press, 1975.

Wolf, Tom. *Colorado's Sangre de Cristo Mountains*. Niwot: University Press of Colorado, 1995.

Yeatman, Ted P. *Frank and Jesse James: The Story behind the Legend*. Nashville: Cumberland House, 2000.

Young, Otis E., Jr. *Western Mining: An Informal Account of Precious-Metals Prospecting, Placering, Lode Mining, and Milling on the American Frontier from Spanish Times to 1893*. Norman: University of Oklahoma Press, 1970.

Audio Source

Dark and Light in Spanish New Mexico: Alabados and Bailes. New World Records, New York, 1995, compact disc.

Online Content

Christiansen, Paige W. *College on the Rio Grande: The Story of a Small School*, web edition, http://www.nmt.edu/about/history/paige/chap1.htm.

Christopherson, Nancy. Huerfano County, Colorado History, http://www.kmitch.com/Huerfano/hist.html.

Elswick, M. S. "Colorado Volunteers 1861–1865." Colorado States Archives, http://www.colorado.gov/dpa/doit/archives/civwar/civilwar.html.

Federal Census of Santa Ana County, NM, 1850. http://webcache.googleusercontent.com/search?q=cache:http://files.usgwarchives.net/nm/santaana/census/1850/index/indx02ca.txt.

Fort Garland Commanders. http://www.fortgarlandmuseumfriends.com.

Hartley, George. *"I Am Joaquín": Rodolfo "Corky" Gonzales and the Retroactive Construction of Chicanismo*, http://epc.buffalo.edu/authors/hartley/pubs/corky.html.

History of Sheriff's Department, Fremont County. http://www.fremontco.com/sheriff/history.shtml.

Mitchell, Karen. "Huerfano County, Colorado: Index to Book I." http://www.kmitch/Huerfano/book1.html.

Old Colorado City. http://historyofthespielmanfamily.blogspot.com/2006/10/history-of-spielman-family-1730-1944.html.

Philbrick. Descendant List of Sergeant Thomas Philbrick. http://homepages.rootsweb.ancestry.com/~nvjack/fylbrigg/pdfs/descendants_of_sgt_thomas_philbrick.pdf.

Philbrick and Cookson Family. http://wc.rootsweb.ancestry.com/cgi-bin/igm.cgi?op=DESC&db=ssgtal&id=I1257.

Philbrook, Robert W. "The Execution of Sgt. Darius Philbrook, 1st Colorado Volunteers." http://www.philbrick-genealogy.org/Civil%20War/Darius_Philbrook_story.htm.

Philbrook, Leander D. Find a Grave Memorial. http://www.findagrave.com/cgi-bin/fg.cgi.

Philbrook, Leander D., Darius A. Philbrook, and Henry Clay Philbrook. http://homepages.rootsweb.ancestry.com/~nvjack/fylbrigg/data/b19748.htm.

Philbrook, Darius A., and Leander D. Philbrook. www.philbrick-genealogy.org/Civil%20 War/civil_war_roster.htm.

Sand Creek Massacre National Historic Site—People. http://ehistory.osu.edu/osu/sources/recordView.cfm?Content=083/0956.

Single Graves and Abandoned Cemeteries, El Paso County, Colorado. http://files.usgwarchives.net/co/elpaso/cemeteries/single.txt.

Slatta, Richard W. "Eric J. Hobsbawm's Social Bandit: A Critique and Revision." *A Contracorriente: A Journal on Social History and Literature in Latin America*, 2004, www.ncsu.edu/project/acontracorriente/spring_04/Slatta.pdf.

Treaty with the Utah-Tabeguache Band, October 1873. http://digital.library.okstate.edu/kappler/vol2/treaties/uta0856.htm.

Index

Page numbers in italics indicate illustrations.